EPISTEMICS & ECONOMICS

EPISTEMICS & ECONOMICS
A critique of economic doctrines

G. L. S. SHACKLE

CAMBRIDGE

At the University Press 1972

PUBLISHED BY THE SYNDICS OF THE CAMBRIDGE UNIVERSITY PRESS
BENTLEY HOUSE, 200 EUSTON ROAD, LONDON NW1 2DB
AMERICAN BRANCH: 32 EAST 57TH STREET, NEW YORK, NY 10022

© CAMBRIDGE UNIVERSITY PRESS 1972

LIBRARY OF CONGRESS CATALOGUE CARD NUMBER: 72–76091

ISBN: 0 521 08626 4

PRINTED IN GREAT BRITAIN
AT THE UNIVERSITY PRINTING HOUSE, CAMBRIDGE
(BROOKE CRUTCHLEY, UNIVERSITY PRINTER)

THIS BOOK IS DEDICATED TO

J. L. FORD

Acknowledgements

This book flows from some forty years of involvement in reading and writing economic theory. That involvement began with an attempt to relate to each other the monetary theories of J. M. Keynes and of Professor F. A. von Hayek, of whom the latter became my supervisor at the London School of Economics and showed me an inexpressible kindness and generosity. His brilliant study of the role of knowledge in economic affairs was an early source of inspiration for me (*Economica*, new series, vol. IV, no. 13, February 1937).

Professor Ludwig M. Lachmann has pursued the same theme with unique force and incisiveness for many years.

Thirty years have passed since a letter from Sir Roy Harrod, commending the heterodox theory of expectation which I had just published in *Oxford Economic Papers*, original series, no. 6 (1942) gave me an immense accession of faith in the possibilities of my theme. His encouragement then and since has been of incalculable value to me

I wish to record my gratitude to Mrs E. C. Harris, who has most generously undertaken the proof-reading of this book, and the setting in order of the items of the index, tasks in which her endless patience, skill and care have for many years rendered me such inestimable help.

14 MARCH 1972   G. L. S. SHACKLE

CONTENTS

CONTENTS

Time and *Knowledge* belong together. The creative acts of the mind need not be reflected in changing preferences, but they cannot but be reflected in acts grasping experience and constituting objects of knowledge and plans of action. All such acts bear the stamp of the individuality of the actor.

The impossibility of prediction in economics follows from the facts that economic change is linked to change in knowledge, and future knowledge cannot be gained before its time.

As soon as we permit time to elapse we must permit knowledge to change, and knowledge cannot be regarded as a function of anything else.

Ludwig M. Lachmann,
Metroeconomica, vol. XI (1959)

PREFACE

Political economy being a theory of the origin, nature and effects of conduct and policy in a class of human affairs, it seems to me natural that in framing it we should begin by considering what is sometimes called the human predicament, what Fitzgerald, or his inspiration, Omar, the great calendar-mathematician, called the Scheme of Things Entire. Omar in the voice of Fitzgerald speaks of 'unborn to-morrow and dead yesterday'.* He may have thought that tomorrow is yet un-created. At any rate it is to us unknown, yet what is most of all peculiar to men is their concern with imagining it, seeking to originate it in the image of their own ambitions. Economic theory is exceedingly shy of this conception. The source of its distaste for *expectation* is not far to seek. Expectation, time itself, is alien to reason, except in the perfect, void freedom of pure mathematics, where time is merely an extensive variable, not the real, enigmatic, unarguable reality, that Guillaume de Lorris so perfectly describes in *Le Roman de la Rose* :†

> Li Tens qui s'en va nuit et jour
> Sanz repos prendre et sanz sejour.
> Et qui de nous se part et emble
> Si celeement qu'il nous semble
> Qu'il s'arrest adès en un point
> Et il ne s'i arreste point
> Ainz ne fine de trespasser,
> Que l'on ne puet neïs penser
> Quels tens ce est qui est presenz.‡

*
> Ah, by my computations, people say
> I've squared the year to human compass, eh?
> If so, by striking from the calendar
> Unborn to-morrow and dead yesterday...

† Guillaume de Lorris *floruit circa* 1240.
‡ The following is the translation given in Mr Brian Woledge's most admirable and exciting anthology, *The Penguin Book of French Verse* (to the

PREFACE

Imagination and Reason are the two faculties that make us human. But whereas Reason has its laws that are the same for all men, Imagination is brought under constraint only when men turn it to practical affairs, in which it is only useful to imagine what is deemed to be possible. Reason is sure, safe, even in a sense simple. The economic analyst has opted for Reason. His guide is a single principle. He assumes that men pursue their interest by applying reason to their circumstances. And he does not ask *how they know* what those circumstances are. It is the effect and consequences of asking this last question, and of going on to enquire what we substitute for knowledge in that vital and limitless area where we are eternally denied it, 'tomorrow', that is my object of study in this book.

In the first of its six divisions (I have called them 'books' in the tradition of our literature) I have been concerned with what are often called General Ideas, ideas which seem to describe the formal frame in which human experience takes place: the faces which seem to be presented to us by time; the idea of novelty or new knowledge; the contrast of our propensity to make a collection of things and assign to it a meaningful 'size', with the ineffable diversity of the things themselves; the essential nature of *the formal* in our construction of theories; the necessity of assigning to things a place for each in a purposeful scheme, if they are to have 'value'; the notion of value itself; the arbitrariness, and consequent danger, of dividing the study of human nature, human conduct, human policy, institutions and history, into such divisions as economics, politics, diplomacy.

Book II seeks to present the brilliant and beautiful conception which arose in the last third of the nineteenth century from the union of mathematical analysis* with the notion that the value of different goods in terms of each other varies according to the relative quantities of them available to the valuing individual, and the further, astonishing demonstration that these valuations, by individuals of the most diverse tastes and endow-

fifteenth century), pp. 146–7: 'Time, who speeds on both night and day, never resting, never staying, and flees from us, and steals away so secretly that it seems to us that he is always standing still, and yet he never stops but endlessly flies past, so that you cannot even seize the thought of present time.'

* We have not, in this volume, resorted to formal mathematical notation, save as the merest occasional auxiliary to a verbal statement.

ments, could, through this diminishing marginal utility, be brought to unanimity by the operation of the market, whose ultimate gift, however, was the pre-reconciliation of the choices of individuals in such fashion that each such choice could be made in virtual knowledge of the others and could thus achieve *rationality*, demonstrable optimality. Human conduct, thus elevated to the plane of pure reason, seemed to allow men an apotheosis even in their most mundane affairs. Such a vision was tenable in the late Victorian world, and Alfred Marshall was able to believe in the perfectibility of human nature. In the troubled times of the world since 1914, it became apparent that the Rational General Equilibrium owed its encompassing completeness, exactness and certitude to its neglect of all that is essentially implied by *time*. The rational, sure and pre-reconciled world is timeless. The belief that the Human Affair in its business aspects could be fully understood in the light of the rational ideal, the theory of value, had to be abandoned.

The dissolution of the rational system was started by the consideration of the nature of money. Knut Wicksell in 1898 had shown that money prices of *goods in general* will rise perpetually, so long as money can be borrowed at a lower annual charge than the annual gain which can be made by its use in commerce and production. And it was evident that banks by their nature were able to lend money at a rate of interest lower than the Natural Rate, since they could create money without cost. *Money was different.* It was not just another good. Was it a good at all, since it could not be eaten, burnt or worn? Who, in a timeless system, would want money in exchange for a good desirable for its physical, technological qualities? Money looks forward. It is wanted so that it can be later exchanged for something whose precise nature need not now be decided. Money makes it possible to divide the act of exchange of real goods between two dates. In a money-using system, time is not excludable. Time, however, goes about in disguise. The natural scientists, especially the astronomers and navigators, have taught us to think of time as just another dimension of space, a set of *co-valid* points. But the time of actuality is *now*, and nothing outside of now. In the solitary present all thoughts take place, including thoughts about yesterday and tomorrow. Tomorrow is figment. Expectation is origination, undetermined for all we know.

PREFACE

Recognition of the consequence of admitting the time of experience to our theoretical system was attained only by painful and confusing stages. It is still distasteful to many minds. In 1930 John Maynard Keynes's *Treatise on Money*,* in 1931 F. A. von Hayek's *Prices and Production*,† both drew inspiration from Wicksell. In the *Treatise* were the Fundamental Equations, a telescoped and incomplete, but essentially matching rival presentation of the idea, invented at that time in Sweden, of sequence analysis. Sequence analysis supposes that the decisions of enterprisers on the quantity of his own product that each shall make in the impending week or month, their decisions how much of it to put on the market, and at what price, at the end of that interval, the decision of each how much to spend at that time on supplies of intermediate products and tools from other firms, are all taken at one and the same threshold-moment of the interval. At that moment also, contracts are signed with the suppliers of productive services as to the quantities and prices of those services to be supplied during the interval. Thus the scene is set for the events of that interval, which emerge at the end of it as a consequence of the decisions taken at its beginning. At that threshold-moment, the enterprisers do not know what their revenues, price times quantity sold, will be, nor therefore what their net revenues will be after deduction of factor-costs. The picture *ex ante* can fail to be vindicated by the picture *ex post*. There can be an unexpected surplus over the revenue just sufficient to pay their factors and reward themselves with a return just satisfying them for their scale of production. Such a surplus, if it occurs, will be what Keynes in the *Treatise* called a *windfall profit*. It can, of course, prove to be negative, a loss. What is the source, in money terms, of such a windfall profit or loss? In the Fundamental Equations it is the difference between aggregate Investment and aggregate Saving. Can there be a difference? Yes, because Keynes defines these two quantities in such a way that, in Gunnar Myrdal's language, one of them is in effect an *ex ante* quantity. And that language of *ex ante* and *ex post* was the key which released economic theory from its subservience to that conception of time which prevails in celestial mechanics, the time which is a mere dimension where the distinction between past and future

* Macmillan.   † Routledge and Kegan Paul.

is meaningless. Myrdal, explicitly (*Monetary Equilibrium*, Swedish original, 1931, German version 1933, English version* 1939), and Keynes, implicitly (1930), set forth the Economics of Fallible Expectation. They gave it a very embryonic formulation. But the theory of fallible expectation is *necessarily, essentially* embryonic, for we can describe what is expected, what is planned, at some present moment, but not what experience and time's new knowledge will do to those hopes.

Professor Hayek's *Prices and Production*, published forty years ago as I write, was a fascinating enigma which, in order to be clearly logically cogent, would have required an explicit framework of time-lags or at least a more distinct statement of the sequential order of events, and an explanation of why some of the discernible phases of its process did not overtake and co-incide with, and thereby obliterate, other phases. Again there was at the heart of its argument a distinction between the lending-price of money and the earning-power of capital-*goods*.

My Book III does not aspire to deal with all this in any systematic fashion. The policy of a book which (making no claim to do more than express its author's intense search for insight) calls itself a Critique, should I think be to select those parts of received theory, or those especially enigmatic passages of the pioneer theoreticians which have become notorious (or those which *ought* to have been so singled out, but have not been), which the author believes himself to have in some degree unravelled and distilled into a sense different from the orthodox understanding of them. Some chapters of the *General Theory*, some themes suggested by that book, fall into this class. Keynes's book was an immensely more destructive subversion of received theory, a more absolute relegation, in particular, of the Theory of Value to irrelevance, than even his admirers have acknowledged. But this failure to take his measure is the more natural, because the ostensible frame and method of the book appear so orthodox. The method has the look of an appeal to equilibrium. Yet the *meaning* is that rational, fully-informed equilibrium is excluded by the denial to us of anything but fragmentary suggestion of what will be the sequel of today's efforts and plans. Expectation is not rational. There are also more special ambushes for the reader who supposes that the argument will

* William Hodge and Co. Ltd.

prove transparent and will proceed on a steady straight course. On the contrary, it goes round the most unexpected corners. Such a one is in Chapter 2. Here, two quite distinct explanations are given of how, despite the marginal productivity theory of wages, unemployment can be involuntary. One of these explanations relies on the distinction between money wages and (as we may say) product wages. The other, an obscure hint occupying only the last page or two of a long chapter, glimpses the far more radical theme which can be discerned, though it is never made quite explicit, in the body of the book, namely, the difference of *composition*, in terms of real goods suitable for consumption or for accumulation, of the product-pay which income-earners desire (high saving ratio) and the product-pay which enterprisers are willing to give (low investment–goods ratio). The nature, origin and determination of interest-rates are necessarily a central theme of the *General Theory*, since if the interest-rate were determined, as earlier theories supposed, by a balance at the margin between impatience to consume and the profit-incentive to invest, there would be a mechanism for pre-reconciling planned investment and saving, and the basic reason for involuntary unemployment would be eliminated. The greatest *technical* innovation of the *Treatise on Money* and the *General Theory* is the liquidity-preference theory of interest. The essence of the liquidity theory, its ascription of interest to uncertainty and the speculative motive, are considerably obscured by the *General Theory's* retrograde resort to the notion of a stable curve relating the size of the money-stock to the interest rate. The appeal to a supposedly stable curve is, perhaps, merely didactic, but liable to be highly misleading.

If there is a fundamental conflict between the appeal to rationality and the consideration of the consequence of time as it imprisons us in actuality, the theoretician is confronted with a stark choice. He can reject rationality or time. The theory which rejects time has certain technical features, often referred to as, respectively, subjective marginalism, the market mechanism, and partial equilibrium, which we try to examine in Book IV. The other road consists in abandoning, not the *word* time, but its meaning of a forceps which grips us between the past which is unchoosable and the future which is unknowable. Instead of accepting the incompatibility of time and reason, and electing to base our theories on one *or* the other, we can de-nature 'time' and make it an artefact, a space whose distinct points are co-valid like those of physical space. A great deal of the work of economic theoreticians has been done within this conception. The theory of capital and the various theories of the business cycle necessarily have aspects which place them in this class. There was, however, one writer who in some measure perceived and acknowledged the dilemma but strove for a compromise. The real character of Marshall's *Principles** seems to me to go almost unremarked by his commentators. Marshall sought to *accommodate* the intractable implications of time in an analysis appealing essentially to logic. He has been accused of lack of rigour. How else, except by a relaxation of rigour, can a compromise between incompatibles be achieved?

Not only Marshall, however, has resorted to a softening of precision and rigour in the effort to simplify the vast, fluid, elusive maze of the business aspects of human affairs. Eco-nomics has, in effect, set itself the task of finding scalar measures of assemblages which exhibit limitless diversity. Valuation and the concept of the index-number are amongst its prime tools. Its essential, unavoidable concern with imprecise and abstrac-tive quantification ought perhaps to be more explicitly acknowledged and its consequences more distinctly recognized. This plea occupies the first chapter of our final division. It is, I believe, overshadowed by a theme which concerns, as it were, the soul of economic theory. If we acknowledge that expectation undermines the view of conduct as purely rational, we ought to attempt some systematizing of our ideas about expectation, in order to see how far a formal system can be built to embody expectation, instead of 'objective' fully-informed rationality, as its essential principle. The chief difficulty in suggesting such a system will be to secure an understanding of the radically different criteria of success between an objective and an expectational system. The former, abolishing time, has no use for any *ex ante–ex post* distinction, past and future are non-existent. The test of success in the objective system is a test of fulfilment *in publicly observable fact* of some stated conditions. The test of success in an expectational system is the maximum attainment of *a good state of mind*, a good state, that is, of *imagi-*

* *Principles of Economics*, 2 vols., Macmillan.

nation, of the conception of states to be attained which cast the warmest glow of anticipation on the present. The expectational test of success is to be applied *ex ante*.

The word *profit* is surrounded by a haze of meanings and of meaninglessness. It would be right for a theoretician to discard it and invent a new vocabulary. But our tradition is to adopt familiar words and define them precisely. By profit I mean a business outcome (of exchange, production, investment in equipment) lying outside the individual business man's inter-focal range for the particular operation in question. This is not the place to define the term *inter-focal range* which, since it does represent an idea, and belong to a scheme of ideas, originated within economic or epistemic-economic theory itself, has a claim to exist despite unfamiliarity. Profit, in the language I propose, is a distinctly counter-expected outcome of a business enterprise or transaction. To be counter-expected is to be *surprising*, to be upsetting to one's established conceptions or assumptions, to be such as to demand a re-thinking of those mental postures. Profit, positive or negative, calls for a review of policy. Profit exists in thought. It is an aspect of the business man's orientation, his scheme of intentions for the employment or destination of his resources. Profit is a difference between two estimations, an inconsistency, a signal and incentive to fresh thought. It is an essential part of the kaleidic process, the sudden emergence of new situations. To develop these ideas is the purpose of my Chapters 35, 36 and 37.

Economics is about thoughts. It is therefore a branch or application of epistemics, the theory of thoughts.* Economics is concerned with thoughts about things, both directly, when business men consider the intended uses of their resources, and indirectly, when they consider and conjecture each other's thoughts about what to do with the resources entrusted to them. The conjuncture, in our title, of the two words Epistemics and Economics expresses with precision my own belief about the essential nature of our subject.

---

* By *epistemics* I mean something other, and more general and inclusive, than epistemology. The term epistemics was first used, so far as I know, by Professor G. Patrick Meredith, a psychologist, but with a specialized meaning different from mine.

BOOK I

Economic Theory and the Scheme of
Things Entire

I

Economic Theory and the Formal Imagination

When the time came to invent economic theory, a number of established, exact and thoroughly explored modes and schemes of thought were ready to hand. They pressed themselves upon the inventors' minds. They gave to economic theories their own shape, derived from other contexts, devised for other questions. The procedure of invention was often to accept some such self-suggesting analogy and make the economic questions fit it; not to ask what is peculiar and essential in economic questions, what is the essential nature of the world to which those questions belong. Thus economic theory took on a character belonging to the manipulable, calculable, external world of *things*, not the world of the conscious mind in its eternal station on the edge of the void of time, the conscious mind whose being consists precisely in the endless gaining of knowledge. *Knowledge* and *novelty*, the essential counter-point of conscious being, was given only a casual and subsidiary role. Un-knowledge, the aboriginal state of man, both in his individual personal experience from birth and in his social-historical life, was simply disregarded and tacitly abolished by unthinking implication. The question of knowledge, of what is and what can be known, the governing circumstance and condition of all deliberative action, was assumed away in the very theories of deliberative action. Or rather, the natural, inevitable and irremediable insufficiency of what is at any moment known was assumed away and largely neglected. This insufficiency of knowledge is permanent and part of the nature of things, for consciousness consists precisely in the continuous gaining of knowledge. If there is always knowledge to be gained, knowledge already gained is therefore always insufficient. The history-to-come which will flow from men's decisions is non-existent until those decisions themselves are made. What does not yet exist cannot now be known. The future is imagined by each man for himself and this process of the imagination is a vital part of the process of decision. But it

1-2

does not make the future known. The absolute and eternal difference between the recorded past and the unformed future, despite its overwhelming significance for the very stuff of human existence, has been often overlooked in our economic theories.

The theoretician assumes that men pursue their interests by applying reason to their circumstances. He assumes that they are both rational and fully informed. Given a complete statement of all a man's relevant circumstances, the theoretician can, by this method and this basic assumption, predict what a man will do. The theoretician has seldom asked himself how this supposedly complete knowledge of circumstance could be attained by the individual. Which of the economist's theories have looked in the face of the genuine predicament of man, the logical non-existence of such complete knowledge? Economic theory for two hundred years modelled itself increasingly on the science of the inanimate creation; upon celestial mechanics for its large-scale conception and upon the isolable, purifiable experiment for the small-scale. The end-product was the neo-classical conception of general equilibrium, the economic system fully adjusted to an underlying body of complete relevant knowledge. Such a method and its models have given us sharp and brilliant tools and illuminations, lightning-flashes in which the scene is stilled to immobility by the brevity of the glimpse. But these fragments have been allowed to mislead us about the composition of the mosaic as a whole. Partial equilibrium has been taken as a pledge of the possibility and relevance of a general equilibrium. The field of economic events has been assumed to be self-contained and self-sufficient, shut off from the rest of humanity's affairs by a wall of rationality. Economic science has been assumed to resemble the basic sciences of Nature, where ultimately *everything that is* might be reduced to, or explained by, a single and solitary 'secret of the cosmos'. Economics, however, is not like this. It is concerned with the thoughts and deeds, not with the ultimate chemistry of man.

May we not say that there are centri-petal and centri-fugal sciences, sciences of the heart of things and sciences of the manifestations of things, the root and the flower? Human nature, conduct, policy, institutions, affairs and history are surely too remote from their conjectural 'ultimate' sources, the bio-chemical history of the individual brain in its earliest development; molecular biology; genetics; sub-atomic events which may set off heritable mutations of the species. However far the physicist may be from an all-embracing, and therefore self-sufficient, theory of the nature and texture of the cosmos, such is still presumably his aim. But how can there be a self-sufficient theory of *one aspect only* of human affairs? Economics is only one colour in the spectrum of those affairs in their general totality: a band in that spectrum, divided from all the rest of human concerns, let us recognize, by the feature of valuation and market price, but still a part of what is in essence a unified phenomenon.

The world of economic phenomena is not self-contained and self-sufficient. The motives and deliberations which we include in it, though having important aspects in common with each other which are not shared by other parts of human nature and conduct, are radically affected and governed in their effects and inter-actions by those other parts. Political motives, so-called, are often in their basis indistinguishable from economic motives, both kinds being concerned with acquisition and with the sharing, or the tearing into portions, of the product of man's collaborative effort. These kinds of action use different methods or levers, the one depending on the vote, the other on the possession of marketable capacities and assets. Yet both, in these days, depend heavily on the arts of supposed persuasion, on rhetoric (in the baser sense of that word) and advertising. Each flesh-and-blood embodiment of 'government' is not merely a formal mechanism for interpreting and implementing what the popular majority desires. It is an *interest*, an entity which is willing to serve the general desire and interest largely because in that way it serves its own. A government, a particular, proper-named body of men in office, is a self-interest, a political party representing the vague consciousness of unity of one part of the whole nation in some degree of opposition to another part. A political party in power trades some of that power for the prospect of its continuance, it takes action contrary to the more extreme of its own inclinations in order to win votes. But such conduct very closely resembles that of the man who trades his leisure for his sustenance, who works at distastefully strenuous tasks in order to live until another day. The polling booth, the hustings, and the market, are institutions distinct from each other in method rather than ultimate purpose. The latter is in both cases the struggle for survival.

If this is so, how can we hope that purely 'economic' explanations will answer our questions about economic effects and manifestations? The inclination of a government for choosing one tax rather than another, for deciding to devalue or not to devalue its currency, for raising or reducing tariffs, is not founded wholly on those considerations which we conventionally call economic. Such action is not purely a matter of business. It reckons upon effects attained through a variety of channels, some of them long and devious and not readily acknowledged.

The motives and calculations of diplomacy are hard to distinguish from those of politics or of business. They again are concerned with acquisition or retention of the sources of wealth. When business is international and world-wide, diplomacy is its indispensable tool and servant. Diplomacy in its turn is supported by culture, by art and literature and science. The boundary which divides economic or business affairs from those of politics, diplomacy, art and science is not a purely arbitrary one, an excellent case can be made out for it. But to suppose that economics can answer all its own questions on its *own terms*, by reference to its internal conditions, is absurd. To make predictions of the economic course of events, which treat economic affairs, *stricto sensu*, as self-sufficient, autonomous and able to snap their fingers at the rest of the thoughts and ambitions of humanity, is folly. And who is to know, at any moment, what those thoughts and ambitions are?

The ultimate indispensable permissive condition of knowledge is the repetition of recognizable configurations. These patterns or stereotypes form a hierarchy in our minds. A pattern of sense-impressions, perhaps from more than one sense, is pinned down as an object or an event. The occurrence, over and over again, of similar objects or events establishes a class of objects or events, a *concept*. Such concepts themselves can then form the building-blocks of more complex and inclusive configurations. Science tells us what to count on, what to rely on. But in doing so it merely imitates and refines the process by which we build, each of us for himself, the homely technology of everyday living. The means of its doing so is the power of survival and re-appearance of types of configuration. Such classes of configurations can have as their medium or subject-matter the most extreme diversity of impressions or phenomena. We recognize by the architecture which its members or instances possess in common a species of living creatures, the heritage of some geological era, the molecule of a chemical substance, the orbit of a planet, the syntax of a sentence, the order of an equation, the mechanism of a steam-engine, the stages of a disease, the spectrum of visible light, the life-cycle of a plant, the technique of an orchestral conductor. Recognition of a stereotype may involve not merely sequence in one or many distinct orderings, spatial or diachronic, but also measurement, proportion amongst the components of the pattern or amongst their intervals, or the scale of the pattern as a whole in comparison with other such patterns. The structure may even be one of logical implication or inference.

Among the stereotypes expressed with greatest precision are those whose form is that of the vectors and functions of mathematics. Let us define a *variable* as a class of measurements actual or conceivable whose members are distinct from each other, such, that is to say, that while all members of the class have in common some one or more circumstances of measurement, no two members are equal. Then any one member of such a class is a *value* of the variable. When some list of variables, each with a distinct subject-matter or set of defining circumstances of measurement, is specified, it may be found that some sets of values, each set containing one value from each variable, occur in Nature or in the particular universe of discourse, whatever it may be. Such a set is a *vector*. If we find a collection of such vectors, and also some rule of operations by which the values composing a vector of the collection (each such vector taken by itself) can be composed into an expression equal to zero, we may say that this collection belongs to a *function* binding together the variables of the list. That function is then contained in the rule of operations itself. What conditions, then, will have to be fulfilled in order that such a function may be found to represent the texture of some observable scene or field of phenomena? One condition will be the suitability of the list of variables included. An interloper in the list who has no business there may obscure the regularity of the relations of the other variables to each other. Or the omission of some rightful member of the team may apparently dissolve the genuine bonds of the others. If economics is not a self-sufficient science, it will be vain to expect that its observed variables can always of themselves compose stable, robust and repetitive stereotypes. We can, of course, construct theoretical models where the functions and their variables are such as to make the model self-sufficient and determinate. But the self-sufficiency is then that of an abstraction, and does not of itself make the model a safe guide to policy.

A more insidious and surprising danger lurks for the economic theoretician from another methodology which he necessarily uses, that of the accountant. For the accountant is compelled by the most basic imperatives of his discipline to account for all items as coming from somewhere and going to somewhere. In accountancy there are, in the language of physics, no 'sources' and no 'sinks' in the ultimate sense. There is a law of conservation. The idea of an economic valutum arising *ex nihilo* or vanishing inexplicably is contrary to the whole meaning of the accountant's operation. Values, for him, are produced by visible and tangible industrial processes; by transforming materials, transporting, storing and dividing them up; values are lost by wear and tear and by consumption. But valuation is an act of the mind. It can be the agreed act of all the persons in a market, or a compromise between their judgements. But such a public judgement rests on, is composed of, individual and private judgements. A private judgement of value is, of its nature, essentially and inescapably, a conjecture of what the valued object or system *will be able* to do, a conjecture of its potentialities, of its future. Valuation is expectation. What is vital is that expectations are conjectures, let us say *figments*, resting on elusive, fragmentary and confusing evidence whose interpretation and suggestion can change from moment to moment with no visible cause. Valuation is expectation and expectation is imagination. This is the mutable and shifting world of lights and shadows which the accountant is supposed to pin down in definite numbers which can change only when we can show from whence they are augmented or by what charge they are diminished. In the accountant's world, everything must be accounted for. By the unaccountable shifts of the expectational kaleidoscope, it must inevitably be disrupted.

The economist's attitude to his art of theorizing is in several ways divided against itself. That art consists largely of the devising of means to give to essentially and incurably imprecise notions an air of exactness and rigour. In this task he has hit upon a number of most ingenious and dramatically successful *tours de force*. Thus though valuation is in origin the personal and private act of the individual mind, yet it becomes through the device of the market a public and objective fact upon which every individual, at least in regard to goods for immediate consumption, agrees. This is achieved by the power of exchange to adjust each person's supply of this commodity and his supply of that other commodity until the market valuation of one in terms of the other is the same as his own marginal relative estimation of the two goods. When all the individual valuations have been adjusted to that market valuation which reflects and is itself determined by them all, the public prices of goods have been established as public and objective facts to which all relevant conduct will in its own interest conform. Prices, given this public authority and validity, enable collections of the most diverse objects to be measured in a single dimension and treated as representing a scalar quantity. Thus the gross national product consists technologically of scores of thousands of different items to which no physical measures in common can relevantly apply. Yet the gross national product is stated as a single number of millions of pounds sterling. The capital of a concern, the volume of imports or exports, the investment performed by a society as a whole or by a single firm: each of these is a diverse collection, reduced by means of market values to a scalar quantity. Such a conceptual sleight-of-hand is the pre-condition for economics, the analysis which treats each of the great aggregates, income, investment, saving, consumption, as if it were a single variable of uniform, homogeneous composition. In this there is obvious danger as well as a great simplifying revelation. Each component item of, for example, the investment aggregate, may or must be influenced by a different set of particular circumstances from every other. Why should they be expected to run smoothly together in harness or behave, in total, as a function of one or a few independent variables of the same composite nature? Economics might almost be defined as the art of reducing incommensurables to common terms. It is the art of heroic simplification, the art of the Gordian knot, carefully tied up in advance, however, by the very man who is going to cut it. But the economist ought to bear in mind that his conjuring tricks have their element of illusion, which he must not allow to deceive himself, despite the strong temptation. For he has before him the astonishing and prestigious record of the natural sciences. Why should he not aspire to their exact formulations and confident predictions? The general considerations which preclude it are well illustrated by the theory of money.

The theory of money illustrates very strikingly how a current of thought, once it has dug itself a particular channel, finds escape extremely difficult. Because money appeared to have no value in use (that is to say, it seemed to possess in its own right no power of giving satisfaction) and to be wanted not for its own sake but only because, by convention and custom, it was acceptable in exchange for goods that were desirable in themselves, the idea became established that the purchasing power of money (or its reciprocal, the general level of prices) was determined in some quite different manner from that which yielded the market mutual exchange-rates of goods which were wanted for their own sake. If money served no purpose but to be exchanged for non-money goods, its duty seemed to be merely to flow, to move around the system from one momentary holder to another. How many units of money were exchanged for a year's production of goods of all sorts taken together, thus seemed to be resolvable into the number of money units existing and the speed with which, on the average of all these units, they moved. This speed, in turn, could perhaps be explained by reference to some sort of mechanics of the passing of money from one person to another. There are habits which dictate the paying of wages, salaries and rents weekly, monthly or quarterly, and the settling of bills at fixed intervals. There are obvious constraints on the frequency with which it is convenient for a shop-keeper or a taxi-driver to take the contents of his till or pouch to the bank. Such examples can easily be multiplied. The speed of technical transit of money from one bank-account to another may depend on the organization of the Post Office. Because of such psychic, institutional and technological facts, a given *stock* of money, it was thought, would imply a given *flow* of money. If goods in general are meeting this given flow of money in a stream whose size is determined independently of that of the flow of money, the money price of the average 'parcel' of goods will be fixed by the sizes of the two flows.

Such in bare outline is one version of the Quantity Theory of Money. It has a very notable peculiarity. In contrast with the theory of the market ratios of exchange of one good for another, which depends on human tastes and circumstances, this Quantity Theory of Money is *hydraulic*. To make an impression upon price, according to this theory, the money must arrive at the spot where it is to be actually exchanged for goods. Mere knowledge of the existence of money in the hands of customers, mere belief in the owners' willingness, intention or need to exchange it for goods, are quite beside the point, quite unable to bear upon the price. The money which matters to the question of price is money which has moved and arrived, money which is as it were 'physically' present, money which can be traced in actual passage from possessor to possessor. Thus the Quantity Theory puts money beyond the control of thought and feeling, making it something inhuman, automatic and quite alien to that Theory of Value which explains the exchange ratios of 'real' goods for one another.

The hydraulic view of money is illustrated also in one of the orthodox presentations of the Multiplier theorem. Suppose that society invariably makes its consumption-spending of week 3 greater than that of week 2 by a proportion k (a proper fraction) of the excess of its income of week 2 over that of week 1. Now if, in circumstances which otherwise would leave the income of all weeks equal, an extra income-stream of A per week is added by means of a public works scheme, starting with week 2, the excess of income in successive weeks over that of week 1, supposing this extra spending is matched simultaneously by extra production, will be:

Week	1	2	3	4	5
Excess of income over that of week 1	0	A	$A+kA$	$A+kA+k^2A$	$A+kA+k^2A+k^3A$

and so on. The excess of income in week n, over the income of week 1, will be $A(1-k^n)/(1-k)$, and since k is assumed to be a proper fraction, this expression will tend to $A/(1-k)$ as n tends to infinity. The assumption that extra spending, due to an increase of income, must wait until the week after that extra income has been earned and received in money form, may have some realism to recommend it, but cannot claim any basic logical necessity in its support. Those who know, because they have obtained a job after being unemployed, that their income of the coming week will be greater than that of the past one, can spend on credit. Those shopkeepers who learn of a large increase of employment in their neighbourhood can give anticipatory orders to their suppliers, who can set manufacturers in motion even before the first additional pay packets have reached their earners' hands. What is vital is what is thought or known about the movements of money, and these ideas can be anticipatory, they need not wait on the physical transit of notes and coin, or the making of book entries. All this does nothing to invalidate the exposition of the Multiplier principle by means of an infinite series. But that series need not wait a week for the realization of each of its terms.

The theory which regards money as a sort of mechanical device running at its own speed determined by its design, was one more instance of a total disregard of the question of what men can know and cannot know in making their choices and decisions, and of the fact that the region of ignorance is as important and as exploitable as that of knowledge. The exploitation of ignorance is called speculation. It becomes possible when one man is willing to trust his own guesswork in preference to that of majority opinion in the market, or to adopt a new opinion earlier than that majority, and this is only possible if he can assume the market to be at least not perfectly informed. It is of course the future of which the market is not and cannot be informed. The value of any thing which has any prospect of durability depends largely on what value people think it may have at future dates, because by acquiring it now and preserving it, they can hope to secure that expected price. But that 'expected' price is merely a conjecture, and there can be as many conjectures as there are persons in the market, even if they only make one 'best guess' each. Money does have a value in use, for it has a *value in possession*, and not merely a mechanical and token value for perpetual exchange at as rapid a rate as the social organization and habits permit. Money is something which is useful to retain. It is useful to retain some money all the time in order to be sure of being able to make payments at those unknown future times when the need will arise. But why not *lend* the money in the meantime? One reason is, as Sir John Hicks has explained, that when only a little money is available to be lent for a short time, the cost and trouble of lending will not be compensated by the price for which the money can be lent. The fact and the *rationale* of a price for borrowed money is the key to the modern conception of the role of money in the economy, and this *rationale* itself rests on the notion of speculation.

For to lend is to part with a known sum of money in exchange for an unknown sum. To lend is to buy a borrower's *bond*, his promise to make payments of stated amount at stated future dates. The borrower does not promise to pay *on demand*. Were he willing and able to promise to pay on demand, he would scarcely be in a position where borrowing is necessary or profitable. The only exception is that of a bank, which borrows in order to re-lend, and which in respect of money which can be re-claimed by the customer on demand, does not pay any interest. But the lender at the moment of lending does not know at what future date he may wish to recover the money he now lends, or such of it as he can get. If such a moment of need arises earlier than the borrower's date of promised repayment, the lender's only resort will be to sell his bond on the market for what it will then fetch. What will it then fetch? No one can know. Thus at the moment of lending, the lender does not know what sum of money he will, in fact, in the event, recover. *Interest* is that excess of the borrower's promised payments, over the sum of money lent to him, which gives the lender some statistical presumption of recovering at least as much as he lends, and which goes somewhat beyond this to compensate him for the discomfort and inconvenience of the uncertainty in which the act of lending will have placed him.

The rate of interest as an element in the working of the modern economic system has unique aspects which distinguish it from all other prices. Its role in the theory of money arises from its bearing on the 'present valuation' of those goods, namely, durable facilities for production and for living, which will render service and earn revenue at dates years deferred. The rate of interest determines, or expresses, the value of deferred money in terms of present money, that is, in terms of spot cash in hand. And thus it determines the value, in terms of spot cash, to be placed on any supposed series of future revenues, and so it determines the value, in today's market, of the durable goods which are looked on as sources of future revenues. The comparison of the value placed by business men on durable goods, with the cost of acquisition or construction of such goods, will govern the incentive to produce them and, eventually, the quantity of such goods which it will pay to produce per unit of time. This flow of investment will influence, by great and pervasive repercussions whose study belongs to the theory of employment and general output, the level of prices of goods in general, that is, the reciprocal of the so-called purchasing power of money.

Investment in fixed capital equipment means, for the economist, the business man's act of acquiring productive tools or systems which are highly expensive, complex, specialized and capable of a long physical life. These qualities of fixed equipment have, for the business man, essential and highly important inter-relations. The expense of acquiring such a tool must be considered in relation to the value of the productive service which it can give in a month or a year. This relation is typically such that many years of service will be required from the tool if it is to repay its first cost. One condition of its doing so is its physical durability. But there is a further condition, the fulfilment of which is much harder to be sure of at that moment when the business man is deciding whether or not to acquire the tool. This second condition is, that the technological services which the tool's design will enable it to render will continue to have a market value. For if a very much more economical method of performing the same tasks which this tool can perform, is going to be invented shortly after the tool has been acquired, the price of the product may be so much reduced that the old tool will cost more to operate (in materials, labour and so on) than is brought in by a sale of its output. And that tool, by assumption, is specialized and complex, and thus cannot be adapted to a radically new method. The implication of these considerations is, that the question which the business man must answer for the purpose of his own policy, namely, whether or not it will pay him to acquire a given tool or system, depends on expectation, the conceiving of the future in imagination. If such work of the imagination is to give the business man a feeling that his act of investment is justified so far as it is possible to judge, he must apply to that work of conjecture some tests and constraints, he must give play to a *practical conscience*. The economist must study what these tests should be.

The body of economic theory bequeathed by the nineteenth century largely, if tacitly, ignored the question of what can be known by the maker of choices amongst rival available courses of action, and concentrated instead on the *logic of comparison* amongst courses having assumedly known results. Economics was said to be 'the pure logic of choice'. When attention was drawn to the possible insufficiency of knowledge, one reaction was to dismiss the question as trivial. If there is not knowledge in the sense of facts capable of simple and precise statement, there is instead probability. We have to consider what this response really amounts to.

Probability has two skeins of meaning of quite opposite nature. In one of these it stands for a type of knowledge and a number of techniques for gaining that knowledge, techniques which differ widely on the surface, but share a vital characteristic, namely, that they all involve the counting of cases. In the other, it stands for a *language for expressing judgements* as to the weight that the individual in choosing his conduct ought to give to each of a variety of rival hypotheses concerning the outcome of some one course of conduct. This language however is not merely a vessel but a mould. Form and content here, in an essential matter, are one. For the language of (subjective) probability is only capable of utterance subject to an all-important mental reservation. It assumes, implicitly, that the hypotheses which have been enumerated, specified and presented for the assignment of weights are *the only relevant ones*. Thus the language of subjective probability is confined to the expression of a certain kind of meaning. And there are other meanings whose exclusion would be arbitrary and senseless.

Probability is thus a word with two quite opposed uses. It is at the same time the name of a kind of knowledge, and an admission of a lack of knowledge. Because of its reference to these two highly contrasting and opposed ideas, the word probability has been seized on as an incantation to perform what reason declares impossible, the prescription of rational conduct in face of ignorance concerning the outcome of rival courses of conduct.

The counting of cases in order to attain probabilities can arise in two ways. Both can be illustrated by the notion of a dice-box with two dice. How often, out of n throws, will the two dice taken together show a total of, say, five? There are two routes to an answer. Inspecting each die, we find it to be symmetrical, a cube, and to have its six faces respectively numbered from one up to six. The symmetry deprives us of any ground for preferring the hypothesis that any one face will be uppermost rather than another. The faces are 'equi-probable'. This is not really a fact about the system constituted by the two dice and the box and the human hand which will shake out the dice, it is a fact about our knowledge of this system. The two dice taken together can make any one of thirty-six different patterns (table 1). Die A can show any number from one to six, and with *each* of these, die B can combine any number from one to six (the total of two particular faces is given by the number at the intersection of the corresponding row and column).

Faces of die B

		1	2	3	4	5	6
	1	2	3	4	5	6	7
	2	3	4	5	6	7	8
Faces of	3	4	5	6	7	8	9
die A	4	5	6	7	8	9	10
	5	6	7	8	9	10	11
	6	7	8	9	10	11	12

Table 1

The table shows that *five* is the total of four out of the thirty-six 'equi-probable' patterns, and so we may say that the probability of a total of five is one in nine. This is a ground, of a sort, for answering the question how often, out of n throws, we shall get a five, by saying $n/9$. We have performed a counting of possible cases and we may call the result an *a priori* probability. Instead of this we can start throwing the dice and recording the results. The record will give us an *a posteriori* probability. It will in general be different for different series of throws, and usually different from the *a priori* probability. But there may be enough consistency of the results to give us a claim to some knowledge about the system constituted by dice, dice-box, hand, air and table-top. The two methods both, in a sense, involve measurement. The difference lies in what is measured. One method measures an 'unchanging' configuration, the other measures one member of a set of biographies. These biographies (each 'biography' a series of throws) are distinct and different individuals, and there is no more reason to suppose that measurements obtained from them will be the same, than that the height of different human beings will be the same. But the height of adult human beings may be found to lie mostly between four feet six and six feet six. This result is knowledge about human beings as a class.

In one of its two opposed and discordant meanings, then, probability stands for measurements. Probabilities, in the sense of measurements actually made and actually numerically expressed, must, as a condition of their being meaningful, have been obtained by examining a concrete, existing and delimited system. When these measurements have been made in a sufficiently methodical and thorough-going way, and when they are used as a description of the system from which they have been obtained, and so long as that system continues to conform to the delimitations specified in the statement of what the measurements mean, these measurements are *knowledge*. They are knowledge in the same sense as measurements of the volume or mass of an object. On the other hand, expressions having a form which superficially resembles the kind of measurements we have been speaking of can be a language for stating judgements reached by a private and personal process of thought, about questions on which knowledge may be practically or even logically out of reach. Probabilities, that is to say, can be knowledge itself, or they can be an admission of the absence of knowledge. But the two situations thus characterized are radically different in nature. When there is knowledge we can, and must, apply reason and calculation. When there is un-knowledge, we have freedom for imagination and conjecture.

That probability which is itself the substance of knowledge requires, as a *sine qua non* of its existence, some underlying stability and invariance of the system being described. Know-ledge and constancy are so intimately related in all science, that we can say that science is merely the recognition and description of constancy.

The method of probability as a measurement procedure leading to knowledge requires us to define some operation which we can perform on the system, or observe as it is performed by the system. The system and the operation must be such that a number of different outcomes of the operation can result. If the system and the operation conformed so exactly to the notion of the ideal controlled experiment, that the result was the same at every instance of the operation (every *trial*), the idea of proba-bility would have no part to play. The role of probability arises when, because we cannot control Nature in the large or because we deliberately accept variability of circumstances in order to construct a game of chance, the circumstances can vary from one trial to another to a limited extent in a number of respects. It is then necessary to make a list of what we shall deem to be distinct outcomes, and this list must constitute an omni-competent classificatory system of such a character that any sequel which the defined operation can produce can be un-equivocally placed under one or other of the outcomes. We are required to make it logically certain that, when a trial is about to be made, its sequel will belong to one or other of the outcomes in the list. From these stipulations it follows that when the frequency-ratios which have been measured up to any stage of the process of observation are added together, they are bound to sum to unity. The set of frequency-ratios which have emerged can vary as the process continues, and there is no ground even for supposing them to approach a set of respective limiting values. But, according to the degree to which the system and the operation are more or less closely confined within certain ranges of variation, the frequency-ratios may show some approximate stability. If so, they can serve their purpose. They constitute knowledge.

The question for the business man deliberating whether or

not to acquire a specified piece of equipment is how the value
of its services, reduced to terms of cash in hand, compares with
the expense of acquiring it. The services will be rendered in
future years and their value in each of those years is conjectural.
The value, whatever it may prove in any future year to be, will
not be received until that year has become 'the present'. Thus
the earnings of the tool must be guessed at and then the results
of that guessing must each be discounted to allow for the fact
that a deferred sum of given size, being obtainable (as one
method) by lending a smaller sum now available, is only worth
that smaller sum in spot cash. When the total discounted value
of any given series of conjectured sums, to be earned by the
tool in future years, has been reckoned, that total can be compared with the cost of acquisition. But that total, being based on
conjectures, is itself a conjecture. Many different numbers of
pounds or dollars can be entertained as possibly representing it.
The cost of acquisition may also of course be in some degree
uncertain. But if one or both of the two amounts is uncertain,
what is to be compared with what?

To be uncertain is to entertain many rival hypotheses. The
hypotheses are rivals of each other in the sense that they all
refer to the same question, and that only one of them can prove
true in the event. Will it, then, make sense to average these
suggested mutually exclusive answers? There is something to be
said for it. If the voices are very discordant, to listen to the
extreme at one end of the range or the other will be to have
most of the voices urging, in some sort of unison, a turn in the
other direction. 'The golden mean' has been a precept from
antiquity, and in this situation it will ensure that, since the
mass of hypotheses will still be in disagreement with the answer
which is thus chosen, they shall be divided amongst themselves
and pulling in opposite directions. Moreover, the average can
be a weighted one, if appropriate weights can be discovered.
There will be a temptation to call such weights probabilities.
But what is to be their source? We have argued that statistical
probabilities are knowledge. They are, however, knowledge in
regard to the wrong sort of question, when our need is for
weights to assign to *rival* answers. If we have knowledge, we are
not uncertain, we need not and cannot entertain mutually rival
hypotheses. The various hypotheses or contingencies to which

frequency-ratios are assigned by statistical observation are not *rivals*. On the contrary, they are members of a team. All of them are true, each in a certain proportion of the cases with which, *all taken together as a whole*, the frequency-distribution is concerned. Rival answers might indeed be entertained to a different sort of question, one referring to the result of a single, particular, 'proper-named' and identified instance of that sort of operation or trial from which the frequency-distribution is obtained by many-times repeated trials. But in answer to the question about a single trial, the frequency-ratios are not knowledge. They are only the racing tipster's suggestion about which horse to back. His suggestions are based on subtle consideration of many sorts of data, including statistical data, but they are not knowledge.

The probability which can be assigned to one of many rival hypotheses is a 'subjective' probability, it belongs to what we called, above, 'a language for expressing personal judgements'. The basis for such judgements can be infinitely various in texture and composition. It can scarcely avoid resting in part on the individual's own history and experience, it can include knowledge of all sorts. But upon a structure which can consist of knowledge, reasonably so-called in a practical sense, there must, for a decision-maker faced with *uncertainty*, rest something which can by no means be proven: which does not follow from this knowledge but is only suggested by it; something including an element of origination.

The procedure of attaching weights to rival hypotheses concerning some question, that is, the procedure of subjective probabilities, has one advantage over conjecture pure and simple. It may lead the decision-maker to attend to the question whether his list of those rival hypotheses is exhaustive and omni-competent or not. If they do form a complete system of classification of all possible answers to his question (an exhaustive set of headings under one or other of which it is logically bound to be possible to place any actual answer) then he can give his various conjectures a consistent relation. For then each of the subjectively-adjudged weights or probabilities will be assigning to its particular member of the list some fraction out of a total which stands for certainty that the eventual answer will belong to the list. We have still to ask precisely what role this kind of consistency performs; whether the air it gives to the whole proceeding, of sharing in the authority which belongs to a statistically derived set of probabilities, is dangerously misleading; and above all, in what circumstances the omni-competence of the system of classification of answers, the list of outcomes, can be logically guaranteed; and if not, what is to be done?

Subjective probabilities assume this omni-competence. They imply the certainty that no answer can elude the list. Thus the first stage of the process of assigning subjective probabilities to the members of the list, the headings of the classification, is the assertion that something will prove to be the case, the assertion that something is certain. When the decision-maker turns to look at individual rival hypotheses, he will not in general feel certain that any one of them will prove true. But what he expresses concerning any one of them is still, in some sense, some degree of positive belief in this hypothesis. He may there-by be saying that he 'half believes' that-such-and-such an answer will prove true, or that he one-quarter believes, or one per cent believes, and so on. Some such fraction being assigned to each heading of the list, these fractions taken together as a whole are consistent with each other in the sense that, no matter how various they are, they divide up the unity which stands for certainty and exhaust it. They add up to unity and thus avoid saying that, for instance, the decision-maker 'half believes' in three or four mutually exclusive hypotheses. In this sense, the language of subjective probabilities ensures coherence in the expression of judgements or expectations. But it still asserts degrees of positive belief in a number of rival ideas. There appears in this to be some inconsistency. But there is a greater drawback.

In order that every answer to the decision-maker's question, no matter what it may prove in the event to be, may be guaranteed a place under one or other heading (hypothesis) of the list, these headings must either be so related, by the speci-fication of each of them, to the context of the question, that they can be logically seen to provide for all answers that can arise in that context; or else they must be mere boxes of unspecified content into which no matter what can be put; or some com-bination of these two things.

A formally all-inclusive classification can be constructed by means of some rule which will reduce any and every answer to a scalar valuation, such as the money value of a gain represented by this answer (let us say, this outcome of an investment), and by dividing up the scale of such values into unit intervals of any chosen size. For since the scale can range over all real numbers, positive, negative and zero, all valuations and therefore all answers can in this way be provided for *a priori*. But the intervals of such a scale are of course empty boxes having, of themselves, no content to which a subjective probability could meaningfully be assigned. The content of any such box would consist of rival specific imagined courses of events, rival specific hypotheses concerning the answer to the question, such an answer as the sequel to the decision-maker's proposed move or course of action. Unless these specified and meaningful answers can themselves be listed on some principle by which the list can be known to be complete, the formal inclusiveness of the valuation-scheme does nothing to make possible a distribution of subjective probabilities. And so far from any such principle presenting itself, the individual's process of imagining such rival histories may be seen by him as endless.

The business man is condemned to dip endlessly in a bottomless bran-tub. If he seeks to make a list of the specified distinct things which can happen (even up to some practical time-horizon beyond which it is not worth-while to take anything into account) as a sequel to any one move of his own, he will in the end run out of time for its compiling, will realize that there is no end to such a task, and will be driven to finish off his list with a residual hypothesis, an acknowledgement that any one of the things he has listed can happen, and also any number of other things unthought of and incapable of being envisaged before the deadline of decision has come: a Pandora's box of possibilities beyond reach of formulation.

If such is the case, if the list of hypotheses in answer to some question is acknowledged to be endless and incapable of completion, requiring thus an infinity of time in face of a need for decision in the present, the language of subjective probability may seem unsuitable. That language distributes a total, representing the certainty of inclusiveness, over a finite number of specified rival answers. Or if not, then instead it includes a

Black Box, a residual hypothesis of unknown content. A language seems required instead which does not distribute anything. A non-distributional uncertainty variable, an expression of the seriousness with which a hypothesis is treated, which refers simply to the character and epistemic circumstances of that individual idea and does not attempt, save as a background, to bring in the infinity of rival suggestions which are waiting to be invented, would avoid the misleading appearance of claiming exhaustiveness and closedness of the system of answers. Such a means of expressing adjudged possibility rather than of apportioning probability, by inverting the problem and considering degrees of doubt and disbelief rather than degrees of positive, but fractional, confidence or belief, will be discussed in a subsequent chapter.

Economics as a discipline in its own right was late in the sequence of such disciplines to be constructed. As a consequence, its inventors found ready to their hands all too many tools and schemes of thought which had been shaped for the purpose of systematizing other and very different fields of knowledge. Not only did these pre-existing means of analysis offer a great saving of inventive effort, since they had already been invented, but they were in the service of sciences of high achievement and prestige. Thus economics took on the posture of physics, physiology and engineering. It has lately embraced cybernetics, the science of communication and automatic control. These borrowings have very greatly enriched it, but like the gift of Bacchus to King Midas, they have carried a heavy penalty. Not everything that economics touches is fit to be turned to certainty and pure reason. By tacitly assuming that the right conduct can always be discovered by taking orderly thought, and that this is how men's conduct is formed, economics has precluded itself from understanding the vast area of human enterprise where disorder is of the essence of the situation, the areas of break-away, of origination, of poetic creation or innovation in elevated contexts or in the mundane one of business, and of conflict and cut-throat struggle. Sometimes the renunciation has been explicit, as when Edgeworth declared that the outcome of bilateral monopoly is indeterminate. Massive general unemployment defeated all attempts to understand it in terms of orderly, cohesive and fully-informed conduct, for it was a *disorder* of the economic organism and could only be understood in terms of disorder. A great paradox, yet one which epitomizes the paradoxical nature of economics, is the Theory of Games invented by John von Neumann and Oskar Morgenstern as a means of treating relations in business as those of warfare rather than of organized collaboration. Success in war has been most conspicuously achieved by the commanders who took their enemy by surprise. The battle of the Trasimene Lake, Gideon's attack by night, the capture of Quebec, and the stunning apparition of Wellington's lines of Torres Vedras which set Masséna in retreat without any attempt at assault, illustrate the most incisive tactic of war. The successful commander in such instances exploits an unawareness which he has taken the utmost pains to preserve. But in reducing games or battles to a mathematical analysis, it was found necessary to grant, by supposition, to each contestant a precise and guaranteed knowledge of what would be the consequence, the 'pay-off', of each possible pair of strategies, one strategy for each of them, that they might adopt. Thus the conduct of each was determined: he must reduce as far as possible the damage which his enemy could do him by choosing that strategy whose worst possible pay-off was, for him, the least bad of all such pay-offs. To ensure a saddle-point, randomness had to be introduced. But full knowledge of pay-offs for each pair of strategies remained.

A discipline, a region of the world of thought, should seek to *know itself*. Like an individual human being, it has received from its origins a stamp of character, a native mode of response to the situations confronting it. Right responses, 'responsibility', will require of the profession as of the individual an insight into the powers and defects of the tool which history has bequeathed to it. This is the first part of the study which this book proposes for itself. The further part, called for, or excused, by the critique of existing theories, is a suggestion merely, seeking to show that other modes of understanding the economic scene and of systematizing our impression of it are, at least, not logically excluded.

2

Time, Novelty, Geometry

Reason unfolds the meaning of the premisses. It can do no more. But if one of the premisses should be: There are things unthought of, that time in its operation will suggest, what can reason tell us about that entirety, which contains both the visible premisses and the unknown things? If the system, or field of experience, which we seek to understand includes in its essential nature this law, that it shall endlessly propose to the investigator or exploiter of it fresh suggestions, fresh hypotheses, fresh figments of a boundless imagination, not implicit in what he has already conceived concerning it; if he acknowledges that the entirety, which he seeks to grasp, is in its nature a source of novelty, of knowledge new to him in more than its superficial aspect; what can reason, based on his existing conceptions, be relied upon to give him truthfully concerning it? Reason and time seem thus to be at odds, for reason is asked for the meaning of premisses always partly unstated. When the premisses, which are accepted and acknowledged, include one which denies the completeness of the system consisting of the rest, we cannot derive from the rest any safe conclusions even about the implications for us of the system that the rest in themselves compose; for the effect and powers of that system may be changed by the adjunction to it of new premisses. That Scheme of Things which includes time thereby incapacitates reason in its ultimate endeavour.

Yet time, in a different aspect of that Scheme of Things, is indispensable to reason. For reasoning takes time. A step of reasoning must start from the results of previous steps of reasoning, and we cannot, in the nature of things, in logic itself, *anticipate* reason: reason cannot anticipate itself. Thus time has men's understanding in a double grip: because the pace of reason is limited, there will be yet unthought of things. Yet the potential, the threatened, the promised and inexorable revelation of some such things to each step of reason, in itself withholds from that reason the true fruits of its endeavour.

We can somewhat differently express this theme. It might be better to say that the premisses cannot be appropriately expressed in the absence of that illumination which time is at all times about to supply. We need to know the hidden premisses in order to have language to state *any* premisses. If paradox, dilemma and contradiction arise in all such attempts as these to encompass the notion of time, it is because the theme is ultimately ungraspable. We may seek to catch this fleeting and elusive idea in yet another way: we cannot claim Knowledge, so long as we acknowledge Novelty. Novelty is the transformation of existing knowledge, its reinterpretation; in some degree necessarily its denial and refutation.

Mathematics can explore the meaning of what is already implicitly stated, of what is already *given*. A mathematical model of a society in its economic affairs can treat the members of that society as gaining access steadily or step-by-step to items in a bank of knowledge which the model in some sense specifies, that is to say which the constructor of the model, the detached, omniscient analyst, in some manner specifies. He must specify in some sense the content of this bank of knowledge, must lay down the discoveries which are available for the members of his invented society to make, or at least the kind of discoveries, and also the mode of operation of the society in progressively gaining possession of this knowledge. Such a model has no place for what we are calling *novelty*. When the analyst or model-constructor is not detached and 'omniscient', but is a participant in the process of discovery of things not deducible from existing knowledge, then no model can encompass the course of the society's history. If the Scheme of Things has unending stores of essentially new things to show us, things such as must surprise us because they go beyond what can be deduced from existing knowledge, then we can construct no model of that Scheme of Things. We can make no model which will immunize us against the epistemic tremors and shocks which it is bound to deliver. Such statements are evidently tautological. To acknowledge that there is novelty, in the sense of fundamentally undeducible things, waiting to be encountered for the first time, is to acknowledge that we cannot build models that will exhibit the course of a society's history over even a limited span of time. Mathematics turns its back on fundamental novelty, except when it is itself undergoing fundamental transformation by the invention of concepts not implicit in what has been hitherto recognized as mathematics. Whether, in logic, such novelty can exist in the world of discourse of mathematics we do not, of course, here pretend to say.

Time is a denial of the omnipotence of reason. Time divides the entirety of things into that part about which we can reason, and that part about which we cannot. Yet the part about which we cannot reason has a bearing on the meaning of the part that is amenable to reason. The analyst is obliged to practise, in effect, a denial of the nature of time. For he can reason only about what is *in effect* complete; and in a world where there is time, nothing is ever complete.

3

Self-subsistent and non-self-subsistent sciences

The distinction we now wish to make is between those fields of knowledge within each of which, taken by itself, the considerations and concepts which are invoked are relatively alike in the modes of description which fit them (as that all, for example, involve position in relation to a frame of reference), and are in a sense unentangled and simple, and are capable of treatment, both conceptually and experimentally, in insulation from those of other fields, on the one hand; and on the other, those fields where a rich diversity in the nature and reference of the concepts and their relations is combined with a continuous, complex and indissoluble involvement with other fields. Kinematics may serve as an example of the first kind, and no better example of the second kind need be sought than economics. We shall suggest, however, that the former kind, which we shall call self-subsistent sciences, have often some claim to lie on the road towards that basic revelation which is presumably the goal of natural science as a whole, a Scheme of Nature from which all phenomena can be shown to stem, while the non-self-sufficient sciences are not interested in such a goal. The kind of distinction here in question cannot determine a precise and unmistakable boundary, nor even offer a simple formula as its criterion. But there is an evident and wide difference (we shall claim) between a science of the effects of gravity and a science of the effects of self-interest in human individuals, a difference still more insistent if we cut off some part of the latter effects and make them into a science on their own.

We need scarcely labour the differences between the operation of gravity or magnetism, and that of the influences which bear on human volitional conduct. The former do not depend on conscious knowledge, memory, past experience, reason or imagination with their more than infinite possibilities of variation in character and combination. The calculation of the effects of gravity can of course be highly intricate (the 'three-body problem' is not amenable to direct functional analysis) but there is also a sense in which even the most intricate pattern of gravitational influences is essentially simple in its nature. It is a network composed of simple threads each expressible (at the approximation needed for practical applications) by the inverse square law. The sources of human conduct cannot be conceived in terms of such a single and simple basic formula. But this consideration is not the main point. Ultimate unifying simplicity is the aim or the dream of natural science in a sense which is not permissible for the study of human affairs. For the disciplines which envisage human conduct, policy, history and institutions, or art in all its forms, are directly and essentially concerned with the manifestations themselves, the manifoldness, the richness and the detailed particular variants and individual facts of these facets of humanity, rather than with dismissing them as the contingent outcomes of some original, general and essential principle which it is the real purpose of science to identify. The science of Nature and the science of Man stand in some sense back to back, the one looking inward at the Origin and the other outward at the Manifestation. The unity of the cosmos of which we are a part does not preclude a variety of approaches to it. It is a pity that 'science' should have to stand for study of the florescence of mankind as well as of his basic nature and his ultimate origins. In this respect again, no unique, determinate and unarguable boundary can be envisaged. For if knowledge of human affairs must be largely a catalogue, so is a large part of the knowledge of the outwardness of Nature, the sciences of botany and zoology in their descriptive aspects. The forms of natural growth may seem as various as those of human action. But the botanist and zoologist are not limited to cataloguing and description. They can turn to molecular biology and genetics to try to understand the unified origin of the outward multiplicity. It ought to be questioned whether any similar thing is true for the students of the forms of human history. If the botanist and zoologist were cut off from a study of physiology and genetic mechanism, they could still resort to classification, and could still derive from classificatory knowledge a great practical competence and skill. Is it possible that the economist, if he concludes that economics does not reach down to the root of things, ought himself to turn towards some classificatory method?

Sir Isaiah Berlin once drew attention to a surviving line of Archilochus: 'The fox knows many things, but the hedgehog knows one big thing'. This saying perfectly epitomizes the distinction we have in mind. Natural philosophers from Pythagoras to Eddington and Dirac have sought 'the essence and principle of all things in the universe', the Single Secret of Nature. Would science, without this ambition as its real driving force, be anything more than a technology, a rule-book for workaday tasks? But is it conceivable that the student of human affairs can deem himself to be even remotely approaching such a goal? Do the phenomena he studies lend themselves to description in terms which could conceivably explain inanimate nature? To work outwards from the really ultimate particles (only three, according to one view) through the unified chemistry of life, to the endless resource of genetic Nature and the wild profusion of forms, may be imaginable. To work inwards from the consideration of what human beings do, to what they are in origin and ultimate constitution, would surely be, at best, only reasonable as a complement to the work of bio-chemistry and neuro-physiology. But as a field and object in itself, the study of human affairs can proceed quite independently in full self-respect and self-belief. To assume, however, that this study can attain or does well to seek a 'minimal description' in terms of mechanism or an axiom-system, from which everything can be deduced, is at present arbitrary and gratuitous. Moreover, what men do goes far beyond what they do within the artificial boundaries of economics. Human conduct, affairs and history do not, in any evident way, lend themselves to the search for 'one big thing'. On the contrary, they require us to know 'many things'. 'Many things', the kind of field which asks for some form of taxonomic treatment; and which, given that treatment, could be split up at will into 'economics', 'political theory', 'theory of conflict', 'theories of social organization'; has been a neglected and even rejected viewpoint amongst economic theoreticians. It deserves examination. For classificatory schemes of knowledge are not mutilated and crippled even by arbitrary divisions, provided these are recognized as such. Mechanism or axiomatics, if established on a too-restricted basis, is by contrast cut off by its design from the things which it has left out. We may go so far as to say that a classificatory scheme invites both the filling of its cells and the extension of the range and capacities of the system, whereas a 'model' seems to claim exclusive rights until a minor crisis of thought overthrows it.

By a self-subsistent science we mean one which, having demarcated a field of concern, claims to dispense with any contribution from or dependence on other fields of knowledge. Doubtless there are very few disciplines to which such exclusiveness can be strictly attributed. Pure mathematics in its modern posture, as the game or business of uncovering *relations amongst relations*, the setting up of an outfit consisting of relations amongst empty symbols defined only by these initial relations themselves (symbols, of which nothing is required and upon which nothing is bestowed, until their relations are postulated, except distinguishable physiognomies), and the endeavour to compose or reveal further relations latent in this initial outfit, represents the extreme and ultimate degree of independence and self-containedness. Cosmological theories can perhaps approach it, if not in exclusiveness (what can a theory of the cosmos *exclude*?) then in self-sufficiency. Cosmology, however, is certain to appeal to physics if it does not incorporate it. Chemistry is indissolubly united to physics, and all the material sciences rest in some degree upon these two. Yet in physics and chemistry there are possibilities of conceptual and technical insulation of strictly describable phenomena, in ways that are suggested by and conformable to Nature rather than imposed by arbitrary abstraction. The controlled experiment is possible because the channels of possible interference are known and can be blocked, even if the possible sources of such interference are not known. But in the study of conduct, policy and history, who can tell what influences may approach by what roads?

If pure mathematics is alone in being able to claim an absolute self-subsistence, we may be inclined to guess that this uniqueness arises from the circumstance that mathematics is a description of the human mind, and that the surprising applicability of mathematics to the phenomenal world of the senses arises from its being the language in which of necessity men describe that world to themselves. The mind, in such a view, is a scheme of taxonomy for filing impressions in a way which relates them to each other, and this scheme (it might be argued) is essentially mathematical. Thus by mathematics the mind can retrieve the ideas it needs in the meaningful pattern required, and thus mathematics appears to 'fit' the natural world. On this view, in short, the human intelligence constructs the phenomenal world in its own image, and that image is the vast mathematical chandelier in which a single light-source is split and multiplied in ten thousand refractions and reflections. On this view also, the more self-subsistent of the natural sciences would be those that lend themselves most readily to mathematical statement. Formal astronomy, cosmology and physics are the obvious candidates. As we move towards the region of knowledge where each science, through the lack of homogeneity in its subject-matter, through the pervasive involvement of its concepts and of the structures and events which it studies with those of other sciences, and through the internal complications of its own fabric, must be called non-self-subsistent, it seems evident that the dependence of such a science on others may be, as it were, vertical or horizontal. One science may climb vertically on the shoulders of another. Geography rests in part on geology and geology on crystallography and chemistry and these upon physics. But the interpenetration of economic, political, diplomatic and military events is not that of foundation and superstructure but of collateral fields of human activity and concern. More than one line of thought suggests that the boundaries between these four fields are somewhat artificial and arbitrary. We may claim, first, that all four are ultimately concerned with acquiring and keeping possession of the means of survival, freedom and enjoyment. Economics assumes directly that conduct and policy are shaped by the desire for wealth. The direct concern of politics is with power, but power is largely wanted for its supposed control of the sharing of wealth. Diplomacy's main purpose is to defend or put forward territorial claims. But these are claims to possession of one of the essential means of production of wealth. Military action has been called an extension of diplomacy, though it is rather the failure and ruin of diplomacy. Diplomacy's end is gain, like that of politics and business. But its method is bargaining. Bargaining is one of the central and characteristic types of business procedure. It occurs whenever a single buyer faces a single seller, as when a trade union leader faces the representative of the employers in some industry. Bargaining calls for many of the resorts of war, to concealment and deception, to menace and the vital effort to gain insight into the opponent's mind. Politics is bargaining first and last. The aspiring leader of a party must offer potential supporters some of what they want in exchange for their allegiance. The two wings which every party necessarily has, pulling somewhat against each other, must come to a compromise if the party is to succeed. The party as a whole must buy power from its potential opponents by conceding some of their distasteful demands. Thus a wide tract of common ground leads through the middle of all four fields. If they are to be deemed distinct, it will be through rather secondary characteristics. Ought these four modes of acquisitive action to be treated as a single field of study? Unity of motive and considerable unity of means; this situation might absolve them from Alfred Marshall's condemnation of Comte's thesis:

There are some who hold with Comte, that the scope of any profitable study of man's action in society must be co-extensive with the whole of social science. They argue that all the aspects of social life are so closely connected, that a special study of any one of them must be futile. But the whole range of man's actions in society is too wide and too various to be analysed and explained by a single intellectual effort. The physical sciences made slow progress so long as the brilliant but impatient Greek genius insisted on searching after a single basis for the explanation of all physical phenomena; and their rapid progress in the modern age is due to a breaking-up of broad problems into their component parts. Doubtless there is a unity underlying all the forces of nature; but whatever progress has been made towards discovering it, has depended on knowledge obtained by persistent specialized study.*

The practical and the aesthetic case for treating economics as a discipline on its own rests on the notion of exchange in a market. It is this which binds together the rival interests of individuals, and likewise of firms and nations, into reconciled specialization. The market makes the actions of all its members

* Alfred Marshall, *Principles of Economics*, eighth and ninth editions, Appendix C, p. 770.

2

in some matters mutually coherent. Diplomacy and politics leave them largely in cut-throat opposition. We need not believe that the clashes of interest at the polling booth or the conference table can be eliminated from human affairs, before we can believe that a means of coherence in one region of human conduct justifies a demarcation of study.

Conflict has in recent years become established as a distinct field of study. It is often treated as a branch of economic theory and its exponents are sometimes members of economics departments in universities. The origin of this development may perhaps be found in the invention of a Theory of Games by John von Neumann and Oskar Morgenstern, published by them in 1944 and 1947. But *bargaining* is conflict, and was treated systematically within economics as long ago as F. Y. Edgeworth's *Mathematical Psychics* in 1881. Politics is the rhetoric of persuasion, but so is advertising, and advertising is marketing and marketing is economics. The marking off of a distinct field of action as economic will be a delicate and tentative matter. Edgeworth may be thought to draw the boundary at a particular place on grounds of taste and morality, but we can at least as easily assign his choice to a resolve to include in economic action only action which can be defended as rational. When action becomes that of a gambler, no less than when it is that of a deceiver, it is not, we may take him to be saying, a fit subject for the economist. And bargaining, we must recognize, since it consists *essentially* of action chosen in face of uncertainty deliberately induced by the other party, is a gambling activity. Thus Edgeworth, in describing the negotiation between Crusoe and Man Friday over terms and quantity of Friday's employment, defines a *contract zone* within which agreement will fall, if any agreement is possible, but within which also, agreement will be indeterminate. Reflection shows, however, that Edgeworth ought to have made clear more precisely the meaning of this indeterminacy, namely, that the agreement is left undetermined by the true tastes or needs of the parties, as those might be confided to a detached and uninvolved third party. In a real process of bargaining, with its series of reactions by first one party and then the other to each other's offers, reactions designed to discover what the other is concerned to hide, namely those very attitudes which delimit the contract zone, it appears that a deeper knowledge of each party's mode of inference and his needs and expectations in regard to other matters than the immediate issue, might in principle enable a determinate outcome to be discerned. To say that a result is indeterminate, which the facts and pressures of reality will inevitably determine, is to renounce a certain region of speculative enquiry and draw the boundary of economics so as deliberately to exclude that region. Edgeworth made his choice, but we are not compelled to adopt it.*

The difficulty of demarcation between economics and politics is perhaps as great, and of greater practical consequence. Whatever technical means may exist in this or that climate of public expectation and assumption, in this or that historical era and conjuncture, to prevent or to halt a continuing rise of prices in general (a fall in the value of money), these means will not be applied if they obstruct the vote-gathering purpose of a Government dependent on popular support. It may be right and desirable that this should be so. We may believe it best that the majority wish should prevail, even if that wish is the product of disingenuous manipulation and a competitive party auction. But the situation, if we have properly described it, means that economic forces (the desire of people for better, more expensive social provision for health, education, infirmity, unemployment and old age, or for roads and concert halls and libraries) may work *through* politics in order to return and achieve economic effects desired and undesired. Where, then, is the distinction between economics and politics?

The influence of economics upon politics can be greater and more terrible than the mere inducement of inflation. In 1930 to 1932 the German, as well as the British, government sought to cure deepening business depression and unemployment by *reducing* government expenditure. This profound misconception of the needs of the case, which Keynes's *General Theory of Employment* was too late to correct, and the grossly perverse and disastrous action which followed from the application of essentially inappropriate theory, provided the situation in which Nazism could flourish. Had the incipient depression been attacked with bold schemes of *high* expenditure (and there is

* See below, Chapter 8, Sect. 6, and *Expectation in Economics* (Cambridge University Press, 1949, 1952)

nothing in the short run to prevent a government from combining this with *reduced* taxation), the war-makers in Germany might never have gained power.

Scientific prediction is *conditional* prediction. A theory binds together certain variable quantities into a set of fixed attainable configurations. It allows as possible any one of these configurations, but excludes all others. But if further classes of measurements are introduced as variables into the list, instead of being treated as an unchanging background or vessel for the experiment, the set of configurations or states of affairs which can arise can be entirely altered. If the volume of a given weight of gas is held constant, its pressure will rise with temperature; but not if it is allowed to expand without constraint. The possible relations between variables even in the original list can become quite different through the introduction of additional variables. A predictive statement begins, explicitly or tacitly, with the words 'If...' or 'Provided that...'. Non-fulfilment of stipulated conditions renders the prediction inapplicable to the case, and if accepted as applicable, it is of course misleading. How can economic predictions be framed in a scientific mode, if they confine themselves to purely economic variables? There must at least be some such phrase as 'If other circumstances remain as at present...'. Those 'other circumstances' include the political, diplomatic, technological and even the fashionable. Yet at any moment, who knows but that the seeds of inevitable change in those fields are already sown? The invention which will revolutionize technique in some industry may already have been made, though as yet unhinted at. The non-self-subsistence of economics is not a mere epistemic detail but a momentous fact of public life.

The inter-penetration of economic, political and diplomatic considerations and events is of what we have called the horizontal kind, and it is this kind which should enjoin upon economists the utmost caution in making predictions and in giving advice to politicians. These connections are obvious and undeniable as to their existence, however incalculable in effect. A more difficult question is whether anything can be found in economic affairs which acts with as universal and, in a sense, simple an effect as gravity does in the physical world. The obvious candidate is self-interest coupled with the assumption that men will act 'rationally'. But the cases are very different. Gravity affects the behaviour of massive bodies without any conscious knowledge or volitional response on their part. Its effect is direct and universal. The effect of self-interest works through the personal needs and tastes of the individual, formed by his history as well as his heredity. Above all, it depends for its precise character upon *what he knows* of his circumstances and of the ways in which they can be changed. 'Rationality' is an empty and idle term until the data available to the individual are specified. If they are incorrect, what is the good of his taking action which would be rational if they were correct? If they are essentially incomplete, conduct which assumes them to be sufficient may plunge to disaster through the gaps of knowledge which it has ignored. For the traveller in the dusk, a bridge with a missing span is worse than merely useless. Economics has gravely and greatly misled itself by a tacit belief that *rational self-interest* is as simple a basis of prediction as the laws of physical motion.

If economics were to abandon mechanism as its model and an easily applied, supposedly fully-informed rationality as its conception of human conduct; if it were to repudiate the economic man, and not merely conceal but expel him from his governance of its method; in what company would it then find itself? The disciplines whose main method is taxonomic have vastly more importance and prestige than one might suppose from the economists' failure to take any leaf from their book. Medicine and Law are in practice classificatory. What is political theory but an orderly setting out of patterns of authority in the state for comparison with one another? In chemistry itself, the bulk of knowledge is a vast catalogue of facts which cannot yet be exhibited as the mere consequence of a few compactly-stated principles. Professor Nicholas Georgescu-Roegen has divided the theoretical sciences from the others, by the test that the propositions which make up a theoretical science can be exhibited as an axiom-system. The propositions or sentences of an axiom-system are themselves divided into those which state, as it were, the formal rules of play, and those which are validated or rendered accessible by these formal rules; as in chess, the pawns and pieces are allowed to move under certain constraints, and these constraints themselves constrain the course of play to one or other out of perhaps some 10^{120} possible courses; except that an axiom system need by no means impose any limit on the numbers of deduced *theorems* which can be shown to follow logically from an acceptance of the *initial propositions* or *axioms*. The advantage of organizing a body of knowledge as an axiomatics is the economy and compactness of the record and the ease of consulting it. To these reasons which Professor Georgescu-Roegen cites, we must add that of beauty. Undoubtedly the unfolding of stage upon stage of implication, the endlessly-proceeding enrichment of the system, no matter how abstract, is at once unreal and overwhelming. Yet how much of knowledge is susceptible to such formulation? Pure mathematics is the method itself rather than a field of knowledge concerning phenomena. We may include physics (though along several lines, not one unique line), the statistical science of genetics, and perhaps some special aspects of many disparate fields. But the great mass of knowledge is a catalogue, not a geometry. To have opted for the axiomatic mode as the appropriate one for economics was a bold and a surprising stroke. Economics was denied the experimental method. Economists could sit and build a theoretic system, or they could assemble something resembling case-law. We shall suggest that this was the choice before them, with a wide liberty to combine the two over some of the field. But the actual decision was for an axiomatic method (in which we include, of course, all those mathematical models which are stated in the form of equation-systems) and therefore for what we have called self-subsistence.

Economics is an attempt to study in outline, by means of an imposed simplicity and precision, some aspects of a subject-matter which in the fullness of its unabstracted nature involves a vast richness of intricate and yet essential detail. Businesses are run by those who understand their subtle and complex physical techniques, the demands they make on the peculiar skills of their work-people, the tactics of rival suppliers, the susceptibilities of customers. In the hands of the economist, all this at best is summarized or proxied, it is encapsulated in hold-all variables which stand only for its broadest meaning; at worst it is ignored. To speak thus is not to disparage economics, but to argue for a cautious and detached appraisal of its proper task. Economics, in its traditional form, is not intended as a guide for the business man. For that we have nowadays linear programming, critical path analysis, operations research and management science in general. (Even these still leave the engineer–artist–designer–technician at the heart of the web.) Economics is for the statesman, the public servant, the student of mankind in its integral nature and ambitions. Again, the air of precision with which an axiomatic method (in the broad sense) is liable to wrap economics is considerably false. Economics is the supremely ingenious device for eliciting scalar quantity from vast heterogeneous assemblies of qualitatively incommensurable things. But this trick only serves certain purposes. It submerges detail, not abolishes it. We shall study this again.

The practice of treating economics as a self-subsistent science would be astounding to a Renaissance scholar. Such a man being accustomed, in any case, to regard all knowledge as a unity, would surely be more than ever baffled by such a mutilation of the General Human Affair. Economics has one chief reason for setting itself apart. It has a means of quantifying the objects of its discourse. This means is peculiar in the extreme when compared with those available to the material or natural sciences. But this inconstancy and mutable meaning of its unit of value is not the worst of the difficulties which stem from its almost exclusive concern with quantity. Quantity obscures form. To be always considering ratios is to be in danger of being blind to the subtle and intricate *jigsaw-puzzle problems* with which engineering, marketing, labour relations and all the real and concrete detail of business confront the business man. Midas could touch nothing without turning it to gold, and the economist likewise turns everything to sets of proportions. This relegation of form, structure and detail in favour of addable scalar quantity is his characteristic method of simplification, it is the essence of the market method which itself is the sole excuse for separating economic considerations from others. We have no ground for cavilling at it unless we are prepared to forgo the understanding which it gives of the most remarkable of human organizational inventions. What is enjoined upon the economist by a recognition of the peculiarity of his method is, of course, caution and restraint in the interpretation of his results.

4

Valuation, Variety and Scalar Quantity

4.1 *Quantity and form*

Economics has concerned itself with quantities and proportions, rather than with shapes, structures and intricate compositions of richly various pieces. The quantities and proportions have their subtle effects and implications for human feelings and human efficiencies and powers, and it is these effects which give economics its chief themes. But this concentration upon *scalar* aspects of business and of the enjoyment of life excludes very much that the business man and the human being in his full nature are deeply concerned with. Economics may be said to have taken as its text the question How much? and to have consciously and deliberately put aside all questions of How? This choice is no doubt the consequence of a desire to construct a system of ideas which may claim an encompassing generalness and wide sweep of application while possessing also the beauty, incisiveness and authority of simple and few principles. Codes of conduct or of management must be simple or they defeat their own end. A flood of instructions will necessarily be ignored. And if the scheme of things in which mankind has been placed is such as to give him a fair chance and an attractive challenge, its rules and its secret must surely be, in the last analysis, simple and arresting? The decision of economics to confine itself to essentially scalar concerns, at any rate on the line of its main advance, is a credit to its practitioners' imaginative clear-headedness. They early chose their policy and have stuck to it.

Economics has adopted as its chief tools such universal mathematical notions as function and derivative, vector and matrix, where quantities, which in themselves are scalars, are associated and compared. This does not affect our contention that it is quantity, and not form, which we study as economists. A function is of course a class of points or vectors, and a point or vector stands in direct contrast to a scalar, but in our concerns as economists it is ultimately the scalar components themselves that interest us. The man who finds beauty in the matricial patterns themselves (and who can help considering them in their arresting, suggestive and meaningful architecture?) is not at that moment an economist but an appreciator of totally non-scalar, non-quantitative, non-numerizable things. Economists are not essentially concerned with: In what arrangement, in what configuration, in what manner of assemblage?, but simply with: How much?

4.2 *Technology as the foreground of business*

Economics gives the superficial impression that it believes the business man to ask himself first and foremost how much of his product he shall put on the market, or at what unit-price he shall offer it, and by what combination of a few broad categories or means of production he shall produce it. But these must in reality be often merely *summary* or *secondary* questions. The first question is: What to produce? and this What? can only be answered by a specification which may run to many thousands of words, to detailed design drawings and precise formulae. The whole engineering question must occupy the forefront of the business man's attention. How much to produce must seem at best to be somewhat overshadowed by the qualitative question, the question of character and design of the product. The question of the proportions in which he shall employ broad categories of means of production will seem to him to call merely for a summing up of the consequences of decisions concerning an immense array of rival possible technologies and details of design. Those choices will be essentially influenced by the respective prices of the alternative practices and tools, but the choices will be constrained by the need for a resulting coherent total process. Despite price considerations, there will be an impression and acceptance of the primacy of technological considerations. To crack crude petroleum into marketable constituents, a large and complex plant is indispensable, and the question whether the distillations should be effected by individuals each using his own hand-fed still does not arise. The business man's *production policy questions* will be framed in terms which include an *essential* reference to technological, viz. engineering, chemical and biological, detail; detail of materials science and soil science, of colour aesthetics, of pharmacological effects; details of practical arts.

Economic theory must appear to the business man a summary and commentary of his methods, or else a viewing of them in an irrelevant and trivial light. Its real purpose is quite other than to offer him guidance in his individual, peculiar, special situation and affairs, where 'marginal cost' is no more than a curious gloss or pale reflection from practical realities. Economic theory has elected to be *general* in its bearing and interests, and those concerned with human affairs at such a level of generalness are politicians and representatives of large masses of opinion, leaders of parties or trade unions. In this it shares, of course, the character and posture of other great disciplines. Moral science as a whole, any system of ethical principles and injunctions, the law and religion, depend for their effect upon a detailed interpretation far beyond the reach of their explicit general statements.

4.3 *How may business be rendered* scalar?

Business, then, is intimately and essentially concerned with the whole technological richness, complexity and manifold variety of life, manifested in its methods, materials and products. Economics is concerned to sweep this army of detailed facts into great classes and collections where their variety is deliberately ignored, and then to measure the size of each such class and treat it, in some sense, as a scalar quantity, a mere number of some kind of units. What units?

We may spare a little further space to insist again on the nature of this paradox. It is the business world, the skein of activities by which means of production are combined and transformed into products, and these exchanged and enjoyed, that forms the basic field of the economist's concern. Yet he must simplify it to a mere handful of variables, either by selecting some small portion of the field as typical, a firm or a household, or else by combining households or firms and their activities into great aggregates. By the micro-economic method of particular equilibrium or the macro-economic method of aggregative variables, or at the best, by matrix methods which can in some degree compromise between the two, he must turn the limitless details, the literally infinite and more than infinite* forms of things, into *scalars*. Economics might almost be defined as the method and exploitation of this *tour de force*. The means of performing it is the most central and characteristic, perhaps, of all economic concepts, that of *market valuation*.

Valuation and exchange are operationally inseparable terms. To value something is to name the number of units of some other thing for which one would be just and only just willing to exchange it. But that number of units will differ from one set of circumstances to another. For what it measures is not an intrinsic character of the object to be valued, but the capacity of that object, given its intrinsic character, to satisfy the needs of a particular individual, with his personal and particular tastes, in some specific set of circumstances in which he finds himself at some calendar date. How is it then conceivable that value can be other than a private judgement differing from person to person and from date to date? How can value provide anything resembling those *public universal* units by which we express length, mass and so on? The answer depends upon two further conceptions which are central piers in the economic construct. First, the observed or assumed fact of diminishing marginal rate of substitution gives the individual a considerable control over his private and personal valuation, not indeed of his entire stock or his entire weekly or daily supply of some commodity, but of an extra *tranche* which might conceptually be superposed on, or removed from, that stock or that flow as it exists. Secondly, by means of this control, which depends upon adjusting the *size* of his personal stock or inflow by exchanging some of it for other goods, the individual can come to an agreement, advantageous to himself and to his partners in exchange, as to the value of the particular commodity in terms of other things. This agreement can advantageously, and by means of the general market, readily be made with all other members of the society who are interested in having some of the commodity

---

* The variety of possible shapes (we may roughly interpret the mathematicians' conclusion) is beyond counting and beyond the cardinality even of the continuum of real numbers.

in question, or with parting with some of it. Thus the agreement concerning the value can be public, universal and unanimous. Thus by means of the market and the principle of diminishing marginal significance, private valuations are reconciled and equalized, and acquire, in a particular sense, some of the characteristics of objective and intrinsic qualities.

4.4 *What question is answered by the theory of production?*

The orthodox theory of production illustrates the scalar pre-occupations of economics. That theory is concerned to show by what formal tests a firm can identify the most economical pro-portions in which to combine the agents of production in order to obtain a given quantity of product in each unit time-interval. The agents are conceived as permanent sources of productive service, the service rendered by each source being distinct from those of other sources, and all being in some degree substitutable for each other. The question of what proportions will yield a given output for the least expenditure depends on two sets of data, the technological qualities of the agents or their services, and the prices of those services. The theory does not restrict the number of agents which are supposed to be involved, but much of its formal insight can be gained by supposing that there are only two agents. The problem can then be treated by means of an equal output diagram where the technological qualities of the productive services and their diminishing rates of mutual substitution are represented by equal output curves convex to the origin, and where the prices of the services (assumed to be constant irrespective of quantity demanded by the firm or industry in question) are represented by the slope of a straight budget line. Equal-output curves and budget line all slope from north-west to south-east, and we argue that since all points of a given budget line stand for the same expenditure, the largest output for this given expenditure will be obtained by combining the two services in the quantities represented by a point of tangency between the appropriate budget line and an equal-output curve. In such a procedure we are of course appealing in essence to the classical method of the differential calculus for identifying a value or values of one or more independent variables which correspond to a constrained extreme value of a dependent variable, namely, to suppose the derivative or differential to be equal to zero and then to solve the resulting equation or equations.

When we consider this 'theory of production' and its maximizing or minimizing procedure, we see that all questions of why or how particular sets of quantities of agents provide particular quantities of product are completely submerged and disregarded. The theory does not concern itself with the arts of the farmer, the cabinet-maker or the tailor as such. It is not in any full sense a theory of production. It is a theory of the *determinacy* of the marginal exchange values of productive services, a determinacy whose demonstration makes possible the solution of the problem of how the value of the product can be precisely and exhaustively distributed among the agents of production on a principle which can claim the 'sanction of the market'.

4.5 *Valuation as a means to scalarity*

In the timeless system where all choices can be made in knowledge of each other, and may thus compose a general solution or equilibrium, prices or exchange ratios of goods can all be unanimous or at least universally consistent and assented. If a sole-moment general equilibrium served our purpose, so would price, and we could claim that a collection of goods, no matter how various its items, could be reduced to meaningful scalar measurability by multiplying the price per unit and number of units of each type of item and summing the results. For thus, in the general, momentary equilibrium, such collections could be compared by means of a unit which meant the same to everybody, a unit of value. Superficially it might seem that valuation can give us the scalar measurability of diversely-composed collections, which the elected aims and methods of economics seem to require. But we have to consider whether this is so.

The mass or bulk of a collection of objects will tell us how many wagons we shall need to transport it, or to transport any given proportion of it, no matter whether in fact we wish to move the whole or only a part. But equality of valuation of two collections of objects, when its meaning refers to prices for exchanges at the margin, need by no means guarantee that these collections can be exchanged for each other *en bloc*. This distinction is entailed by, for example, Marshallian consumer's surplus. Value at the margin is valid only for marginal exchanges. Length or mass, by contrast, is valid not only for marginal differences of length, but for the whole object at once. Value is not an intrinsic character of an object, but a surface reflection of the way in which that object is placed, as it were, in relation to the needs of individuals. Value expresses a complex and subtle inter-action between the technological and aesthetic character of an object, and the needs, tastes, knowledge, judgement and expectation of individual persons. Value depends upon circumstance, and even if circumstances can for one specially organized occasion be so chosen that all persons agree on the relative valuations of things, circumstances in the world of many moments and not of the single moment, will change from moment to moment. Value is mutable and even inherently self-changing, compelled to disillusion one or other of the bodies of opinion which determine it and so to destroy its immediate basis. In the world of natural or practical sciences, a unit is ideally required to be invariant against changes of the identity of the observer, and against changes of place or date, or of any circumstance whatever. Value cannot meet any one of these requirements. Valuation cannot by any ingenuity reduce essential diversity to uniformity, and no subtlety of reasoning nor ruthlessness of assumption can enable a unit of value to measure the same sort of thing as is measured by units of length or mass.

Let us now concede that the sheer scale and variety of some of the great collections, such as *income* or *capital equipment* in the aggregate, paradoxically robs the objections against valuation-scalarity of some of their force. *Income* embraces all the material or technological desires of mankind, it can claim to be a measure of the material fulfilment of life. The term *standard of living* expresses or implies this claim. There is a temptation to defend in the same way the scalar measurement of the capital stock or of its process of development, namely, investment. But here there are special dangers.

The value of a piece of durable equipment, a productive

facility or tool, is the value of the hopes it represents of net earnings in future years. Those hypotheses, or ranges of hypotheses, are themselves figments tenuously related to data concerning the present and the past. They are not observational knowledge, nor rigorous inference from sufficient data. If we are candid, *knowledge of the future* is a contradiction in terms. But this is not the only source of mutability of the value of the aggregate stock of equipment. Even if firm guesses are made about the size of the net earnings of a piece of equipment in a series of future years, those conjectured amounts, being deferred, are not worth in spot cash their nominal amount. The existence of a bond-market makes it possible to buy for a given sum the guarantee of a dated sum greater than the price of this bond. A deferred sum must therefore be discounted, at any 'today', at the market interest rate prevailing at this today. Changes of interest-rate can greatly affect the present value of promised income-streams, or of hoped-for and conjectural income-streams, which stretch far into the future, and moreover, these changes of interest-rate have a widely different effect on the present value, according to the distribution over future time of the sums promised or hoped for. The measurement of a stock of diverse capital goods by valuation can thus have latent in it great changes in the basis and meaning of such valuation if the rate of interest changes, and the revaluations or distortions of meaning will be unrelated to any physical or technological change.

To treat a collection of very various things as a quantity expressible by a single number is, of course, to ignore the diversity of the composing items. In many aspects and purposes of business, politics and administration, the diverse particular details are of the essence of the matter. Form, structure and quality, even variety for its own sake, may lie at the heart of our aims and methods. Here, the economist's instinct to sweep everything into a few conceptual hold-alls is dangerous. This appears, perhaps, most dramatically in war, where a statistically superior force may be defeated by a smaller one: Pizarro's minute band overcoming the Incas, or the Royal Air Force's victory in the Battle of Britain. Economic considerations are in this sphere a third step backwards from the battlefield itself. Tactics is the actual management of battle as it proceeds, strategy is the organizing of battles in advance, the economics of warfare is the study of whether given strategies are available, the study of their feasibility, not at close quarters but on grounds which are remote, abstract and technically blurred and indistinct. Yet economic insights are real, and are dependent on this very procedure of broad, gather-all accountancy. The need, and it is important, is to recognize economic scalarization for what it is.

Ingenious expedients have been resorted to in order to achieve some quasi-physical measure, or index, which shall not depend on valuation. Keynes in the *General Theory* uses, as an indicator of the changes of size of general output, the total number of persons in employment in conjunction with an equipment which, for society as a whole 'in the short period', can be taken as given. Even here valuation must be resorted to. Labour of different degrees of skill cannot reasonably be treated as homogeneous. Thus

in so far as different grades and kinds of labour and salaried assistance enjoy a more or less fixed relative remuneration, the quantity of employment can be sufficiently defined for our purpose by taking an hour's employment of ordinary labour as our unit and weighting an hour's employment of special labour in proportion to its remuneration, i.e. an hour's employment of special labour remunerated at double ordinary rates will count as two units.*

But if the prices of different kinds of labour can be treated as fixed, why not treat as fixed the prices of products themselves? Keynes in the passage we have just quoted cuts the ground at one stroke from under his three preceding pages of condemnation of just such a scalarization-by-value.

4.6   *The use of economics*

Economics is that body of descriptive method and of inference which treats as scalar quantities certain collections of extremely diverse objects and activities, consciously and deliberately ignoring their non-homogeneity. Thus it gains insights of a peculiar sort, without which the economic world would appear

* *General Theory of Employment, Interest and Money*, p. 41.

a mere chaos of proliferating and unintelligible detail, reasonable and orderly only in the small, in space and time, and otherwise altogether lacking any sense or architecture. This achievement of broad intelligibility and visible structure, out of so vast a flood of minutiae and such limitless diversity, is a very great and remarkable achievement. Economics has shown a long reach, but its very success has led to some abuse of its real powers. It has far outstripped in useful conclusions the other social sciences, but it cannot altogether escape the inescapable, the inherent limitations of a most special, peculiar, tantalizing and unique subject-matter, that of human conduct and affairs.

5

Formal Codes and their Efficiency

5.1 *The concept of* code

A set of terms or symbols, and a set of operations or transforms producing one of these entities out of one or more others, constitute what I mean by a formal code. This conception is meant to be envisaged in the most general and thus in the first place the most abstract sense. A sentence of verbal language is the production of more complex meaning out of the simpler meanings of words. The transform or operation involved is here grammatical. Algebra operates upon quantity-symbols to produce other quantities, and frequently the initial quantities (terms, exponents and so on) and also the quantity produced from them, belong each to its respective class of quantities and is thus a variable, so that the produced quantity is a function of the initial quantities. The operations here are evidently the operations of algebra: addition, subtraction, raising to a power, differentiation and integration, and so on. Instead of *code* we might have used the word language. However, we wish to include under the heading of code some techniques or procedures which are less general and flexible, less capable of *novelty by specialism* than ordinary language or mathematical language are. Novelty of thought, when invented, can be expressed only in an *existent language*. How is the contradiction resolved, between what is existent and thus not novel, and what is novel and thus only coming newly into existence? It is by specialism. The particular in such a case is novel, a new meaning attained by an advance from the generalness and abstractness of the forms of language or notation to the greater concreteness of a particular realization, by the use of one general meaning to restrict and specialize another, as a cross-bearing specializes a compass-bearing by means of a distance. But a code in our sense may have only a limited capacity for serving as a vessel of novelty. It can be a working formula or a

[50]

rule of thumb, a technique. As an example we may take the method of determining which algebraic values of the argument of a function correspond to extreme values of the function. Again, the solving of a differential equation in order to disclose the consequences *in extenso* of a given structure of rates of change is such a technique. These encapsulated methods are tempting. A field of phenomena can appear to be reducible to order by such means. A code may present itself as a means of release from anarchy or intolerable variety.

The criterion of success for a code is the contrast between the disorder and diversity of what we seek to understand, the complexity and anarchy of the field of observation, on the one hand, and on the other the encompassing unity and simplicity of its appearance when illuminated by the selective light of the code. The code offers something which can be discerned in all instances in common. It produces a class of situations. In every situation, it shows that one and the same series of steps, beginning with certain terms, or names of classes of entities, will yield a further entity which is the one we seek to understand. Understanding, insight, command of the environment, intuition of future transformations, consist in such discernment of repetitive forms of arrangement of simpler entities into more complex ones. The code is an instruction for practice. To explain an observed situation or event, the code says, look for such and such elements and apply such and such operations to them. If this procedure results in a situation like the one to be explained, we have 'explained' it. For we have rendered it familiar. Understanding consists in the recognition of familiarity. To bring about a desired situation or event, the code says, assemble such and such circumstances and allow them to inter-act. To gain suggestions, at some moment, of what will happen next, apply the code (the sequence of operations) to what can be seen of the kind of circumstances it concerns itself with. The code thus serves as theory, as technique, and as means of conditional prediction. If the code itself is complex and must labour to attain its result, it is not fully successful. The swiftness of the leap from initial elements or circumstances to the final product of the cerebral procedure, the spareness of what intervenes between beginning and end of the operation, is what adjudges the code to be efficient. This also is what accords it beauty. By its brevity and simplicity the code is efficient and elegant; by its unifying of great ostensible diversity, it is powerful. The elegant and powerful codes of one field or discipline are tempting to the analyst engaged in other fields. Once adopted, such a code steers him inexorably down one path of thought. It may or may not in the end be apt to provide him with knowledge worthy of that name.

5.2 *Analytic versus constructive theories*

Theories in economics divide themselves into those which describe situations or states of affairs, and those which describe steps or movements of transformation by which one situation is carried into others. The former we may call analytic and the latter constructive. We shall later show that this is not quite the same distinction as that between static and dynamic. In mathematics, the analytic method consists in supposing a problem to have been solved, and considering what conditions the solution must fulfil. The analytic theories of economics do the same. In the theory of consumer's behaviour, we ask what will be the detailed marks and characteristics of that situation in which the individual income-disposer is getting the most possible satisfaction of his desires out of a given market value of weekly or annual income. The theory shows that when he has attained that situation, his expenditures on two commodities will be such that his marginal rate of substitution between them is equal to the ratio of their prices. It does not discuss any exploration by him of different degrees of satisfaction attainable by different distributions of expenditure. That knowledge is supposed to be instinctively or intuitively available to him, or to have been already arrived at by steps of experiment with which the economist is not concerned. The theory offers no account of any genuine heuristic process. We can if we wish refer to the individual as moving along his budget-line until he comes to its point of tangency with an indifference curve. It says nothing whatever of the prior question, how does he know the shape of the indifference curve? Those curves express a connection between his psychic responses, on one hand, and certain pairs of quantities of consumed goods, which can give rise to those responses, on the other. How does he know what the form and precise character of that connection is? We are not told. Indeed, the question is never raised. Such theories thus pre-suppose a boundary already drawn around the economic field so as to exclude problems of how knowledge may be attained. This pre-disposition of the economist's concern has had immense consequences for his theories and their usefulness, or lack of it. How did this pre-disposition arise? May it not have been the consequence of adopting codes appropriate to the science of *inanimate* events, where the question does not arise, how massive bodies come to be aware of their duty to attract each other with a force proportionate to the inverse square of their distance? In the pursuit of elegant simplicity, analytic theories have a natural advantage over constructive ones. For in the nature of things, in the nature of the human imprisonment in time, constructive theories must describe a process of groping experiment and gambling for knowledge, of being wrong many times in order to be ultimately right, while analytic theories describe what things will be like when, if ever, they have attained rightness. And this contrast of character and of goal between the two types of theory shows us that we cannot simply treat beauty as another name for efficiency. Efficiency is more than spare incisiveness of means. It is also the dramatic, sweeping and surprising scale of the result.

The meaning of analytic theories is epitomized by the word equilibrium. Equilibrium is the expression and result of un-hampered rationality, subject only to each person's renunciation of force and fraud. Rational conduct is that which is demonstrably the most advantageous open to the individual in view of his circumstances. In order to demonstrate its superiority, even if he can do so only to himself, he must know what those circumstances are. Knowable circumstances can be those only of an immediate present. Situations and events removed into the future are not observable, and thus not knowable, for there is no proof of any rigid implication of the future by the past, and such an implication would contradict the notion of originative choice. Rational conduct is thus confined to a time-less or a momentary world. The circumstances which will affect the outcome of given conduct include the actions of other individuals. In order that each person may choose his conduct in effective knowledge of the contemporaneous choices of others, there must be pre-reconciliation of all choices by means of a declaration and pooling of conditional intentions. Equilibrium is the prescription of each person's conduct in accordance with his own preferences thus declared, which emerges from that pooling as its solution, if such exists. The analytic method may thus produce an answer which is unique and unarguable, to the question: How would things be, in a momentary world of perfect pre-reconciled choice? It is the demonstrative character of this answer, its reliance on pure logic or mathematical inference applied to an extremely spare axiomatic base, that gives it its claim to efficiency.

Reason applied to circumstance in pursuit of self-interest is a commanding formula. Why should we not allow it to command us? No formula or code can be expected to illuminate every angle and detail of so intricate, finely-spun and self-deceiving a fabric as that of the general human organization, or even its business aspect alone. Is there not a great gain in having one incisive principle for all questions and situations, one which is understood, because of its ultimate simplicity, by everyone concerned? The analytic method embodied in value theory, with its central idea of equilibrium, answers questions that defeated all previous attempts for centuries. To explain the sharing of the total produce of the society, measured by its market (that is, publicly agreed) value, amongst those who contribute to its making, by merely combining the two notions of marginal product and perfect competition, is a Copernican stroke. Rent, wages, interest, as ostensibly different as the colours of the visible spectrum, are all unified by a conception having almost the simplicity of the inverse square law or the notion of the wave-length of light. Such results showed theory performing with a consummate efficiency its highest duty, the one task which it alone can perform, the satisfying of the pure questing curiosity of the intellect. Men are human because they wonder about things which are for practical and material purposes seemingly useless. Questions whose answers are 'no earthly use', which present to us life and the cosmos *sub specie aeternitatis*, are the ones which release men from their daily frustrations, privations and despondencies. It may seem perverse and absurd to place economic questions, of all things, amongst those which are not materially oriented. Yet to enquire into the nature of rationality, into the sources of conduct, into the admissible meanings of 'choice', is not banal or undignified. Men have been urged by their most revered guides through the ages to 'know themselves'. When economic theory turned in an age of tranquillity to look into the foundations of some aspects of conduct, it was perhaps making the right and appropriate use of a privileged era. However, the late Victorian era was not only an opportunity for an unusually detached and abstract reflection, it was by its nature also a source of deception and a false view. When Victorian optimism was destroyed by the great wars, the theory of basically rational and predictable conduct turned out to be helpless. It could not explain the seemingly irrational and unpredictable events of the 1920s and 1930s, the immense unemployment and the neglect of available resources in the midst of scarcity and poverty. Nor can it explain the apparently impending destruction of currencies and of the orderly price system by runaway inflation in the early 1970s.

5.3 *Business cycle theories*

Constructive or transformational theories purport to show some regularity, some elements of necessary sequence, in the historical succession of states or events. One type of such theories claims that history in the large, as described by great aggregates such as general output, employment or general price levels, broadly repeats itself in a constant pattern of phases of prosperity and depression. Such theories have something in common, and some characteristics widely at variance, with analytic theories.

Business cycle theories assume the society to have a design, such as that of a steam-engine, which prescribes that each 'part' or measured aspect (aggregate general output, aggregate income, total employment) shall move through its own repetitive cycle of phases, tracing a time-path approximating a sine curve with, perhaps, an exponentially growing or diminishing amplitude and a rising trend. The theory may account for this picture by showing how each phase or segment of the wave is necessitated to grow out of the preceding one through market, technological or epistemic features of the mechanism. Or the pattern as a whole may be presented as the solution of a system of difference or differential equations whose character the theory does not attempt to account for. In either treatment there is a reliance on some permanent character of the society, a character which dictates the systematic repetitive movements of its aggregative measures, so that these are in some broad sense predictable. Society is thus looked upon as analogous to the solar system, and its mechanics are compared to celestial mechanics in their regularity, whether or not they are shown to proceed from some single and incisive principle corresponding to the inverse square law. Compared with equilibrium theories, such accounts gain something in realism at a very great sacrifice of the direct appeal which equilibrium theories make to the most prized and peculiar human characteristic, the power of reason and imaginative penetration of circumstance. For business cycle theories give men little credit for any capacity to learn from experience or to legislate co-operatively for an improved working of their affairs. They are assumed to behave in a mechanical, habitual and imperceptive fashion, no more capable of insight or control over their destiny than the valves and pistons of the steam-engine. Business cycle theories are in some sense and degree constructive, in attempting to show how situations are transformed, rather than show merely what a uniquely determinate situation will be like, but the changes described are in another sense no changes at all, since they merely reflect an essential permanence, the fixed design of an 'engine' whose working is always the same.

Theories of the business cycle well illustrate also the use of pre-existing formal conceptions to represent economic phenomena. Wave motion has long been studied by physicists. If the formal properties which imply that waves will be generated by certain physical systems, can be imputed also to economic organizations, a ready-made 'model' of the business cycle will have been provided, which can be described by differential equations or by difference equations. Economics has found the latter more congenial to its own subject-matter. In this method, the equations associate with each other values of the variables which are separated by a time-gap or lag, given which, it can in certain models be shown mathematically (that is, by purely formal argument) that fluctuations, repetitive cycles of phases, are bound to be produced. Does such a model perform the most characteristic duty of a theory, namely, to satisfy the mind's wish for a perfect matching of the hitherto unfamiliar and puzzling, with something which is instinctively and intuitively part of the mind's own constitution? Since there can be no 'explanation' which does not involve a comparison or analogy, we cannot deny the claim of formal models which bestride two streams of subject-matter to be genuine explanations of each in terms of the other. But there are degrees of mind-satisfying power in such appeals.

Let us dispose of a possible misunderstanding. The formal description of systems in such a way that we can infer for each of them the character of an inherently natural behaviour is plainly indispensable. But it is not the whole task. Theory should go beyond the description of modes of behaviour and suggest their sources in some aspect of the nature of things. Doubtless 'the nature of things' does not establish a uniquely meaningful boundary between the formal, on one hand, and, on the other, what can by appeal to intuition bridge the gap between mind and Nature, between Descartes's *res cogitans* and the *res extensa* with which it must cope. But aspects of theory fall plainly on one or other side of even a vaguely conceived boundary. The distinction is illustrated by those theories of the business cycle which view history from outside, which are constructs in the mind of a detached, non-participant analyst for whom distinct dates can be co-valid elements in a structure, rather than the mere projections, from a given, solitary moment, of the thoughts entertained in that moment. The more powerful a formal description is in condensing appearances to a single, simple, all-inclusive principle, the more deeply it contrasts with an argument which puts together, as it were, the mind's direct intuitions without intervening gaps.

5.4 *Time-lags and the transmission of influences through time*

The time-lag theories take as their starting-point a formal assumed association between a measurement of one variable made at one date and a measurement of another variable made at another date. When several such correspondences have been discerned and expressed as equations, the elimination of some variables by substitution for them of expressions which are their equivalent in terms of other variables may yield an equation where differently-dated values of one and the same variable are exhibited as depending on one another. Then an examination of the mathematical character of this equation may show that the variable in question will fluctuate, or that it will move monotonically towards some limiting value, along paths prescribed by the design of the system expressed in its equations, and also on the particular values of its variables during some 'pre-history'. But such a scheme must lead us to ask what vehicle conveys from the situation or event of one date the influence it is supposed to exert on those of another? How do things grow out of each other through time?

Such a question could be asked about the physical world, and it is obvious that in the most fundamental sense we cannot hope to answer it. Insight is comparison, and for the ultimately unique phenomenon, of which one supreme example is time itself, there can of course be no comparison. Our explanations of the physical constitution of the cosmos rest, not on something ultimate and transcendental, but on an appeal to analogies of experience. Even the Democritean atoms, exerting pressure on massive bodies which shielded each other and thus were pushed together (as we should say, by 'gravity'), must have possessed some mass in order to exert that pressure by their impact. But this does not tell us 'what mass is'. In our own problem, it is plain that the physical arrangement of things at any moment (the total physical configuration) is a constraint upon what can physically happen 'next', and also that if there is a tendency or capacity of things to remain in some sense as they are, the state of affairs established in the physical world at one moment can condition the events of a later moment into which that state of affairs is preserved. We can also accept the notion of 'trains' of physical events. The planting and germination of seed will produce a crop in due time, erosion of mountains by weather will form a landscape, and so on. But in human terms the vehicle which carries an influence of the events of one moment to affect or generate those of a later one is human thought: memory, insight, expectation, intention. It seems plain that a theory belonging to what we have called the constructive class, even if it is only a theory of cyclical recurrence, ought, if it is to appeal so far as possible to the foundation of things, to give some place to human thought in a broad sense. Business cycle theories of a purely formal kind, such as neglect the humanity of the stuff they deal with, are asking to be out-witted by man's ingenious mind.

Some analysts of the business cycle find a positive virtue in renouncing any attempt to peer behind a formal mechanism. When they have arrived at a mathematical model which repro-duces the broad movements of the principal aggregative variables describing the economy, over some period of the past, they are content to declare that the business cycle has been 'explained'. They regard as unnecessary and meaningless any selective linking together of individual phases by a suggestion as to how one of them is generated by the other. The mechan-ism, in their contention, is to be viewed as one whole, every aspect, phase and part of its performance being inherent in that self-subsistent unity, and every such part or phase being an expression of its unified design. Thus we are not to ask how recovery takes place from a depressed level of general output and employment. Recovery is inherent in the design of the machine, is as much a part of its nature as the return of the piston of a steam-engine from one end of the cylinder to the other at each revolution of the crank. Yet we are entitled to point out that the unity and repetition of the machine's pattern of movements is visibly accounted for by its mechanical linkages. What is the nature of the linkages in the business cycle machine? They must be the inferences, judgements, decisions, in short, the thoughts, of the business men. Those thoughts need by no means embrace any such abstraction as an entire business cycle and its formal mechanism, they can and will concern themselves at any date largely with the details of the current situation and what has immediately preceded it. Business cycle theories thus offer us a contrast and a conflict between formal elegance and an insistence on seeking insight into the shaping and even the origin of thoughts.

5.5 *Self-transforming expectations as a business cycle theory*

A business cycle theory that seeks such insight, or makes suggestions concerning the problem, need not on that account fall short of a very high degree of unity. Every phase of the business cycle and its mode of transformation into the next and the next phase can be exhibited as belonging to a thought-mechanism, a sequence of states of mind growing naturally one out of another. The Multiplier theory elaborated by Lord Kahn and Lord Keynes shows how an additional continuing stream of output, of goods of a kind which cannot directly satisfy the desires of consumers, will be associated sooner or later with further additional streams, but of directly consumable goods, so that, for example, an addition to the aggregate flow of net investment will lead to a total addition to the stream of general output, larger than the extra stream of net investment itself. If the Multiplier principle is not understood, or not sufficiently reckoned with, by business men, they may regard the consequence of its operation, at a time when they have spontaneously increased their aggregate flow of net investment, as evidence of a further, unexpected improvement of business prospects, and they may on this account further increase their outlay per unit of time on improving and enlarging their equipment. Such a sequence of actions and thoughts may be several times repeated, so that general output appears to have, for reasons not apparent to business men, an upward trend. If, after some time, they come to accept this trend as a reliable feature of the scene with a momentum of its own, they may step up their investment to a degree which is only warranted by this supposition that general output, and its corresponding aggregate income, will continue to grow. The next 'instalment' of such growth will then merely confirm the rightness of the action of which it is itself the consequence, but will not lead to any intensification of that action. Investment will remain roughly constant at its new high level. However, with this cessation of growth of investment, the growth of general output will also cease, and this will disappoint and disconcert those expectations on which the new, steady high level of investment was based. That level will thus appear excessive, and will begin to be reduced, and the growth-phase will thus rapidly dissolve into a cumulative downward movement which will eventually be arrested and reversed by an exactly parallel mechanism working in the opposite sense and generating a fresh boom.

5.6 *Impressions, classes, concepts, stereotypes. Description via abstraction*

Such an account, whatever degree of greater or less realism or realistic suggestion it may have, is evidently an account of what we may properly call a cyclical mechanism. It refers to men's thoughts, but it treats those thoughts as parts of a machine with a permanent design and mode of operation. It makes men robots, or mere circus animals, going through their routines to the guidance of those cues or signals which a peculiar kind of experience has taught them to recognize. But men in the end are more resourceful, more masterly, more ingeniously dissatisfied than that. The real question is, what ultimate building-blocks of conduct, if any, are elemental enough, are sufficiently part of the nature of things and of human nature, to be indispensable to all human endeavours to cope with their essential circumstances, their 'predicament', and are thus the ultimately reliable stuff of theories? A theory will only be efficient if it uses ideas which are elemental in this sense, the irreducible *tesserae* out of which any mosaic of human affairs must be composed. Large-scale formal structures, by contrast, are fragile.

A discipline begins with the separating out of impressions from the general scene and their association with each other as having something in common. To describe a thing or an event is to place it in a class pre-existing by general public convention, a class constituted by means of a name. Such a class, with its name, is a concept. Description is conceptualization. It both uses and stabilizes concepts or named classes. The abstract has thus already been introduced. Description, however, has not finished when objects or events of a general character, conceptual objects or events, have been constituted by means of classification and cross-classification, for these can be seen as forming arrangements or configurations, as occurring in association with each other or in temporal sequence, as forming stereotypes or stable patterns which recur and repeat themselves as the general scene is surveyed or watched. Recurrence, repetition, regularity are names for essentially the same idea. Regularity, 'scientific laws', can be discerned only when the observer's eye sweeps over the scene, moving from one place to another in a succession of moments. Regularity appears as repetition, and repetition, even if in Nature it may mean co-existence of similar things, must in human observation involve temporal sequence. Description rests essentially and indispensably upon abstraction and the formation of concepts, and is thus already theoretical. Nonetheless theory has a distinct process of its own. Stereotypes, the robust and recurrent patterns in which objects and events seem to present themselves in fixed relations, can be subsumed under successively larger and more general or more fundamental configurations. Such constructs may be further classifiable under formal codes, as examples of such codes. Here too the mind appeals to what has already been invented. Codes are borrowed by one discipline from another. Such borrowing can claim a merit of its own, for when one and the same formal code has been imposed upon the phenomena of several fields, progress has ostensibly been made towards the unification of science. Description involves theory, yet there is an axis of thought on which description, with the minimum of theory, forms one pole, while the endeavour to unify, simplify and generalize, the search for the single secret of things, forms the other. Between those who turn their faces towards one or other of these poles, there arises a natural tension. To encompass more and more aspects and lineaments of the general scene within a formal, simple scheme seems to produce science, but it seems also to abandon and discard the 'particulars', the items, each perhaps in some way unique, which compose that general scene. It is for the disciplines concerned with human affairs that this opposition is critical.

5.7 *Tools versus systems*

Let us try to examine the matter empirically, and ask which are the most successful codes that economics has adopted. Let us approach the question, not with a set of pre-conceived tests of abstract qualities or capabilities, but by simply considering which theories, methods, or constructs have been most admired, and which have been most employed, by those intent on insight or on application. The conceptions of our discipline can be classified as tools or systems. Systems arrest the attention of mankind and fire their imagination. They assure us that the world is designed and orderly, not a random and meaningless chaos. They give the individual his sense of having a part to play. They confer meaning and purpose on the circumstances and demands of life. They constitute the Great Institution. Institutions are subject to some human shaping and control, so a system may lend itself to the purposes of policy. Tools, by contrast, so far from relieving the individual of his burden of responsibility, impose one on him, and demand from him, decisions as to what he shall do with the powers which the tools confer. Tools are versatile, passive, waiting for the guiding hand or commanding brain. They do not instruct or orientate their owner, but only constrain him in some degree by their specialized technological powers. Systems, thus, envelope and incorporate the individual, but tools equip him for an adventure on his own. Economics very early enjoyed the prestige of a system, that of the Physiocrats who assimilated the economic aspects of society to the natural world itself, and regarded society as an organism, as a system of inter-necessary activities each sustaining, and each sustained by the system as a whole, just as the living body sustains and is sustained by its individual organs. The Physiocratic system of economic society was compared in importance to the Newtonian system of the material universe. It located the various activities of men in the scheme of things and showed the nature and mechanism of their need of each other. The *Tableau Economique* was admired in its day, and in ours has provided a model for the most successful, in terms of the importance attached to it by governments and the money spent in applying it, of all the methods of the economist, the Leontief input–output analysis. What is it, in these two conceptions, that gives them their ascendancy? The Leontief scheme has several very striking characters. It illustrates, visually and vividly, the notion of a manifold unity. It can involve ten thousand, or a million, input co-efficients, the number of these being the square of the number of sectors

(industries) which the system distinguishes, and the division of
the economy into a hundred, or a thousand, sectors is plainly
still insufficient to secure the homogeneity of the product of each
sector. Yet each of these many input co-efficients performs the
same duty in the scheme: we see a large regiment of quantities
marshalled in row and column and capable of a unified and
dramatic drill, the inversion of the Leontief matrix, which at a
stroke turns the knowledge of the dependence of quantities
available for final use upon total outputs, into a knowledge of
the dependence of total outputs upon final use requirements.
The array of input co-efficients, and that of the co-efficients of
the inverse matrix or solution, is of course a perfect square, and
thus the scheme offers the eye a symmetry which need not be
thought beneath notice. The data required by input–output
analysis are, in principle, data of the direct, undoctored kind
which Leontief himself has recommended as the proper material
for econometric models: the facts directly gathered from the
book-keeping records have a tangible and retainable meaning
which averages and other calculated statistical entities lose in
the process that cooks them up. In sum, input–output analysis
has the virtues of comprehensiveness (every product can find a
place, every source of demand is brought to bear); of essential
simplicity (the notion of solving a system of logically simultaneous, i.e. co-valid, equations); of visual symmetry reflecting
the central economic principle of the dependence, actual or
potential, of every industry and firm upon every other; of importance for practical affairs (the programmes of development
of un-industrialized countries need it as a base); of intelligibility
(the notion of converging streams of supplies to his firm, and
diverging streams of his own output, is necessarily familiar, and
insistently present, to the mind of every business man). 'Leontief' is a model of the whole productive machine, and it is a
model of what a model should be. Lastly, for those with a
sensuous eye for notational elegance, it enjoys the 'coherence
and beautiful simplicity'* of matrix algebra as its vehicle.

The Leontief method belongs to the class of theories which
are for application rather than for insight. It contains only two
economic ideas, that of the inter-necessity of the sectors or industries that compose production as a whole, and that of the self-

* The words are Mr C. F. Carter's.

sufficiency of the system as a whole, residing in the fact of the value supplied by each individual sector to all purchasers taken together being exactly matched by the total value of its intakes. These ideas in combination make up the great contribution of Quesnay in his *Tableau*. It is mathematics rather than economics that gives to input–output analysis its sweeping power and efficiency, and does so by means of a simple and basic procedure, rendered applicable, in face of the great volume of arithmetic which it requires, by the electronic computer.

The hunger of economics for techniques, both for formal codes in our sense, and for the more purely manipulative methods offered by mathematics and statistics, and its catholicity in adopting them, are indeed great sources of its attraction. No one need feel that the tools he brings are unlikely to be useful. In this respect a notable example is the *contour-line*, invented by cartographers in the early eighteenth century to map three dimensions upon two dimensions, so as to represent latitude, longitude and altitude on a flat surface. The indifference curve, the equal-output curve and a score of other applications have shown this brilliant tool to be the economist's best visual aid, almost able to think for itself. It enables him to handle three variables together (his minimum necessary team for many purposes) in Cartesian form, gives him the *point of tangency* to express at one stroke the equality of two functions and the equality of their first derivatives, at some point thus marked out as critical, and brings *economic* considerations (indifference, the optimum, the rate of exchange which clears the market, etc.) into the heart of a formal, simple yet subtle diagram. In the indifference map, economy and geometry form a perfect union, economical in two senses, cutting out a thousand verbal circumlocutions. Edgeworth, Pareto, Barone and Sir John Hicks here endowed economics with a master tool.

The calculus, the Cartesian system, matrix algebra, the notion of mapping, that is, the interpretation of quantities referred to one reference-system in terms of quantities referred to another, are all of them mathematical methods adopted by economics in virtue of its claims as a logical-quantitative discipline. Once it discovered a few of the enormous riches with which mathematics can endow the logical manipulation of measurements, economics was tempted to consider itself one of the 'exact sciences'. It is not even the lack of exactness in its measurements (the more fundamental and inherent imprecisions are those of meaning) but the extent to which their subject-matter consists of *thoughts* and not of *objects*, which makes the assimilation of economic analysis to mechanical science dangerous. Thoughts are transformed invisibly and radically with baffling swiftness, stultifying the accountant's careful additions and subtractions of quantities which become obsolete before they are printed. Even the market only reveals the marginal façade of agreement amongst thoughts whose main depth and direction it is profitable to conceal. Often the market's equilibrium is poised on conflicting conjectures, not reconciled needs, and waits to be destroyed by the essential restlessness of speculators. After all, then, has not economics had ideas of its own, of a character peculiar to itself?

5.8 *The teleological nature of economics and the subversion of determinacy*

It is perhaps the complex skein of ideas gathered under the unified heading of income and capital which is most representative of economics, which, more than many others, is its own invention, and which illustrates most arrestingly its essentially subjective, epistemic and teleological nature. Economics is the analysis of that conduct, and its results, which originate from what people look forward to; conceive, upon fragmentary evidence, as possibly attainable; and devise their policies to achieve: conduct springing from imagination and hope, dependent upon the confined but flowing stream of knowledge. Capital is the discounted assessment of an income-stream, income is expectation; or, income is the change in the capitalized value of supposed deferred receipts of the means of sustaining and enjoying life, the change brought about as the deferment of those expected things is steadily reduced. The two notions, or bundles of notions, capital and income, are intimately related. In natural science, what is thought is built upon what is seen: but in economics, what is seen is built upon what is thought.

Erik Lindahl's 'The concept of income', published in *Essays in Honour of Gustav Cassel* in 1933, proposed that all income, no matter what the basis of those expected receipts on which it rests, can be regarded as appreciation of capital value due to the passage of time. Since the passage of time (or the movement of the 'present moment' along the calendar axis) continually carries the future via the present into the past, there is, inseparably linked with income, the notion of the destruction or transformation of the expected receipts or 'instalments', as they arrive at the present. The resources which any such packet represents are necessarily either consumed or invested. And this introduces the real difficulty into Lindahl's conception. For the size and number of the future instalments which can be counted upon depend on what is done with the instalments which arrive at 'the present'. If the latter are re-invested, an extra series of expected packets is generated whose appreciation with the passage of time means extra income; the size of income thus depends on the intentions concerning the use of future instalments arriving at the present. An infinite regress of the re-investment of the results of re-investment comes into view, and short of a complete plan or policy for disposing of all future packets as they become available, income becomes indeterminate. We have referred to this as a 'difficulty' of Lindahl's conception. But it might be called the chief merit of his conception, for by the surprising conclusion to which it can lead (Lindahl did not carry his argument so far) we are compelled to acknowledge the dependence of the *meaning* of what we now do upon everything that we intend to do in future, and upon everything that our present means, suitably employed and re-employed through all their future generations, can conceivably enable us to do. The teleological concern of economists is thus forced upon us with dramatic impact. The present includes and consists in the future, that invention and figment of imagination. Erik Lindahl's theory of income has high virtues from the viewpoint we are taking in this chapter. It is ostensibly incisive and simple, yet on examination subtle and somewhat elusive. It is sweeping and inclusive in scope. It rests immediately on a central aspect of the Scheme of Things, the 'human predicament', namely, the flow of time. It goes to the heart of things, and in doing so reveals the unsubstantial, mutable and fictional basis of our book-keeping values.

Elsewhere in this volume we have used the word *orientation* to name comprehensively the idea that the value of things depends on what is intended to be done with them. The meaning and effect of such intentions, concerning any one individual item, depends evidently on what use is intended for all the other items in the visible catalogue of our possessions at any moment. The problem of valuation thus becomes essentially arbitrary in principle and theory, and it becomes in some degree, as we shall suggest, a matter of convention. The material frame of business life, as it exists at any moment, can support infinitely many teleological interpretations. Balance sheets are 'strong' in a degree which increases with the proportion of assets which remains *uncommitted* to a particular orientation: assets which are 'liquid'. Yet, of course, liquid assets would be valueless were there not the prospect and assurance of the future availability of non-liquid, that is, of specialized, enjoyable and employable things.

The driver of a car travelling towards a distant row of houses lining his road, will see the surface they present gradually growing in apparent area. As he passes the first house, its disappearance behind him abruptly reduces the visible total area of walls. This may serve as a picture of Lindahl's conception. Perspective here represents the process of discounting for deferment. The movement of the car is the passage of the present moment towards later and later dates on the calendar axis represented by the road, increasing the image or 'present value' of the instalments represented by the houses. Lindahl thus looked with new insight into familiar matters. He left his theory as a new statement of the meaning of income. However, it seemed necessary to us to see where that suggestion leads, and we have sought in the foregoing to draw its highly charged implications. They contribute to that total subversion of determinacy in the economic scene, which seems to us to have emerged from the work of the last forty years.

5.9 *Capital theory and the nature of economics*

We turn now to a thesis which hangs differently upon time as its central strand. Böhm-Bawerk's theory of capital is one of the purest of economic conceptions, borrowing little from other disciplines. He sought to answer the question: What service is rendered by the man who accumulates a stock of material goods, so that the mere existence of such a stock in his possession entitles him to an income and provides its source? The process of accumulation consists, Böhm-Bawerk says, in making longer and longer the interval which elapses between the performing of work, or the application of natural forces, and the moment when the consumable fruits of these inputs become available. The existence of the stock, once it has come into being, makes possible an improved organization of production, by means of a technology which uses labour and the powers of nature more efficiently, and yields a permanently larger output for a given input of these 'original means of production'. Thus the distasteful acceptance of the once-over postponement, till next week, or next year, of some enjoyments which past work had promised for this week or this year, is rewarded by the prospect of larger enjoyments in every year thereafter. An acre of forest is planted each year and grows for thirty years, each year the acre which was planted thirty years ago is cut. But if, for once, the cutting is postponed for five years while the planting continues, the trees in *every* subsequent year, after the five year moratorium, will be thirty-five years instead of thirty years old and will be correspondingly heavier.

Böhm-Bawerk's conception illustrates our claim that a theory's power to give insight is independent of its aptness in framing policy or serving as a basis for statistical studies. Before we can enquire about the source or the justice of rewards for building up a stock of capital, it will be natural and necessary to ask: What is capital, and how is it measured? Is capital the physical facilities of modern industry in their immense variety and specialized complexity, together with the mines, wells, drained fields and planted forests that supply them with materials? How can this vast catalogue of diversity be measured as a scalar quantity? It is plain that the items and quantities in such a list must have what we have called orientation if they are to have the most effect, for given sacrifice, in increasing the product of given inputs of labour and natural forces. But once this fullest efficiency is attained, a further gain in the productivity of the 'original means of production' will require the extension of the capital stock in some directions, there will need to be more tools, more goods in process, of certain kinds (even if of different kinds from any which existed before). How are these additions to be made? They will require work to be done which will add nothing immediately to the outflow of goods ready for consumption. There will need to be a prolongation of the average lapse of time between input of work, by men or Nature, and the output of final product. The Böhm-Bawerk theory proposes to measure the size of a capital stock by means of a variable which, in an evident broad sense, increases monotonically with that stock. The *average period of production* unifies all types of capital goods into an operational concept, giving us, in principle, a method of scalar measurement. It has proved extremely difficult to show precisely how this method is to be applied in practice. We shall seek to dissect these difficulties in Chapter 29. The idea which informs the 'Austrian' theory of capital can be summarized in the expression *capital is time*. Heavy and subtle qualifications are needed before this statement will do. Yet it gives a simplifying insight which makes an immediate appeal. Strangely, there is a modern substitute for Austrian capital-theory which might conceivably offer some hope of actually measuring an 'average period of production' in a modern industrialized nation, namely, the input–output analysis which starts by *sectorizing* the productive machine as a whole. If just one such sector could be briefly interrupted while the rest of the vast apparatus continued at full flood, the speed of the spreading ripple of effects might just conceivably be measured so as to trace the *time-structure* inherent in the *technological structure* of production.* By observing many such ripples, having their respective origins at many different sectors, we might build up a picture of the time-lapses between inputs and outputs over the productive apparatus as a whole, and weight them by the values of the inputs so as to obtain the relevant average. Thus one of the most applicable and practical of economic theories might be married to one of the least applicable, but most insightful, whose modern form owes its high suggestiveness and subtlety to F. A. von Hayek.

* Such a proposal is made in my *A Scheme of Economic Theory*, Chapter vi (Cambridge University Press, 1965).

5.10 *Economic conduct is engendered by thoughts about thoughts*

Impressions of the general scene; configurations which seem to associate these impressions in fixed relationships, and to repeat themselves; classifications of these patterns; general propositions embracing many ostensibly distinct patterns; schemes in which some such propositions are shown to be related to others as logical consequences; something needs to be done with all such thoughts. What we have called a formal code is a means of orderly disposal of these thoughts, a settling of them so that curiosity, mystification, disconnectedness, surprise, are set at rest. The prime duty of a theory is to tidy the mind, leaving it clear for practical activity. Theory also offers techniques, prognosticates the results of given conduct. All such intellectual clearing-up involves imposing order and tidiness upon material that in various degrees is unsuitable for it, and resists it. Economics is faced with special difficulties in this regard, for while natural science is in its first approach concerned with impressions (observations) themselves, economics is composed of thoughts about thoughts. Its subject matter, namely, desires and needs, valuations, the filling of gaps of knowledge, or the filling of a vast field (where knowledge is denied us by the Scheme of Things), by means of invented ideas and suppositions, the drawing of inferences from a composite of knowledge and conjecture; all these are themselves the products of thought and imagination, yet these are what economics has to talk about. Competitive, speculative and bargaining conduct is conduct based on conflicting, mutually exclusive assumptions, conduct in fields where only conflict of opinion or intention can bring a *concert* of action. In battle the opposing sides agree to fight because each expects to win. How can a uniquely true, 'objective' account be given by the analyst, when for the participants, truth is plural and self-contradictory? Economics is concerned with the public aspect of affairs. Exchange must be at an agreed price. Values must be added together into great aggregates or averages: general output or national income; consumption and investment; the general price-level; the quantity of capital. Each man's contribution to such a total will have its own meaning for him, different from the meaning that others would ascribe to it. An average, by its nature, is true of an object composed of particulars, of each of which the average may be false. Economics for these reasons is fundamentally, essentially, imprecise and blurred. It proceeds, in its essence and of its nature, by lumping things together in a way which is, in the last analysis, arbitrary. It ascribes to its composite entities a permanence of meaning, an individuality and determinate character which it knows them to lack. In this fluid, eddying and dissolving subject-matter, what kind of theories or formal codes are 'efficient'?

They will be those which present to the world a double face, while openly insisting that this duality can be resolved only by mental operations lying outside of logic and consistency. A theory, to be useful, must be capable of being seen as exact, simple and essentially unchanging, and to be not misleading it must, in economics, be the vessel of cloudy, fluid and elusive conceptions. Keynes solved this problem by a bold (if somewhat accidental) resort to what I have elsewhere ventured to label a kaleidic method. Situations are portrayed by curves (or their equivalent) in two dimensions, connecting at most three variables (as can be done by the contour-line device, not used by Keynes). But the meaning of these situations is that of momentary, ephemeral glimpses at selected and rare points of a mainly un-adjusted, groping and speculative process, involving vast numbers of variables subject in many cases to an inherent restlessness and precariousness. The jump from one aspect to the other of this two-faced presentation consists formally in the liability of the curves to abrupt, unexplained shifts. We do not ask for explanations of these shifts except on the most *ad hoc* basis, appealing to 'special factors'. The type of theory we are describing renounces, of its nature, any claim to offer a general, permanent frame of explanation of the shifts. This renunciation is the essence of the method. It is what enables the theory to tell its complex and elusive tale in simple and convincing language. But if theory pretends only to give an account of particular, peculiar and special moments (such as may be scarcely ever attained in fact) and repudiates any hope of connecting them by any intelligible, permanent mechanism allowing prognosis, then the theory ought explicitly to be a classificatory one, putting situations in this box or that according to what *can happen* as a sequel to it. Theories which tell us what *will* happen are claiming too much: too much of independence from their turbulent surroundings, too much capacity to remain upright in the gales of politics, diplomacy and technical chance and change, too much internal simplicity for even the world of business itself. Kaleidic theories give insight: preparedness for what cannot, in its nature, be known for sure or exactly or in detail, but which need not spring a total surprise. Classification is no second-rate technique. It is the method of medicine (the doctor classifies disease); of the law (cases are classified as resembling previously decided cases, or as differing from them); of the organization of libraries and museums; of stellar (as opposed to planetary) astronomy (stars are red giants or white dwarfs, they are variable or not, young or old, etc.); and, of course, of botanical and zoological organization of orders, genera and species. Even the procedure for finding solutions of differential equations is a question of groping in a catalogue of possibilities. The efficiency of formal codes is the efficiency of classification.

6

Orientations

6.1 *Choice amongst thoughts*

In the foregoing chapters we have suggested grounds for doubting whether the master-method of the precise sciences of the behaviour of *things* is appropriate to an essentially never-ending pursuit of the originative, elusive, ever-dissolving behaviour of *thoughts*. Economics is about choice, but choice is amongst pure creations of the mind, for experience of the actual is already unique and past the opportunity of choice. Economics studies conduct guided by reason, but guidance is for the future, while reason can base itself only on premises about the past. The theorems of reason concerned with still-choosable conduct must have half their axioms supplied by imagination, for the real axioms are concealed by time. The variables appropriate to the establishment of exact metrical relationships in a model which can be grasped, must be pure and homogeneous, few, permanent in nature, and capable of being insulated from the rest of the cosmos. All four of these conditions are the opposite of what prevails in the economist's field of study. If his variables are to be few they must be aggregative, the opposite of homogeneous. How are they to be permanent, when the whole endeavour of man is continually to transform his circumstances by seeing new meanings and possibilities in his physical surroundings? Or how can any action he takes escape the dependence of its outcome on everything that exists and happens in the world? How can economic variables have uniquely precise meanings, when they purport to make scalar quantities out of the immense diversity of objects composing society's general output or its equipment or its general level of prices?

The exact model expressed in equations whose form and co-efficients are invariant against all changes of circumstance, is unsuitable to the economic subject-matter for several reasons.

A variable is a class of recorded or conceivable measurements. To be deemed to form a class, the instances of measurement must be performed on like objects by like procedures. But the matters of essential concern to economics do not offer us such opportunities. The conduct of individuals who continually gain knowledge and originate thoughts upon it will not appear consistent. To out-rival their competitors, the most effective means will be invention, the exploitation of novelty. But novelty is that which is not necessarily intelligible by reference to the past. Thus a *variable* (a class whose members have some relevant character or circumstance in common) will be in many subject-matters of measurement an unsuitable vessel for collecting the operations of an individual. The same effect will be seen in aggregative variables, for individuals are imitative and suggestible, and will swing off together on new courses rather than give an effect of consistency through the mutual independence of their responses and the 'law of large numbers'. But aggregative variables, indispensable if a general model is to be interpretable and meaningful to intuition, have their own capacity for generating inconsistencies. Their composition can change and thus the relative weights of diversely behaving components. Such internal sources of dissolution of the subject matter and essential meaning of a variable are paralleled by those which affect the model as a whole. The parameters of any model are inevitably permeated by non-economic influences of commanding importance, from politics, diplomacy and power-hunger in general; from demagogic rivalry; from the intense pursuit of technological improvement. *Ceteris paribus* is a mere pedagogic device or means to insight, and cannot be turned into practical experimental insulation. Most alien of all features of the economic field to the concept of an exact and stable associative pattern amongst variables of reliable content is the co-existence of multiple valuations of one and the same object, arising from the totally different orientations which can exist simultaneously in different minds or even in one mind. An *orientation*, a scheme to exploit in a particular way the economic scene as it presents itself to some individual at some moment, will assign to the object its role in the total scheme. But schemes can be innumerable. The transformations which a scheme can undergo can be continual and endless. Thus, a thing is not one thing but many different things, according to its possible uses and involvements. If the essential quantities of the economic discipline are valuations, how can a variable of stable content, or a function of stable form, be constructed from them?

6.2 *A kaleidic society*

In face of these difficulties which the orthodoxy of natural science encounters when it enters the economic field, something new might at least be excusably attempted. The business scene and its participants can be looked on as staging a contest of rival orientations, rival ambitions, rival exploitations of the world. It is capable, for all the analyst can tell *ex ante facto*, of realizing some one or other of these visions in some degree, and thus of presenting an appearance of momentary or temporary orderliness during the ascendancy of one orientation and its sponsors. Or the contest may be inconclusive and sterile, and result in a period of rudderless backing and filling of the sails and of untidy, blind struggle and groping for decisive policy. It will be a *kaleidic* society, interspersing its moments or intervals of order, assurance and beauty with sudden disintegration and a cascade into a new pattern. Such an account of the politico-economic process may at various epochs or in the course of various historical ages appear less or more suggestive and illuminating. It invites the analyst to consider the society as consisting of a skein of *potentiae*, and to ask himself, not what *will* be its course, but what that course is capable of being in case of the ascendancy of this or that ambition entertained by this or that interest. The rival orientations, in the pure form of each if it were conceivable that one or other would be perfectly realized, would define the boundary of the possible situations, or transforms of situations, through which the society might pass in the course of a few years or a few decades. The partial or mixed success of several would lead to interior paths within this boundary, or to the temporary loss of a sense of direction. Such a loss of direction, in the economic aspect of affairs, might consist in a catastrophic slump or an uncontrollable inflation and the destruction of the currency and the society's confidence. The orthodox approach of science, even in the era of Heisenberg

and Gödel, proposes to look on the course of affairs as determinate. The kaleidic approach proposes to deem those affairs to
be bounded, but within those bounds to offer a rich manifold of
rivalry and indeterminism.

The course of history can be envisaged as a succession of
states of affairs (situations) or as a succession of transformations
of one state into another (events or transforms). If we wish for a
formal notation, we can express a situation as a vector of as
many elements (measurements, values of variables) as will
present the desired degree of detail. Two such vectors, representing situations at different dates, can be carried one into the
other by a diagonal matrix of the ratios of the corresponding
elements or subject-matters. Thus a historical succession will
appear either as a series of vectors, or as one (column) vector,
the 'initial' situation, multiplied on the left by a series of
matrices or transforms. A formal scheme of this nature may be
helpful to our present mode of conceiving the economy. Its
events will be of two kinds. There will be physical, 'visible' and
public events involving objects; and there will be thoughts
assigning to these objects, uses, involvements and valuations.
The formal scheme need not distinguish between the two kinds.
But any instance or example of such a scheme will be the work
of one individual mind, and every mind must have its own. The
course of business, the course of history at large, will be made up
of the endeavour to follow out what are believed to be the
intentions of policies which are in force; of the seizing of
ascendancy by one group of interests from another and the
substitution of the former's policies for those of the latter; and
the origination of new policies by any interest or individual,
whether or not he can immediately give effect to his ideas. The
source of this whole stream of history will be the ideas, and the
ideas will come, not by continuous and gradual change, but by
discontinuous, decisive shifts. If so, the appropriate scheme of
analysis is one which starts from the notion of multiple, mutually
inconsistent conceptions of the momentary states of affairs and
of their potential sequels, multiple orientations entertained by
different individuals or, some of them, even by one, and of a
play of shifting light ('the news') which endows first one and
then another with relevance and influence. The freedom for
arbitrary division of history into shorter or longer intervals, and

the description of the content of any interval by means of a set of co-efficients or ratios of change, may itself be advantageous in reflecting what may in some true sense and degree be a discontinuous process. At least such a scheme will not encourage us to see emergent history as implicit in its own past, nor as unique, objective, manifest and public. What seems, is; and what seems is what seems to each and any one of us.

The kaleidic movement of affairs, the interspersion of abrupt shifts and intervals of ostensible stability, is a natural social response to uncertainty. When 'the news' is fragmentary, conflicting and incoherent, men's only resort is to wait for some extra pieces of the puzzle to appear and some persuasive suggestion of meaning to emerge. In high uncertainty, a man feels himself surrounded by possible false steps and perhaps far more to be lost than gained. There is a general truce and withdrawal. But the current of those affairs which are necessary in order that men may stay alive will eventually render untenable some of the frozen positions which have been taken up. Some interests will be driven to break out of increasingly insistent difficulties, the incipient movement will gather adherents to various interpretations of its meaning, and the landslide phase, of lesser or greater importance, will have begun. The business scene, moreover, is made up of smaller and larger pieces. The interpretation and manipulation of the larger pieces, the policies of governments, the outcome of political and diplomatic ambitions, of the greater commercial schemes, are momentous and intimidating. There will be hesitation to take the first step. Meanwhile, play can go on with the smaller pieces. Play with the smaller pieces will constitute stability, until a clear advantage for some one or other party to the large-scale game appears. Finally, there is the desire of ambitious men to transform only a part of the scene, their own standing, against a background of stability in the rest. For only within a stable environment can success have a clear meaning and measure. The man whose frame of reference is rotating, whose world is adopting new valuations, cannot establish his claim to success in his own or others' judgement. There will be a desire to preserve the general order of things. Ambition and conservation have a large interest in common. On such grounds, we may claim that the kaleidic model is realistic. The analyst can in some degree adapt himself to it.

The kaleidic analyst must, of course, recognize the real market as a speculative market. Even in the value-theory market for perishable consumers' goods, unanimity is at the *margin*. Intra-marginal valuations can differ from each other unconstrained by the marginal agreement. Consumer's surplus is determined by personal individual tastes and circumstances. But in the markets for storable goods, for durable goods, for producers' systems of equipment, for bonds and, in general, for *assets* whose whole essence resides in their reference to the future, the intra-marginal basis of valuation can even be in total contrast and contradiction: when Bears and Bulls have brought the securities market to a temporary rest, this may be at a price which Bears judge to be so high as to presage a fall and which Bulls judge to be so low as to promise a rise. Whatever the market does, whether it moves in one or other direction or remains still, it will disappoint or frustrate one or other camp and induce action which will affect the price. A speculative market is spontaneously restless. The analyst of such a market can seek only, so far as there is time, to dissect the evidence, suggestions and interpretations on which the dissentient camps have built their views, to gauge their sensitivity to the varieties of conceivable 'news', to classify according to some scheme the types of orientation which have generated, and been generated by, the existing posture of the market. The Stock Market is only the most obvious and volatile aspect of a modern society's pervasive character of multiple, divergent orientations. What classificatory principle can give insight into such a character and its consequences?

7

Reason versus Knowledge

7.1 *Self-consistency of purpose and of action*

What the economist is concerned to do, according to some, is to work out 'the pure logic of choice'. Reason has attracted man since the Greeks, because it was something that a man could find within himself. A few ideas or statements put together became a powerful entity. These propositions were like the several faces of a prism. They could be seen simply as what they ostensibly stated, each on its own, and viewed thus they formed a mere collection. But when light was viewed through the prism as a whole, so that several faces had a part in the matter all at once, there were surprising revelations of the colours of the spectrum, latent meanings of the set of propositions taken as a whole became apparent. Men seemed to be equipped with a power to discern and elicit such inner meanings. The process of eliciting them could be pursued indefinitely. A geometry capable of endless elaboration could be envisaged. The process yielded the pleasures of surprise and of invention. Truth appeared to be limitlessly rich and manifold, yet capable of condensation to a nucleus of a few simple statements. This conception must surely reflect the essential nature of some important thing. Was that thing the cosmos itself, outside of the human mind? Or was it the attainable human picture of the cosmos, something that could exist only within, and in virtue of, the mind? Or was it the mind itself? Or, finally, were all these things one and the same thing?

Reason, it seemed evident, represented and insisted upon one character which truth must have: truth must be consistent with itself. Any description of what is, any account of the cosmos, must be a unity. It was useless to present a collection of ideas about the cosmos, some of which conflicted with others. And by the same token, there was something unsatisfactory, something to be remedied, in any scheme of actions whose individual elements partly defeated or obstructed each other, *unnecessarily*. Economics, seen as the pure logic of choice, takes as its task the pointing out of such avoidable clashes. Conduct, as well as understanding, ought to be a unity. Each part of it ought to be designed and adopted in awareness of the other parts, potential conflicts must be arbitrated, the opposing expeditions must be brought to a halt before they collided.

The acceptance of this view meant that certain other ideas had also been accepted, or must now be accepted. The whole notion of self-consistent action implied and rested on the supposition that there was some test or criterion of whether one set of actions produced results more desirable or less desirable than those of another set. Indeed, the whole meaning of consistency (beyond that of mere physical or technological compatibility) required some purpose or end, or some scheme of ends, to be stated. For in its absence, an action would have no value or meaning, good or bad. And this requirement required in turn that the effects of given actions should be assumed to be known or knowable. Economics as pure logic was thus pure in a very extreme sense. It applied a test to any proposed scheme of action, a test in respect of a formal characteristic, that of self-consistency in the pursuit of a unified scheme of ends. These ends themselves, in order to deserve to be called a unified scheme, would have to be reconciled with each other. Beyond requiring such unity of the ends, economics was wholly unconcerned as to their nature. But the test which it was concerned to apply could only be applied in certain circumstances, namely, when any contemplated scheme of action could be seen to have one and only one possible result (a result uniquely specified in relevant matters, no matter how complex the whole), and was certain therefore to attain that result. This was the austere view taken by the 'purists' of the nature and duty of economics. But the question arises of the limitations imposed by this austerity on the application of economic theory.

7.2 *Logic and the attainment of data*

One such limitation is what we may call the assumption of the single maximand. Even this problem falls into two parts.

Robinson Crusoe might have found difficulty in deciding between two courses of action, if he had been unable to weigh one sort of satisfaction against another. If he had been unable to find within himself some psychic weighing machine which declared that in some specific situation an extra daily gallon of milk was more important to him than the leisure he could enjoy by having fewer goats to milk, he would have faced an insoluble dilemma. But there evidently is such a weighing machine, and 'tastes' as a whole do provide a man with a unifying criterion, a single maximand of comfort, satisfaction or call it what we will. It is far less clear that a society has such a weighing machine. It would have very little claim to have one, were it not for the market. The vote is no substitute. The member of a minority party may find his views and wishes quite unrepresented in government policy. Even a member of a majority party may have been given no clear idea of what that policy was going to be, he might find large parts of any declared policy distasteful, and even if a wholly acceptable policy were declared in advance, he has no guarantee that all or any of it will be adhered to when his party attains power and is faced with the pressures and distractions of responsible office. But the market is very different. The report which the market furnishes of what the society desires is partly written by each individual member. His influence is real if not easily perceptible; it is continuous in time; it carries effective sanctions against those who ignore it, or fail to watch for its signals. In politics, it pays best to be one of a large crowd. In the market, however, it is often best to be one of a few. The man with rare capacities and skills can sell his work for a high price. But above all, the virtue of the market is that each member of the market can adjust his own affairs so that his relative valuations of different goods are those of the market. To do so is to practise 'economy', which is a quite distinct thing from parsimony, and is something which every distinct *interest*, every person, firm or government, does well to have at the back of its policy making. For to be antieconomical is to be inconsistent, it is to engage in actions which are at odds with each other, it is to be less effective than one could be. The detail of a formal consistency, in such matters as the best output of goods which can only be produced in fixed proportions, or such questions as the imputation of costs of productive facilities common to many products, can be subtle and complex. It is this formal guidance that economics, in the sense of 'the pure logic of choice', can give. Such guidance still requires to be brought down from the formal and abstract plane to that of concrete detail and practice by the engineer, the chemist, the soil scientist and other technologists.

The market, then, enables the individual to adapt his conduct to his circumstances, and thus elicits from all individuals taken together a certain kind of unanimity as to what should be produced, and by what means. It solves, for society, subject to one proviso, the problem of the single maximand. That proviso is an essential and difficult one. It is that the endowments of individuals, in their quantities and qualities whatever these happen to be, both personal capacities and possessions, are accepted as right or just or unalterable, or else that such as can be altered are deliberately adjusted before the individuals bring their tastes to bear on the market.

The other, and more intractable, limitation from which economic theory suffers through the abstract and formal character of its concerns is that of knowledge. Economic theory indicates what to do in face of certain data. It does not suggest how they are to be come by, except for the consultation of the market. To advise a man to buy such weekly quantities of this good and of the other, that his marginal rate of substitution o. one of them for the other is the same as the ratio of their market prices, is very well. But how does he discover his marginal rate of substitution, if the goods are unfamiliar, either through being newly invented, or because they have only now come within reach of his income? This may seem a trifling difficulty, though not so trifling when it involves the choice of a place to live in. But there are greater difficulties. The goods amongst which he is to choose may depend for their usefulness on circumstances of the future, which now can only be conjectured. And the question what it is now worth his while to pay, in exchange for some specific good, depends also, if that good is storable, on what the *price* of that good is going to be in future. The market cannot solve the problem of expectation. The only price it can distil, for a storable non-perishable good, is one which divides the potential holders of that good into two camps, those who think its price will rise and those who think its price will fall.

For at the moment when all are agreed on the direction of the next movement, that movement, paradoxically, will prove to have already taken place.

7.3   The bounds of rationality

What does economic theory, in its traditional form called value theory, do in effect? It defines the nature and necessary conditions of self-consistent action for an individual, and of general pre-reconciliation of action amongst the members of a society. Pre-reconciliation ensures that each individual, given his endowment of skills, capacities and material possessions or purchasing power, gets the most satisfaction which is possible for him in his given environment of other individuals with their respective desires and endowments, on the supposition that every one of all the individuals is to be exempt from force and fraud, to have equal freedom to make exchanges with others, and equal and perfect knowledge of the exchanges which are available. What we seek here to insist on is the extremely limited range of situations in which the necessary conditions, for giving such rationality its full meaning and effect, are fulfilled. To discern what specific action is rational is only useful *ex ante*, but is mostly only possible *ex post*.

We may venture on a bolder and more incisive statement. Rationality cannot span a temporal succession of situations. Each situation in such a series includes within its specification a specific collection of data available to a given individual. These data in the nature of things are confined at most to the present and the past. But what is relevant for choice of action is the future, except in so far as available action is strictly confined to the immediate now, a single moment divorced from any temporal sequel. Each present moment by itself can, conceivably, be so dealt with by suitable organization that its actions can be pre-reconciled. But everything that one moment bequeaths to a subsequent moment, everything now present which depends for its meaning, purpose and value on a subsequent moment, removes choice of action from any possibility of being rational, in the strict sense of demonstrable superiority of outcome over all other available courses; demonstrable, that is to say, *in advance* of the taking of action.

Strict rationality, the claim of a chosen action to be based on full relevant information and to be demonstrably superior in its results to any other available, is of course not the only basis on which an action can be recommended with good conscience or adopted with equanimity. But it *is* the only basis to which traditional value theory appeals. Such a criterion *forbids* the study of the question of what men in any given context and situation can know. If we refuse to examine their problems of choice, save on the assumption that they know everything relevant, plainly the question of what they can or cannot know is transformed into the question of what situations we shall or shall not allow to be part of the economic field of study. And in excluding all situations where the chooser is not fully informed, or even where he is not able to prove himself fully informed, we are evidently rendering value theory in its rigorous form only obliquely relevant to the practical concerns of life. It has its powerful bearing on our conduct; but that bearing does not consist in propositions directly applicable to real conduct, but in propositions *directly* applicable only to an abstract system which shadows forth one aspect only of the problem of practical affairs, a system designed to highlight the question of internal consistency of any scheme of action. This abstract world, the class of problems amenable to perfectly rational solutions, is the setting in which the nature and necessary conditions of consistency can be most sharply illuminated. To press home the meaning and value of consistency is a service of prime importance which value theory has rendered. The lesson is one which some systems of economic organization have neglected to their detriment.

How did it come about that the field of knowledge chosen by economic theoreticians in the Victorian era should be circumscribed with such extreme narrowness? We can answer only speculatively. We may be inclined to refer to the immense prestige of the reasoning discipline in its most far-reaching form, mathematics; to the simplicity and unity achieved in the seventeenth century by celestial mechanics, and to the grandeur of its subject matter; to the conviction of determinacy in the cosmos, and to the inference that this determinacy must necessarily include human affairs, and to the natural consequent desire to find a simple, single principle of such determinacy. That principle was found in the supposition that men pursue their ends by applying reason to their circumstances; and this supposition was taken to be equivalent to supposing that their circumstances directly govern their actions. In fact, however, an important and essential part of that governance is exerted not directly but through men's knowledge and thoughts; and by that fact the whole scheme of things is divorced from the physical analogy. The study of the pure application of reason drove out and logically excluded the question of the possibility, nature and source of knowledge. The part which reason can play in organizing a body of knowledge, and the part it can play in determining the best action, stand sharply in contrast; for the validity of the knowledge of general principles is independent of the historical calendar, but the question: What is the best action? is wholly dependent on the unique historical situation; and any knowledge of that situation, which is lacking when it is needed, is effectively lacking for ever and is for ever too late.

BOOK II

The Rise of the Rational Ideal

8

The Construct of Reason

8.1 *Two questions examined by economic theory*

Economic theory has asked two questions: How will things happen? What will things be like? The former leads to a study of diachronic forms, of a series of situations growing in some sense one out of another and thus composing a unity spread along the calendar. The latter leads to the construction of an exact, encompassing, timeless adjustment. Our purpose is now to consider this contrast of method and of the insight which the two methods seek. Both methods, in the nature of things, must study *what is* at some (one or more) *moment*. For existence is existence at a moment, the moment of existence is solitary and by itself. In the diachronic method, however, what exists is assumed to have, as a whole, such a character that it must needs transform itself into something different in the next moment. In the synchronic method, transformations have merely a potential existence as a background to throw into relief the adjustment which has been attained. The water in the lake is level and still, it is perfectly adjusted to the shape of the basin which contains it. If it were ever to find itself high up on the hillsides round about, it would flow down them. But this hypothetical event is invoked only to explain the meaning of stability. Part of the essence of the adjustment is that it has within itself no inherent propensity to change. The water, if we wish, *has* flowed down the hillsides, but it will not of its own accord flow up them again.

The posture of mind and the basic pre-suppositions from which one of these methods springs is different in essential ways from those of the other. The dominant principle of the equilibrium method is that men's conduct is guided by reason and that it can shape its affairs to the demands of reason. In the diachronic method we are shown, by contrast, those affairs being borne on the broad current of self-determining, or organically

evolving, history. It is too much to suppose that men can discover a set of biographies, one for each of them, such as would
fit together in a pre-reconciled fashion and give to each of them
the best he could get, subject to the equal freedom of other men
to seek their 'best'. The notion of a wholly foreseen and wholly
constrained biography-to-come is nightmarish, let alone the
inconceivable complexity of the task of pre-reconciliation and
the general implausibility of the logical existence of a solution.
A general solution, or general equilibrium, has accordingly to
be conceived as a state of affairs and not a course of affairs.

8.2 *Rationality dependent on synchronicity*

General equilibrium is the natural and even the logical arrival
point of that procedure of theorizing which assumes that men
pursue their interests by applying reason to their circumstances.
Here we have reason in a double role. Men's conduct, springing
in given circumstances solely from reason, can be understood
by a reasoning analysis. The particularity of the circumstances
themselves can be made to vanish or become irrelevant by
framing our explanation in terms of general or universal
principles. The theory of value, which names this procedure
and its results, adds no more than broadly-stated *classes* of
circumstance to those formal, abstract and general principles
which mainly make up its substance. The theory of value does
not give usable guidance or prescription, since it does not tell
how in practice and detail to apply its precepts, save in a few
respects or in a few matters abstracted from the difficulties of
reality. It is proper to claim that insight, not guidance, is this
theory's business. Even its insight, however, is of a special kind.
It is insight into a system of actions by a number of individuals,
a system which, by the conditions required to be fulfilled by the
value-theory procedure itself, must logically be *timeless or
momentary*. For reason can only be applied to circumstances in
so far as those circumstances are taken as known. But the
circumstances relevant to the choice of actions include other
men's chosen actions. If the solution is to be *general* or *symmetrical*, if it is to accord to any and every person, no matter
whom, a freedom and knowledge formally identical with those

of every other person, if the rules of the game are to be precisely the same for all, the various actions of all these persons must be pre-reconciled. But choices which are pre-reconciled are effectively simultaneous. Actions dictated by impeccable and demonstrable reason must base their justification on their membership of a general system of synchronous actions, a system whose essential character of synchronicity will not be impaired by letting these actions be complicated and involve 'sequential' phases.

To act by reason, a man must be fully informed of his circumstances so far as they bear on the outcome of his action. For a circumstance whose character he does not know, but which by being one thing or the other will affect what he achieves, must leave him in doubt of his best course. Whatever course he chooses will then not be *demonstrably* the unique best one. We may go further, and say that this demonstrable superiority of his action requires not only that he be fully informed of all circumstances bearing on those aspects of the outcome which interest or concern him, but that he be able to demonstrate this completeness of his information. Such a condition may in practice be hard to fulfil, and conceivably, save in special cases, impossible in logic. To analyse conduct on the assumption that it is fully guided by demonstrable reason thus leads the analyst to ask the second of our two questions: What will things be like? For his chosen method allows him only to study the character of a general and encompassing pre-reconciliation of action, a static and timeless system of adjustment. *Sequential* actions, transformations of one situation into a subsequent and different one, occurring successively, are excluded in the nature of things from being studied as the consequences of pure reason, unless these successive transformations all belong to simultaneously pre-reconciled plans. Thus the analyst who wishes to ask: How will things happen? must suppose conduct to transgress the bounds of demonstrable reason. The *static method* in economic theory, the choice of the question: What will it be like? imposes itself on those who are resolved to treat human conduct as rational.

8.3 *Value theory's relaxations from rationality*

Value theory has of course not been content to remain within the confines thus imposed. It is worth while to consider some list of the things which they exclude. The timeless equilibrium can accommodate exchange, and treat exchanges as the outcome of the confrontation of tastes and endowments of goods. Pre-reconciled plans could cover the technological preparation of goods whose exchange was agreed upon, there could be 'production'. But there could be no *enterprise*, no place for Cantillon's merchant whose function and source of gain was to buy at a certain (i.e. known) price with the purpose of selling later on at an as yet uncertain price. There could be no bilateral monopoly, no bargaining, where success depends upon deception, upon an imposing of ignorance or misconception by one party on the other. There could be no investment in long-lasting specialized equipment whose value might be eroded or destroyed by innovations. Indeed, how could there be saving, in a system essentially timeless? But above all, novelty, *new* knowledge, invention and origination are wholly alien to the rational, timeless, static system. There could be Game Theory in the von Neumann–Morgenstern sense, but not real games or tactical contests where the greatest secret of victory is *surprise*. For in Game Theory there is no surprise but only calculation.

Value theory, the construct of reason, the postulator of reason in conduct and the explainer of conduct as the interaction of circumstance, interest and reason, had in practice to make some concessions to the unreasonable aspects of the human state. Though actuality is a moment, it is a flowing moment continually changing. The future moments or their transformations can be imagined in endless rival forms. These contending expectations help to generate the actual course of things. Value theory was under strong pressure to acknowledge a flow and not merely a moment of time. The expected moments were sequential and displaced each other into a more and more 'remote' future. A part of conduct would be directed towards the further and not the imminent future, there would be a concern to build up wealth as provision for remote times, or to take advantage of the 'elbow-room' of future time. There was

conduct whose principle was the very opposite of pre-reconciliation, and was instead the intention to take others by surprise, to disconcert their plans while concealing one's own, to
foster and to exploit the others' *lack* of knowledge. All this
implies that choice of conduct involves far more than pure
reason. Value theory has responded to this challenge in three
ways. In some cases, as in Edgeworth's theory of bilateral
monopoly, illustrated by his picture of Crusoe bargaining with
Man Friday, the theory repudiates all concern with those
aspects which cannot be reduced to reason: the price in
bilateral monopoly is *indeterminate* within the contract zone. In
other directions, value theory has adopted constructions no less
unreal than the timeless system of pre-reconciled actions, but
able, by drastic abstraction and artificiality, to accommodate
some aspects of the flow or the extension of time. Such is the
stationary state.

8.4 *The insidiae of particular equilibrium*

Thirdly, value theory has resorted to *particular equilibrium* and
ceteris paribus. Economic society is seen as composed of a few
types of building-blocks, each type able to be understood by
studying a representative. The nature and conduct of each type
is studied by considering how its interest dictates that it should
act when the conditions and environment of this action are
prescribed and *passive*. Finally, it is supposed that this insight into
the parts is insight into the whole. This is the method of Alfred
Marshall, lending itself to detailed observational study as well
as theory, and to the formulation of precise statements, but
tempting the analyst to leave unexamined the nature and
meaning of the aggregation or scaling-up of partial systems into
the general one. Particular equilibrium is the method of
natural non-human science. There, uniformity is assumed with
proven justification. Nature falls into classes of elementary
particles, atoms, molecules, crystals, living organisms, rock
formations; and into classes of events uniform in essentials.
Inanimate objects do not cheat the scientist by behaving
differently today from yesterday in 'the same' conditions
external to their thoughts. They have no thoughts, or not

scheming, illusive and disconcerting ones. Nature is not political. Natural science uses the controlled experiment, in which one circumstance or measurable characteristic alone is deliberately varied by a measured amount, and the accompaniments or sequels of this change are noted. The observed association of changes in different respects is held to reveal part of the architecture of things. In economic theorizing this is the method of *ceteris paribus*. It conceals a most insidious danger. It overlooks the governance of human conduct by *interpreted* circumstance. The massive body falling freely in a vacuum does not inquire into the intentions and hidden thoughts of the force of gravity. But the human contestant with a rival or an enemy does. In prescribing what shall be treated as constant, the analyst in that very prescription unavoidably and necessarily prescribes what questions the subject he is studying need not and cannot concern himself with. If demand conditions for a firm's product are to be taken as *given*, the conceptual firm is relieved of any need to consider selling methods. It need not ask itself whether rival firms will be so noticeably affected by its actions that they will make a direct riposte of unknown character. If in analysing the firm's choice of what, how and how much to produce, the analyst confines himself to the 'short period' in which the firm's durable facilities are *given*, he absolves the firm from making investment decisions. The firm's insistent, oppressive, overriding difficulty in real business life is how to gain *knowledge* of its situation, how to read the thoughts of technical originators whom it cannot name, of rivals whose order-books it cannot inspect, of trade-union leaders whose intentions are carefully misrepresented, of fashion-setters whose guiding aim is capricious change. The analyst of particular equilibrium assumes these difficulties away, providing his conceptual firm with supposititious knowledge without minding how this could be attained. Thus by the nature of his method he desiccates and sterilizes the problems.

Partial equilibrium can also mislead us by the very simplicity of its geometric language. For by supposing that nothing changes except price, amongst conditions which could affect the weekly quantity demanded of some goods, it can represent the mode of association of price and demand by a Cartesian plane curve. And by a similar supposition it can represent the association of price and weekly quantity offered by another plane curve. Then it can assert that price will change until it reaches the point of intersection of the two curves. In such an account one question has not yet been asked: How can we be sure that price can alter without bodily shifting one, or both, curves and compelling us, at each movement of price, to re-draw them? For a movement along the supposedly stable supply curve, implying a change of both price and quantity, implies thereby a change in the income of the producers of the good. But can a section of society have its income increased without spending more than before on every commodity? And if it does so, what becomes of the supposed stability of the demand curve? Is it not impossible in logic for the two curves each to be stable and unshifting, and *each at the same time* to be meaningful as representing concomitant variation of price and quantity? It is not implausible or unreasonable to assume that *demand is unaffected by supply*, provided the production of the good in question is only a minute proportion of the society's aggre-gate income. For then, since the demand for any one commodity will depend on the incomes earned in producing all commodi-ties, the mutual influence of the demand and the supply of one commodity can be neglected. Partial equilibrium is, precisely, a method appropriate to so small a part of the economy that the reflection upon it of the effects of its own actions, from the great absorbent bulk of the rest of the economy, is negligible. If the mutual independence of demand and supply conditions is to be legitimately assumed, the relative smallness of the partial system is essential. Yet before 1936, value theory tacitly assumed that in the labour market itself, money wage rates could be reduced without affecting the flow of monetary demand for commodities and thus for labour to make them.

8.5 *The limitations of the relevance of reason*

Insight into the parts is not sufficient for insight into the whole. Reason is not sufficient for the guidance of conduct. These two propositions explain why economic theory was unable, in the early 1930s, to understand or even to believe possible the catastrophe of business depression and massive general unemployment which had occurred. Economic choice does not consist in comparing the items in a list, known to be complete, of given fully specified rival and certainly attainable results. It consists in first creating, by conjecture and reasoned imagination on the basis of mere suggestions offered by visible or recorded circumstance, the things on which hope can be fixed. These things, at the time when they are available for choice, are thoughts and even figments. In matters of immediate physical performance, experience or expertise is a sure enough guide. Practical life can be lived, and what we expect is usually broadly realized. But business does not consist solely in hand to mouth operations. By contrast, it looks into remote years and continually seeks technological innovations which will render much of its own calculations obsolete. In mathematics and in other kinds of science, reason can find novelty. But if we wish to claim that reason by itself is a sufficient guide for conduct, we need to claim, not that reason can find novelty, but that it can find *all* novelties and thus *exhaust* novelty. Only when novelty is eliminated and all is known can reason be the sole guide of conduct. It is only in the timeless fiction of general equilibrium that reason can prevail alone.

It is not only time which is at odds with the supremacy of reason. Duopoly is that situation where two interests face each other in isolation from all others. Cournot supposes that the whole supply of a uniform product is in the hands of two sellers. Their combined output (daily or weekly quantity which can be sold) is a stable function, known to each, of the price, which is necessarily the same for both. The product is costless to each seller. Each seeks to maximize his revenue, that is, his own output times the common price, by adjusting his own output. Each has therefore, in deciding on his action, to make an assumption about his rival's responding action. The game is tacitly assumed to be played with formal courtesy, each making a move in turn. At the outset of the game, each seller has a certain output. Seller A is to make the first move, and Cournot supposes him to assume that B will keep B's output unchanged in face of any change in A's. If B makes an assumption symmetrical with A's, A's assumption will be falsified. Yet what ground has A for assuming that B will think differently from A?

A's next suggestion to himself may be to assume that B will adjust B's output on the supposition of constancy of A's output after one adjustment. Then A must design that 'first' adjustment to exploit the notion that B will adjust B's output to take B's best advantage of it. But may not B have in mind this second possible step of A's thought? The only end to the otherwise infinite regress of mutually out-reaching thoughts is a recognition of its futility. The dilemma has a profound and simple meaning. Victorious aggression is not possible for both of two contestants. If rational conduct is that which brings victory, it is not symmetrically and generally available. And each contestant should ask himself why he, and not his opponent, should be privileged to make use of reason. The duopoly problem in its essential nature implies that reason in some circumstances can fail in its guidance and defeat itself.

8.6 *Bargaining and the meaning of indeterminacy*

Bilateral monopoly is the situation where one sole seller faces one sole potential buyer. It is the case of bargaining. Attempts at formal analysis fall into two classes, the same two classes which we named at the beginning of this chapter. The analyst can ask: What will things be like, when reason has been given full opportunity? or he can ask: How will things happen, when reason is a flickering lantern on an unknown road? The former, the equilibrium treatment, will concern itself only with what is mandatory upon one party or the other in view of his tastes and circumstances. But there is no general ground for supposing that this sort of guidance will be sufficient to prescribe his conduct. It is as though a traveller should ask: Since I wish to travel to the next town, what must I do? and his guide should say: Avoid falling into the river over there, and do not get lost in the forest. Equilibrium is a solution, and there is, in the most general frame of thought, no guarantee that a problem which presents itself, unchosen and undesigned by us, will have any solution, or that it will not have an infinity of solutions. In either case, there is no prescription of conduct.

Edgeworth* showed that the tastes and circumstances of the

* F. Y. Edgeworth, *Mathematical Psychics*, 1881.

two parties in bilateral monopoly, their *interests*, do not, except by the most unlikely accident, determine what their conduct should be. These data merely circumscribe an arena within which, in Jevons's words quoted by Edgeworth, the 'transaction must be settled upon other than strictly economical grounds'. What grounds are deemed strictly economical is evidently at the taste of the analyst. Edgeworth and Jevons excluded from the economist's concern the essential bargaining *process*. This process was not reducible to fully informed reason.

Edgeworth supposes Crusoe and Man Friday to be seeking an agreement about the number of daily hours that Friday shall work for Crusoe and the pay he shall receive. If distances northward from the origin in a Cartesian diagram (see Fig. 8.1) represent Friday's hours of work, and distances eastward his pay, any point in the north-eastern quadrant will represent a contract. The longer the daily hours proposed, the more distasteful to Friday the marginal minute will be, and the greater the increment of pay he will require if such a minute is to be accepted. Even the first minute will have some minimum pay which will make worth while its inroad upon leisure, and further minutes will require successively larger additions to total daily pay. There will be a curve, extending north-eastwards from the origin and bending towards the east, such that points north and west of this curve will represent contracts less desirable to Man Friday than no contract at all. This is for Friday an indifference curve. For Crusoe a curve also starting from the origin, but lying southward and eastward of Friday's and bending northward, will mark a boundary on whose south-eastward side will lie those contracts, which to Crusoe are less desirable than no contract at all. This is for Crusoe an indifference curve. Edgeworth does not show in his own diagram any other indifference curves than these two. However, it is plain that any point on the west–east axis can be the start of an indifference curve for Friday, and that if such a starting point is distinct from the origin, no point on its curve can coincide with, or lie to the north-westward of, Friday's *origin indifference curve*. Any point in the north-eastern quadrant, lying to south and east of Friday's origin indifference curve, can be deemed to lie on one or other of an infinite family of Friday's indifference curves densely covering the north-eastern quadrant. In the

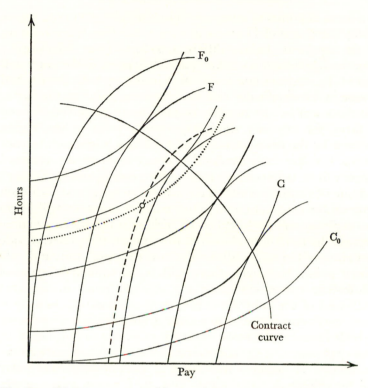

Fig. 8.1. Distances eastward from origin represent total pay given by Crusoe. Distances northward represent total hours worked by Man Friday. F_0: Friday's origin indifference curve; C_0: Crusoe's origin indifference curve. Contract curve: locus of tangents of F and C curves, specimens of which are labelled F, C. Broken line (- - -): F curve containing a randomly-chosen point lying SW of the contract curve. Dotted line (. . . . .): C curve containing same randomly-chosen point. The tangency lying between the broken and dotted lines lies on Crusoe's preferred side of the dotted line and on Friday's preferred side of the broken line. Consequently the tangency is preferred to the random point by both Crusoe and Friday.

same way, the north-eastern quadrant to the north and west of Crusoe's origin indifference curve will be densely covered with indifference curves for Crusoe. If we assume, plausibly, that Friday's indifference curves are all convex to the north-west, and Crusoe's curves are all convex to the south-east, there will

be a locus of points of tangency between pairs of curves, one of
Friday's and one of Crusoe's in each pair. This locus gives us,
by an argument slightly different in form from Edgeworth's
own, the Edgeworthian *contract curve*. Any point to the south and
west of the contract curve will be rejected by both Friday and
Crusoe in favour of some one and the same point on the curve,
and there will be any number of such points preferred by both
of them, for any one randomly chosen point in the region
enclosed by the contract curve and the two origin indifference
curves. For any such randomly chosen point in the enclosed
region will lie between two indifference curves, one of Friday's
and one of Crusoe's which have a point of tangency with each
other on the contract curve. That point of tangency will lie on
the *preferred side* for Friday of Friday's indifference curve
through the randomly chosen point, and on the preferred side
for Crusoe of Crusoe's indifference curve through the randomly
chosen point. Moreover, there will be an infinity of pairs of
indifference curves enclosing any random point in the area
south-west of the contract curve. Any randomly chosen point
to the north-east of the contract curve will similarly be rejected
by both Friday and Crusoe in favour of some one or other of an
infinity of points on the contract curve. Once some point on the
contract curve becomes the object of discussion, neither party
will be willing to move away from it. For any move north-
westward *along* the contract curve, meaning more work for less
pay, will be unacceptable to Friday, while any move along the
contract curve south eastward, meaning more pay for less work,
will be unacceptable to Crusoe. Any and every point on the
contract curve, lying between its points of intersection with
Friday's and Crusoe's respective origin indifference curves,
will, if they can once agree upon it, be more advantageous to
each of them than no agreement at all. But of any two such
points, one will be more advantageous to Friday, and the other
to Crusoe. Which point will they agree on, and how will they
arrive at any agreement?

   Which point? It is this question which the data admitted by
Edgeworth as proper to the economist's method cannot answer:
'Contract without competition is indeterminate'. If we are
prepared to admit other data, and can obtain them, we may be
able in principle to answer the second question: How will they

settle on some one point? But to think on these lines is to transform the question from: What will things be like? to: How will things happen?

8.7 *Value theory's choice of question*

One idea, whose formal beauty and efficiency are hard to overstate, enabled value theory to suggest that when the respective interests of the members of a society are collated within the timeless frame of fully informed and perfectly ingenuous reason, there will plausibly emerge a unique solution prescribing one action and one only for each member. This idea was the assertion that the marginal efficacy of a commodity, or of a means of production, in satisfying need or contributing to output, would diminish as its proportion to other commodities or factors was increased. *How* collation of individual interests could take place was not really a problem to which value theory felt obliged to address itself. Such a matter was not the stuff of which elegant works of the theoretician's art are made. Let this collation be shown to be logically conceivable, and let the solution be shown to be determinate, that is, unique, and value theory would have achieved its triumph, its construct of reason would have been perfected. The policy of attempting the question: What will things be like? rather than the question: How will things happen? would thus possess one powerful justification. For it is very difficult to conceive that there could be shown, on any assumptions short of caricature, to be only one single way in which things could happen, one uniquely possible course of events; diachronic models are arbitrary in a way that equilibrium theory is not. There are, perhaps, three options. We can elect non-arbitrary abstraction, or else arbitrary quasi-realism; or we can abjure the search for rigour and exactness, and find some other means of organizing our perceptions.

9

Subjective Marginalism

Economics is a search for the method of getting the most out of things. But this assignment taken literally would sink it in a morass of detailed technology. There are so many senses and respects, so many kinds of things, in which such an endeavour could be applied. Economics wished to concern itself with general principles, with an over-riding logic. Only so could it be a *system* of thought, a discipline, a means to a unifying insight. Getting the most out of things (or getting what was wanted out of the least quantity of things) had a formal language. There must evidently be something adjustable or tactically manoeuvrable about the 'things', else nothing could be done. Something about the 'things' must be capable of variation, there must be an independent variable, 'independent' in the sense that *we* are free to manipulate it directly, either in thought or fact. Then the desired result must respond in its degree to our manipulation, it must be a dependent variable. If once the desired result could be regarded as a function of something which was both constrained and adjustable, the whole business fell into shape as a classic maximizing problem. There was a problem: What must the lines or rules of conduct be, to find what (algebraic) value of the independent variable gave the locally largest, or least (algebraic) value of the dependent variable? Economics needed a question to answer, and one which could be answered with great generalness. Here was one. The answer flowed at once in precision and detail from the differential calculus.

The calculus procedure does not directly interpret itself as an economic problem. That colour must be given to it by our description of the variables. To make the formal problem (namely, the finding of a value of the independent variable such that the corresponding value of the dependent variable is a locally extreme value) into an economic problem, we have to interpret the range of the independent variable as a range of choice of the use to be made of some resource limited in quantity. But if we are to avoid a plunge into technology which would quite destroy any hope of generalness, the nature of the choice must be simple. Since we are stipulating a limited quantity of some (presumably homogeneous) resource, the simplest kind of use will be an *exchange* into some one or other set of quantities of other things. In the simplest case, our independent variable will be a proportion between two quantities of things into which the exchange can be made. Besides giving our problem an economic content, we have to show that this content implies the *existence* of an extreme value of the dependent variable. By satisfying the first requirement by means of an independent variable representing proportions, we thus satisfy the second, for changing proportions have an effect on human satisfactions and on technological efficacy that guarantees the existence of maxima or minima. There thus resides in the logic of economy, or making the most out of limited means, a remarkable unity of its formal and its psychic aspects, which must surely in part explain the fifty-year ascendancy of an ultimately somewhat arid and complacent doctrine. Economics was brought to a halt by having arrived at a terminus, the end of a road. Subjective marginalism, conferring determinacy on the conception of general equilibrium, brought one system of economic theory to perfection.

In mathematics the analytical method consists in supposing the problem solved and considering what must be the characteristics of the solution. For practical purposes, in a sense, the procedure thus starts from the wrong end. The method offers tests of whether or not a proposed solution is a solution, rather than a heuristic policy for determining what the solution can be. One of these two kinds of answer can of course throw light on the other. In the problem of maxima and minima of suitably differentiable functions, we know that at an extreme value of the function its first derivative will be zero. Then the practical problem is pushed back a stage, and we can search for a value of the independent variable which makes the derivative vanish. But this may hardly be easier in practical terms than a direct groping for the maximum or minimum. It may amount to precisely the same thing. The consumer's expenditure should be so distributed over two goods, that his marginal rate of substitution of one for the other is equal to the ratio at which these goods exchange for each other on the market. But what the consumer really knows is which basket of goods he prefers. His marginal rate of substitution is not so much a *route* to a knowledge of the best basket, as an inference from that knowledge. The business man who is adjured to use such quantities of various factors of production as to equalize their marginal products per weekly £10-worth, may feel that successful experiments in cheapening his process may be deemed to have attained their result quite directly, rather than via a study of difference quotients. His real problems are technological ones, and they are not limited to choosing between a given list or range of possible combinations of *quantities* of known and specified materials and skills. There is not just one cook-book, but an endless number, and new ones are all the time being brought out. Even without novelty, technology involves an indescribable richness of form and fact which cannot even in logic be reduced to number. The notion that quantity and metrical fact are the whole of science, if not indeed the whole of knowledge, would be too grotesque to be worthy of rebuttal, were it not so pervasively insidious and had it not shown itself so attractive to economists.

The formal notion of pre-reconciled choice solves, within a highly artificial and abstract frame, the problem of how men can make their choices of action in full knowledge of each other's simultaneous choices. Such a solution is necessary to the notion of strict rationality, the exercise of reason upon complete relevant information, since the latter must include the intended actions of others. But pre-reconciled choice does not of itself ensure a unique solution. If no other condition were imposed, each man might find himself indifferent between so great a diversity of situations that the members of the society would be able to accommodate each other's wishes in countless different systems of actions, and equilibrium would be indeterminate. Diminishing marginal rates of substitution, whether of goods to please the consumer or of factors to be used in production, is the foundation of whatever determinacy, whatever limitation in the number of solutions, can exist in any society. The means of establishing this is itself one of the peculiar ingenuities of economic theory. It is persuasive rather than rigorous. If the society is numerous enough, the individual's actions within it, with his negligible proportion of its total resources, can be what he will without noticeably affecting it. Thus in making his own choice he can be taken to face a *given* situation, expressed in a set of given market prices. These and his wealth expressed in terms of any one available good define his opportunities in the form, for example, of a straight budget line in a two-good system, while his diminishing rate of substitution of these goods for each other is manifested by the convexity of his indifference curves to the origin. Then a unique point of tangency between an indifference curve and the budget line indicates his unique preferred action, namely, the exchange of such quantities as are necessary, in view of his initial set of possessed quantities, to bring him to that point. Thus demonstrable determinate general equilibrium rests, in the traditional value-theory analysis, on the tripod of pre-reconciliation, diminishing marginal rates of substitution, and the assumedly negligible effect on society as a whole of the portion of it (individual or firm) which constitutes the representative subject of 'partial' analysis. Determinacy can, of course, be a character of systems where the individual income disposer or the individual firm cannot be treated as having negligible influence on the rest. But if so, economic theory would need a different approach from the one built up in the thirty or forty years from 1870.

The outcome of those years was a theory which satisfied to an extraordinary degree some canons of conceptual beauty. It answered a list of questions which seem to form a closed circle and to achieve a self-subsistent completeness. It invoked very few ultimate principles. It achieved a unified simplicity which powerfully commands assent. On its own terms it explained everything. All this had its price. Value theory cannot accommodate time. But time is in any case alien to reason. Value theory was the construct of reason, with only a minimal appeal to experience.

The principle of diminishing marginal efficacy was the main part of that appeal. Only by observing his own or other people's choices could a man establish the principle that when n or $n+1$ unit flows of some good were offered as rival opportunities, the incremental flow of some other good, sufficient to induce him to choose n, diminished as he contemplated larger and larger n obtained by sacrificing more and more of his supply of the other good. Only by comparing the outputs attained when n or $n+1$ units of some factor of production were employed along with given quantities of other factors, could a man establish that the difference of output diminished as n increased. To choose one thing rather than another is in effect to exchange one thing for another, and choice or exchange was recognized as the central economic phenomenon. Choices were pre-reconciled, or exchanges were brought into a general relation with each other, in the market. Production also is exchange, the exchange of forms of resources. When all choices and available technological transformations (that is, all exchanges, simple or via production) were pre-reconciled on the market, the whole of the activity, the entire phenomenon, which concerns value theory was present and could be exhibited as self-determining. Thus value theory attained its aesthetic goal.

The questions it could be said to answer, within its frame of a single, synchronous system of actions, were: What things and how much of them will be produced, and who will receive what quantities of these things? Inputs, outputs, exchanges, prices and 'income' distribution could all be discerned in the picture, the whole subject-matter of static analysis was present in it. Complete specification of all actions and their complete mutual pre-reconciliation deprived any lapse of time or sequence of moments of any role or meaning. It was a unity, satisfying, if we like, the canons of dramatic unity. Neo-classical value theory sought insight, but sought it along lines governed by taste, by the desire for elegance and perfection.

Value theory as the expression of the rational ideal of conduct could find no place for time. Reason requires completeness. The things and the conditions with which it is to deal must be in view. Neither what has happened and is unalterable, nor what has not yet happened and is invisible can be manipulated by reason. Reason deals with the abstract, the conceptual. It is perhaps insufficient to say that the neo-classical construct was concerned with the momentary present. It dealt with a world removed from time, a world to which time was alien. The whole mystery of things resides in the experience of time, but reason has no truck with mystery.

Time suggests a skein of numberless ideas. Some of these have little to do with the experience of the flow of transformation and the engenderment of history. Some such selected aspects merely provide a dimension along which situations or events can be sequentially arranged. It is felt that the quantities of which value theory must speak ought to have the formal character of flows, ought, that is, to be of dimension xt^{-1}, where x is dollars, litres, kilograms, etc., and t^{-1} is an expression meaning 'per hour' or 'per annum'. Or it is felt that the contemplator of value theory will wish to know how the pieces fall into place, there will need after all to be room for some aspects of the question: How do things happen? The great fact obtrudes itself that at every randomly-chosen historical epoch there has been accumulation to bring some things to their existing state. Must not value theory somehow take account of the motives for accumulation? Value theory therefore has not completely elided time, but has retained a mask composed of time-like features. In particular, it allows itself questions about *stability*, it resorts to the stationary state and to comparative stationary states, and annexes a province called the theory of capital. In so far as these things are concerned with the time of actuality and experience, they have no rightful place in value theory's ideal of rigour. In so far as they do find a place in it, the time they speak of is an artefact.

10

The Concept of Value

10.1 *Value as a shadow of conduct*

Value arises from the possibility of exchange. Until one kind of thing can be had *instead* of another, the question does not arise of what quantity of one is equivalent to a given quantity of the other. The exchange need not involve two parties. Technological exchange of one potential possession for another, when each can be produced by the same set of available resources, is a choice confronting Robinson Crusoe and every free individual who has his time and powers to direct into this channel or that. It is thus that *value* comes to occupy so central a place in those theories of conduct which speak of 'freedom' and of 'choice'. When we spoke of a free individual, however, we meant one unconstrained by other men. It is needless to labour the dilemmas on which we are impaled by any attempt to say what is meant, in a profounder sense, by 'freedom' and by 'choice'. Economics has run headlong and heedless into the thicket. It offers to analyse and explain 'free choice' by assuming that men pursue their advantage down the path, supposedly unique, which reason and circumstance point out. They go, that is, where they must go and do what they must do, for is not their free choice dictated by reason and their situation?

The value of 'value', then, is as an analytical, explanatory, linguistic token. Value, like an index number, is an answer to a calculation, not a 'thing in itself'. In the dilemma of choice and freedom versus completely explained conduct, conduct fully accounted for and explained away, it is choice and freedom which are words out of place. The value-construct is a determinist system, its aim and essence are the reduction of action to mere response. 'Value' is an auxiliary or instrumental notion, a shadow cast by men's actions and employed to interpret them. Like a shadow, it abstracts from the reality the mere outline of a complex and involved structure, a structure, in this case, of thoughts, knowledge, tastes and feelings. It reifies a mere collection of measurements. Yet in this, of course, it conforms to the modern notion of a concept, something whose meaning is fixed by the nature of the operations by which it can be quantified.

10.2 *Value and aggregation*

Through all its historical phases, except for Keynes's massive, brilliant but still ineffectual attempt to persuade men differently, economics has remained an endeavour to scalarize, mechanize and determinize conduct and the consequences that flow from the inter-action of conduct. Value is the instrument, not only of the determinism of value theory but of the scalar mechanics of macro-economic aggregative theory. Aggregation requires the items which are to be added together to have some common measure. 'Value' provides that measure. It is assumed that market values, being public values which, though determined by individual actions *en masse*, re-act upon those actions, are homogeneous and render addable, despite their diversity, the objects to which the market assigns value. But such public values are merely the surface of things. They are often the meeting-points of opposites in expectation, interpretation, intention and potential response to any shift of visible circumstance. They reflect entirely dissimilar orientations, in the sense which we have proposed for this word in Chapter 6. Market values are not the lengths and masses of the engineer, but they tempt the social accountant, and the enterprise accountant, to treat them as such.

10.3 *Value and consumer's surplus*

When they are the prices of consumable goods, market values can claim a unanimous acceptance, because consumers, the disposers of incomes, adjust their expenditures on this good and that good so that each individual brings his marginal rate of substitution into equality with the relative market prices which the demands of the individuals as a body have helped to determine. As we have recognized at least since Marshall, such an equilibrium price does not express the average 'utility' or 'significance' to the individual of his units of a good. The total importance to him of the daily or weekly quantity of a good that he buys is not measured by multiplying this quantity by the price he pays. He has a consumer's surplus. And yet it will be meaningless to add his consumer's surpluses, measured for each good in the Marshallian manner, together. For the Marshallian consumer's surplus in respect of any good is a 'particular equilibrium' concept, calculable only for one good at a time. The Marshallian consumer's surplus for a good, for some particular individual, is arrived at by securing his answers to the questions: How much would you pay for (e.g.) one sole ounce per week?; for a second ounce per week?, and so on. But when these measures of the importance to him of the individual successive 'layers' of his weekly intake of one good are added together, and when the same is done for every good, the grand total of notional weekly expenditures will come to far more, of course, than his actual total of weekly consumption expenditure, and very likely more than his weekly income, unless his weekly supplies are limited to smaller quantities than those which, at market prices, he is actually able to buy.

10.4 *Market values and the defacement of reality*

Market values are thus insidious. The scalar calculations which they permit seem to have a meaning and relevance which closer consideration must deny them. But even the market values themselves are less firmly grounded in stable fact than they may appear. For we have to consider the effects of shifts of demand and supply conditions, shifts which, in particular analysis, will be expressed by bodily deformations and displacements of curves. Price elasticities of demand such as are, let us say, numerically small, imply that a physically larger flow of some good on to the market will be reflected as a flow which in market value terms is smaller. In this way a technological advance can reduce the market measure of the society's income, at least in the short period. The deliberate destruction of part of a bumper crop of some foodstuff can actually increase the market valuation of that income. Such possibilities may be swallowed up in the general conformity of market-price measures to physical changes, but they mean that the market measure of aggregate income is a rough one and of debatable meaning. We have referred to technological advance. It is plain that change in general, in technology, taste or social organization and policy (in especial, the after-tax distribution of income) robs market values of meaning for historical comparisons over periods longer than a very few years. By its insistence on measuring the unmeasurable, economics bludgeons the face of reality, the detail and vitality of human concerns are flattened to an unrecognizable tedium.

10.5 *Value and expectation*

Price-unanimity can prevail amongst buyers of goods for their own immediate consumption. This unanimity refers to an equilibrium and to the margin. It depends upon an all-inclusive pre-reconciliation of choices, and is thus confined to an effectively timeless system. It refers to one particular point on each consumer's schedule of desire for each commodity, the point where his social and physical environment have halted the further extension of the satisfaction of those desires. It is thus intimately related to the supposed circumstances of a single-moment system of endowments, desires and choices. It is needless to insist upon the unrealism of this conception. How could it be more remote from experience? It has one sole purpose: to exhibit men's actions as dependent upon reason and circumstance alone. This is a purpose that it is needful and right for economists to perform, for men are indeed guided and misguided by reason. But men take thought for the morrow, and it is then that reason loses the aid of fact. Where reason must work with suggestion, expectation and figment, market prices are a still less direct reflection of men's total thoughts than in the world of immediate and future-less consumption.

The speculator holds particular assets because he *disagrees* with the market's valuation of them. His valuation of them is private, for if it were publicly agreed his hopes of gain would be gone. The existence of 'futures' markets is a mere technical gloss on the essential situation, and leaves essentially untouched the freedom of opinions about the future to diverge from each other and from the pronouncements of any market.

If the price of any durable or storable good is to remain even briefly at rest, it needs to have attained a level which divides the potential holders of this asset into Bulls and Bears of its price. For if all of them suddenly come to think alike, at that moment the price will change abruptly. Yet the public values of many goods have a greater stability than the speculative possibilities that essentially, ineradicably inhere in all but the most ephemeral objects might lead us to expect. If price stability, in reality, is not ensured by a direct governance of prices exerted through human reason by visible, objective circumstances which are themselves stable, then the practical needs of business and the workability of life demand that it be conjured *ex nihilo* by tacit, instinctive agreement, that is, by *convention*. For price stability of some degree is an indispensable support for stability of the rules of the business game and those of the broader game of survival itself. Stability by convention, by indolence, by letting 'well' alone, by the strong instinct to preserve a frame of sanity, by the need of humanity's self-esteem to pretend to control its affairs, has to serve instead of stability determined by reason and knowledge.

10.6 'Value' or values?

The word 'value' has played perhaps too great a part in our literature. There is not 'value', but there are values. There is no constant, permanent, isolable thing called 'value', there are only the ratios in which goods exchange in the particular circumstances of a particular day and hour on a market. Market values are the solutions of the practical task of pre-reconciliation of actions. They are signals and expressions of a situation in which tastes or needs, endowments, expectations are the real elements, elements which are some of them ephemeral and scarcely to be traced to any source observable by more than single individuals, and perhaps not even by them: the speculative hopes and anxieties, the expectations conjured from scarcely recognized suggestions and principles of interpretation. *Value* suggests something intrinsic to physical objects or performances, subsisting in its own right, capable of being stored up in vessels of guaranteed security, and poured from one such vessel to another. Value is, instead, in each momentary and special instance the child of circumstance. Even prices, exchange values, were declared by Pareto to be 'auxiliaries, to be finally eliminated, leaving us in the presence of tastes and obstacles alone'. The weight that Marshall put on the possibility of measurement of the strength of motives by money was part of his reliance on the study of 'particular' small parts of the economic scene. He well knew that a given quantity of money meant the same thing only in appropriately similar situations. If economics is found by some to be a mean and unedifying study, this attitude is partly the fault of economists themselves, who have allowed the flavour of their subject to be disguised by the distasteful associations of a word. The subtlety, elusiveness and fascinating difficulty of political economy are not well rendered by the word 'value' with its somewhat sordid accretions of modern meaning.

I I

Quantity versus Form

Value theory is the study of variable proportions. It is interested almost exclusively in the effect of having one rather than another set of relative quantities of various kinds of thing in the consumer's shopping list or the producer's outfit of factors of production. The 'kinds of thing' are the merest abstractions, assigned only such qualities as being necessaries or luxuries, as being slowly or quickly adjustable in quantity, as being in more, or less, elastic supply. The economic analyst renounces all concern with the technical or artistic character of these ingredients, with questions of how or why they delight the consumer or serve the purpose of the artisan. The analyst is not interested in *form*. His characteristic question is not How? but How much? This blinkered vision of the economist, no matter whether or in what degree unavoidable, desirable or essential to some of his purposes, has powerful consequences which must be examined if we are to be clear what kinds of insight his methods can and cannot provide. Linked with this enquiry is the question of how it has come about that economic theory treats quantity alone as important, and neglects or abjures all interest in the real internal structure or visible conformation of things, in how they work physically or how they appeal to instinct, taste and judgement or fire the human imagination by suggestion of beauty.

From this cause, from his disregard of *form* in a very general sense of that word, the economist's advice to policy-makers must often appear crude and be misleading. Thus he gives the impression that investment policy is a matter only of millions spent per year, no matter on what. Efficiency is for him a matter of best mixes, not of best shapes. He seems to treat knowledge as a stuff, obtainable in measurable quantities for a known expenditure, and guaranteed to produce effects knowable in advance; he believes that we can know in advance precisely what it is, in all essentials, that we are going to find out. Better a contradiction in terms than acknowledge a chink, let alone a gaping rent, in the armour of rationality. The economic theoretician's guidance is like the navigator's lines of latitude and longitude, a necessary frame of reference but no substitute for the details of the chart, the soundings and the outline of the coast. The analyst's concerns are a thin gruel, but he takes no pains to make this understood. He counsels the firm to set its output where marginal cost equals marginal revenue, as though this were an applicable recipe in itself, instead of a step made relevant at the very last, by a vast process of review of products, methods and materials. His analytical bent and training lead him to start at the end, with a test which tells whether the answer is right, instead of telling how to begin finding it. How did economics come to limit its purview in such a manner, and was this policy a good one or not?

It is possible, perhaps, to see broadly how economics has come so sharply and explicitly to eschew technology and the concrete and particular *arts*, as distinct from the abstract and general logic, of making a living. In brief, those arts and technologies are overwhelming in range and in change. To try to embrace them in detail would be to make economics synonymous with applied science as a whole. Yet economics is the study of business, and applied science is the very image that modern business has of itself. Can there, then, be a *general* theory of technics, a *rationale* of the productive arts, a body of principles which would unify and simplify the panorama of production so as to illuminate it as a source of history? Economics has sometimes glimpsed the problem. Marshall, profoundly conscious of the flowing tide of technology and responding to it with his greatest innovations, asking himself whether any principles were conceivable which it would not wash away, still found it worth while to study the physical operations of the carpenter and to understand the technical details of many a trade. What general theoretician nowadays would dream of emulating his example?

The goal of science is to unify, to exhibit diverse phenomena as examples of a single principle or an intimate connectivity of principles. A discipline which merely catalogues its items, even on some universal plan claiming to be *raisonné*, is only a data

bank. Professor Joan Robinson has pointed out how the variegated and colourful denizens of the sea, so ostensibly different
from each other, look far more alike when reduced to bare
skeletons. Science aims to *skeletize* phenomena. But the methods
of modern industry cannot be skeletized in any way useful to
individual industries and firms. Their detail is their essence.
Things are done *just so and so*, not 'by the principle of the lever'
or 'by burning out impurities with oxygen', though even those
prescriptions would not be much of a unification. In becoming,
or aspiring to become, a science, economics had to turn its back
on pin-making *per se*. Adam Smith could have found a hundred
examples of the division of labour. His great discovery was a
rare example in economics of a substantive, rather than a
logical, *principle*. There is one great difference between the arts
and crafts, the technologies, on one hand, and the sciences concerned with insight and truth on the other. Technique is
essentially the particularity of detail. Science is abstraction,
generalness; and abstraction is the negation of detail. In electing
to be a science, economics was obliged to confine itself to some
aspects of business which are generalizable. Thus it reduced
business to quantities, and quantities to market values.

However, there was another possibility, another course which
economic theory might have taken, and which it has given
some hint of taking in some of its specialist branches such as
agriculture and transport. It might have sought to formulate
general principles about technologies. Likenesses and uni-
formities might have been hypothesized in trades based on a
particular feature: the cutting edge, the use of high tempera-
tures, the use of hammering or grinding processes, dependence
on particular soils or climates. And a hint might have been
taken from modern chemistry and genetics concerning the
importance and essential governance of outcomes by spatial
configuration and dimension. The molecule and the atom are
not mere baskets of ingredients, they are architectures. The
codes of heredity depend upon arrangement and not mere
combination. What account has economic theory taken of the
sequence in space or time of the elements or ingredients of the
phenomena it studies? It has done so in macro-economics, in
theories of the business cycle. But in value theory, and especially
in that branch of it known as the theory of production, there is

great neglect of conformation, of shape, arrangement, design and physical, as distinct from mere proportional, general characteristics. The search for such principles, the pursuit of useful hypotheses about threads of uniformity running through ostensibly diverse sectors of production, might call for audacious ingenuity, but it would open fresh fields of suggestion where at present economic theory seems to be running into the sands of over-refined logic.

If James Watt, Nasmyth or Maudslay had watched and reflected upon the pin-makers, he might have arrived at much of Adam Smith's conclusions: but from that point, where would he have carried economics? Power, friction, hardness, strength, plasticity, might not these have become the categories of an industrial *general* science? Would this have been merely the science of engineering? No, for we can conceive the emergence of a notion of technological exchange-value, the gaining of strength at the sacrifice of lightness, the balancing of desirable qualities at the margin, perhaps a concept of industrial general performance. Would this have been no more and no less than economy, the greatest result from given means? It would have expressed in those terms the result, not of relative quantities only, but of shapes, curvatures, spatial organizations, materials, critical paths, and general productive address. Economics, in truth, has sought to simplify and unify the phenomena of business by means of the heaven-sent general scale of measurement, *exchange-value*. By means of exchange-value, everything of every kind, colour, aptitude and form can be reduced to a scalar quantity. In the interest of additiveness, all distinctions, specialisms, identities can be blotted out. Two questions offer themselves: Is scalarity compatible with a sufficient insight? Is there no other road to simplicity and unity than exchange-value? We may consider the things that the physical chemist does, that go beyond mere weighing, his use of the electron microscope to examine spatial relationships, his construction of models of molecules in which the constellation, the spatial arrangement, is the basis and explanation, at sub-molecular level, of the properties which substances exhibit in the large. As to the second question, we may feel inclined to answer that the phenomena of the market, the instrument on which the existence of exchange-values depends, are important and interesting in their own right, that they are the signals which pre-reconcile conduct and make it coherent. It remains true that exchange-value is an expression of need confronted with means, of tastes confronted with obstacles. Pareto regarded price as secondary. His indifference curves are combined, not with a budget line but with paths of physical transformation. There have been times, and minds, which veered distinctly towards an economics of *qualities* and not merely of quantities and values. It would have to be a classificatory economics. That, too, might provide new revelations.

Between theory and 'fact' there is a perpetual tension. Theory (the complaint goes) makes its way by ignoring any details, complications or questions that would spoil the classic simplicity of its elected scheme. But these details and difficulties (the theme continues) are the substance of the business man's and the administrator's affairs. Life, business, politics, diplomacy, history, are made up of 'accidents', non-conformities, deviations, the ironies, idiosyncrasies and individualisms of people and their fates. Theory at best, it is said, is a mere datum line from which to measure the departures of reality from a non-existent ideal which has no referend and represents nothing in itself. Let 'facts' speak then for themselves, let the investigator *describe what is* and allow it to tell its own tale. However, we must protest that there are no facts without categories, for no perception can be given an identity, named, placed in a category and located in a scheme of things, until such a scheme has been invented and its categories set up. There are no such things as 'objective' facts, only judgements (of similarity, association, separateness, etc.; measurements (a classificatory operation), selection (according to criteria provided by personal background, sensitiveness, 'ear'). The role of theory is to be an illuminant. It throws features of the scene into relief, gives them substance by eliciting a shadow, defines profiles and lends colour. The illuminating beam is not itself the object of study, and it will not do to mistake theories for realities. But without the illumination there is nothing to be seen. It is absurd for economics to claim (if it ever does) to tell a total and self-sufficient story. It deals with only a small part of the business man's total anxieties and pre-occupations, it is only a superficial statement of the politician's perpetual dilemma between the efficient and the practicable. The business man is concerned with customers, tastes, fashions, selling points, needs, demand; designs, specifications, materials; physical, chemical and biological properties; suppliers, workers; experts; laws, licences and taxes. In this rich, proliferant, accidented country he must find his way. Economic theory gives him a compass-bearing, a formula for recognizing his goal when, if ever, he finds himself at it. Nor does it give much more help to the statesman. Deep social tides are not to be conjured by some simple formula. The world is full of *shapes*, classifiable perhaps by a thousand different schemes, but not countable, not even a countable infinity, too many even for the cardinality of the real line, the numberless numbers of the continuum.

12

The Rational Ideal as the Core of
Economic Theory

In the *Tableau Economique* we see a small number of parts
composing a whole to which each part is necessary, and which
itself is necessary to each part. This formal description could be
applied to the theory of value. It attains an extreme of spareness
and of efficacy, in a word, an extreme of efficiency. It enables
us to prove the answer Yes to the question: Can the participants
in a general inter-action each act with perfect rationality? It
thus enables the analyst to understand all action as a rational
response of self-interest to completely known circumstances.
Tastes and endowments being supposed given, action is determinate. Thus value theory performs its task with incisive and
consummate power.

With the ascendancy conferred by such an accomplishment,
value theory might almost be allowed to claim that the field of
economic phenomena should be defined as the field of rational
action. Thus the problem implicit in the title of this chapter
would not arise. Value theory would be, not the core, but the
whole, of economic theory. We have to consider how far it is
expedient for this claim to be allowed. We can ask either of two
questions: Where, if at all, does value theory fail to conform in
its premisses to the conditions of our human predicament, the
nature of the Scheme of Things?, or: What phenomena, if any,
are unexplainable if we suppose all action to be rational? The
former question reveals by its answer the source of the astonishing accomplishment of value theory. Value theory neglects the
implications of time. For time denies us that complete knowledge which is indispensable to rational choice of conduct.
Value theory in its rigorous form requires that all choices be
pre-reconciled, that is, simultaneous. Thus time is reduced to a
single moment. If we believe that there were past moments and
accept the suggestion which this belief offers that there are
moments to come, we cannot be satisfied with value theory.
On the contrary, we shall expect the answer to our second

question to be a vast catalogue of events and situations which patently deny the inclusive rationality of the action which produced them. And so it proves. And yet, can we willingly resign a tool of such beauty and force?

If the choosing of conduct requires no other kind of thought than the self-interested exercise of reason, the analyst's task is nothing more than to trace out that reason. He need only ask himself: Given the complete relevant knowledge of his circumstances which we are supposing to be guaranteed to him, given a perfect understanding of the powers of these circumstances to afford him various kinds of satisfaction, what ought the participant of action to do in order to experience the utmost available satisfaction? When he has answered this question in general terms, that is to say, in such a form as can be applied to any set of circumstances confronting any coherent set of tastes, the analyst will have constructed a theory of value, indeed we may say, *the* theory of value, and if the tastes and the circumstances of any individual are described to him in full precision and detail, he will be able to predict that individual's choice of conduct. When we examine such a claim from a detached viewpoint, we must find it astonishing. There is, at first sight, even some suggestion of *unconditional* prediction. Can economics, then, really go beyond natural science (which takes care to be conditional) and speak with Euclidian certainty about the construction of the very frame of Human Affairs? We have to remember that value theory speaks in *general* terms. Prediction of particulars of action will only be possible if particulars of circumstance and taste are stipulated. Value theory has the appearance of transcending conditional limitations, because it is in its nature merely a reflection of an aspect of logic, and logic is a pervasive characteristic of our world-picture. We believe the world to be self-consistent,* and therefore to be, up to some point, understandable by logic. When Sir John Hicks asked 'How did the rabbits get into the hat?' (*Value and Capital*, p. 23), his answer was, in effect, that they were put in by the assumption that differences in the composition of equally-esteemed baskets of goods could be exhibited as composing a curve which is everywhere convex (to the origin of the indifference map) and differentiable. This seems to me to be the

* We have not yet adapted our mental pre-dispositions to Gödel's discovery.

appropriate gloss on his own expression 'absence of kinks' in the indifference curves. Sir John seems to me to be saying that if the world is, indeed, self-consistent, so that, for example, its members' preferences do not exhibit sudden capricious gaps and jumps, but show (mathematical, not chronological) continuity of change, then we can understand that world by taking *the world itself, and our own minds,* to reflect each other in their construction. Sir John does not give any hint that he may thus be understood. But perhaps this is a permissible extension of his own step towards explaining 'apparently *a priori* propositions which apparently refer to reality'.

By a double audacity, value theory does in fact seem to claim that the business scene, the economic aspect of society, can be isolated from all other aspects of society and conduct, and treated as a world in itself and on its own, self-contained and self-determined; and that this isolated economic world reflects in its structure the mind's logical design, so that by examining our own thoughts we can gain insight into the world's action. To discard, as irrelevant, all other human concerns: politics, diplomacy, technology, pure science, art and religion: is a bold stroke enough, and an exceedingly dangerous one. But to discard *time* is a thousand times more reckless still, and essentially transforms in nature the business of choosing conduct. For in value theory the choice of conduct is in effect a choice amongst alternatives *given*; in the Scheme of Things in which we live, choice of conduct is choice amongst things imagined, originated. For our knowledge is knowledge about the *present*, but choice is choice of what we hope for. We cannot *choose* the present: it is too late. The present is unique, but choice requires rival possibilities. It is mathematically impossible for choice to concern itself with the unique present. The present is uniquely determined. It can be seen by the eye-witness, and the present alone is open to the eye-witness. The past exists only in traces perceptible in the present, and in memory. For the rest, it is (however vividly suggested by those traces) merely figment. What is the future but the void? To call it the future is to concede the presumption that it is already 'existent' and merely waiting to appear. If that is so, if the world is determinist, then it seems idle to speak of choice. Choice, if it means what our instinct and workaday attitude assume, is originative, it is the start of a new train of influences. If so, we cannot know what choices will be made at moments still to come. And this essential and vast gap in the 'relevant knowledge' required for rational choice cannot be overcome, if the world is what all our talk implicitly supposes. The timeless system of pre-reconciled choice, in extreme contrast, is a fusing of present and future which makes possible both choice and knowledge.

It falls to the economic theoretician more than to most scholars to ask and to adopt an answer to the question of whether conduct is rational or originative. His *analysis*, at its heart, rests on the assumption that conduct is rational and can be so understood. His *posture*, his conception of the Scheme of Things, tacitly accords to choice an active and generative role, and not merely that of an element in a rigid determinist structure. Choice, in the instinctive view of the economist as of most of us, is a *source* of events. If future choices will engender history, how can that history be now inferred? Some are content to say that men are free to choose unwisely, but that in fact they choose by reason. If we also suppose that they are relevantly fully informed, it then follows that they choose correctly, that is, in such a way that their conduct is demonstrably the best in their own interest. However, there is another path of thought by which we can claim for them both a real freedom and also an obedience to reason.

At what moment can a test of the efficacy of a proposed course of action be usefully applied? At the moment when that course is to be adopted or rejected. And what can such a contemplated course be required at that moment to achieve, upon what can it bear, what can be the nature of its effect? Its first and crucial effect is upon the individual's state of mind. We shall go so far as to say that the purpose and the proper criterion of a choice of conduct is to afford the chooser, at the moment of choosing, a good state of mind. The orthodox view is different. That view prescribes the application of some public standard after the event, when the 'objective', publicly observable outcome of the action can be seen. A public standard is inappropriate because the conduct has not been chosen in view of circumstances of publicly agreed character, but of circumstances privately supposed by the individual. A standard only applicable after the event is plainly useless as a guide to choice.

A standard which assumes the possession of data, and the power to base choice on data, that the chooser of conduct cannot in the nature of things possess, is non-logical. We shall seek later in this volume (Chapter 34) to examine the problems of choice of conduct when, as must be the case if imagination of possible courses of events has to take the place of non-existent and logically impossible knowledge of not-yet-existent things, the conduct-chooser must entertain plural rival (mutually con-tradictory) hypotheses about how things will be and what will result from this or that course of action selected by himself. The essence of the matter, for our present purpose, is that the business of choice of conduct will have two stages: first the conceiving, for each available course of action, of a skein of non-excludable outcomes, and the representation of this skein in some way which will enable a choice to be made amongst these available courses; secondly, the comparison of those representations and the choice amongst them.

The view we have just been suggesting accords to reason as essential a place in the *choosing* of conduct as the system of timeless pre-reconciliation does. It is in the *inter-action* of the individual courses of conduct that we find an obvious radical difference. For the achievement of the timeless system is, pre-cisely, to cause that particular conduct to be chosen by an individual which will validate the conduct-choices of other individuals. The timeless pre-reconciliation achieves one form of a Hayekian equilibrium.* The latter conception is that of a perfectly co-ordinated set of individual plans. The timeless pre-reconciliation exemplifies such an equilibrium by a system of choices of inter-active conduct which assigns to each chooser his most advantageous course of action, given his tastes, his endowments and the equal freedom and equal and perfect knowledge ensured by the pre-reconciliative system to all participants. But when we relax the supposition that an organ-ized pre-reconciliation takes place, and consequently fall back on the supposition that each individual must originate part of the 'data' on which reason is to work, there is no longer any guarantee of sufficient common ground amongst participants for their courses of action to fit together in mutual verification.

* See the classic article by F. A. von Hayek: 'Economics and knowledge', *Economica*, New Series, vol. IV, no. 13, February 1937.

In what we have called elsewhere* the *kaleidic* view of the business world and of economic society, all endeavours can still be supposed to be directed by reason (deliberative or intuitive), but by reason basing itself on a flow of suggestions rather than on well-jointed information, a flow which occasionally achieves coherence for all participants at once (though not necessarily, or even with the smallest probability, the *same* coherence) and leads to a state of affairs which has some public air of being generally co-ordinated. The principles of value theory are the principles of logic applied to self-interest. The human mind appears to work by reason and to assume a logically coherent and self-consistent world. The part of that world which it can observe and have direct knowledge of is a minute fragment of the relevant world. Thus the mind is always exploring, experimenting, guessing and gambling, and is constantly misled. But in order to follow its operations the analyst still needs to see them as employing reason and therefore as employing the principles which are dissected and laid out for study by value theory.

We have sought to show that rational inter-active conduct is confined to a timeless system. If by rational we mean demonstrably optimal, it follows that conduct in order to be rational must be relevantly fully informed. Full information for each individual must include a knowledge of the choices to be made by others. It follows that the choices of all individuals must be pre-reconciled, that is to say, simultaneous. The universal moment of choice must include all choices of all individuals, since any choice allowed to be made at any other moment would either destroy the completeness of information for the other choices or itself lack full information. The system can have but one moment. Such a restriction seems to cut off the rational system from all relations with the real Scheme of Things. Yet the very faculty which we have of reflecting upon things seems by its existence to compel us to suppose that reason enters largely into our choice of conduct. To overcome the paradox or bridge the gulf, we have open to us two entirely different courses. We can argue, as we have done in the preceding pages, that men are not concerned with objectively optimal conduct, with conduct optimal in the eyes of the omniscient detached

* *A Scheme of Economic Theory*, p. 5 and Chapter IV (Cambridge University Press, 1965), and Chapter 37 below.

observer, or in the eyes of a participant in a system which ensures full information, but only with subjective optimality, with the enjoyment of the best accessible *state of imagination*. Such a state of mind must find its ultimate self-consistency in the acknowledgement that access to the best hopes is bought by acceptance of some anxieties. There is in such a state of mind an inevitable tension and polarization. The mind and imagination are alive to a dramatic world of confused, conflicting but powerful and insidious suggestions battling for ascendancy, a world full of promise and threat.

To the writer, this recourse for the analyst seems the right one. This is the frame of thought, I would say, by which men's instinct of reason can be supposed to be applied in a world where the data necessary for objective and demonstrable best conduct are excluded in the nature of things. But economic theory has taken a different view. To the orthodox theoretician, the picture to be described by theory is the one seen, not by the participant, but by the detached observer, capable of surveying the public scene entire. He does not claim to explain this scene in any and every 'present moment' randomly chosen from the whole past or potential course of history, nor even at particular historical moments, but only to explain what this scene would be under certain conditions. His method is to ignore the questions raised by the moment-to-moment conduct of business, by the need for decision in the heat and fog of battle, by disequilibrium situations as a class, and to be concerned only with the kind of equilibrium or settled and adjusted state which, given a long enough respite from non-economic events, the economic society would achieve by trial and error in the 'long period'. Value theory, when it sets itself to be practical and realistic, adopts the stance that policy need consider only comparative long-period equilibria. By this attitude, value theory exploits and justifies its self-isolation and self-sufficiency. For it defines the economic field as those affairs of men which can be understood in the light of a single principle, the reasoned pursuit of self-interest. In conditions guarded from interference, guarded from the incursion of social, political and technological changes, this pursuit can be supposed to be successful, given time. The application of value theory is by comparative long-period statics.

The timeless system, on one hand, and the long period, on the other, make a paradoxical contrast. Their formal assumptions appear to be at opposite extremes, the one abolishing extended time, the other prolonging it indefinitely, with the vague phrase 'a period *long enough*. . .'. Yet this contrast is somewhat misleading. Both conceptions treat time with disdain, the one dismissing it utterly and allowing it no role and no existence, the other treating it as of so little consequence that any amount can be used up. Both recognize implicitly the great obstacle to rational inter-active conduct: the difficulty of being sufficiently informed. One relies on organized pooling, solution and diffusion of information, the other on trial and error. They suffer almost equally from the need for drastically unreal assumptions. The timeless system is a candid cutting of the Gordian knot. Its sole concern is to satisfy logic, and since any concession to realism must entail a derogation from absolute rigour, it will have nothing to do with realism, and nothing to do with that arch-spoiler of logic, time. The long period, on the other hand, makes limitless demands upon the notion of *ceteris paribus*. Nonetheless, it is upon the long period that we must rely if we are to urge the rational ideal as a policy guide for the statesman. We may fairly tell him that the best he can do is to legislate for conditions as he sees them, take account of what he can observe; set a goal for the improved situation he would like the society to attain; assume that his constituents, its members, will respond with reason to a gradually clarifying set of circumstances, and will recognize as transient much of the immediate consequences of his measures and their own and each other's responses to them.

The timeless system is for the theoretician who (rightly) wishes to base every analytical excursion upon a starting point of unquestionable clarity of meaning and rigour of reasoning. Let us decide, he may properly say, *what the rational ideal would be like*, and only then consider what approximation to it can be attained in practice. Let us establish (he may say) the logical existence of fully rational inter-active conduct, in no matter how abstract and remote a world-picture. All theory is abstraction, he can argue, and the logic must be followed where it leads. In the timeless system rationality can be sharp-edged and untainted, derived from the minimum conceivable axiomatic base. This very purity and formal spareness are what make the timeless system efficient, and thus beautiful, from the theoretician's viewpoint. They are what satisfy the purpose of theory, to set at rest the mind's desire for order. The long period is the means to justify theory in the eyes of the administrator. The problem for both methods is how the necessary knowledge of his circumstances, in particular those of his circumstances which consist in the impending actions of others, can be assured to every participant. The timeless system achieves this by pre-reconciliation. The long period achieves it by *tâtonnements*, by trial and error. But those *tâtonnements* have to be in a peculiar kind of sequence and harmony with each other if they are to achieve the desired result rather than its opposite. The famous cobweb theorem shows how *tâtonnements* can result in progressive divergence from equilibrium. We can devise assumptions which will, instead, lead to convergence. But how can we know, or show, that these assumptions are the realistic ones? We can do so, of course, by insisting that the long period means long enough, that trial and error must be supposed to continue until all error has been exhausted and wisdom at last distilled. But this leaves us more than ever at the mercy of technological, political and moral *ceteris paribus*.

Value theory is constructed on a tacit premiss which, for the early economists, was perhaps too obvious to need expression. It is that men's ends are thrust upon them by the nature of their world. The supreme end, the pre-condition for attaining every end, is survival, to keep going from day to day. This is the *instinctive* end, built by Nature into human nature and underlying the miracle of the persistence of the human species through millions of years when their numbers were small and scattered, beset by predators, diseases, natural disasters and the general indifference or hostility of their environment. They bent their remarkable minds to overcome their natural hazards, they had no need to ask themselves: What shall we attempt, what will keep us busy, what will engross and entertain us, what is there to do? Their purpose in life, on the secular level, was to go on living, and therefore their immediate and pressing purpose was to provide themselves with the means of living in face of the fact that these means were hard to come by. For strength, tools and time were scarcely enough to make such provision possible. There was scarcity. Scarcity imposed economy, and economy called for reason.

The need for economy has been throughout human times a permanent constraint, ever present at the back of men's minds in their waking and their dreams and in every policy and enterprise. There was no need to justify the study of economy, whether that study was by practice in a harsh world or by theory when a few men had leisure for contemplation. Economy called for reason, and the conditions which imposed economy also provided the unmistakable data to which reason must be applied; so it would have seemed, had they reflected upon the matter, to countless generations. For most of history the *rules of the game* have not been too hard to discern. Techniques have been traditional, commodities have seemed to be defined and designed in their character by natural laws. No one needed to ask: What kind of grain shall we sow, what flocks shall we herd and breed from, what stuff shall we build with, what use shall we make of this and that? The pieces were on the board, the rules were laid down, it remained only for reason to find out how best to play. Thus *economy* became identified with *reason in living*.

13

Cost and the Meaning of Choice

13.1 *Origination, reason and freedom*

Economic theory is unified by its teleological account of human affairs. What happens, it says, is the outcome of men's strivings to attain their desires or realize their ambitions. Traditionally, it has given little attention to the nature or source of the desires themselves. They have been tacitly deemed to be the natural reflection of men's biological constitution, their dependence for survival on food, fuel, clothing and shelter. If these basic needs have shown a fantastic efflorescence of variety and complexity, this has not affected the policy of taking tastes as 'given'. Marshall taught that at first needs give rise to activities, but that then activities give rise to needs. He mentioned beauty in their possessions as a proper concern of men. Does not this concern have a suggestion beyond anything that economists have made of it? The conscious conception and creation of beauty in our surroundings is uniquely human. But what should interest us is the peculiar gift of mind which this pursuit betrays. In a less elusive form it is the source of men's whole capacity for developing techniques, tools and scientific theories. Art, poetry, science and mathematics are the products of imagination, the creation of forms for the sake of their form. Whatever form it takes, the possession of the imaginative gift transforms the problem of accounting for human conduct. For now it is not a question of how *given* needs are satisfied. Deliberative conduct, *choice*, the prime economic act, depend for their possibility, when they go beyond pure instinctive animal response to stimulus, upon the conceptual power of the mind. Choice is necessarily amongst thoughts, amongst things imagined. For when experience is actual and proceeding, outside the realm of ideas, it is unique and already chosen. When men's exertions are directed to the attainment, the rendering actual, of products of their imagination, then indeed we are as much concerned with the source and process of that imagination as with the reasoned plan for the pursuit. Moreover the assigning of results to means or of means to ends is, in great regions of life, conjectural and itself a field for originative thought. Is it not by their access to these creative aspects of their choice of conduct, that we can suppose men to have freedom, without being obliged to deny them the exercise of reason?

13.2 *Cost, reason and determinacy*

The essential form of economic concepts and theories is that of counterpoint. Two ideas are found in this pattern to be set in partnership, comparison, contrast and opposition with each other. Such pairs are ends and means, needs and satisfactions, sacrifices and rewards, costs and results, desires and obstacles, input and output, argument and function (in the mathematical sense). Our discipline makes use of words which contain a comparison within their meaning: *economy* compares the means with the result, so in a narrower sense does *efficiency*. *Maximum* and *minimum* make implicit comparisons between values of a variable. This structure reflects the basic teleological viewpoint, since there can be no purpose unless there are obstacles. A purpose unopposed would be instantly self-realizing. Purpose requires opposition, even if this consists only in deferment. Similarly the existence of an obstacle, the possibility of viewing a circumstance as an obstacle, depends on the existence of a purpose. This structure has also, however, had formal and methodological consequences. It has encouraged and strengthened the additive and scalar character of economic theory. When there are 'two sides' the natural and inevitable question is: Which is the stronger? Which is the greater? This is perhaps part of the explanation why economic theory has leaned so strongly towards quantity and away from shape and configuration.

'Ends and means', 'ends and obstacles' express two slightly different views of our place in Nature. It is perhaps better simply to regard man's circumstances as something neutral, but transformable and exploitable by thought and action of his own. His central economic activity is then that of choice, and the notion of *cost* is clarified to that of displacement cost. The cost of any chosen course of action, and of the results which can be envisaged for it or looked upon as an aspect of it, is then anything which could have been done, or had, instead. Since these available alternatives are themselves in rivalry with each other, the effective displacement cost of some course and its envisaged result, or array of possible results, is the most desired available alternative.

It is perhaps allowable to notice yet again the pre-supposition, the settled choice of world-picture, which is betrayed by the terms which the economist has adopted or accepted. *Cost* implies the availability of rival (i.e. mutually exclusive) alternatives. For the cost of something is the rejected best alternative which could have been had instead. Thus it implies that if the cosmos is determinate, that determinism works by way of men's responsible, reasoning and capable self-interest. Men's instinct to seek advantage (for themselves in some restricted sense, or for the interest or the institution or the idea with which they identify their own purpose of being), and their power to know what will conduce to that advantage, are supposedly relied on by Nature to bring about the destined course of events. The world-picture which speaks of cost but also regards the course of things as determinate treats men as responsible choosers, as being faced with rival alternatives yet sure to choose a particular member of the array. We must allow that this view can find a place for error, if we are willing to descend from the heights where men's reason and knowledge are *themselves* the essential mechanism of history. If men are confronted with mutually exclusive alternatives within reach, if the choice they make is nonetheless uniquely determinate, yet could be made via a process of erroneous reasoning or false information, then Nature must supply *something else*, in addition to her incorporation of men's moral and intellectual qualities in her Machinery of Destiny, to *make men make the right mistake* to lead them to the destinate action. We are, in this case, retreating from the extreme elegance and simplicity of the construct of value in its purest form, where men's conduct is determined by their pursuit of their advantage by means of correct reasoning on correct and sufficient data. The picture we are thus presented with is of freedom of a sort: 'freedom' within determinacy. *Cost* is then a term and a concept belonging to this highly special world-picture, by which the governance of men's affairs by reason and their resulting determinate conduct can be reconciled to their ascription to themselves of freedom of choice. I believe that if opinions on this matter were canvassed amongst economists who have given any thought to it, some such view as the foregoing might attract more assent than any other. The need for any such balancing on a razor-edge arises, perhaps, because of the neglect of the question of knowledge: if, because men (necessarily) lack much of the data required for rationality, and are therefore free in some measure to supply their own suppositious circumstances, there is another door open for the access of indeterminate thoughts and consequent actions.

13.3 The non-arbitrary system

From the urge to survive, and its extension into the urge to ensure survival by gathering wealth; from the assumption that survival and wealth will be pursued by reason applied to a relevantly complete knowledge of circumstances; from the evident inclusion of other men's conduct in each man's circumstances and the consequent need for pre-reconciliation as a necessary condition of rationality, that is, of demonstrably best action; economics derives the notion of value, agreed ratios of exchange which are consistent throughout the whole range of exchangeable things. Universally pre-reconciled exchange-values, a unanimous system of public prices, appear to afford a universal unit for scalar, additive measurement. By this means, men's activities are *measured and brought into account*. The account exhibits all the activities as constituting a closed, self-contained system where the source and destination of everything is to be seen as belonging to an inter-contributory, multiple exchange of equal values. Economics displays business affairs as teleological, rational and closedly accountable ('book-keepable'). Closedness was illustrated by the *Tableau Economique*, its determinacy explained and established by the General Equilibrium of marginal adjustments.

The ultimate and conclusive success was the proof of the exact exhaustion of the product by the factor-payments, this ultimate closedness of the system following logically from its own principles of rationality and equal freedom. In assessing this great scheme of thought, we are likely to be swayed by a personal bias towards formal beauty and completeness (one of the first criteria of theoretic excellence, since it is this which enables a theory to perform its chief duty of setting the mind at rest) or towards realistic usefulness as an insight-tool into practical problems. One of its most powerful claims arises from the comparison with other economic theories. Nothing else in economics approaches its unity and sweep. For the theory of value and distribution, in its austerest form, is single-minded, aiming to establish the supremacy of the human reason in human affairs, human conduct as part of the Natural Order, and the whole as intelligible. The rest of economic theory views business affairs, on the one hand as either mindless or mistaken, or on the other as exploiting chaos in a spirit of adventure. The theory of money is either mechanical (the Quantity Theory) or speculative, a contest against uncertainty (the Liquidity Preference theory). The theories of the business cycle aim to show the effects of error or of unavoidable lack of knowledge. The theory of employment depends on a theory of investment where, in diametric opposition to the theory of value, enterprise is shown as essentially and inherently lacking the data necessary for rationality. Enterprise and investment are seen in it as activities where knowledge is necessarily substituted by originative figment: activities whose nature is incompatible and at odds with that of the rational general equilibrium. Some return is made towards a self-regulating system in the conception which has emerged in recent years of the Assurgent Economy, where relations are between simultaneous time-rates of growth, and inflationary general price-rises induce sufficient spending, by consumers and investing business men, to keep the economy pressing against its full-employment ceiling. Perpetually-rising general prices come to be expected, and induce pay demands whose effects justify the expectation, which in itself is a promise of money profit for enterprise and investment. Such a conception, however, is far from possessing the internal coherence and self-subsistent logic of a genuine system of pre-reconciled actions. Its stability depends on a fragile relation of expectations to experience, which some accident could destroy or which, for all its theory can tell us, may be essentially self-destructive. The strength of the timeless system is that it can be self-contained, totally independent of any world outside itself. Any system which exists in time and includes expectation is exposed to the whole conceivable range of non-economic events. For how can we limit the classes of events which can offer suggestions to expectation? To abstract from them would be arbitrary in a sense in which the comprehensive abstraction of general equilibrium is not.

Those who wish to disparage a plea for or against some course of action often describe its arguments as 'emotive'. In this they perpetrate a nonsense which ought to be exposed by any who hear it. What is action but the response to feelings? What action would there be if there were no desires, no consciousness of dissatisfaction, no longing for a 'good state of mind'? What is *motive*, except emotion? We choose, and take, action in pursuit of an end. What is an end if not something upon which our desire concentrates our thought and effort? Again, what is desire if not emotion? Reason, logic, are in themselves purely formal, without force. Those who disparage their opponents' plea by calling it 'emotive' mean merely that those opponents' desires, the object of their *emotions*, are different from their own.

In circumstances sufficiently known, reason may tell what action will lead to what end. But reason will not tell *what end ought to be chosen*. It will not do so if the end in question is to be an ultimate, irreducible expression of taste, temperament, character; an expression of the original fibre of personality, those things (whether formed by genetical endowment, or the earliest bio-chemistry of the embryonic brain, or the experience of the individual in life) which make the individual what he is. There is a basic source of choice beyond which no analytic penetration can be made except to the individual's constitution. Reason will not tell what end ought to be chosen, if the alleged 'choosing' of an end is, instead, the *origination* of an end, the outcome of a creative thought. Reason shows the route, *given the goal*. Does a railway time-table tell me, of itself, what ticket to buy, what train to take? To require that action be free from emotion is to require that a journey be without purpose. Without feelings, desires, demands, the mere terms efficiency, economy, lose all meaning. Reason comes into play only after the end is chosen. One route may be preferred to another, but that merely means that the chosen end is the attainment of some result in a particular way. If route and goal are unified, choice of this unified entity is choice, not reason. Choice and reason are things different in nature and function, reason *serves* the chosen purposes, not performs the selection of them. Loose expression and looser thought are betrayed in those who speak of a 'reason' for such-and-such an action, and fail to acknowledge to themselves that their 'reason' means merely the logical implication of a choice already made, a purpose already taken for granted. To claim that one's conduct is 'guided by reason' and is therefore superior to, better founded than, that of a person 'guided by emotion' is a crude confusion of thought and abuse of words.

14

Perfect Competition and Conceptual Illusionism

14.1 *Perfect competition: definition and sufficient conditions*

The value-construct of 1870 to 1900 employed only four principles to achieve its picture of inter-dependent rational self-interest. These principles were pre-reconciliation, action in pursuit of self-interest, diminishing marginal efficacy and perfect competition. In earlier chapters we have sought to show that pre-reconciliation, itself a necessary condition of rational action, entails that each distinct interest be allowed only one occasion of choosing, and that all such choosings must belong to a synchronous or timeless system, having no concern with any subsequent moment or later system of actions; we have suggested (in line with orthodoxy) that diminishing marginal efficacy (of goods in giving enjoyment to consumers, and of means of production in adding value) is what confers determinacy upon the solution, the system of actions or choices. We wish now to show what part is played by perfect competition in achieving simplicity of analysis and unity of explanation.

The restriction of each interest (each person or firm) to a single occasion of choosing does not preclude the chosen action from being complex or even from comprising several 'stages', provided these form one integral and rigid configuration. Such an action can thus comprise both the technical exchange of resources for product (the act of production) and the market exchange of one product for another. The value-construct, that is to say, can include the analysis of production. Since in the value-construct there is no extension of time, we can speak simply of the quantity of product offered or demanded by a member of the society, without referring to any time-interval. Whereas in reality production must be measured per day or per year, the value-construct has no use for such a dimension.

Nonetheless we shall speak of those who offer products on the market as firms.

A firm of given productive capacity is selling its product in a perfectly competitive market if the price per unit does not vary on account of changes in the quantity it offers within that capacity. The price can of course be affected by circumstances outside the firm's choice. When all circumstances are given except the quantity offered by an individual firm, the test of perfect competition is the invariance of the price against changes of that quantity. Various sets of stipulations, each set taken as one whole, concerning the product, other firms, and the buyers, might comply with this test. One particular set, however, is envisaged by those who formulate this test. The conditions which they lay down are that no possible buyers must have any preference for the product of one firm over that of another; that the firms offering the product must be so many, and so similar in productive capacity, that no one of them could noticeably affect the aggregate of the quantities they offer by varying its own; and that the price of every offer must be universally known. The last of these conditions is merely an aspect of a necessary condition for all rational conduct, namely, that the chooser of conduct shall have complete, perfect and guaranteed knowledge of all relevant circumstances, and shall know that his knowledge of circumstances is of this kind. The first condition is necessary, because if any buyers placed firms in an order of preference, as sources of products which were otherwise identically similar, less preferred firms might be obliged to charge a lower price than more esteemed ones in order to sell their product. When looking at successively lower hypothetical prices, a firm might thus find that lower prices were associated with larger quantities able to be sold. Its situation would not then be one of perfect competition. From the need for buyers' indifference amongst firms, a conclusion follows about the entity which consists of the products of all the firms composing a perfectly competitive market in the sense we have defined. Unit specimens drawn at random from those products must be in all respects indistinguishable from each other, since otherwise an order of preference would be established by some buyers, on the basis of the differences amongst specimens, which would destroy their perfect mutual competitiveness in the same way as a preference for one source of the product over another source. We may say, therefore, that perfect competition applies to a *natural commodity*, specimens of which cannot be technologically or physically distinguished from each other, a collection of products uniform by nature, and that the technological character of this uniform product must be the only quality of it, or circumstance of its offer, which is of interest to the buyers. The need for the second of our stated conditions of perfect competition arises from our use of perfect competition as a principle of the value-construct. For the value-construct embodies also the principle of diminishing marginal efficacy of goods in giving enjoyment to consumers. It follows that when the aggregate of all the quantities offered by all the firms is noticeably increased, the price will have to be reduced. A firm whose offered quantity is more than a 'negligible' proportion of this aggregate offer will thus also have to reduce its price in order to sell a larger quantity, and thus will not be selling under perfect competition.

14.2 *Three features conferred upon the value-construct*

We have now defined perfect competition in its demand aspect. We have stated the particular set of necessary conditions for its presence, which are conventionally regarded as the relevant and interesting ones. We have thus sought to show that perfect competition refers to a natural commodity technologically and physically defined, something whose characteristics, in all relevant respects, can be established by the chemist or the engineer. The first notion we must link with perfect competition is thus that of the *commodity on its own*. Perfect competition then in turn confers upon the value-construct three features essential to that coherence, simplicity and beauty which are its chief claim. These features are, first, the simultaneous determination of price and quantity by the intersection of mutually independent demand and supply curves; secondly, the solution of the problem of the exact exhaustion of the product by the aggregate of the factor bills (the *adding-up problem*); and thirdly, the formal description of production at minimum unit cost. We shall describe these features in turn.

14.3 *Particular equilibrium*

The value analysts were concerned, on one hand to show that an encompassing system of rational self-interested and inter-conditioning choices could be conceived; on the other to examine these choices at close range to understand their variety of detailed circumstance. The former was general equilibrium and the latter partial or particular equilibrium. Particular equilibrium considers the individual in his private capacity; the firm, that is, the individual employer or supplier; and the individual natural commodity. The early posture of economics was extravert, directed to things rather than thoughts, and the commodity is the cardinal central object of particular equilibrium analysis. The two primary questions about the commodity were: At what price will it be exchanged? and: How much of it will be produced and sold? In partial or particular analysis, *equilibrium* names the idea that the two questions can be answered at one stroke, given the tastes and the endowments of the members of the society. On one condition, the answer could be given a striking and appealing simplicity, the condition, namely that the market should be perfectly competitive.

The simplicity which we achieve by confining the analysis to a single commodity and to perfect competition rests on the mutual independence which this double restriction ensures between the supply and demand conditions. The single commodity represents in its production so small a part of the income of the society as a whole, that changes in the quantity produced will leave that income almost unaffected, and so in that respect will leave unaffected the society's demand for the commodity; and the single commodity absorbs so small a part of the society's factors of production, that changes in the quantity produced will leave unaffected the cost-conditions of producing substitute or complementary commodities, and so will not bring about price changes in these commodities, which would affect the demand for our commodity. These two implications of perfectly competitive particular analysis mean, in short, that a movement along the supply curve will not require us to re-draw the demand curve. There is, however, a further kind of mutual involvement of the supply and demand conditions, which is eliminated by assuming perfect competition. To examine this we must consider the nature of the supply curve.

The supply curve of a commodity names for each hypothetical price per unit, P, the number, Q, of units which will be offered. The value-construct assumes that the firm will choose Q with a view to make as large as possible the excess of revenue, $R = PQ$, over the cost S of providing Q units. Net revenue, $U = R - S$, will have an extreme value where

$$\frac{\mathrm{d}U}{\mathrm{d}Q} \equiv P + Q\frac{\mathrm{d}P}{\mathrm{d}Q} - \frac{\mathrm{d}S}{\mathrm{d}Q} = 0,$$

that is to say, where marginal revenue $P + Q\,\mathrm{d}P/\mathrm{d}Q$ is equal to marginal cost $\mathrm{d}S/\mathrm{d}Q$. Perfect competition being that condition where $\mathrm{d}P/\mathrm{d}Q$ is zero for all relevant Q, the rule for choice of Q for a firm selling under perfect competition is to bring marginal cost to equality with price. This formal rule expresses the consequence of a market mechanism. A natural commodity being such that no buyer cares which firm supplies him with it, and every buyer being aware of the price at which any offer of the commodity is made by any firm, no firm can sell at a higher price than any other, nor need sell at a lower, so that a uniform market price will prevail. Because each firm can offer only a small part of the industry's total offer, no firm can affect the market price by varying its own offer. Thus a price is imposed by the market upon each firm, at which it can sell as much as it likes within its capacity. Since buyers do not react in any way to a variation of the firm's offer, beyond buying whatever quantity it offers, subject to the price being that of the market, the firm can disregard completely the question of demand, and in determining the quantity it shall offer, need pay attention only to its own costs and their relation to the market price. It will not pay the firm to offer $n + 1$ units rather than n units, if the difference of total cost of these offers is greater than the price per unit. For the price is the difference of revenue of offers which differ by one unit. But if the difference of cost of $n + 1$ units and n units is less than the price, the firm will gain by offering $n + 1$ units instead of n units. Amongst quantities in that range where the cost difference between n and $n + 1$ units increases with increase of n, it will pay the firm best to offer that quantity which makes the difference of cost equal to the difference of revenue, that is, where marginal cost is equal to price. If at the lower of two prices this rule would put every firm, which is able to offer the commodity, on a rising part of its marginal cost curve, then at a somewhat higher price every such firm will somewhat increase its offer, since the higher price will cover the higher marginal cost corresponding, for each firm, to an appropriately larger offer. The collection of all firms able to offer the commodity (the firms composing the *industry*) must evidently be taken to include those firms whose offer rises from zero to some positive quantity; it must include, that is to say, those firms who, in the process of pre-reconciliation of actions, would be induced by the substitution of a higher for a lower price to 'enter the industry'. With this understanding, we can say that the supply curve of the commodity will be obtained under perfect competition by aggregating, for each hypothetical price, the quantities which will respectively make the marginal cost of every firm equal to this price. When a commodity is sold under perfect competition, the supply curve of this commodity is its *industry marginal cost curve*.

Before we go on to contrast this situation with that of non-perfect competition, we ought to consider what the smallness of the individual firm's offer in relation to that of the industry is required to mean. Under what interpretation will an increase of the firm's offer make a 'negligible' or 'unnoticeable' increase in the industry's output? Only if we invoke a limiting process, where the number of firms is conceived (not historically but by abstract supposition) to increase beyond all bounds while the output of each continually shrinks. Either this, or we must admit that economics deals in essentially *imprecise* ideas. (And, of course, it does.) However, the former alternative itself involves us in a dilemma. If, as that alternative would have it, the industry in relation to the individual firm is infinite, the output of each of those parts of the industry into which it would be divided up by buyers' preference amongst firms might also be infinite in relation to the individual firm, and if so, buyers' preference would not lead to a southward-sloping demand curve facing the firm. (An infinite class is one which is no larger than some of its parts.) If we are prepared to ignore that dilemma, we may be tempted to say that the industry comprising infinitely many firms is an abstraction quite consonant with the other unrealisms of the value construct, no more to be objected to than its timelessness.

Non-perfect competition can consist in the non-fulfilment of any of our necessary conditions. We saw that if there are buyers' preferences amongst firms (*a fortiori*, if the 'commodity' does not conform to the definition of a natural commodity whose significance to buyers resides solely in its objective technological qualifications) or if the firm is not a 'negligible' part of the industry, the demand curve facing the individual firm will be southward-sloping, dP/dQ will be negative and not zero, and thus the right choice of Q will depend on the conformation of that demand curve facing the firm. Let us note what we have concluded. In these circumstances of other than perfect competition, the quantity offered by a firm and therefore the quantity offered by the industry will be influenced by demand conditions. Thus disappears the simplicity of the analysis which, under perfect competition, can confront with each other a market demand curve and an industry supply curve which are drawn in disregard and mutual independence of each other.

14.4 *Exact exhaustion of the product*

The purpose which in the end best justifies the value-construct is the demonstration of the possibility (the logical 'existence') of rational conduct and the determination of the necessary and sufficient conditions for it. For this purpose it needs to be a system complete and self-sufficient in its own terms. Any failure to determine some unknowns or to explain the source of quantities which play a part, any gap or breakdown in the mutual epistemic support of the parts by each other, would destroy the claim of actions to be rational, since they would then be founded on incomplete or meaningless data. Complete knowledge, in the essential sense, must be about something complete. If the value-construct is to include production, we must therefore require it to show how the whole product, or its equivalent, is accounted for by its exchange for its necessary means of production. For if this balance-sheet is not established, we are leaving some question with *no answer in the required language*, the language of rationality. The problem which, looked at from one side, concerns the disposal of the product, and looked at from the other side, concerns the reward of the suppliers of means of production, is the problem of the distribution (sharing) of income, the well-named *adding-up problem*. By providing a solution for this problem, which springs naturally and inevitably from the premises of the value-construct itself considered as the necessary frame of rational conduct, the value-construct attains a summit from which it can surely never be displaced.

In its most rigorous and efficient form, the value-construct assumes that every resource and every product with which it deals is measurable and perfectly divisible; that it can appear under the guise of continuously variable quantities. And it assumes that amongst the vanishingly small 'particles' which are classed as composing any one resource or any one product, there prevails a quality of being in every way indistinguishable from each other, so that no member of the economic society is in the smallest degree concerned as to which such 'particles' he acquires. The value-construct assumes also that by some means, perfect relevant knowledge is possessed by every member of the society. These assumptions lead to the inference that the production function will have a form giving constant returns to scale, or in an alternative language, that it will be homogeneous of the first degree.

The production function is a formal statement of the association of quantity of product with quantities of the various means of its production. Self-interest equipped with perfect relevant knowledge ensures that any set of quantities of means or *factors* of production is used to the greatest possible technical effect. Then the quantity of product can be taken to depend on the quantities of the factors. If in the term *factors* we include (as our first assumption above intends to do) every circumstance which bears in any way on the size of the product, then since every such factor is deemed to be both measurable and perfectly divisible, there is no apparent reason why a simultaneous doubling, for example, of every factor quantity in the list of factors should not double the product quantity, a trebling treble it, and so on. Such a multiplication of every factor quantity simultaneously by one and the same number, s, is called a change of scale. If a change of scale in a ratio s changes the product quantity in the same ratio s, we speak of constant returns to scale. When the production function gives constant returns to scale, the most economical use of factors at given rates of pay in terms of product will result in the precise exhaustion of the product. For the mathematician, the proof that a linear homogeneous function of several variables is equal to the sum of the numerical values of those variables, each multiplied by the partial derivative of the function with respect to it, was provided (well in advance of the economist's need) by Euler.

Between the value-construct and the adding-up problem there thus subsists a mutual reinforcement. Within a framework of stark abstraction, the value-construct shows that the adding-up problem has an answer. The demonstration of that answer is the crowning achievement and chief justification of the value-construct. It remains for us here to consider just what is in question when we describe the relevant framework of assumptions as an extreme abstraction. In conforming to the requirements of Euler's theorem, the value-construct is obliged, not surprisingly, to ignore three out of the four walls of the human prison and to discard large items of its real economic furniture.

14.5 *Unrealisms of the formal solution of the adding-up problem*

First, then, is the universal matter of what the conduct-chooser can know, in comparison with what the theory of value supposes him to know. He cannot know the future, therefore there must be no future, and the value-construct, and every part of it including the adding-up problem, ought, if we are to be strict, to be regarded as timeless. (But this need not exclude from it the problem of income-distribution in its most formal guise.) But by this abolition of time and un-knowledge, we solve another difficulty: the un-realism of perfect divisibility. For the most indivisible thing is the enterpriser himself. His duty is to fill, with inventions and figments, the gap between what can be known and what needs to be known. When there is no such gap, there need be no enterpriser in the sense of policy-originator. We need not then strive to persuade ourselves that his powers of intuition, his nerve and ambition, can be 'multiplied in the ratio s'. There are other indivisibilities, those of equipment in particular. We have shown that a 'time-less system' can allow for a process of mutual accommodation of *plans*. It is the conclusive, irrevocable acts of *choice* which must be *co-determined* and in this sense, simultaneous. The scale on which equipment shall be built can, despite an appearance of paradox or unrealism, be included in such mutual adjust-ment of plans, so that in effect the timeless system becomes assimilable to the 'long period' of perfect fluidity and perfect mutual adjustment. Pre-reconciliation by means of simul-taneous choice, on one hand, and infinite time for trial and error, on the other, aim at the same result.

14.6 *The two contributions of perfect competition to solving the adding-up problem*

There is an essential matter still to be considered. We have been supposing that the suppliers of productive services (services of themselves or of their material possessions) are paid in *product*. If they are paid in a *numéraire* or in money itself, the question arises what is to be assumed about the price of the product in terms of this *numéraire*. If the product is to be sold in a perfectly competitive market, where the quantity offered by the firm will leave the price unaffected, the measuring of the product in market value instead of in physical quantity is merely a change in the unit of measurement, and leaves the argument about the production function still effective. But if the price of the firm's product depends on how much of it the firm produces, then all is altered. This is one of the two essential roles of the assumption of perfect competition in the solution of the adding-up problem.

The other duty which the assumption of perfect competition has to perform is to explain why the employed quantity of each factor of production should be paid at a rate equal to the dif-ference made to output by the presence or absence of a marginal unit of that employed quantity of that factor. (This difference, in perfect competition, can be measured indifferently in physical or value terms.) When innumerable suppliers of any one productive service (of themselves or of their possessions) are in perfect competition with each other, no one of them can secure a higher price than the market price by withholding his supply. And when innumerable firms are competing with each other for supplies of a productive service, none of them can get it at a price below the market by reducing the quantity that firm demands. Thus a 'market price' will be established.

14.7 *Two dilemmas of perfect competition*

The value-construct is still not quite free of all troubles. There remains the dilemma whose discovery can be ascribed to Cournot, to Marshall or to Sraffa. It is the dilemma that if no circumstance, of technology or the market, causes the unit cost of product to rise as output is assigned a higher conceptual level, and if no circumstance causes the unit price of product to fall as the weekly (etc.) quantity put upon the market increases, there will be no intersection point of marginal cost and marginal revenue to determine output at any finite size. What, then, becomes of the perfect competition on which this con-clusion itself is based? Perfect competition, if taken to apply throughout the economic system, appears to be self-contra-dictory.

There is another aspect of 'perfect competition' in the formal sense which theory must impose upon it in order to make it serve the desired purposes, which is equally destructive though more subtle. It is effective, for the desired purposes, only so long as we confine it to *particular equilibrium*. When the single firm is considered in isolation, the price it can obtain can be deemed independent of its own output. But if we try to apply this semantic fudge to all firms at once, we are involved in a form of the fallacy of composition. For they cannot *all* increase their output simultaneously, in any finite degree, without increasing, substantially and noticeably, the total flow into the market. When we examine the dependence of the formal value-construct on the formal notion of perfect competition, we find it more elusive than even its timelessness alone would make it.

15

The Value-Construct in the Round

The value-construct envisaged a society where people were all subject in economic matters to the same laws, and where these laws were mainly concerned to prohibit force and fraud in their dealings with each other. The affairs of such a society would evidently have to be explained by reference to the conduct chosen by individuals. It would be possible and necessary to study the *general individual*, an abstract person equipped with only those tastes and capacities which are common to everyone. The tastes and capacities themselves would be described only in very general and abstract terms. The individual would have needs for the means of survival, and the capacity to render useful service. It was necessary to state some principle on which he would act, and then to consider what would be the consequence when all individuals acted on this principle. Since all were equally forbidden to constrain or cheat each other, the agreements that were come to would have to be acceptable to both parties. The result would have to be a sort of general settlement, where individual conduct had successfully adapted itself to the desires of others. In selecting his assumed principle of individual action, the analyst must be able to apply logic to understand the action of the general economic subject, the 'economic man'. For he was deprived by his subject-matter of the possibility of making experiments.

The simplest way to apply reason to the task of understanding conduct was to assume that the conduct itself was based on reason. The analyst would thus open for himself a route into a field where experiment was impracticable and direct observation was confused by the inexpressible complexity, intricacy and mutual involvement of the phenomena. Besides this, he would be attributing a highly plausible posture to the individual, who could be counted on to think intensively and carefully about his situation, for the reason that his poverty required him to *make the most* of the possibilities confronting him. The analyst's instinctive method of attacking his problem was indeed itself based upon most plausible reason. It aimed at a *geometry* of conduct and its outcome, in the old sense of the word, which we should nowadays render by an *axiomatics*. A few propositions, whose factual truth was exempt from demonstration but simply *assumed*, were to serve as the basis for logical drawing of inferences, the construction of theorems as the logical consequences of the axioms. Economics was to be a deductive science, bound therefore to resort to high abstraction, fewness, generalness and simplicity of principles. The conceptual elegance and austerity which resulted became strikingly evident when the value-construct was given mathematical expression (of a kind which improved in conciseness upon the pioneer attempts) as a system of simultaneous equations. The 'simultaneity' of such a system is, of course, a logical simultaneity, meaning that the equations are *co-valid*. It does not refer to simultaneity of date, and indeed a system of simultaneous equations can (so far as mathematical considerations are concerned) involve situations or events at a number of distinct dates, provided some dates are in common between the equations. But again reason came forward with a powerful, if unformulated suggestion. An attempt to answer the question: What course would things take? might be susceptible of infinitely many answers. The question: How would things settle down? might yield a single answer. The formal, abstract answer of principle to this latter question was the concept of general equilibrium.

A system of simultaneous equations is a set of conditions to be fulfilled. The question to be answered by solving such a system is: What set of numerical values of the variables, one value for each variable, will satisfy every equation of the system at once? The algebraist has his formal procedure for such a purpose. Thus he may be in a position to say, of a given set of equations, that it has no solution (the equations being mutually incompatible), or that it has infinitely many solutions (there not being enough mutually independent equations, i.e. equations not deducible from each other, to determine the given number of variables): or finally, he may say that the system has one and only one, unique, solution. If in any given case this last is his conclusion, he will be strongly tempted to be satisfied. The system, he will declare, is *determinate*. The question that this leaves unanswered is: Who, in a society of independent individuals, discovers the specification of the set of equations which will describe the society's collection of tastes and capacities, and is thus in a position to solve it?

In the type of economic society which the value-construct envisages, it is of course the market which makes possible some approach to a pre-reconciled solution. Walras and Edgeworth were each conscious of the need for idealizing the design of the market in order that it might be conceived to be in this respect wholly efficient. Walras accordingly spoke of *tâtonnements* and Edgeworth of re-contract, each meaning that sets of prices would be tried out until a set was found which, taken together with the quantities which individuals would buy and sell at those prices, would offer to each person that particular exchange of goods for goods, which he would most prefer. When we examine this suggestion, we see that it is no more than a formal acknowledgement of a problem, the problem of how (by what institutional arrangement, by what organization of affairs) the equilibrium prices are to be discovered. Repeated trial and error, while the market stands in suspense awaiting the outcome, is not a practical resort. The number of distinct trials, even if confined to discrete steps of price and quantity, would be so immense that the necessary 'market day' would extend beyond human life-times. Not even the electronic computer could cope with such a task. Moreover, the market's endless flux in pursuit of the ever-elusive equilibrium is not so far inferior to the theoretical ideal pre-reconciled solution as might appear. For the theoretical ideal applies to mutually *isolated* days or moments, each to be treated as perfectly self-contained and looking to no yesterday and no tomorrow. But the real market is dealing in goods inherited from yesterday, and in means of production whose products will not be ready till tomorrow. Meanwhile the non-economic circumstances are changing and rendering each successive equilibrium obsolete. There is little point in demanding minor concessions and relaxations of the abstract, timeless general equilibrium. The light it can throw on human affairs is thrown by its most austere and formal version. We are not concerned to ask: How could it possibly work? The useful question is: What does its logical structure imply?

The value-construct, being a work of theory and therefore an abstraction, was selective. It selected what was perhaps thought to be mankind's most distinctive and distinguishing characteristic, his power of reasoning. It was natural that the reasoner, the theoretician, should elevate above the rest that particular faculty which was his own especial tool. In making this choice of the aspect upon which he would concentrate, the theoretician was perhaps unaware of the degree to which he was carrying abstraction. We have sought to show that he was dismissing *time* from his concerns. He did so because *time* and *complete knowledge* are utterly incompatible. Time is what brings *new* knowledge: how then could the old knowledge ('old' at any given moment) be complete? The reasoner's conclusions, no matter how rigorous his logic, are only valid in relation to a given set of premises. If those premises are not the whole of our real circumstances, if they are even *not known* to be the whole, his conclusions as to the best conduct have no imperious and unarguable validity. He cannot *demonstrate* that one course of conduct is in fact the best of those available. Time is alien to reason. Reason works within the frame of axioms *taken to be valid*. The *assumption* of their validity is absolute. For the purpose of the argument in hand, we take them for granted. Thus if economics is to be the pure logic of choice, the dismissal of time was necessary. The paradoxical human mind can see in the one scheme of things where we are placed, on one hand time, novelty, uncertainty, the three strands of consciousness itself, inseparably spun together; and on the other hand, pervasive ostensible consistency, the pre-condition of reason. The value-construct edifies reason into a claim to represent the whole. But the invalidity of this claim does not invalidate the claim of the value-construct to throw light on our affairs.

BOOK III

The Dissolution of the Rational Ideal

16

Expectation: the Dissolution of Determinacy

16.1 *Expectation and price-indeterminacy*

The rational ideal is the conception of men's conduct as a part and aspect of the orderliness of Nature. Have we to think of that orderliness as something imposed, complete in all respects, once for all, or as a principle whose detail is being continually realized and unfolded? On the biological level, the answer was clearly perceived that there is evolution. On the level of human consciousness, it may be hazarded that there can be something other than pure rational response, and that indeed there must be something other, because of the asymmetry of a time-world where knowledge lies upon one hand and the whole field of choice lies upon the other, so that, circumstances of choice being only partly and unsurely known, and partly a field open to conjecture, rational response in the sense of a uniquely and demonstrably best action is logically excluded. Rational response, in the strict sense of a perception of a complete set of relevant conditions and a conforming with them in pursuit of an interest or purpose determined by tastes, themselves inborn or at least determinate, is not possible if that set of relevant conditions is not visible, *a fortiori* if the exercise of imaginative conjecture is an element in creating them, so that at the moment of choosing, they must be said not to exist.

If assured knowledge is fragmentary and disconnected, if there are voids which must be filled to complete a system of knowledge, the manner and means of this filling is a question of elemental importance for insight into the nature of conduct. At the least, this filling of void spaces in knowledge, or finding of places for the insufficient fragments of knowledge in a com- pleted mosaic, cannot be a matter of mere rational inference, for it is in conscious knowledge that the void spaces exist, and if their filling could be done by inference alone, that would be tantamount to the existence of sufficient knowledge. The general configuration, the mosaic as a unity, the meaning of that whole to which the fragments belong, must be in some sense invention. Such a view of conduct can apply to moral or to mundane decisions, and to the principles or the particulars of the world, but even when they refer to ephemeral detail, such detail makes up the substance of history and can play vital parts in its most momentous events.

The idea of perfectly rational, that is, fully informed, conduct in a human basic situation of continual gaining of additional or incongruous and surprising new knowledge, shaking and confusing the existing conceptions, is a fundamental contradiction. So far as men are concerned, *being* consists in continual and endless fresh *knowing*. How can this be reconciled with the idea of even relevantly complete information as the basis of action? The economic aspect of conduct could be defined as that part of it which is mediated or guided by valuations, by assessments of ratios at which it is worth while to exchange things. If exchange is interpreted in a rather general sense, so as to include the technical exchange of means of production for products as well as products for each other, we can say that economic conduct consists of exchange. Then, valuations, and the business of forming valuations, is essential and central to it. In a world of timeless pre-reconciliation, valuations could be determinately based on tastes and on full relevant knowledge fully diffused. But in a world where things can be exchanged either today or on some subsequent envisaged day, all such possibilities of subsequent exchange have a bearing on the exchanges which are worth while today. The price which it is advantageous to accept today can only be judged in the light of the price which it will be possible to get tomorrow, and on any of the tomorrows, and in what sense are those future prices determinate? For each of them in turn will depend on the prices which are going to be obtainable on its own tomorrows, in the infinite regress of time. Expectation and determinacy are incompatible and mutually exclusive. The rational ideal must therefore exclude expectation, and expectation, since it is real and insistently present and accompanies all activity, must destroy the rational ideal.

16.2 *Speculation limited by the urgency of exchange*

The ultimate price-indeterminacy which follows logically from the fact of expectation is, of course, heavily restrained and modified by other aspects of the business of being, and keeping, alive, aspects which are no less fundamental. There are perhaps three such influences of dominant importance: poverty, urgency and convention. Those who must consume or exchange what they have in their hands in order to live through the day or the week cannot concern themselves with the notion of getting a better price next week. Even those who possess reserves of wealth are compelled by technical facts to exchange it in some cases. Water-power will run to waste at the mill if there is no grist for it to grind or yarn for it to weave, and so water-power must be exchanged *now* for the material upon which it is to operate. Both the farmer and the miller need to exchange their respective goods and services, if the water-power of today is not to be lost for ever. But the services of machines and buildings in general are in the same case. Houses that stand empty are losing money which their owners could have had. Time and what could have been done in it run away. There are urgency and pressure to use it, and in the highly specialized economy, use of time means exchange of goods and of services for goods and of means of production for products. There must be exchange continually if life is to continue and if it is to continue in the richest flood it can achieve. Exchanges which must take place, in this day and this hour, must find a price by some means or other. The easiest price to hit upon is the one that prevailed yesterday, modified perhaps by circumstances which both parties can recognize or by a convention that, for example, prices rise gently all the time (the convention of the years since 1945). Poverty and urgency *demand* a price, and convention supplies it. The more nearly the economic society is confined to a hand-to-mouth existence, the more nearly, in principle, can its operations approach the rational. For when the goods dealt in on the markets are perishable and ephemeral, they must be exchanged at once and therefore find a price at once, and there will be no considerations bearing on that price except the immediate needs, tastes and momentary endowments of the members of a society. Prices in such a society *must* be formed; they *can* be formed because they are properly based on definite and simple data. It is the introduction of 'wealth', of assets which promise and represent permanence or persistence, that must destroy the basis of rationality.

16.3 *Speculation requires irreconcilable expectations*

We have sought in earlier chapters to show that rational conduct, that is, conduct logically arising from sufficient data, must be pre-reconciled conduct, since the necessary data include the intentions of other members of the society, and it is only by a scheme of pre-reconciliation that those intentions can be brought to bear in effect on each individual's choice. However, it can by no means be inferred that pre-reconciliation ensures rational conduct. To suppose that this converse proposition holds is fallacious. For in *speculative* markets there is pre-reconciliation, but a speculative market is one where each dealer hopes to exploit the general insufficiency of knowledge, and hopes to do so despite the recognized insufficiency of his own. Speculation by its nature is opposed to rationality. We may summarize the matter by saying that the notion of a market is roughly equivalent to that of pre-reconciliation, but that the pre-reconciled intentions of the parties in a speculative market are respectively based on wholly *irreconcilable* conjectures about the sequel.

16.4 *Durability engenders non-rational conduct*

The speculative economy is one in which a particular price seems worth while to one party because he judges it to be lower than tomorrow's price, and worth while to the other party because he judges it to be higher than tomorrow's price. In the event, when it shall have appeared, one or both parties will be proved wrong in their guess. How will the disappointed party respond? This question is wholly beyond the reach of any data that the analyst or observer can possess, save by an arbitrary process of simplification which would leave the answer worthless. If the disappointing event itself is the fact to which the dealer chiefly attends in the new situation, his action will depend on his interpretation of what has happened, and that interpretation itself will arise from all the details known to him of the circumstances of his misjudgement, the gaps of knowledge or the false beliefs which made it possible, the true circumstances which engendered an opposite movement of the price to what he expected. This body of detail can plainly vary from case to case in numberless ways which it would be an endless task to try to enumerate even in broad categories. A counter-expected event destroys in some degree the basis of assumption and inference on which the disappointed expectation had been built. What will replace that disrupted basis, in the mind of the expectation-former, is unguessable, because the detached analyst and observer can hardly have any knowledge of the contents of that private individual mind which must re-form the structure. To assert in general and in the abstract that expectation-forming is non-logical might be thought an un-supported *ipse dixit* or an exaggeration. But if the even momentary stability of a speculative price depends on the existence, in the market, of two opposite views about the impending price-movement, both of which cannot be right, it is plain that the data or the reasoning which form an expectation of price-movements can be at fault. If the data can be at fault, the expectation-former is either at fault himself in supposing the data to be sufficient, or he is drawing inferences from data which he recognizes to be insufficient, and thus is engaging in a non-logical procedure. The observed existence of speculative markets where temporary price-stability is nevertheless estab-lished, proves that expectation-forming of a non-logical kind occurs. The rational ideal cannot apply to speculative markets and cannot include them. Yet storable and durable goods of all kinds necessarily constitute a medium of speculation. Perma-nence and durability, if we see them around us, imply that we shall not find around us the perfectly rational conduct which the value-construct describes. The two things are logically mutually exclusive.

16.5 *Money allows the deferment of choice*

A money-using economy is one which acknowledges the permanent insufficiency of the data for rational choice. For money is the means by which choice can be deferred until a later and better-informed time. The passage of time will of course engender all sorts of questions of its own in an endless stream, and will not bring 'better information' in any comprehensive and permanent sense. But it will illuminate such questions as what particular goods will best serve the needs of some particular date at present lying in the future. Money saves the seller of services or other goods from having to make up his mind, at the moment of selling, what in detail he wishes to receive in exchange. Not only what will be bought, but when, can be left undecided by the possessor of a stock of money. But if all necessary data were present in his mind, why should he desire to defer his choice? Amongst all assets, money depends to the least possible degree, namely, a zero degree, on specialized technological powers of its own for its value in exchange. Any assurance it has of being exchangeable arises from a convention, from an aspect of the texture of society, a tacit understanding. It is not rational, in our strict sense, to hold technologically useless money instead of serviceable goods. But it is unavoidable to do so, for life consists in coping with one minor crisis after another, and not with discrete moments of general, comprehensive pre-reconciliation of choices which will solve all questions of conduct for a definite impending period and leave all beyond that period unaffected. Money is the purest embodiment of *liquidity*.

16.6 *Rationality defended by the Theory of Games*

The word liquidity was made common coin of discussion among economists (as distinct perhaps from bankers and accountants) by John Maynard Keynes, for whom it was an indispensable and central strand in an argument which ended by rejecting the claim of economic conduct to be capable of rationality. Keynes approached this position of nihilism by unconscious and irregular intellectual strides. His ultimate vision, or discernment, of the chaotic in the business world might have been extended and opened out, made explicit and anatomized in detail, by the authors of the Theory of Games, had they happened to achieve some spasm of radical doubt. But on the contrary, by an extraordinary paradox, the Theory of Games turned out to be a supreme intellectual effort to defend the rationality of conduct in face of a recognition that business, and life in general, is a conflict of cut-throat ferocity. The Theory of Games of von Neumann and Morgenstern makes conduct rational despite the head-on collision of interests, by supposing that this is the conflict, not of real life in the fog of deliberately engendered uncertainty and misconception, but instead the conflict of a *game with known rules*. Each of two contestants is assumed to know what pay-off, what result for himself, will be the consequence of any pair of strategies, one adopted by himself and the other by his opponent, and also to know the complete list of strategies available to himself and the complete list of those open to his opponent, but not to know what will be the opponent's choice of strategy out of the finite list available to him. From this situation of each opponent is deduced the rational conduct for each: the maximin strategy by which each player minimizes the harm that, at worst, his opponent can do him. The Theory of Games thus supposes the players to have knowledge of all the possibilities: *surprise*, the most powerful and incisive element in the whole art of war, is eliminated by the theoretical frame itself; and novelty, the *changing* of what appeared to be the rules of the game, the continually threatening dissolution of the conditions and circumstances in which either player may suppose himself to be operating, is eliminated also, by the supposition that each player, like a chess player of super-human intellectual range, knows everything that can happen. There is thus, for each of the contestants in the Theory of Games, a quasi-rational choice of conduct: he does not have *complete* knowledge, for he does not know *which* thing his opponent *will* do. But he knows what things his opponent can do.

16.7 Ex post *equilibria necessarily conceal their own origins*

Keynes wrote three versions of his *theory of output as a whole*. In the *Treatise on Money* he introduced the essential leaven of novelty which was going to transform economic theory: the notion that a *speculative* market, the bond or loan market, operates at the heart of things. Before the *Treatise*, the interest-rate was determined by tastes and objective circumstances, by the persuasibility of income-earners to transfer consumption from the present to the future, and the desire of business men to transfer the means of enterprise from the future to the present, thus altering the productive possibilities and enlarging the prospective income of the society including themselves. An interest-rate which was determined by the inter-action of reluctant thrift and the extra productivity of labour and of Nature when applied via machines and man-made industrial facilities, depended also on an assumed sufficiency of knowledge. Interest was one of those prices which disseminated to all members of the society the necessary information for rational, that is, fully relevantly informed, conduct. In the *Treatise* we are shown the bond-market as it exists in real life: a speculative market where a price, with an identity and a momentary stability, can only exist if there are two camps of dealers holding opposite views of the impending *movement* of bond prices. Where, then, was determinacy and where was rationality?

Keynes did not, in the *Treatise*, exploit or even properly assess the meaning of the great undermining which had thus happened to the theory of value. In the *General Theory of Employment, Interest and Money*, that most paradoxical of books, he abandoned in some part his discernment of the full speculative nature of the bond-market and of the nature, meaning and consequences of speculation. The speculative motive for holding money, as its role is elaborated in the *General Theory*, becomes gradually debased and de-natured, until the demand for a stock of money, for money to *hold* as an *asset*, became something which could be reduced to a demand curve, a *stable* relation between the size of the demanded stock of money, on one hand, and the rate of interest on the other. Such a stable relation is a total denial of the essence of speculation. In

Keynes's own mind, such a relation between the interest-rate and the size of the society's stock of money was merely an aspect or an element of his curious methodology in the *General Theory*, where what is displayed to the reader is a range of 'equilibria' of the most precarious and ephemeral kind, and what is really at the heart of things is the precariousness itself and its natural sequel of a disorderly non-equilibrium sequence of events or states, leading perhaps to another no less precarious situation of the kind where things can be deemed to be in a sense again adjusted to each other. Keynes's resort to some kind of 'equilibrium' conception may be conjectured to have sprung from three sources. He was trained in Marshallian economics; secondly, he had the mathematically trained man's instinct to adopt the analytic method, which starts with the hypothesis that a solution exists and proceeds to specify it by considering what characteristics are dictated for it by the conditions of the problem; a method which it is fatally easy for the economist to translate into starting with an *ex post* situation and regarding that situation as containing *in itself* its own explanation; and thirdly, he was divided in mind by the contradiction between his two purposes, namely, the purpose of explaining what things are like and the purpose of showing how they can be controlled. On the face of it, these two purposes seem to be naturally unified, since one must have some insight into an institution or a mechanism in order to obtain desired behaviour from it. But Keynes's search for an understanding of business led him to the conclusion that business is essentially, irremediably non-rational, not through its defects of organization or mistaken choice of ends or of methods, but in the nature of things at their most fundamental level; it is logically inconceivable for business to be rational. But if there is no consistently operating mechanism, how can any reliable levers exist for managing it?

The full measure of his own conclusion did not come to him until he wrote his third version of the theory of employment in answer or in dismissal of his critics. In the *Treatise*, he had nearly broken clear of the notion of an economy describable in terms of stable functions and predictable reactions. In the *General Theory* the pressing need to prescribe action for the government and to persuade the scholarly community, and perhaps the desire to build something scientifically positive and self-sufficient, led him back to a Marshallian frame. Only in Chapter 12, which contradicts its own title in a long digression, he glimpsed the message he ultimately had to convey. That message came out unmuted in the *Quarterly Journal of Economics* one year after the book itself.

16.8 *The infinite regress of expectations*

It is not, of course, only the bond-market which is speculative. All asset-markets are speculative, since today's valuation of every asset depends on suppositions about tomorrow's valuation of it, in the infinite regress of expectations concerning expectations. A speculative market is subject to bi-polar forces, the desire for positive gain and the desire to avoid loss. Richard Cantillon defined the activity of the business man as the buying of goods for a known price with a view to selling them at a price which, at the moment of his buying them, is unknown. The goods, of course, need not be bought in the physical form in which they are sold. They can be meanwhile transformed, 'produced'. But Cantillon at the beginning of the construction of economics penetrated to the heart of things, the truth that a world which looks to tomorrow is a world bent upon exploiting uncertainty, un-knowledge. It is a speculative world. When it has over-reached itself in the hope of gain it will retreat precipitately upon *liquidity*, the means of avoidance of commitment.

16.9 *The world of perfect foresight would be timeless and event-less*

Money, otherwise than as a mere accounting unit to express the price-pattern of a general equilibrium, has no place in the value-construct. Money, as something which can introduce a time-interval between selling one thing and deciding what to have in exchange for it, can evidently have no place in a system whose logic requires all its choices to be comprehensively simultaneous in order that they may be pre-reconciled and thus fully informed. Money is the means of stopping half-way in the complete transaction of exchange, the means of avoiding or postponing the hazardous and expectational choice of a concrete, specialized asset whose value is a conjecture about the relation of its design to future technology and markets. *Liquidity* is a denial of the rationality of the only economic world we have evolved. Value-theorists, balking at the open acknowledgement of timelessness in their construct, have sometimes invoked perfect foresight. It is, of course, simply another name for timelessness. If every event can be perfectly foreseen, there is no event. An event is something which *becomes* known. To look down the complete vista of all relevant history-to-come is to see a still picture where nothing happens. In such a world, as in the overtly timeless world, there would be no need for postponement of choice, no need for liquidity. In chapters which follow we shall seek to show that an interest-rate, the price of liquidity, is itself the expression of the fact that lending is the exchange of a known for an unknown sum of money. Interest-rates, determined in the speculative bond-market, are held steady, if at all, by the momentary balance of power between two camps, the Bulls and the Bears. Since one or both of these camps must be expensively wrong in their opinion, the interest-rate will change of its own accord, it will be an *inherently restless variable*, able, and obliged, to alter the values of assets, since their value depends on conjectured future exchanges discounted to the present. But alteration of asset values is alteration of the wealth of individuals or of the firms they control, and thus must affect the values of all exchangeable things, whether or not they are long-lasting. Uncertainty comes full circle and engenders its own source.

17

Chapter 2 of the *General Theory*: Two Entrances for Involuntary Unemployment

17.1 *The paradox of involuntary unemployment*

It will pay an employer to employ any man whose weekly wage does not exceed what that man's presence adds to the weekly value of the firm's *production*, the weekly *value added* by the firm's activities to the inventory with which it starts the week and the materials, etc. purchased during the week. By taking the value, at prevailing prices, of the collection of materials and tools (in the widest sense) which the firm possesses at the beginning of the week, and adding to this the value of materials and tools that it buys in from other firms during the week, and subtracting this total from the collection of materials, tools and product with which it ends the week, plus any product sold during the week (all of these taken at prices unchanged during the week), we have a measure and operational definition of the firm's production in the week. A man whose presence adds more to the weekly product, thus defined, than the weekly pay he receives, is adding to the firm's net revenue. It will pay the firm to take extra men into its employment, up to that number (other circumstances given) where a further man would cost it more than the difference made by one man of his quality to the firm's value added. Why, then, should not any and every man be able to find employment at a wage which is not greater than this *marginal product of value* of men such as himself? If he refuses employment at such a wage, is not his unemployment voluntary? This is the prior question about involuntary unemployment which Keynes recognized in the first main chapter (Chapter 2) of *The General Theory of Employment, Interest and Money*.

Numberless objections to the posing of the question in the bald and uncritical form we have given it spring instantly to mind. Some are quibbles, non-essential distractions from the real point. Some amount to the invoking of frictional unemployment. This is a genuine minor contribution to explaining the paradox of involuntary unemployment. When unemployment is on the scale which occurred in Britain, the United States, Germany and much of the industrialized world in the early 1930s, something altogether more fundamental is plainly needed. There are some important questions about the meaning of the paradox, when formulated broadly as above, which are not quibbles, but ought to be answered or attempted if we are to claim that the question has been properly posed. But these semantic matters are still beside the point, and do not touch the substance. Vast numbers of men were *despairingly* unemployed. It is futile to call their unemployment 'voluntary'. There can be, there was, such a thing as massive, general, involuntary unemployment. What was its nature, where does the argument about the wage and marginal product go wrong or miss the point, what explains the logical existence, the possibility as a concept, of men desiring to work, being willing to accept almost any wage, yet not finding any offer of a job? This is the question which Keynes had to answer at the outset of his book. In Chapter 2 he proposes two entirely distinct, virtually independent explanations, and neither in this chapter, nor elsewhere, explains the relation between them.

17.2 *Product too cheap in relation to money wages*

The first of the two independent explanations offered in Chapter 2, as to how unemployment can be involuntary when a worker's acceptance of a sufficiently low reward, in terms of product, would make it profitable for an employer to engage him, is that the product may have become too cheap in terms of money, so that at the prevailing money wage the unemployed worker is asking too large a wage in terms of product, namely, a product wage greater than the marginal product which men of his capacity and skill would be producing at a larger volume of employment than the prevailing one. In such circumstances, three things will be true:

(1) There will be unemployed workers who would gladly work for the prevailing money wage, in view of the high product wage it represents.

(2) There will be no employers willing to engage these men, in view of the excessive product wage that the prevailing money wage represents.

(3) The workers, in the trade union institutional setting, will be unwilling to accept a lower money wage.

In stating this explanation, we have referred to 'product wage' instead of 'real wage' or wage in terms of 'wage-goods'. The latter is Keynes's own term. There is in the present theme an instance of the unavoidable rough edges which occur in economic argument. From the employer's viewpoint, what matters is how much of his own product he has, in effect, to pay a man. From the man's point of view what matters is not, directly, how much his money wage will buy of the product, but how much it will buy of enjoyable goods in general. But when employment in the economy as a whole is in question, the two ideas are effectively the same.

The question which this explanation leaves still to be answered, is how it comes about that the product becomes too cheap in money terms. Why do not the employers raise the money prices of their goods? The answer which most readily suggests itself is that the employers believe that any such action would lead to smaller quantities of goods being sold, so that some of their output, at its prevailing size, would be left on their hands, and their revenue* might perhaps actually contract. But this answer is not contained in the 'first explanation' which we have sought to set out above. That explanation, in itself, offers no suggestion as to how goods become too cheap in relation to wages. What it does is to show that in a money-using economy, involuntary unemployment is logically possible on certain institutional assumptions.

17.3 *Workers' lack of power to reduce their product-wage*

In his second explanation, Keynes advances to a quite different problem. Supposing that trade unionism, or the workers' fear of falling behind each other in the matter of wages, did not inhibit their acceptance of a reduction of money wages in order to increase employment, would such action be effective? His

* Revenue, i.e. price per unit times number of units sold.

answer is that it would not. A general reduction of money wages would leave the body of wage earners as a whole with a smaller aggregate income. Out of this they might well spend less than before on consumption goods. Then with given weekly or yearly quantities produced, the prices per unit would have to be lower, so that the effect of money wage reductions might leave things largely as they had been.

17.4 *Escape from the dilemma by a change in the composition of real income*

Keynes's first argument thus shows that unemployment can be involuntary in the sense that it arises from the money wage being too high in view of the prices of the products, and that for institutional reasons or reasons of rivalry there will be no willingness on the part of workers to allow money wages to be reduced. His second argument shows, however, that even if workers accepted a reduction of money wages, this would not necessarily, or probably, lead to a reduction in their real wages. But in the mid-career of this second argument, Keynes by a sudden swerve of his chariot brings into view an answer to a third question: What action on the part of wage-earners would enable employers to offer them an acceptable reward at a higher level of employment than that prevailing? The answer is not given explicitly in Chapter 2, it is not really even hinted at, but it can be inferred, at any rate by the reader who knows what later chapters contain. If the workers were willing to spend on consumption a larger proportion of their incomes, then the contraction of quantities of product sold, due to a lowering of money wages, might be avoided.

Keynes's second argument thus hints at something entirely independent of the question how involuntary unemployment can logically exist. What hovers elusively on the threshold of perception in the last page of Chapter 2 is the idea, never stated by Keynes but almost implicit in his subsequent chapters, that the discrepancy between offered and demanded product wages is not one of size but of composition. Wage-earners, or rather, the whole body of suppliers of productive services including even the business men themselves in their capacity as income-receivers and disposers, rather than as enterprisers and employers, desire a wage, or other pay, which in product terms consists partly in provision for the future rather than enjoyment in the present. But at certain conjunctures in their affairs, at certain historical epochs, employers are unwilling to offer a product wage of this composition, because in fact they themselves would have to stand proxy for the income-earners and act as the nominal *de jure* owners of the *real provision for the future*, the industrial facilities and equipment which alone enrich society as a whole, while the real owners, the income-earners who had made possible the accumulation of those tools by saving part of their incomes, merely lent the saved money to the employers. At times of depressed business or uncertain politics, at times of threatened technological change, employers do not want to become debtors in money in order to gamble on the fortunes or misfortunes of technically specialized, invention-vulnerable, market-dependent concrete equipment.

17.5 *Chapter 2 finds its inspiration only on last page*

The structure of Chapter 2 is thus peculiar. That chapter raises a question essential to the whole enterprise of explaining the origin and nature of involuntary unemployment, namely, the question whether such a thing as involuntary unemployment is logically possible. It shows that the contrast of nature between money wages and what we have called product wages opens the possibility that money wages will be set at a level where, in view of the prevailing prices of goods, they imply a product wage higher than the least which labour would work for at the prevailing level of employment, and higher than the marginal productivity which labour would have at full employment. At a later stage it then turns to the question whether this discrepancy can be eliminated by action on the part of wage-earners. It shows that mere reduction of money wages will not have the effect required. Then on its last page, virtually apropos of nothing relevant, it introduces the question of the relation of saving to investment. Later chapters show that this question provides the basis for an explanation of involuntary unemployment, quite independent of the question of too high a product wage. When the desired saving gap (desired excess of income over consumption spending) of the society as a whole, at some given level of employment, is larger than the business man's desired net investment available for filling that gap, it will be impossible for the business man to sell the whole product of that level of employment. Thus Chapter 2 distributes itself most oddly over its subject-matter, giving all but one of its nineteen pages to questions of definition and logical possibility, and only one page to a glimpse of the heart of the *General Theory* itself.

17.6 *The distinction of* employed *equipment from* existing *equipment*

The reader of the foregoing will have questions and objections to raise. We have spoken sometimes of wage-earners and sometimes of income-disposers. Keynes himself may even be said in Chapter 2 to have attended too narrowly at first to the question of wages rather than the more inclusive notion of rewards of the suppliers of productive services. For the consumption function, or propensity to consume, is concerned with spending or saving out of the aggregate of incomes of all kinds, and on the last page of the chapter it is the consumption function which is coming into view. Keynes's own argument, in the earlier part of the chapter, is also open to question. He treats the *existing quantity* and the *employed quantity* of capital equipment as identical, and thus argues that in the short period, because the stock of equipment existing will have remained undiminished while the number of employed workers has declined, each of that smaller number of employed workers will be aided by a larger quantity of equipment than before, and thus the marginal product of workers will be higher at low than at the former high employment. If the unemployed are to be re-employed, it will then indeed be the case that they must accept a lower real (or product) wage, which can be achieved by a rise of money prices of products unaccompanied by a rise of money wages. This approach to the conclusion, however, seems questionable. Can machines and buildings be treated in this respect like farmland, where the fields in a sense are fully employed no matter whether five men or ten are working on them, and where in consequence a decline in numbers of men does really give each man more land and thus increase the product per man? Technology may, on the contrary, dictate one lorry, one loom or one type-setting machine per worker, and if so, unemployment of machines will keep step with that of workers. Then the marginal product of the employed workers need not reflect a changed relation of *existing* equipment to employed workers, but only the *unchanged* relation of employed equipment to employed workers.

17.7 *The two comparisons of saving and investment: Keynes's unfulfilled promise*

Let us return, in conclusion of this chapter, to the essence of the explanation of unemployment which Keynes's theory really leads to. On the last full page of his Chapter 2 there is a passage of great interest, seeming to hold out a promise which, regrettably, Keynes never fulfilled:

Similarly it is natural to suppose that an act of individual saving inevitably leads to a parallel act of investment. Those who think in this way are deceived. They are fallaciously supposing that there is a nexus which unites decisions to abstain from present consumption with decisions to provide for future consumption; whereas the motives which determine the latter are not linked in any simple way with the motives which determine the former.

From the standpoint of those (like the present writer) who believe that the theme of the *General Theory* requires the language of *ex ante* and *ex post,* this passage is irreproachable. For it speaks in terms of *decision,* and decision is *ex ante.* This passage expresses the heart of the arithmetical aspect of Keynes's thesis in a single sentence of plain English devoid of any hint of technicality, clear and precise in meaning as the most elaborate notation could have made it. Can saving and investment differ? Are they not two sides of the same account, two names for the same thing? Is not saving the excess of money income over expenditure on goods for immediate consumption, while investment is the excess of production of all goods over the equivalent of those bought for immediate consumption, and income is, precisely, the money measure of production? All these things are true, when we examine a self-consistent record of the past. Their implication, in that context, is that saving and investment are identically equal. That implication, however, is not valid when they refer to a time-interval of the future, concerning which there can now be only intentions, decisions, plans, depending for their power of realization on their compatibility with each other and with the course of non-human Nature, and with the undeliberated human conduct of each moment. For there is 'no nexus' between those figments, which we call expectations, invented by one person or group of people, and those invented by another, except the tenuous and delusive indications which are perhaps available to both persons, or both groups, in common, in the record of the recent past, in so far as they happen to make use of the same parts of it. If Keynes had maintained throughout the *General Theory* the practice he begins here of referring to decisions (or intentions or expectations), that is to say, to forward-looking, conjectural ideas, personal to each individual mind and shaped by all the details of that mind's personally unique experience and heredity; and if he had drawn from this language the implications it has for the essence of his argument, much confusion in his readers' minds, much illegitimate 'short cut' reasoning in his own, would have been avoided.

17.8 *Employers' and earners' disparate desired 'mixes' of consumption and wealth-accretion*

Chapter 2 offers a puzzle and hints with infinite elusiveness at a skein of solutions. The puzzle concerns the relation between the two, or perhaps three, quite distinct themes there presented in an accelerating and increasingly disconnected argument. The thread of guidance which we wish here to suggest is a spinning together of two strands. One of these strands is the idea of non-compatibility between the 'mix' of consumption and wealth-accretion desired at full employment by the income-earners, that is to say, the suppliers of productive services of all sorts, to whom the produce of industry as a whole necessarily belongs, and the 'mix' which the business men, in their capacity as such, the risk-bearers of industrial processes which are technologically compelled to look years ahead for their consummation and reward, are willing to give. For the income-earners save *money* which they lend, in one way or another, back to the business men (the income-earners, of course, *include* the business men). But money, for society as a whole, for the body of income-earners all taken together, is no use as a provision for the future; only equipment, real tools and facilities, can constitute such provision. However, these tools and facilities will have to be formally and legally the property of the business men. The business men, when they invest with borrowed money, become hostages to an incalculable technological and fashionable future. The extent to which they are willing to do so may not match the extent to which income-earners (including the business men in their private capacity) wish to save *out of the aggregate income corresponding to full employment*.

17.9 *Money as measure and money as liquidity*

The curious duality of Chapter 2 can be expressed in again another way. Its two parts correspond to two views of the nature and effects of money. In offering his explanation of how unemployment can be involuntary, Keynes appeals to the notion that at one date the product wage which the prevailing money wage will buy does represent a barely sufficient compensation for the marginal disutility of employment; but at another date, while the money wage is unchanged, the marginally-sufficient product wage may have come to cost less than that money wage. Then a rise of prices of products would bring about *the offer and the acceptance* of more jobs. Money in this argument is simply a unit of account in terms of which prices of products can be expressed, and in terms of which they can change. But in the last pages of Chapter 2, money has taken on an extra dimension. It has become a means of escape from the hazards of ownership of specialized and crystallized forms of wealth, exposed as they are constantly to obsolescence and loss of value. Money represents general purchasing power, a form of wealth which enables a man to put off making up his mind what his savings shall buy for him; to put it off, possibly, for ever.

17.10 *The symbiosis of money and uncertainty*

Chapter 2 of the *General Theory of Employment, Interest and Money*
presents in microcosm the same paradox as the work in its
entirety. Nineteen-twentieths of its length are devoted to
answering questions which are beside the point, to the removal
of debris from older constructions, to the author's need to free
himself from an obsolete frame of thought. Only a paragraph
in this chapter hints at the cataclysm which Keynes was
eventually to release. The effect of his long-drawn and groping
exploration, begun in the *Treatise* and continued beyond the
volume of the *General Theory*, was the dissolution of the rational
ideal to which economic society had been conceived, by the
Victorian theoreticians, to approximate. Until its last page or
two, Chapter 2 is concerned to show how the rational principle
of equalizing the marginal disutility and the marginal productivity of labour, valid when both are expressed in terms of
their equivalent in enjoyable *product*, can be defeated by their
representation in terms of money. But this looseness of the
joints of theory is a mere trifle, its exposure is not much more
than the clearing up of a vague discomfort of argument. It is
when the wage demanded and accepted by the suppliers of
productive services is expressed wholly in money, in general
non-specific purchasing power, and that which is paid by the
employers is expressed partly in concrete, specialized and
durable equipment, that a great gulf can open up between the
composition of the wage (or other pay) desired by the income-
earners in terms of consumption or saving, and the *composition*
of the pay which the employers are willing to offer, in terms of
consumable goods or investment goods, at a level of aggregate
general output and income corresponding to full employment,
so that full employment becomes impossible. The point, thus
expressed, was perceived more clearly by Myrdal than by
Keynes, but Myrdal did not follow the logic quite to the end of
the path and push, as Keynes and Hugh Townshend did in the
early months of 1937, the theory of value over the edge of the
rubbish pit. Neither in Chapter 2, nor in the *General Theory* as a
whole, does Keynes express the obstacle to full employment in
terms of incompatible real composition of wages demanded

and wages offered. Myrdal in interpreting the concealed implications of Wicksell's *Geldzins und Güterpreise* did refer explicitly to a mis-match between the ratio of saving to income and that of investment to production, all four of these quantities being conceived *ex ante*. This still does not quite attain the full proposition. I do not think its explicit formulation in unequivocal terms is to be found in either Myrdal or Keynes. But each saw the essential clue. Chapter 2, after no matter what distractions, does eventually glimpse the central theme: the intimate symbiosis of money and uncertainty, and their combined effect in undermining the basic assumptions of the rational ideal of economic orderliness.

17.11 *Marginal value-productivity not* measurable *at a time of high uncertainty*

The question of how unemployment can be involuntary, when a man (it would seem) has only to offer his work for less than it is worth to an employer, has something more to teach us. We have not asked *how an employer knows* what a man's work is worth to him. We gave at the outset an 'operational' definition of a firm's weekly value added. That formula referred to the value of the firm's inventory at the end of the week. How does it value that inventory? Part can be offered on the open market, and actually sold. But part must be retained, in order that the firm may continue to exist and operate in the subsequent week. Some of that part which is retained will be durable equipment intended to be used for years to come, some will be the firm's own product waiting to be sold in future months, some will be partly processed products. At a time when the market for the firm's goods has rapidly shrunk, what value is it to put on goods partly finished or ready for sale? There is no knowing at what price, or when, they can be sold. How is an employed man's contribution to the firm's value added to be measured in such circumstances? The firm will acknowledge its ignorance about the money value of its production, and keep as much of its assets as it can in the form of money, whose value in terms of goods appears at such a time to be increasing quickly. At such a time there is no measurable or knowable marginal product of value for the labour which the firm might employ. It may be plain to the firm that the best guess as to such a marginal product is that it is zero. To add to its inventory of goods ready for sale may merely depress their prices by a larger proportion than it increases their amount, so that the marginal product of value is negative. But the essential point is that in such circumstances the concept of marginal product, as something measurable, has dissolved into meaninglessness. *That* is why there is involuntary unemployment. There is no price of labour at which labour seems worth employing. There is the question of timing. Why employ a man now, when in a few weeks his wage will have gone down by a quarter? What we have to learn from such considerations is that economic theory does not deal with tangibles, with measurements that can always be made with the same meaning and in the same terms today as yesterday. Sometimes its task is to find fixed relations amongst the wisps and eddies of a flowing mist.

18

Kaleidic Investment-Values

18.1 *Investment-values as constructions on merely suggestive evidence*

Investment is a department of exchange, and exchange itself embraces everything that is characteristically economic amongst human activities. Exchange is the giving up of one thing as a condition of getting something else. Production is the exchange of resources for products or of inputs for outputs. Market exchange merely transfers ownerships reciprocally. Investment is the exchange, by production or by market, of some forms of technological resources for a different form. It is a stage on the way to produce consumables, but so important a business, in its influence throughout the economic life of society, that it is an object of study in its own right. In creating a source of income, that is, of a flow of output, it creates in that source a stock of wealth. Investment is the acquisition, and from society's point of view the production, of items or systems which are counted on to aid other production for a stretch of time to come. Its worth-whileness is therefore a judgement about situations, and their sequences, which cannot be directly known by being observed and tested. They are a figment, no matter how powerfully suggested by evidence present to the mind of the business man. His mode of gathering, construing and exploiting such suggestions, in order to invent and to value investment plans, is our immediate theme.

18.2 *Expectation rejected by the economic analyst*

A good is an object or an organization which *promises* performance. Its essence is the belief entertained by some person that it is *capable* of doing specific things, or of providing some class of services. A good is a skein of *potentiae*, of things hoped for.

[178]

These hopes may look to the immediate next moment. Food hot and ready to be eaten is a good. But they may look instead to distant years and generations. A good is like a wheel whose usefulness depends upon its whole circumference, although only a minute proportion of that circumference is at any moment in contact with the ground. The contact-point, the present moment, and the conditions which prevail at that point, are an essential part of the evidence for the soundness of the wheel. But the comparison is poor, for the structure of the wheel can be examined and so can the nature of the track on which it will have to roll, whereas the demands to be made upon a tool or some durable productive aid are not visible but only imagined. The valuation of investment-goods depends in the nature of things upon expectation, and expectation is a structure cantilevered out from the present over a void. But such a picture of expectation suggests very poorly its elusive mutability and subtlety, its manifold rival forms co-existing and mutually conflicting even in a single mind, and its propensity to reproduce with enormously magnified effect the changes of the fragments of evidence from which it springs. Expectation, in fact, is almost the worst conceivable material for the operations of reasoned analysis, for how can we reason about something almost impossible to identify or to specify? This basic difficulty has had in economic theory a paradoxical effect. It has led writers to treat the *state of expectations* as a fixed configuration, so that the valuations which depend upon it can be analysed in total disregard of it, and treated as varying only with the percentage per annum which at any present moment the bond market decrees shall be used for discounting future *assumed* payments or receipts to the present. This paradox is very strikingly present in Keynes's *General Theory of Employment, Interest and Money*. Book IV, on the Inducement to Invest, contains in its one hundred and twenty pages, thirty pages on expectation and eighty on the interest-rate, a proportion which reverses and even caricatures the relative importance of the two kinds of influence on investment-values. Keynes had a great deal, of high originality, brilliant insight and basic importance, to say about the source and behaviour of interest-rates, and these eighty pages were his intense effort to replace an irrelevant theory of what interest would mean in a non-monetary economy, with one based on the inherently speculative nature of lending. By contrast, he had, essentially, only one thing to say about expectation: that it eludes reduction to clear and stable principles and laws, and is a law to itself. That can be said in a paragraph, and is said in a few pages of Chapter 12 of the *General Theory*. But it is perhaps possible to single out one ascendant influence on the expectations which underlie investment values, namely, the trading revenue earned by existing equipment in the immediate past. This is a prime element in what Keynes called 'the news'.

18.3 *Magnified influence of 'the news'*

It is not news, at tea-time, that the clock has advanced from four o'clock to five. It is not news that the tide has come in about an hour later today than it did yesterday, nor that the leaves have begun to fall in October. Those facts do not add to or change our knowledge, there is *nothing new* in them. News is something that was in some sense and some degree unguessable. At least it reports as actual, something which was only conjectural; it adds detail and depth, it fills out knowledge and pushes it out one further step across the untrodden ground. 'News' means what it says, it is a datum containing an element of novelty, unexpectedness and surprise. The prime and instinctive duty of the mind in face of news is to assimilate it. The *tessera* which has just been dropped into the mosaic makes what existed before look somewhat different, gives it a changed significance and elicits from it unthought-of suggestions. Earlier knowledge and understanding of things must be re-assessed. This digestion of the news requires that attention be concentrated upon it, it is given a place at the focus of thought, we dwell on it and see it in magnified proportion to its background. We assume that news shows the direction of things. News is that part of history that we have not yet come to terms with, that may pose a threat or disclose an opportunity; it demands and receives special attention and therefore special weight. News worthy of the name reports events which contain some element of the counter-expected, that is, of ideas whose possibility was considered and rejected; and some element of the *unexpected*, the unthought of, the unentertained idea, never considered or assigned any degree of possibility, high or low, because it never entered into thought. News may thus disrupt the former structure of a man's expectations, or may shift that structure bodily, as it were, towards the more sanguine or the less sanguine appraisal. Especially it may do this latter in a direct and simple way, if it is itself quantitative and closely involved in the subject-matter of the system of expectations in question. The value assigned to an investment-good, an item or system of industrial facilities, rests on the trading revenues which it is conceived to earn, or to contribute, in the stretch of future months and years of its economic life. As those years or months become the present and the past, the assumptions formerly held regarding the trading revenue of each particular named interval can be compared with its actual performance, and that comparison is plainly a most relevant matter for the business man faced with the question whether his valuation of an existing piece of equipment, or of an investment-plan existing only in his thoughts, is well founded or not. It may be worth while to formalize this idea.

18.4 *Elasticities of surprise*

Valuation is thought, and thought occurs at some moment, but its content can be the conceived situations or events of any range of moments, and in valuation, these must be expected moments. The stretch of time which we can think of as composed of these expected moments can be divided into unit intervals labelled $1, 2, \ldots$ by counting them forward from the present. The general element on which a business man must base his valuation of an item or system of equipment (a plant) is the difference which he can imagine to occur between the cost of the materials, energy, labour and other necessities for operating the plant during some such interval, say interval i, and the market value of the objects which are formed from these inputs by the operation of the plant during interval i. This difference, Q_i, being construed from suggestions existing in present thought and springing from present evidence, about times not yet observable, ought by its nature to be allowed by

the business man to range over numerical values from important losses to important gains. The notion of focus-gain and
focus-loss supposes that beyond some level of loss or gain, each
further numerical increase will be associated with a deepening
of scepticism as to its plausibility or possibility, and that at
some numerical value a determinate maximum of the combined
effect of these influences, in giving rise to concern or interest,
in arresting attention, on the part of the business man, will be
found. Between the focus-loss and the focus-gain will be found
some neutral (numerical) value, perhaps a zero value, which
will appear neither favourable nor unfavourable, from which
the size of the focus-gain and that of the focus-loss can indeed be
most meaningfully measured. Let us write g for that numerical
hypothesis of Q_i which represents the positive focus of these
hypotheses in the sense we have just indicated. By g is to be
understood a hypothesis prevailing in the mind of the owner of
an existing plant, concerning its trading revenue Q_i in an impending unit time-interval labelled i. When that interval i shall
have elapsed, it will be possible to compare the actual and
recorded trading revenue of that interval with the focus-
hypothesis g hitherto entertained. Let the excess of the recorded
amount over the focus-hypothesis be written Δg. Now a valuation of the plant by its owner must correspond to some self-
consistent set of supposed or hypothesized trading revenues, Q,
one for each of the unit intervals composing the remainder of
the plant's effective life. Given such a series of hypotheses of Q,
and the rate of interest r dictated by the bond-market, we can
write the valuation v of the plant as

$$v = \Sigma \ Q_i(1+r)^{-i}.$$

It is evident that since the number of such series of Q's which
can be legitimately entertained by the business man in face of
the evidence available to him is unlimited, his arrival at an
effective demand-price for such a plant as the one he possesses,
a price such as would seem just worth while for him to pay for
it if he were not its owner, will entail a complex and subtle
path of reasoning and judgement. Let us, however, write such
a demand-price as u. We can surely assert that u will be affected
if the recorded trading review of a just-elapsed interval exceeds
the formerly entertained focus-hypothesis for that trading

revenue, and thus it will be reasonable to define an *elasticity*, which we shall call the valuation elasticity of surprise for gain of trading revenue,* as $(\Delta u/u)/(\Delta g/g)$. The chief assertion of this chapter is that this elasticity will be typically of a magnitude far greater than the ratio of g for interval i to the sum of the g for all the remaining intervals of the plant's effective life. The business man's demand-price for such a plant that he owns will, in other words, be rather elastic to favourable divergences if realized from 'best-expected' hypotheses of trading revenue, even though the measured trading revenue is only, say, for the just elapsed year or half year in the life of a plant which may continue in use for twenty years.

18.5 *Kaleidicity of investment-values*

Expectations are *kaleidic*. Like the symmetric pattern of colours in the kaleidoscope, they can be changed comprehensively and radically by a slight shock or twist given to the instrument, or to the evidence in the mind of the expectation-former. 'Stretch of time' is a figment, it is memory or else imagination engendered by the evidence existing in the *actual present*. But the value to be assigned to a so-called 'durable' tool or plant can be based only on the supposed content of this figmental stretch of future time. Expectational value is a structure of thought resting at only one point on the ground of visibly recorded evidence. A small irregularity as the wheel rolls forward can lift it bodily or even deform and destroy it. The consequences of the kaleidicity of investment-values can be formidable and far-reaching.

Some of those consequences can be formalized by defining two further elasticities of surprise. The change in the business man's assessment of his existing plant may induce a change in

---

* Instead we can define an elasticity of investment-gain (from an existing plant) with respect to the excess of recorded over focus trading revenue, as $(\Delta j/j)/(\Delta g/g)$, where j is the excess of the hoped-for value u of the plant over its cost of replacement; or again we can give j a retrospective meaning as the original excess of valuation over construction-cost of the existing plant as these were reckoned by the business man at the time when he decided to construct it. This alternative meaning was the one which I originally gave. See *Decision, Order and Time*, second edition (1969), pp. 288 and following.

his intentions for further investment in plant. If his intended investment in some future intervals, say intervals $i+m$ to $i+n$, is increased from I to $I+\Delta I$, we may call the ratio $(\Delta I/I)/(\Delta u/u)$ the investment elasticity of surprise for gain of valuation, and the ratio $(\Delta I/I)/(\Delta g/g)$ the investment elasticity of surprise for gain of trading revenue. Elasticities referring to a numerical excess of recorded trading *loss* over the focus-loss for the just-elapsed interval can be correspondingly defined. The investment elasticity of surprise for gain of trading revenue, which we can write more neatly $(\Delta I/I) . (g/\Delta g)$, is of course the product of the other two elasticities, for we have

$$\frac{\Delta I}{I} . \frac{g}{\Delta g} = \frac{\Delta I}{I} . \frac{u}{\Delta u} . \frac{\Delta u}{u} . \frac{g}{\Delta g} .$$

Kaleidic effects, typically the response of asset values to 'the news', the abrupt and necessarily unforeseeable reaction of expectation-formers to announcements which in their nature are unheralded and of a purport quite unknown in advance, pose important problems of notation. The basic and essential character of the kaleidic phenomenon renders inappropriate the accepted methods of analysis of *fully-known problems*. It is the fact, astonishing and yet natural, that in economics we habitually and, it seems, unthinkingly assume that the problem facing an economic subject, in especial a business man, is of the same kind as those set in examinations in mathematics, where the candidate unhesitatingly (and justly) takes it for granted that he has been given enough information to construe a satisfactory solution. Where, in real life, are we justified in assuming that we possess 'enough' information? What would be the test of 'enough'? How many years would have to elapse before that test could be conclusively applied? How could we console ourselves, when the lapse of those years had shown our data to have been insufficient, incorrect or irrelevant, for the disappointing results of applying sound reason to unsound premises? It may be thought surprising that we refer to the consequent difficulty as one of *notation* or of *language*. Yet the point in the exploratory process, where we are most in danger of being unconsciously misled, is that very early point where we seek to write down the terms of the problem. All habit, instinct and training lead us to use the notation and the language, the formal frame of thought, which assumes and takes for granted that the task in hand is one of reasoning on complete data. We write some variable y as a function of x. What does $y = f(x)$ imply? What does its validity depend on? It pre-supposes that the association of values of y with those of x is unambiguous, one-to-one, stable and *ascertainable in principle*. If that association is in fact the expression of surmise and almost fictional elaboration; if it is the expression of conjecture, not merely concerning objective and ultimately observable matters, but about *the conjectures being made by others* about these matters; can we then make that association the subject of an analysis which assumes it to be knowable, stable and exact? Keynes's eloquent analogy is well known. The dealer in Stock Exchange securities is like the competitor in one of those contests where a prize is offered for selecting from twelve portraits of girls the most beautiful girl. What the competitor is concerned to guess is not which girl is in some basic sense the most beautiful, but which one will be so selected by the majority of voters, for that *consensus* is the test which the adjudicators are going to use. The price of a share on the Stock Exchange rises when many or most potential or actual holders of such shares believe that it will rise; whether or not there is any 'objective' reason for such a rise is of no concern whatever to the short-term speculators. When such fluid, transient and dissolving wraiths of thought are the basis of the association between two variables, how can the matter be represented by a formal notation which insists (by its conventional and established meaning) that the values of each are permanently and unequivocally deducible from those of the other?

18.6 *Meaning, notation and the transience of thought*

We have spoken of this difficulty as one of notation or of language. But language is the outward shape of thought, the form which is inseparable from the content, and we here confront in fact the most radical of questions about method: Are the presuppositions of algebraic (functional) analysis, in however carefully safeguarded a form, appropriate to a subject-matter where uncertainty and its deliberate exploitation, and even its deliberate creation, belong to the essence of the phenomena? The methods of orderly thought are not confined to measurement and the comparison of its results. Some systematic disciplines depend on the study of yes-or-no questions: genuine or false, descended from or not descended from, guilty or not guilty (measurement and yes-or-no become one and the same in the binary scale and the computer's use of it); many disciplines depend on an elaboration of the yes-or-no dichotomy, namely, upon classification: mineralogy and paleontology, botany and zoology in their taxonomic aspects, and the whole art of pathology in medicine, where diseases are classified rather than measured, are classificatory disciplines. Classification itself can be looked upon as the most general of a hierarchy of ideas within which the idea of mathematical function takes its place. For *function* implies *cross-classification*. Values of y are classes, albeit classes in each of which there is room for only one member; and values of x are the same. When we declare that y shall be looked on as a function of x, we are saying that there is a cross-classification in which each vector (x, y), falling necessarily in one and only one class of y, thereby falls in one and only one class of x. Classification even includes measurement, for to measure the length of an object is to place it in the class of objects whose length, say, is greater than one metre and less than 1.01 metre. A systematics, or classificatory method, might have something to contribute to the problem of notation and language with which the ostensibly mutable and elusive associations of economic phenomena confront us.

19

Lender's Uncertainty and the Nature of Interest-Rates

19.1 *The* formal imagination *the origin of science*

The question is as old as history, whether formal speculation can throw light on the nature of things. Mathematics is in the ultimate degree formal and abstract, yet its origin and its being are not untouched by the work of the senses. Sense provides the notion of the separateness of things from each other and the integrity of each within itself. From this the feeling of plurality follows, and the need for a measure of plurality. Standard plural collections, arranged so that the minimum step carries the mind from one to another in a succession of ever greater plurality, provide the means of counting. From such beginnings an unending invention of relational structures can proceed. If such a structure is in any way grounded in the work of the senses, it seems at least conceivable that the same constraints which govern the natural cosmos including humanity should also govern the basic fibre of thought, so that the purest inventions of the enclosed but unfettered mind should at various points seem to reflect the perceptual world of sensual exploration. Music is another world where form and physical sense seem fused into an absolute unity. Moreover, it seems plain that without the inventions of thought there would be no facts. Crystallizations of sense impressions must take place and be named. These 'objects' and 'events' can then be the building blocks for constructions of any degree of complexity, constructions both of narrative, that is, of forms which claim to be merely unique and particular, and of principle, that is, forms which claim to be found in limitless repetition throughout history and throughout the momentarily co-existing world.

The formal imagination, we may thus claim, is the originator of science. It discerns or composes the primal pieces, the elementary *nominanda* which provide the stuff of discourse. It may be said that we are here merely re-naming the familiar concept of perception. But if perception means no more than the discernment of the things to be named, it stops short at the point where science begins. It is in distinguishing patterns of patterns, stereotypes in which objects and events appear repeatedly, 'regularly', in the same relations of time and space to each other, that systematic knowledge starts. In some fields the imaginative deployment is more efficient and economical than in others, and approaches mathematics in the spareness of the materials which enable some whole aspect of the world to be encompassed. Can we find any such aspect, and any theme where the formal wholly dominates and overshadows the factual, in economic theory? Such a theme appears most arrestingly, I believe, in the question of the origin and determination of interest-rates. The theory which emerges from their study has implications for the whole of economics.

19.2 *Uncertainty and its governance of the bond market as the genesis of interest*

A rate of interest is expressed as the proportion of itself by which a debt grows in a unit of time. When a lender parts with P money units in exchange for a borrower's promise to repay $P(1+r)$ money units after one year, the rate of interest is r per annum. A bond can stipulate any schedule of repayments, and the instalments need not be equal or at equal intervals, provided that the sums and their dates are stated when the loan is made. In expressing the terms of a bond, it is convenient to use a unit time-interval short enough for each instalment to be deferred an exact number of intervals from the date of making the loan. Let us consider a loan of P which is to be repaid in one instalment after i time-units at a rate of interest r per time-unit. After one time-unit from receiving the loan, the borrower will owe $P(1+r)$. It is this increased sum which he in effect reborrows for the second time-unit, and at the end of that second interval he must add to his debt a proportion r of the amount $P(1+r)$. At the end of the second interval, the debt will thus have become

$$P(1+r) + rP(1+r) = P(1+r)(1+r),$$

which we can write $P(1+r)^2$. At the end of i intervals its amount will be $A = P(1+r)^i$. A *principal* P is said to *accumulate at compound interest* to an *amount* A. If we divide both sides of the equation by $(1+r)^i$, we have an expression of the sum of spot cash which must be lent in order that the amount of the debt after i unit intervals at a rate of interest r per interval may be A, namely

$$P = A/(1+r)^i,$$

or

$$P = A(1+r)^{-i}.$$

P may now be called the *present value* or *discounted value* of a sum A deferred i time-units at an interest-rate r per time-unit. The schedule of deferred payments which a bond promises may be related to the price paid for it, at the moment from which the intervals are counted, by means of the formula

$$P = \frac{A_1}{1+r} + \frac{A_2}{(1+r)^2} \ldots + \frac{A_n}{(1+r)^n},$$

where the instalments $A_1, A_2, \ldots, A_n$ (no matter whether equal or unequal) are each provided with a subscript showing the number of time-units of its deferment from the date when the bond is bought. Writing $(1+r)^{-i}$ for $1/(1+r)^i$, the formula can be written

$$P = \sum_{i=1}^{n} A(1+r)^{-i}. \tag{19.1}$$

A lender cannot recover from the borrower the money he has lent except by waiting for the borrower to make the promised payments at their due dates. Meanwhile, his only resort in case he needs the money is to sell the bond for what it will fetch, thus transferring to a third party the right to receive the borrower's repayments as they fall due. What *will* the bond fetch? At the moment when he makes the original loan, neither the lender nor anyone else can know what price it will fetch if it is offered for sale at some subsequent date. Nor can the lender be sure, when he makes the loan, that he will not need to sell the bond rather than wait for the payments which it promises. A conclusion follows from this which is essential to the nature of bonds, loans and interest-rates: to lend is to part with a known sum of money in exchange for an unknown sum.

In order to give themselves some presumption of getting back at least as much as they lend, lenders will require the promised repayments to exceed, in total, the principal which is initially lent. That is to say, they will require the sum of the instalments A_i to be greater than P. For a further reason also, such an excess will be insisted on. For when he parts with a known in exchange for an unknown sum of money, a lender subjects himself to mental discomfort. The excess of the series of A_i over P will be partly required as compensation for this. That excess is of course not to be measured simply as $\Sigma A_i - P$. Its relevant measure is that rate of interest r which, when applied in discounting every instalment A_i, brings the total of their discounted values to equality with P. Thus, given P and each A_i, the rate of interest is determined (pinned down) by equation (19.1) above.

In what manner and in what sense are P and the A_i given? It is not the case that a would-be-borrower and a potential lender will settle the terms of their transaction by a face-to-face negotiation in disregard of all other persons and circumstances. On the contrary, a market exists for bonds, and the price for which a newly created bond, promising a specific schedule of repayments, can be sold will be intimately bound up with the prices which prevail for existing bonds offering schedules of still-outstanding promised payments somewhat similar in their character to that of the proposed new bond. Indeed, in established and mature markets for bonds, the state of affairs on any day will be dominated by the great mass of existing bonds, created at various times in the past and not yet fully redeemed by the borrowers, which can at any moment be offered for sale in competition with any new bonds which may be created on that day. The rate of interest represented by any particular bond, given that bond's remaining schedule of payments still to be made, is determined by the market price of bonds offering a similar remaining schedule. It is evident from equation (19.1) that as this price, P, rises, so the interest-rate, r, declines. This is true as a mere arithmetical fact. From this dependence of r on P it follows that in order to gain insight into the manner in which interest-rates are determined, we need to study the character and logic of the bond market and the circumstances which influence its happenings.

19.3 *A pure gambling model embroidered to represent the bond market*

In order to examine the bond market, it will not be extravagant to invent what we may call the pure gambling counter. This is a token which has no qualities desirable in themselves, nor any which are useful in producing goods. These tokens need not even be exchangeable for goods. Their only relevant property is to be exchangeable for some kind of entirely abstract scoring points like the 'runs' which appear in the score-book of a cricket match. There is a market in the gambling counters in terms of the scoring points, and the object of the players is to buy counters for as few scoring points as possible and to sell them for as many as possible. We can suppose that sessions for exchange of counters for scoring points take place at discrete intervals. Players offer to buy or sell counters at prices which are undetermined except by self-generated movements away from the last price of a transaction. If that last price appears 'low', some player may think it promising to acquire some counters at this 'low' price, and therefore bids a shade higher than that price. The price of counters then appears to be rising, and other buyers will come in, causing it to rise further and faster. The rise gains momentum, until it has gone far enough for some players to consider it advisable to 'take their profits'. Then these players begin to sell, the rise of price is slowed, and may be reversed as other players see a selling cue. And so the game goes on. We do not intend this fantasy as a piece of mockery of the serious and by no means senseless business of exchanging bonds. Three additions to our scheme will link our abstract game with something more solid. First we will introduce a set of superstitions. Certain events in the room where the game takes place will be conventionally accepted as indicating an impending rise or an impending fall of price. The clouding-over of the sky, the dinner-gong, the barking of a dog or the hooting of an owl, for example, may have somehow imposed themselves on the reasonless convictions of the addicts of the game as omens which it goes against the grain to ignore. These omens will then have a *real* power to bring about a rise or fall of price. Every time it is obeyed by a number of players, such a superstition will seem to have been a true portent of the effect which this obedience produces. Every such occasion will strengthen its grip on the minds of the players. Secondly we will have upper and lower conventional limits. These also we will treat at first as pure superstitions. When the price of gambling counters has fallen to a certain level, there is a convention that it can go no lower. Then, of course, it never will go lower, since to sell at that low price is a gratuitous forfeiting of the gain to be made at the next price movement, which, convention says, must be upward. Every occasion of the due observance and respect for the lower limit (and similarly for the upper one) strengthens its claim to represent something 'real' and imperious which a player ignores at his peril and against his instinct and conviction. Thirdly we will take the important step of allowing the scoring points to be exchangeable for *goods*, that is, for things having qualities wanted for their own sake. Now the question in a player's mind at a particular moment of the real historical calendar (a date with a proper name, such as 23 April 1970) whether to sell gambling-counters, will be influenced by his need for goods for consumption or as aids to production, and by all the further considerations which this one immediately allows to bear on the market for gambling counters, namely, his ideas about future prices and demand for those real goods, and all the considerations which suggest and help to form these goods–price expectations, and so on in an infinite regress of influences influenced by influences which are influenced. . .

We have at last uttered the word which has been implicit in the whole picture, that of expectations. In the light of that picture, we may now surely speak of *pure* expectations, that is, suppositions (about the course of subsequent events) not able to appeal to demonstrably decisive factors and situations, but engendered by an arcane process of exchange of suggestions, themselves untraceable to observation and reason. Is, then, 'pure' expectation mere folly? For some operators in a market, at any time and all times, it cannot be so stigmatized. For at all times in a gambling market, for every man who sells cheap what he bought dear, there are others who sold dear and have now bought cheap. Gambling on such a market need not be a perfectly zero sum game, but it is near enough to that status for the greater part of the truth to reside in such a characterization. It is not foolish to be lucky, but the nexus between luck and wisdom is a tenuous and elusive one. Expectation, no matter how pure, is not folly, for on the contrary it is as inescapable as drawing breath. Founded or unfounded, the guesses must be made from hour to hour.

By *convention* we mean of course that spontaneous coalescing of thought which is so powerfully fostered by the very absence of 'real' clues to the future, in those markets where such clues are least evident and least plausible. The fact that others seem to hold an opinion is itself accepted as evidence for that opinion. One person arriving in doubt at a country bus stop will be in half a mind to give up waiting for the bus. But if a second person, equally uncertain when he sets out, arrives at the stop, the presence of one will fortify the belief of the other. A *conventional* belief in the bus will have begun to develop.

19.4 *The bond market at the centre of a universal web*

We have sought the formal meaning, the logical source and the mode of determination of an interest-rate in the following way. We showed that the relation of a series of promised sums of money deferred to various dates, when this series is considered as one whole, to a single sum of money available at once, can be expressed as a proportion of the size a debt has at the beginning of some unit time interval, which the debt is deemed to add to itself at the end of that interval. Then we showed why lenders, for good reason, require a borrower's deferred promises to exceed the sum now handed over to him. We showed that this excess of repayments over the lent principal arises from the lender's uncertainty as to how much money he will in fact receive, but that this uncertainty has nothing to do with any distrust of the borrower's honesty or capacity. It arises from the logical situation of the *lender*. Lastly we presented a fantasy concerning a gambling game using counters which served no other purpose than this game, and suggested how such a game, even when totally isolated from any influences from outside itself, could have a self-motivation which might set it and keep it in motion. But we proceeded to equip this game with three

7

additional features, namely omens or superstitions; upper and lower limits for the movements of value of the counters; and a quality of exchangeability of the counters for real goods. We now proceed to draw these strands together into a thread which will lead us from the notion of lender's uncertainty, through a complete circuit of ideas including the formal notion of a pace of proportionate growth of debt, the variation of this pace inversely with the price of a fixed schedule of deferred payments, and the existence of a market for such schedules or bonds, to the idea that such a market is primarily a gambling arena where the price of bonds is pushed up and down by the vagaries of a pure speculative restlessness, and back at last to the pinpointing of this speculative indeterminacy as that particular facet of the uncertainty of life at large, which is one half of the explanation and source of lenders' uncertainty. Is this argument, then, circular? No. It is grounded on a fact observable by every individual at any moment when he cares to pay attention to the matter; the ineluctable ignorance we live in throughout life about what is going to happen. This ignorance is doubtless a vital condition which renders life tolerable, that otherwise if conceivable at all, would be oppressive beyond expression. Lender's uncertainty is the beginning and end of the essential explanation of interest rates. But it does not itself demand or allow explanation: there is no explaining *the scheme of things entire.*

The first necessary step in the drawing-together of the strands suggests itself at once: there must plainly be some influence of the outside world upon the gambling activities of the bond market. For there are two channels of reciprocal influence of bond prices and prices of other things. A borrower's wish to borrow may arise merely from his activities as a speculator. He may have decided to buy assets with borrowed money, in the hope of an extra gain beyond what he could put himself in the way of with money of his own. But a more ordinary reason for borrowing will be a wish to buy real goods wanted for the sake of their own qualities. This wish, and the implications of satisfying it, will be affected by price-changes of such real goods. And the terms on which such borrowing can be done will themselves affect, in ways which we shall consider, the prices of real goods. This is one of the two channels of reciprocal influence which we have just referred to. The other is the fact that ownership of bonds provides an income, namely the interest paid by the borrower, and the desirability of holding bonds for this reason, at any *given market price of bonds*, will depend on the comparison of the rate of interest which corresponds to that price with the income which could be obtained from other forms of wealth. If the price for which the bonds could be sold would bring in a larger income when used to buy other assets, there will be a motive to sell the bonds, and such an action, especially if adopted by many holders, will reduce their price and thus raise the rate of interest which they offer to any buyers of them. In this way, operations in the bond market or in the markets for other assets will be intended to bring into line with each other, at the margin, the advantages of holding this kind of asset and that other kind throughout the range of different kinds of assets.

Assets of all sorts: farms, forests, mines, flocks and herds; houses and other property; shares of companies; 'fixed interest' securities, so called because the *schedule of payments* is fixed (the rate of interest corresponding to any such schedule varies of course according to the market price of the security in question); all these categories and everything that comes under them, and even portable property such as jewels and antiques, compete with each other as means of 'holding' wealth. This latter expression is not a very felicitous one, for it gives the impression of wealth as some kind of fluid substance able to retain its quantity while being poured from one vessel into another. Wealth, on the contrary, is an elusive conception encompassing all the potential types and quantities of usefulness of every thing that can be listed or imagined. There is no 'law of the conservation of wealth'. There is a perpetual endeavour of each owner of any kind of assets to sell those whose prospects the market values more highly than he does and to buy those for which its hopes are lower than his own. Thus the speculative valuation of *assets* differs radically in purpose and principle from the consumer's valuation of goods for enjoyment. A man might, conceivably, hold only one kind of asset, because he was convinced that its market price at some deferred date would have increased, over its present price, by more than in the case of any other asset. He might be joined in this opinion by no one else at all. Then there would be nothing even formally resembling the unanimity at the margin achieved by consumers regarding the *flows* of goods which they are regularly buying for consumption. Assets are not *flows* but *stocks*, and this fact also fundamentally distinguishes the asset markets in general from the consumers' goods markets. The two kinds of market meet, of course, in the market for producers' goods, which goods are both assets and flows on their way, eventually, to be consumed.

19.5 *Interest rates and the productivities of physical assets*

Let us return to two notions which we have tried to emphasize. Interest rates are set in the bond market, and the bond market is influenced by what is happening in asset markets of every kind, and in other markets of every kind, and ultimately by everything which can bear on any market. Thus in insisting that the bond market is the locus of determination of interest-rates, we are saying nothing which excludes or diminishes the influence of politics, diplomacy, technology or fashion. Amongst such influences the extent of accumulation of wealth in real forms, the quantities of developed farms, mines and wells, the quantities of machines and plant of all kinds, the durable producer's goods to which we referred in the preceding paragraph, is the one which appears most prominently in the literature of our subject. It is justly regarded as important since it may be said to set a kind of norm, indefinite and lacking in authority, but discernible, around which the interest-rates responding to other pressures fluctuate. On a farm, an extra horse will make some addition, which in principle can be measured, to the farm's yearly value added, after counting the cost of feeding and caring for the horse. There will be a marginal product of horses. And broadly in industry as a whole there will be a marginal product of trucks, tractors, printing presses, machines of each different kind. For a given population, with a given provision of natural forces, at a given historical epoch with its given technology, there may be some valuable and valid meaning in the statement that if it were possible to vary over a considerable range the quantities of durable equipment associated with that society's labour force and other forms of wealth, the marginal product of this equipment would diminish as the quantity of equipment increased. This marginal product must be regarded in the first place as expressed in technological terms. An extra horse on the farm will increase the crop by so-and-so many bushels. The translation of this technological relationship into a relation in terms of values is the economist's instinctive desire, but, except in a roundabout and loose sense, it is indeterminate. It depends, of course, on the price of the crop per bushel and the price of horses. We can argue, in this particular type of example, that the crop will serve to feed horses, and thus there is a basis for valuing horses in terms of crop, and it will plainly not pay to breed so many horses that the breeding and subsequent feeding of the marginal horse costs more in oats or hay than it is going to contribute during its working life to the output of the farm. The claim of the technological marginal productivity of tangible specialized equipment, that is, producer's durable goods in general, to provide a kind of anchorage or steering point for rates of interest, must rest on such roundabout considerations. There is nothing otherwise to obstruct the flow of influence in the opposite direction, the governance of equipment values themselves by the prevailing interest-rate.

19.6 *The formal difference of motive between speculation and consumption*

The bond market, then, is not a gambling casino where players draw only on the abstract promptings of the course of play itself. We shall suggest later that such a mechanism does play a subtle and intricate role. But plainer forces are at work. The market is subject to an immense variety of influences varying widely in their directness or roundaboutness, their quickness, their certainty or fallibility, and their strength. All these influences merely serve to enrich the sources of suggestion or stimulus which the bond market draws on in its central character of a speculative market. In that character it differs essentially in several respects from a market where flows of goods are valued according to the tastes of the consumer. Most strikingly, the two kinds of market differ in the basis and relevance of the notion of balance at the margin. The consumer experiences diminishing marginal rates of substitution. But why should the speculator do so? If he is convinced that the price of asset A is about to rise in terms of asset B, why hold any of asset B? The holding of a mixture of assets can be explained only in terms of lack of conviction.

19.7 *The nature of a market in* stocks *as distinct from* flows

The objects traded on the bond market are a collection to which new items are added, and from which existing ones are removed, only in amounts which in any day or even in any year are small in comparison with the existing collection. That collection has predominantly the character of a *stock*, measured as so-and-so many items or units, rather than that of a flow measured as so-and-so many items or units *per unit of time*. This character of a stock belongs also to the 'scoring-points' or money units for which the bonds are traded. Items of each of the two stocks are exchanged for those of the other in the knowledge that extra quantities of either kind can appear in the future, or even that some part of the existing stock can disappear, and this knowledge, and any indications or clues which may herald such an event, are part of the flow of suggestions continually pulsing through the market. At any moment, nonetheless, the practical task for the market is to find willing temporary possessors of the stock of bonds, and willing holders of the stock of money, as those stocks exist at that moment. It is as actual or potential possessors of parts of a permanently existing stock, not as consumers or *users-up* of a perishable flow, that dealers are concerned with the bond market. The means which the market has of solving its problem from moment to moment are two: the *price* of bonds in terms of money can change so that some members of the market who formerly were unwilling possessors of one or other kind of asset become willing ones; and bonds can be *exchanged* for money between members who have become unwilling holders of the kind of asset they happen to possess. What the market is continually doing, therefore, is to shuffle the ownership and the terms of exchange of the items, so that as nearly as possible each stock is in the hands of those who are content with it at the prevailing terms of exchange.

19.8 *The interest-rate as an* inherently restless *variable*

In this speculative market, willingness to hold bonds will depend on a belief or conjecture that the next movement of the price of bonds in terms of money will be upward; and a willingness to hold money will depend on a belief or conjecture that that next movement will be downward. The willing holders of bonds, and the willing holders of money, must have opposite convictions, or at least must incline to opposite opinions, concerning the immediately future course of bond prices. At a given bond price (or set of respective prices for different types of bonds), the collection of existing bonds will have a determinate money value. If there is not at that moment a group of members of the market, who at that price are willing holders of bonds and whose aggregate wealth (assigned to potential bond-holding) is equal to the aggregate prevailing value of the existing stock of bonds, some change must take place. Its character can be any one of a great variety of types. The price of bonds may fall, and this may lead some of those formerly distrustful of an impending price-*rise* to believe in it, and to buy bonds or keep those they have. But a fall of bond prices may have the opposite effect, and generate an expectation of a further fall. If the market is equipped with the kind of 'superstitions', or with well-founded reasons, for supposing that a lower limit exists below which bond prices cannot fall, the price has only to approach near enough to that floor for its fall to be arrested. The price can *come to rest*. But it will only do so by convincing enough members of the market that the prospects are now for a rise. The necessary condition for its coming to rest is a suitable *division* of opinion concerning the movement of the price in the coming days or months. Evidently the convictions can be strong or weak, they can amount to no more than a slight inclination one way or the other, or even a mere acknowledgement that no special hints are present to discredit a particular change. The price will *not* be at rest if there is any preponderance of opinion distinctly believing in a move in one direction. For those who have *come to believe* in a rise will buy bonds with money which, so long as they distrusted the prospect of a rise, they were willingly holding. Their action, unless offset by a contrary change of opinion in former willing holders of bonds, will push the price up, and this movement in itself may have any one of many possible effects. It may re-inforce, or it may exhaust and eliminate, the new-found expectation of a rise. A speculative market does not operate by seeking out a stable adjustment to a set of governing conditions extraneous to itself. A speculative market is *inherently restless* in a sense and mode that we shall try to examine in detail below. Some members of such a market desire price-movements for the sake of the opportunities of gain which only such movements can provide. Other members are obliged to be alertly responsive to such movements even if they do not desire them. All members are like the units in a moving crowd, some thrusting forward to attain a desired location, others pressing one way or another in mere self-defence. The market seethes and eddies, it does not move towards anything that, in more than the most ephemeral sense, can be called a dependable equilibrium, though it responds to Government monetary policy and can be in some sense manipulated by the Government.

It is of the nature of speculative assets that their price will be continually changing 'of its own accord'. With bonds this *inherent restlessness* takes a special form. The holder of a bond has two sources from which he can hope for gain, but from one of these there may instead come a loss. As the present moment advances through an interval of the calendar axis, the due dates of the borrower's promised payments are brought nearer, and their present value, or discounted value, at a given interest rate, is increased. But meanwhile the price of the bond may rise or fall. Let us suppose that at the rate of interest prevailing at some moment, for bonds promising a schedule of remaining payments like the bond in question, the time-rate of the former process in the immediate future will be s money units per time unit, and let us write the bondholder's expectation of price change of the bond in the immediate future as dp/dt. Then if, algebraically, $dp/dt > -s$, the bondholder will be assuming that some net gain is to be had from holding the bond for a further short time. If, algebraically, $dp/dt < -s$, the bond will be promising, in the bondholder's thoughts and estimation, a net loss. Let us then imagine a society where the only tradable type of asset is a single kind of bond, and let us suppose that at some moment all members of the market, whether or not they are at this moment holding some bonds or only money, set $dp/dt = -s$. The holding of bonds will now offer neither gain nor loss in terms of money, for the short period to which the expectation dp/dt refers, and thus there seems to be for the time being no reason for any buying or selling of bonds, whose price will accordingly stay constant. But *constancy* of the bond price is contrary to the expectation on which it depends. When it has persisted for some brief while, members of the market will presumably become conscious that the interest, s, which they are foregoing is being sacrificed for no reason. If they therefore begin to buy bonds, or in the case of those who already possess bonds, to raise their judgement of what bonds should now fetch, the bond price will rise where it had been expected to fall. The further consequences of such an initial rise could only be deduced if we made a long list of further assumptions: broadly there is no telling. It is only in a model as ultra-simplified and ultra-insulated as ours that even the initial price-rise can be established as a reasonable inference.

Now let us suppose that instead of a unanimously held opinion, two opposite opinions prevail in the market, and that the ownership of bonds is so distributed that, for the time being, all existing bonds are held by those who believe in an imminent rise of price while all non-holders believe in an imminent fall. Until some new source of suggestion about impending events outside the market intervenes, there will again be no reason for any sales or purchases. But again the *actual behaviour* of the bond price will belie the expectations which are holding it constant. For those two expectations, though different from each other, are neither of them expectations of *constancy*.

What state of market opinion will lead in fact to constancy (however brief) of the bond price while being itself justified and confirmed by that constancy? There is no such state of opinion. The bond price, and, as an arithmetical and rigid consequence, the interest rate is an *inherently restless* variable.

19.9 *Deferment, 'impatience' and the nature of liquidity*

We do not wish the foregoing argument to be regarded as more than an abstraction, for the sake of logical simplicity in examining one facet of reality, from the ineffable real complexity of things. It serves two particular purposes. It gives, first, an insight into the uniquely special character of the rate of interest as a variable helping to compose the economic scheme of things. Secondly it illustrates yet again how wholly mistaken and misleading must be any conception of that economic scheme of things which neglects, let alone rejects, the central, vital and essential part played in human affairs of every sort by expectation, the act of imagining the future.

Let us take a general view of the interest rate scene which emerges from the foregoing pages. We have presented a market where bonds and money are exchanged for each other. A bond is an entity which, very exceptionally in the tissue of human affairs, has no relevant characteristics except a highly formal and comparatively simple configuration, namely a schedule of dated payments of stated size. The relevant part of this schedule is that which lies, at any moment, still in the future, and thus the mere passage of time changes the effective character of a bond. Given the configuration of payments still to come, the rate of interest represented at any moment by a particular bond depends wholly on the price of that bond in the market. Thus whatever the richness, complexity, subtlety and even universality of the influences which affect interest-rates, they can do so only by affecting the price of bonds.

Bonds are a means of exchanging money now for money in the future. The time gap involved was looked upon in traditional theories as afflicting the lender chiefly with impatience: he would rather spend his money now on some specific specialized and tangible or enjoyable goods of complex character, but he is induced by a rate of interest not to do so, but to lend it instead. The reality of this impatience is far from clear. To be compelled to decide at once what to buy might very often be a positive embarrassment. To surrender general purchasing power, able to be turned in any direction when the moment comes, for all the hazards of commitment to something of detailed and crystallized form, may in many circumstances seem a positive disadvantage. And those who spend less than their incomes are often those who positively wish to accumulate wealth, and feel no desire to spend all their incomes on immediate consumption. It is not impatience, but ignorance, which enters upon the scene through the time-gap between lending and repayment. When the lender lends, no one can know precisely how his action will affect him. He requires an excess of promised repayments to offset this disadvantage. But the time-gap has effects on a larger stage than the individual mind. It makes the bond market a speculative arena, where events are in some measure free to shape their own course autonomously, rather than merely to respond to pressures of 'real' demand and natural scarcity. Scarcity can be in a sense self-generated, for what is scarce rises in price, and what is thought to be going to rise in price is speculatively scarce.

19.10 *The* non-additivity *of economic conceptions illustrated by 'the stock of money'*

There are, however, despite this bounded autonomy, some constraints which impose the bounds. At any moment, a *given* stock of money and a *given* stock of bonds have each to find willing holders, or else to be in process of exchange for each other between owners who, in the circumstances of the moment, are unwilling holders. The stock of money at any moment we define as the total of all payments which could be simultaneously made at that moment by all individuals, firms and corporate bodies outside the list of banks in the strict sense, the institutions having the power to *create*, and not merely mobilize, money. This definition needs some comment. We shall not spend much time on refuting a charge of circularity. Every dictionary is circular, and every explanation or definition except those which are purely ostensive. We shall assume it to be agreed that we know what a payment is. Money is that with which payments are made, and payments can be made by handing over legal tender notes or coins, or by writing a cheque. A cheque can be validly written by a man who has at the bank *either* a credit balance *or* unused permission to overdraw. We accordingly define the size of the stock of money as that size which results from adding together all legal tender money outside the banking system proper, all bank balances standing to the credit of non-banks, and all unused permission to overdraw, at the moment in question. The difficulty, even for an individual, of knowing how much unused permission to overdraw he has *effectively* at his disposal may be considerable; the very *meaning* of an aggregate of such permissions, which if all exercised at once would perhaps create a disturbing situation or a violent change, must be questioned. But this fact is only one more illustration of the *non-additivity* of economic conceptions in general, to which we shall return. The very value and acceptability of money depends on its holders *not* attempting to spend every shilling in their possession at the first moment they possess it; an infinite velocity of circulation would render money valueless and meaningless.

We have referred to 'banks in the strict sense'. A moneylender is not a bank, for he does not lend his customers *obligations* of his own, but obligations of the central bank or of a bank in the proper sense. If a moneylender, Mr J. Blank, handed to his customer a piece of paper saying I.O.U. £10, and signed it J. Blank, Mr Blank would be a bank in the proper sense, for his own obligations would be circulating and he would thus have acquired and demonstrated the power to *create a medium of payment*, as a bank does when it allows a customer to draw cheques against permission to overdraw.

Our last comment is on the *simultaneity* of the payment-potentials which are to be aggregated. 'Simultaneous' is here to be interpreted in a strict sense. Two payments are not simultaneous if one of them cannot be made until the other has been received.

19.11 *The matter in sum*

We can now condense the whole essence of our theme into a sentence. Bond prices will be under pressure upwards or downwards until all the bonds existing are in the hands of willing holders of bonds, and all the money existing, except such part as is being held in readiness for being paid away in the course of productive business or for consumption, is in the hands of willing holders of money. Willingness to hold bonds will rest upon a 'practical judgement' (something short of complete conviction but sufficient to determine action in face of the imperative, insistent, now-or-never need of every successive moment for *decision*) that bond prices are not about to fall; and willingness to hold money will likewise rest on a practical judgement that bond prices are not about to rise.

20

Liquidity: Its Nature

20.1 *Money as the means of deferment of decision*

A valutum which has no physical properties that are of any interest to its potential owners, that serves no aesthetic or epistemic purpose; an entity with which nothing can be done except to exchange it for something else; is at first sight paradoxical. Why should a thing be valued, which is useless except in virtue of what happens when it is got rid of? Why should such a thing ever be accepted in exchange for goods useful in themselves and desired for what they are? An answer which suggests itself is that the seller of something useful in itself may find it inconvenient to accept immediately in exchange any other object useful in itself. He wishes, that is, to put off receiving his *quid pro quo*. But evidently such casual circumstances as lack of transport or storage space would not account for an institution which plays so universal a part in life as money. There must be, to account for the acceptability of money, a reason as universal as itself. That reason appears in *lack of knowledge*. If the market, or some more exact and perfect system, provided every participant with full relevant knowledge of what he could get in exchange for his own offered goods, why should he not there and then name what he would accept? Let us deal with the objection that such a system, market or other, might be able to tell him only about goods available now, and not about goods that might become available subsequently. This objection infringes our stipulation. If the system cannot give complete and universal relevant knowledge, it does not meet our requirements. And if complete and universal relevant knowledge is only possible in a timeless system, then a timeless system must be supposed. Money enables people *to put off deciding what to buy*.

20.2 *Money as a* medium of search

The inconvenience of barter is the inconvenience of ignorance. Money makes it unnecessary for a would-be acquirer of goods to find by his own efforts the parties to a suitable multi-lateral trade. He can leave them to find each other. Much has been made in the text-books of the need for a barterer to find the man who wants what he can supply and can supply what he wants. *To find*: this is the difficulty of barter. We can conceive, in these days, of a computer which would pool all conditional offers of goods and match them without the exchange of any medium. At most it would use a unit of account. The text-books never speak of barter except as bi-lateral. This is plainly a travesty. Barter could be many-sided, and in fact what used to happen at a country market was multi-lateral barter, arranged by means of money in order that the task of matching the exchanges should become the light work of many hands. Money is a *medium of search*.

20.3 *The 'transactions motive' : money held while* waiting to decide *what to buy*

Money is the means by which a seller gains *time* in which to acquire *knowledge*. By enabling him to put off deciding what to buy, it enables him to make his choice at a moment when his relevant knowledge seems to him to be less insufficient than usual. In a famous article, Sir John Hicks asked why a man who comes into possession of money does not *lend* it. But there is a prior question: Why does he not *spend* it? Sir John did not ask nor answer that question, nor did Maynard Keynes ever raise it. We are not here asking why a man should direct his income partly to the purchase of equipment rather than wholly to the purchase of consumables, but why, for a time after receiving his pay-cheque, he should direct it to the purchase of nothing at all. The prime task of liquidity is, in a sense, the opposite of what the 'transactions motive' ascribes to it. It is fair to say that we do not hold money in order to be ready to spend it, but because we *are not yet* ready to spend it. Again we might say that those who used to speak of money as a 'veil' were strangely misleading us. It is that which enables us to take time for *penetrating* a veil, the omni-present veil of pure absence of knowledge. Knowledge is not pervasive and automatically available, like the air we breathe. It has to be manufactured. And manufacture takes time. Liquidity is a raw material of knowledge, and knowledge is a 'raw material' of value. Those objects are valued, which we know to be useful. The value we assign to them depends on the precision of our supposed knowledge of their capacities to please and sustain us.

20.4 *Generalized and particular wealth: a reasonable illusion*

Once there exists something whose sole interesting quality is to be exchangeable, by an unspoken convention, for anything we like at any time, and which thus enables choice to be postponed until some moment when choosing shall appear convenient, there arises on the basis of this 'something' a structure of characteristic operations and preferences. Through the three versions of Keynes's theory of employment there runs a single commanding theme. There lies open to the free enterpriser a field of spectacular success and spectacular ruin. Its openness consists in the universal condition of men, that they cannot know for sure, or precisely, or completely, what effect upon the interests of each will be produced by his choice of this course rather than that. This uncertainty is at some times more oppressive than at others. In a world where wealth consisted only in objects which took much making and were desirable and useful in themselves for their technical, physical or aesthetic qualities, there would be no escape for the business man from risking his present wealth in making specialized and obsolescence-prone objects in order to increase that wealth. It is when wealth can be held in a perfectly non-specialized abstract and general form, the form of money, that there exists a unit for the expression of the value of objects, which makes it seem unprofitable to produce them. It is the existence of a money which allows things to be sold without anything being bought; which provides the illusion of the possibility, for the society as a whole, of saving without investing; which provides a means of comparison where 'real wealth' appears as a self-defeating and self-negating conception; where it seems unprofitable to use tools to produce more tools, even though by this same token, the tools to be used are as cheap as those to be produced.

20.5 *The meaning of Chapter* 17 *of the* General Theory

Let me not be understood to suggest that this gloss on the triad of Keynes's works, the *Treatise on Money*, the *General Theory of Employment, Interest and Money*, and the apparently quite unread 'The General Theory of Employment' in the *Quarterly Journal*, can be found set out in those works in the form here offered. The theory of employment at which Keynes arrived can be expressed in half a score of different languages. Several of these are visible or half visible in the *General Theory* itself. It is this protean and many-sided character of the theme that has exposed it to charges of obscurity or fallacy, and it is this inherent many-stranded elusiveness which has in some chapters led Keynes to open an argument with passages of tortuous complexity that have baffled the reader for no good reason. Something of the sort seems to have occurred in the notorious Chapter 17. In that chapter, as in some others, it is better to pass quickly into the middle of the chapter, where Keynes seems himself to arrive suddenly at a clear and simple statement:

There are three attributes which different types of assets possess in different degrees:
(i) Some assets produce a yield or output q, measured in terms of themselves, by assisting some process of production or supplying services to a consumer.
(ii) Most assets, except money, suffer some wastage or involve some cost through the mere passage of time (apart from any change in their relative value), irrespective of their being used to produce a yield; i.e. they involve a carrying-cost c measured in terms of themselves...
(iii) Finally, the power of disposal over an asset during a period may offer a potential convenience or security, which is not equal for assets of different kinds, though the assets themselves are of equal initial value...The amount (measured in terms of itself) which people are willing to pay for the potential convenience or security

given by this power of disposal (exclusive of yield or carrying-cost attached to the asset) we shall call its liquidity-premium l.

It follows that the total return expected from the ownership of an asset over a period is equal to its yield *minus* its carrying cost plus its liquidity-premium, i.e. to $q - c + l$...It is characteristic of instrumental capital (e.g. a machine) or of consumption capital (e.g. a house) which is in use, that its yield should normally exceed its carrying cost, while its liquidity-premium is negligible; of a stock of liquid goods, that it should incur a carrying cost in terms of itself without any yield to set off against it, the liquidity-premium in this case also being usually negligible as soon as stocks exceed a moderate level;...and of money that its yield is *nil*, and its carrying-cost negligible, but its liquidity-premium substantial...It is an essential difference between money and all other assets that in the case of money its liquidity-premium much exceeds its carrying-cost, whereas in the case of other assets their carrying-cost much exceeds their liquidity-premium. Let us assume that on houses the yield is q_1 and the carrying-cost and liquidity-premium negligible; that on wheat the carrying-cost is c_2 and the yield and liquidity-premium negligible; and that on money the liquidity-premium is l_3 and the yield and carrying-cost negligible...Taking money as our standard of measurement, let the expected percentage appreciation (or depreciation) of houses be a_1 and of wheat a_2...It is easy to see that the demand of wealth owners will be directed to houses, to wheat or to money, according as $a_1 + q_1$ or $a_2 - c_2$ or l_3 is greatest. Thus in equilibrium the demand-price of houses and wheat in terms of money will be such that there is nothing to choose in the way of advantage between the alternatives; – i.e. $a_1 + q_1$, $a_2 - c_2$ and l_3 will be *equal*. (*General Theory*, Book IV, Chapter 17, pp. 225–8.)

These passages (which we have somewhat condensed, by ellision, from the original) establish the formal frame of the argument of Chapter 17. Keynes then proceeds to draw his conclusions:

Now those assets of which the normal supply-price is less than the demand-price will be newly produced; and these will be those assets of which the marginal efficiency would be greater (on the basis of their normal supply-price) than the rate of interest [on loans of money] (both being measured in the same standard of value whatever it is). As the stock of the assets, which began by having a marginal efficiency at least equal to the rate of interest, is increased, their marginal efficiency (for reasons, sufficiently obvious, already given) tends to fall. Thus a point will come at which it no longer pays to produce them, *unless the rate of interest falls* pari passu [italics in the original]. When there is *no* asset of which the marginal efficiency reaches the rate of interest, the further production of capital-assets will come to a standstill. *General Theory*, (p. 228.)

Keynes's argument is about the expectations and consequent valuations and production decisions which wealth-owners entertain at some moment. For the sake of formal simplicity we are to suppose each of them to look forward to some one future date, ignoring what may happen in the meanwhile or afterwards. Our next step of exposition must already be to add something to Keynes's statement. Expectations, valuations and decisions are thoughts, and we ought evidently to begin by considering those of a single individual. Keynes's q and c are best thought of, for the purpose of formal analysis, as proportions of its present size by which a stock of some asset will grow or shrink, in its own substance, between the individual's present moment and the future date to which he is looking. Thus since houses do not of themselves produce more houses, we can instead think of trees increasing in weight. The trees of a particular plantation are counted upon by our individual to increase, during the interval, to a weight $(1 + q)$ times their present weight. Or the volume of stored spirits will evaporate until it is only $(1 - c)$ times its present size. Thirdly, as he contemplates the coming interval, the wealth-owner may take such comfort from the disposability which his asset will at all times have, that he ascribes to it a *notional* growth to an ultimate size $(1 + l)$ times its present size. Keynes assumes that all assets can be distributed into three classes: those (let us say equipment) for which q is q_1, a positive number, while c and l are negligible; those (inventories) for which c is c_1, a number positive in itself, and q and l are negligible; and those (money) for which l is a positive number l_1, and q and c are negligible. Now q, c and l are expressed in terms of the substances themselves of the assets. But for comparisons of profitability, or rather, of general advantage, all three classes of assets must be valued in terms of one of them.

Suppose that our individual expects equipment to be worth, at the deferred date, $(1 + a_1)$ times as much per unit in terms of money as it is at his present, and that he expects inventories to be then worth $(1 + a_2)$ times as much per unit in terms of money as at his present. Then his relevant comparison will be between the left-hand sides or the right-hand sides of

$$(1+q_1)(1+a_1) = 1+a_1+q_1+a_1q_1,$$
$$(1-c_2)(1+a_2) = 1+a_2-c_2-a_2c_2,$$
$$1+l_3 = 1+l_3.$$

Neglecting the second-order quantities, Keynes speaks simply of the amount which the lapse of time will add to the money value of each asset, according to the individuals' expectations, or in the case of money, the notional addition which, if he had it in prospect, would just compensate him for the loss of the assurance, given him by money in contrast with any other asset, that an abrupt, unforeseen and unprepared disposal of his asset would entail no disadvantage as compared with a prolonged search for the best market and the most favourable historical conjuncture. Keynes's comparison is thus between (a_1+q_1), (a_2-c_2), and l_3.

The source of the 'mystery' which is sometimes found in Chapter 17 must lie, I think, in Keynes's having failed to explain precisely the meaning of the a_1 and a_2 and the manner in which they are determined. Let us suppose the individual at his present moment to assign definite numbers to q_1 and to c_2 and to the money price per physical unit which equipment and inventories will respectively command at the deferred date. Then if the market price which, for example, equipment commands at his present moment is so low in comparison with that of inventories as to make $(a_1+q_1) > (a_2-c_2)$, he will be inclined to sell inventories in order to buy equipment, and will thus press the present price of equipment up and that of inventories down; that is to say, he will thus diminish a_1 and increase a_2. When we say that *the individual* will thus affect the market, we are of course introducing a new assumption: that the individual we are considering will be typical of wealth-owners as a body, who *will share, at least qualitatively, his expectations*. Theorizing and abstraction are inseparable and almost indistinguishable companions, and Keynes had every justification for ignoring, in a complex and subtle argument which sought the foundations of truth in his central problem, even so prominent a fact as the divergences of expectations of individuals. But it is right for the critic to point out his complete neglect of it. Keynes's next step is to point out the consequences if the 'present' market price of, let us say, equipment falls (as it can, of course, if wealth-owners take the opposite views and actions to those we have just considered) and reaches a level below its 'present' supply price, a level below the price per unit at which it can be newly produced. Those consequences will evidently be the decline or cessation of the flow of investment. And then the final step. The typical wealth-owner must evidently compare $a_1 + q_1$ and $a_2 - c_2$ not only with each other but with l_3. The 'present moment' prices of inventories and of equipment may both fall below their supply prices, if, because l_3 is high, wealth-owners are all selling out of inventories and equipment in order to get into money: to get into money with its high liquidity premium. What, then, is liquidity that it can command a high and resistant premium?

20.6 *'Liquidity' handled in the* General Theory *as an indefinable*

Keynes's dealings with that skein of ideas which he refers to as 'liquidity' and 'liquidity preference' are tantalizing. Throughout the scattered observations, paragraphs and pages which bear on it in the *General Theory* we find acute, original perceptions of the necessary characteristics of those assets which are to possess 'liquidity'; of the kind of conduct which a desire or need for 'liquidity' induces in wealth-owners, enterprisers, income-earners; and of the effect upon the volume of investment (in equipment), and on the volume of general output and of employment, which will be exerted by the availability of a 'liquid' asset in terms of which the prices of tangible tools and inventories may be driven so low, in comparison with the liquid-asset price of labour (the wage-unit), that it does not pay to give employment in producing them. Keynes encompasses, in a profound and coherent system of ideas, the role of an indefinable which he calls liquidity. But except in a brief sentence he leaves its essential nature as an untouched mystery: 'Finally, the power of disposal over an asset during a period may offer a potential convenience and security...' (p. 226). *Why* does it offer a convenience or security? How, against what, through what circumstances, by warding off what dangers, by

solving what problems, by dissolving what difficulties, by re-
moving what obstacles, by giving what consolation, by armour-
ing a man's thoughts and feelings in what respect, does it offer
'convenience' or 'security'? Keynes does not say, nor ask,
except by way of a catalogue of situations. 'Liquidity', if
interpreted with imaginative span and depth, lies at the heart
of his whole scheme of thought. In Chapter 17 this essential,
central role is pursued in a spirit of unsparing and unflinching
abstraction and ellipsis, by an argument which the reader
needs to probe, criticize, fill out and emend for himself by
repeated study; by learning to disregard, in this process, an
esoteric language which is in some degree beside the point; by
making allowance for the purpose which is driving the argument on into seeming obscurities, the purpose of uncovering the
foundations of 'involuntary unemployment'. Yet despite all,
we are not told what 'liquidity' is.

We are told many things about it. 'One reason for holding
cash is to bridge the interval between the receipt of income and
its disbursement.' But *why should there be* an interval? An
answer is to be found, if on our own responsibility we are prepared to apply some materials of the chapter to this purpose;
but the question itself is not asked. Keynes could perhaps
answer: In order to let someone else bear the carrying-cost of
goods useful in themselves. For in explaining why 'the rate of
interest is insensitive, particularly below a certain figure, even
to a substantial increase in the quantity of money in proportion
to other forms of wealth', he says

In this connection the low (or negligible) carrying-costs of money
play an essential part. For if its carrying-costs were material, they
would off-set the effect of expectations as to the prospective value of
money at future dates. The readiness of the public to increase their
stock of money in response to a comparatively small stimulus is due
to the advantages of liquidity (real or supposed) having no offset to
contend with in the shape of carrying-costs mounting steeply with
the lapse of time.*

Yet not all goods useful in themselves have high carrying-costs,
not all, by any means, have carrying-costs in excess of their
yield of services. Why should not the income-receiver buy tools

* *General Theory*, Book IV, Chapter 17, p. 233.

or land, if inventories are too troublesome, or expensive, to store? The main answer seems plain: Because of the trouble of deciding what to buy, of finding suitable specimens of it, and the prospective trouble of finding for these specimens a buyer when some consumption goods shall eventually be needed. The key word in this sentence is 'finding'. *To find* has a meaning inseparably connected with another, that of *not knowing*. The clue to the meaning and nature of liquidity lies in its avoidance of the trouble arising from not knowing.

20.7 *The intimate fusing of safety and success*

Even if we thus claim that the nature and need of liquidity springs in all cases from one root, namely the need to postpone choice until the data are more adequate or their interpretation more distinct, yet we have to admit that this tree spreads into many branches. The transactions motive and the speculative motive may, by the appeal to their common source in lack of knowledge, be shown to be essentially the same. In all but this basic origin they appear perhaps very different. Yet they have one further character in common. In both, the boundary is blurred between defence and attack, between avoidance of loss and the making of profit, between safety and success. This is in the nature of things. Those theories, in any part of the field of economic phenomena, which make a sharp distinction between profitability, on one hand, and safety, or power of survival, on the other, are evidently neglecting uncertainty. What meaning do such theories assign to high profitability, if they regard it as necessary to speak separately of risk of loss? And if what is in question, in the real Scheme of Things, or the real Scheme of Thoughts which a business man can entertain, is a freedom to conceive (without conscious absurdity) of high gain or serious loss, each being a *potentia* of his circumstances and his capabilities and his policy as they appear to him, what essential basis is there for distinguishing from each other policy features which aim to avoid loss from those which aim to increase gain? Gain–loss is a single variable, and the business man's endeavour is to push the outcome of his enterprise as far as he can in the sense of gain. If his measure of gain is the net present worth of his enterprise, the policy which he sees as best for maximizing that measure is likely to include provision for a long life for his business, and a long life will depend upon survival through many vicissitudes and the freedom to take audacious gambles without final catastrophe, and that survival and freedom will depend at many a crisis on liquidity.

20.8 *Lack and expensiveness of knowledge as the ground for desiring liquidity*

We say, then, that insurmountable lack of knowledge, or the expense of gaining knowledge, lie at the root of liquidity preference. Were it not for a problem of lack of knowledge, there could be no need for liquidity. Liquidity is, in some sense and degree, a *substitute* for knowledge. At great expense and trouble, a man might contrive to match precisely, in amount and date, his incomings with his outgoings. The necessary knowledge for this purpose would be more expensive than the liquidity which dispenses with the need for it. This is the transactions motive for holding money. Money held continuously and thus available *on call no matter when* is the only guarantee against having to sell non-money assets when their price in terms of money is down, for the moment of such need is unknown. This is the speculative motive for holding money. As for the precautionary motive, it is simply the speculative motive, since non-liquid assets could provide a reserve against contingencies, were it not for their exposure to capital loss. Thus the two famous motives for holding money are both rooted in one circumstance: our lack of knowledge of how things will go.

20.9 *The thesis and its difficulties in Chapter 17*

Let us return to the thesis which Keynes argues in Chapter 17 of the *General Theory*. It may be condensed to the following. Physical assets are expected by the business man to yield services or suffer wastage in the course of some interval on whose threshold he stands. This benefit or damage can be expressed in terms of the material of the assets themselves, by saying that it will be as though the present size of his stock of any such asset were expected to increase or diminish, by the end of the interval, in a ratio $(1 + q - c)$. The smaller this ratio, the lower will be the money value per unit that he will place on the asset in comparison with an assumed money value per unit that it will have at the end of the interval. The market price which such assets will represent 'today' will depend on such judgements arrived at by the business men in general. This *demand price* will be conceptually wholly distinct from that *supply price* at which producers of this kind of asset would be willing to supply such-and-such a daily or weekly quantity of it. If the demand price is less than the supply price assets of this kind will not 'today' be produced: the flow of investment in them will be *nil*. Now (Keynes argues), according as the existing stock of any such asset is larger, its yield, q, will be smaller and its carrying-cost, c, probably larger. Thus (we may articulate the thesis in a less elliptical form than Keynes's) if we consider a series of historical dates within a period when a flow of positive net investment in this kind of asset has been proceeding, so that stocks of it have been increasing, we shall see its demand price lower at each successive one of these dates, until the demand price eventually, perhaps, falls below the supply price and production of this asset ceases. The argument up to this stage evidently raises a number of questions, some of which Keynes himself propounds and seeks to answer. First, why does not supply price fall *pari passu* with demand price? Secondly, as we move to each successive date and see, as it were, the business man looking forward from that date over the number of weeks or months, etc., which constitute 'the interval', what basis has he for assigning any particular money price per unit as that which the asset will command in the market at the end of the interval? And thirdly, what is to be gained by his retaining money as such, even if the purchase of physical assets offers only a very low, and continually declining, marginal efficiency $(q - c)$?

20.10 *The two faces of the* General Theory

These questions, and the difficulty of giving them conclusive and satisfactory answers, have their bearing on the nature of the

General Theory as a book with many faces and purposes, heuristic, persuasive, nihilistic. Chapter 17 seeks to exhibit the operation of a *mechanism* of secular depression or stagnation. But mechanism in its nature is at odds with the nature of the entity which is being examined. For the stuff of that entity is thoughts, and a thought which works by mechanism is not, or not evidently, capable of attaining essential novelty. Novelty, moreover, makes nonsense of the idea that marginal efficiency of capital must decline as the capital stock increases. Invention and new knowledge transform the whole basis of reckonings of investment-gain. The *General Theory* is, throughout, in two minds. It turns instinctively towards stable functions, uninterrupted movements along curves, under-employment 'equilibrium', secular stagnation, step-by-step declension (for example, of the level of interest-rates: *General Theory* Chapter 15, p. 204, last paragraph). Yet the message spelled out by all this creaking semaphore is that intended (designed, *ex ante*) investment is a law to itself, dependent (if at all) on too elusive and involved a skein of subtle influences, too eagerly clutching at the straws of suggestion whirled along by 'the news', to be ever captured in any intelligible, let alone determinable, equation. It is not really the shapes of the curves, but their broad bodily shifts and deformations, that contain the meaning of the argument.

20.11 *A seeming circularity in the relation of wage-stickiness and the liquidity of money*

The implication of Keynes's argument in Chapter 17, namely, that supply price of physical assets will not fall *pari passu* with demand price, must rely on his general assumptions, first, that money wages are 'sticky', and secondly that money wages are dominant in the composition of prime cost. Here, we come upon an intriguing complication: 'It is because of money's other characteristics – those, especially, which make it *liquid* – that wages, when fixed in terms of it, tend to be sticky'. (p. 233.) This remark, unfortunately, is left without explanation. A little later, there is a hint of circularity: 'The fact that contracts are fixed, and wages are usually somewhat stable, in terms of money unquestionably plays a large part in attracting to money so high a liquidity premium'. (p. 236.) But again: 'The expectation of a relative stickiness of wages in terms of money is a corollary of the excess of liquidity-premium over carrying-costs being greater for money than for any other asset.' (p. 238.)

Chapter 17 is no doubt one of the most difficult parts of the *General Theory*. It seeks to reach down, at one plunge, to the heart of the matter of an insufficient investment flow. That insufficiency is attributed to the existence of an asset whose utility, being derived solely from its exchange-value, need not decline as the stock of it increases. We come near, in Chapter 17, to the proposition that money is 'liquid' because of a belief in its power to retain its exchange-value, and that this belief is due to its 'liquidity'. Yet this seeming circularity is very far indeed from being meaningless or futile. It points to the vital part played in economic affairs by *convention*. The dependence of an exchange medium, *as such*, for its efficiency, upon convention, is, after all, a very old and long-recognized truth.

21

Prices As Convention

21.1 *Three categories of price-governing circumstances*

An antithesis of our title might be 'Prices as necessity'. What would this other title be claiming? It would suggest that prices are bound in some manner to certain kinds of circumstance, certain features of the general scene, and that the particular measurements or other relevant characteristics of those circumstances and features were inexorably beyond the power of conscious policy to control. Self-interest (in however enlightened a sense) being supposed dominant, tastes and desires of individual interests being 'given', the endowments (material and personal) of these interests being at any moment the outcome of history, and finally, essential and all-important, knowledge or knowledge-substitutes being given for each individual chooser and policy-maker, there would, it seems, be no escape from the conclusion that prices must reflect this frame of governing conditions. Given those details, prices, we should claim, could not be other than they were. Broadly, there seem to be two routes of escape from the conclusion that prices are determinate in some such sense. One is to deny the reality of the 'bondage to circumstance' in which the theory of determination supposes prices to stand. The other is to suppose that those circumstances themselves can be deliberately modified.

To adopt the first of these means of escape would be to abandon any attempt to gain insight into the behaviour of prices. If they do not obey any rules, it is useless to seek for rules or to study prices in relation to circumstances in which the prices arise. If we are to practise analysis, we are obliged to assume that prices are influenced, or governed, by something in some regular and stable manner. But this does not and must not preclude us from considering the nature of that something, and the mutability which may be implied by its nature.

We suggested that prices are governed by tastes, endowments, and what we may call epistemic circumstances. The traditional view refers only to the first two of these three categories. Value theory describes the interaction of tastes and *known* circumstances, and includes in the latter everything relevant to choice. Thus choice is determinate (can *choice* be so-called, if it is *determinate*?) It is within the unconsidered category of epistemic circumstances that we must look for any source of freedom. There are, perhaps, five ways in which the epistemic circumstances of a real situation can depart from that condition where everyone possesses perfect knowledge. First, there may be no adequate organization for pre-reconciling the simultaneous choices of different individuals. Secondly, present valuations may be made in awareness that choices will be made in future, with which no pre-reconciliation is, in the nature of things, possible. Thirdly, present valuations may express speculation on conjectural future valuations. Fourthly, present valuations may have regard to the unpredictable mutations of technology, fashion, politics and diplomacy, and of every facet of the evolving general scene. Fifthly, there are the deliberate deceptions and concealments practised by those engaged in bilateral monopoly (bargaining) or in duopoly or oligopoly, and the very breakdown of logic which the latter virtually entails. In all these kinds of situation, prices depend, not only on tastes with their reasonably presumed stability, and on endowments with their short-period constancy, but on thoughts, the *formal* contents of the mind, dependent on no slow-moving or tangible elements but swiftly composing, combining and dissolving themselves from moment to moment. In such circumstances, an agreed or accepted price will be, for each individual, a mere façade concealing a mass of reservations, of evolving judgements and intentions. But many prices will be allowed to remain as they happen to be found, because there is no time to investigate, no new source of data or suggestion, no impulse to attempt a change.

21.2 Conventional *valuation*

A price can be called *conventional* when, for example, it is left undisturbed, not because it is subject to 'necessity' in the sense we have sought to describe above, but on a principle of 'let well alone'. Such a situation is illustrated by the *kinky oligopoly demand curve*. Here, because his rivals are few and he has a large part of the market for some product-group, or because he has a product which is in some respect peculiar to himself, the supplier assumes that a larger weekly (etc.) supply of his good can only be disposed of at a lower price. But how much lower need this price be? Under 'necessity' we should assume the supplier to have in mind a well-defined demand curve for his product. But instead, because his rivals are few, he assumes that the effect of a change in his own price on each of those rivals, respecting the weekly quantities they can sell of their own respective products, will be very marked and will not escape their notice. Then he fears that if he reduces his price, they will reduce theirs, but if he raises his price, they will hold theirs constant and take part of his market. The price-elasticity of demand for his product, at its prevailing price, will there be assigned by his judgement a smaller numerical value for a decrease than for an increase of its price. It is perhaps difficult to speak meaningfully of 'the' demand curve for his product, since its shape is a conjecture based on conjectures about the reactions of his rivals to hypothetical actions of his own. But if he represents any one such conjectured curve on paper, it will show an abrupt increase of (downward) steepness at the point representing the prevailing price and weekly quantity sold. At this kink the marginal revenue is indeterminate. The price is 'conventional' since its constancy depends on a tacit mutual recognition between our supplier and his rivals that there shall be immobility on both sides for fear of worse consequences for all. Conventionalism, however, spreads far beyond such cases.

21.3 *Chapter* 12 *of the* General Theory

Commentators of the *General Theory* have on the whole paid very little attention to Chapter 12. The contents of that chapter must have appeared to early readers of the work distinctly digressive and somewhat perverse, since although the title is 'The state of long-term expectation', the strong tendency of the chapter, and much the greatest part of its length, are taken up with showing how much obstructed with unprofitable labour and natural

discouragements is the path of those who might seek to form
well founded and carefully reasoned opinions concerning the
returns to be expected from particular ventures of investment
in plant and industrial or commercial facilities. Keynes explains in the liveliest way how the valuations placed on company shares by the Stock Exchange are those of speculators
who look for quick gains, rather than of persons who intend to
retain permanently, and for the sake of dividends, the shares of
companies whose trading prospects in remoter years they have
tried to assess. As he expresses the matter, the great bulk of
buyers of shares on the Stock Exchange are speculators, not
entrepreneurs. And speculators, he points out, are engaged in
trying to guess what will be the opinion, later in the day, the
week or the year, of *the majority* of their fellow-speculators,
regarding the value of various shares. Keynes makes it clear,
indeed, that Stock Exchange assets are, for the Stock Exchange,
principally gambling counters, and that each fluctuation of the
value of any one of them is (we may gloss his discussion) the
apex of a pyramid of guesses about guesses about guesses...A
valuation which is arrived at by a speculative market whose
members are trying to guess the forthcoming opinion of their
own majority is what Keynes calls a *conventional* valuation.

It is an illuminating irony that Keynes himself, while
writing the *General Theory*, saw Chapter 12 as a digression:

There are not two separate factors affecting the rate of investment,
namely, the schedule of the marginal efficiency of capital and the
state of confidence. The state of confidence is relevant because it is
one of the major factors determining the former, which is the same
thing as the investment demand schedule. There is, however, not
much to be said about the state of confidence *a priori*. Our conclusions must mainly depend upon the actual observation of markets
and business psychology. This is the reason why the ensuing digression is on a different level of abstraction from most of this book.*

There is an irony in this passage, because it is mainly (though
not quite exclusively) in Chapter 12 that there is to be found the
germ of Keynes's ultimate thesis, the nature of which he perhaps
only came to recognize when the book was finished and published, and his critics came forth with their objections to this and

* *General Theory*, Book IV, Chapter 12, p. 149.

that feature of the mechanistic, determinate and mathematiz-
able theory which they read into his book. That ultimate thesis
was brief and destructive. It declared that economic actions,
and most of all, the commanding activity of investment in
durable facilities, were governed in their scale, character and
timing, by expectations, and that expectations can be transformed, and the 'confidence' which gives them their ascendancy can be dissolved, by a breath of suggestion from 'the
news', so that the size of the stream of general output, and the
quantity of employment, rest upon the most mutable and
elusive of all economic elements. Where, in such a vision, is any
place for theory which assumes that conduct and policy can be
rational, calculated, efficient and sure of success? Where is the
basis of mechanistic, or 'hydraulic', determinism, which for
orthodox analysts was the pre-supposition and *sine qua non* of
analysis? Where is the mathematization of economic theory?

It is ironic in high degree that this subversion of economic
rationalism and determinacy, of the putting of men under
necessity of reason, should have been spoken of by Keynes
himself as a 'digression'. Chapter 12 has been neglected (almost
at Keynes's own invitation) by serious seekers after a theory
which would belong in their own tradition and be new only in
detail, would be familiar to their outlook and training, conformable to their instincts as subscribers to the ultimate orderliness of human affairs. Chapter 17, the other maverick chapter,
which continues and deepens the theme of Chapter 12, has also
been pushed aside. It is declared 'mysterious' and unnecessary.
It is, indeed, a difficult chapter for the most open-minded and
adventurous reader. For the reader armoured with orthodoxy,
both chapters must evidently appear to be the means by which
Keynes 'got something out of his system.' What that something
was, it has seemed hardly to matter. Chapter 12, however, is
the chapter where we find explained the nature of 'conventional' judgements and valuations, and where the word *conventional* is given a strict meaning as a technical term.

For Keynes the word *conventional*, applied to a market's
valuation of assets, combines two ideas. These concern respectively the manner in which the valuation is arrived at, or the
principle on which it is based, on one hand; and on the other,
the characteristics of a market judgement arrived at on the

principle in question. The principle itself is that of the search by the market for the opinion of the majority of its own members; not, indeed, the opinion they hold at this moment, but the opinion they will hold tomorrow or next week or month. For when a majority (in a 'weighted' sense, where more power belongs to the wealthier members) holds the view that asset prices are about to be higher than at present, they will buy and drive up the prices. The profitable action, for the speculator, is to place himself today, while there is yet room enough and time, on that ground which the crowd will occupy tomorrow. Every member of the crowd desires to do this. If the eddies and currents of the surging crowd take on, by accident or by some natural means, a seemingly purposive coherence, and suggest that the general movement will be in one particular direction, that will in fact shortly become the direction of general, 'conventional' movement. The notion is elusive and difficult to bind into words. For it is exceedingly difficult to give a precise definition and recognizable distinguishing marks to the boundary between *today's opinion of what will be tomorrow's opinion,* and the actual, prevailing opinion which has *anticipated tomorrow* by being generally adopted today. Expectation and its self-disseminating capabilities are fluid and elusive beyond description.

Let us try to summarize the matter. Conventional judgements are those which, by some more or less accidental coalescence of ideas or some natural but hidden means of communication, are adopted by a mass of people who cannot find, and are not really concerned to find, any 'solid', 'objective' and genuinely meaningful basis for any judgement. They are willing to agree with the majority, for this is what it is profitable to do, if only the majority's impending view can be discerned a little time in advance.

The character of judgements, opinions and valuations thus arrived at will be a capricious instability. For what is there to hold steady and constant an opinion of what opinion is going to be? The self-energizing speculative market has an engine, the restlessness arising from the dependence of gain on movement of some sort, but it has no steering gear. Conventional valuations are at all times (for all anyone can tell) liable to collapse through a sudden acknowledgement of their objective baselessness. Yet, as Keynes explains in this same Chapter 12, it is these speculative and ephemeral Stock Exchange valuations which can bear upon decisions to order the construction of the real and concrete tools and facilities of industry and commerce, whose construction is the basis and necessary condition of high employment in a society given to saving.

21.4 *Mr Hugh Townshend on price indeterminacy*

The meaning of Chapter 12 was understood, disentangled from the encumbrances of orthodoxy still clinging in some degree around Keynes's efforts to emancipate himself, and re-expressed with incisive force by one man, Mr Hugh Townshend, in two contributions to the *Economic Journal* in its great year of debate on the *General Theory*, 1937. One of them was a review of Sir Ralph Hawtrey's *Capital and Employment*, a book which illuminates with Sir Ralph's invariably sympathetic clarity several of the main monetary contributions of the 1930s:

[Sir Ralph] Hawtrey has, I think, failed to get to grips with Mr Keynes. I believe, indeed, that he has altogether missed his central idea, which I conceive to be the *direct* causal influence of expectations on *all* prices. The mechanical analogy breaks down; as it surely must, if prices are influenced, through liquidity premium, by *mere* expectations. There is no position of equilibrium. The foundation of the theory has disappeared. The future is not merely unknown to the economic man; it is also undetermined. The prospect of future returns (whether from enterprise or from the realisation of accumulated assets) is not expressible as a mathematical expectation.*

Mr Townshend makes expectations to work upon prices via 'liquidity premium', that is, through those uncertainties, that void of knowledge, which accounts for the existence of a rate of interest. Interest, in Keynes's view, was the price men will pay for freedom from fear of capital loss. A lender cannot know when he will find himself driven to sell his bond for what it will fetch, and he cannot know what, at that unknown time, it *will* fetch. Thus to lend is to exchange a known for an unknown sum of money. To buy any other capital asset has, of course, a similar effect, unmitigated, perhaps, by any schedule of dated specific payments which a borrower promises by the terms of his bond.

* *Economic Journal*, vol. XLVII, pp. 321–6.

The desire for liquidity is the desire for freedom from 'capital uncertainties'. The price of non-liquid assets must stand at all times at such a level that their cheapness makes their possibility of future gain seem attractive enough to enough people, owning enough wealth, to provide all those assets with willing owners. But the value of assets which can be manufactured, in comparison with their cost of manufacture, constitutes the inducement to invest, and investment, directly and through the Multiplier, pushes general output up or down the supply curve of output as a whole. Thus prices swing to the tides of liquidity preference, of greater or less insistence of uncertainties. Chapter 17 comes into its own.

21.5 *Price stability, efficiency, rationality and illusion*

Mr Townshend concludes his other contribution, 'Liquidity-premium and the theory of value', with an echo of Chapter 12: 'Perhaps economic (price-) stability really depends on the prevalence of custom in regard to price-offers among the majority who all 'think' alike, combined with the prevalence of a divergency of views among those who think for (literally for) themselves.' This passage concisely brings together the two modes of determination of price which can be called conventional. Prices which have stood at particular levels for some time acquire thereby some sanction and authority. They are the 'right' and even the 'just' prices. But also they are the prices to which the society has adapted its ways and habits, they are prices which mutually cohere in an established frame of social life. To upset one of them would be to upset all of them, in an exercise of general unsettlement and general groping for re-adjustment, which would promise no advantages commensurate with the work, expense and uncertainty which it would entail. The hills and the weather of our native land form for us an environment which exacts toil, but provides expected and familiar conditions. Stability is a valuable, an *invaluable*, source of efficiency. Does not practice make perfect? What we can do without thought leaves us time for those things whose essence and delight is thought itself. A stable system of prices has great advantages. That the middle years of the twentieth century have seen so wild a departure from the notion of conventionally accepted prices, and have produced the evils which have so plainly flowed from continual and endless price-upheaval, makes the present a strange background for discussion of conventional prices. Value theory declares that prices should be fluid, because it argues that at any moment there is a notional set of prices which would constitute rationality, and that actual prices should move freely in pursuit of the rational equilibrium. But if the rational equilibrium is an illusion, basically at odds with the human condition, the Scheme of Things, if it neglects the fact and meaning of time, that pre-script of the Rational Calculus is itself an illusion.

22

The Dissolution of Rational Determinacy

22.1 Rational determinacy must exclude speculation and novelty

Self-sufficient completeness, extreme economy of basic principles and assumptions, essential unity and simplicity, a claim
to explain all economic conduct as the dictate of reason, and the
assent which this whole notion gave to the intelligibility of the
world's design: these were the lineaments of the value-construct
which had in the main been perfected by the end of the nineteenth century, and which by then represented the consensus of
'established' scholars in many countries. These characteristics
had a unity amongst themselves. The primacy accorded to
reason made simplicity and unity in the account of things more
plausible, and this simplicity accorded well with reliance on one
or two all-pervasive principles by which the system was seen to
hold together. The conception in fact was the work of logic
selecting its premisses with a view to their efficiency, their
power to explain everything at one stroke. Thus was achieved a
conception of great beauty, in the sense in which mathematical
demonstrations can be beautiful by their element of surprising
conjuration, the sudden, astonishing revelation of necessity.

In attaining this height, the value-construct severely restricted its own applications. The acropolis is a narrow space.
We have sought in the foregoing chapters to set out the limitations which are the price of the elegance of value theory. We
may briefly survey them as a whole.

We have made one elemental claim: that the rational value-
construct must be timeless. This contention rests, first, on the
argument that if *rational conduct* is to have a clear, definite and
assessable meaning, it must mean conduct which is demon-
trably the best for stated purposes. To be demonstrable, its
superiority must be related to a complete set of relevant circumstances. If the statement of circumstances leaves open the
possibility that things unstated and unknown can still intervene;

that circumstances which are included have been only partly, or vaguely, or perhaps wrongly described; that, in fact, the terms of the problem are shapeless, clouded, uncertain and above all *open-ended*, nothing in the nature of a demonstration can be given. But short of a rigorous demonstration, what can be usefully, convincingly done about assigning a meaning to *rationality*? 'It is the best makeshift, in view of the irremediable lack of data.' If there is a lack of data *how do we know* it is 'the best' makeshift? What is the test of 'best'? A space of emptiness in the fabric of knowledge of circumstance is something which can only be remedied either arbitrarily or by appeal to other faculties than logic. If it be granted that rationality in conduct means the application of fully-informed reason, then, secondly, we argue that full information must include those choices of others which will affect the outcome of the choices of the individual. But those choices can only be known by the *general* individual, the individual who can be anyone and is, in turn, everyone, provided that all choices are pre-reconciled. Pre-reconciled choices are simultaneous, that is, timeless choices.

The need for timelessness rests, however, on more general grounds than the need for simultaneity of all choices. A world of plural moments, a world where at one moment, other moments can be envisaged, a world of expectation, must allow the unobservable situations of other moments to bear, by imaginative conjecture, or by mere unsupported and evidence-less hope or misgiving, on the situation of the present moment. In turn, the situation at a non-present moment will be influenced, when that moment comes, by the expectation of still other moments. The infinite regress of expectations, moreover, cannot be put aside or rendered innocuous by an appeal to the discounting principle. It is true that discounting will render innocuous the consideration of a sufficiently distant time, in its *direct* effect on the present. But its effect on intervening moments is discounted with less power (because over a shorter time) and that effect can *qualitatively* alter the content of the present expectations concerning that intervening moment. The infinite regress of speculation must render prices in the present *indeterminate by objective and stable data*. If there is stability, it will in principle and in essential nature be momentary and self-destroying, depending on a balance of mutually contradictory views, those of the Bulls and Bears. Analysts who were candid with themselves and their readers have found it necessary to exclude expectation from their analysis in order to make it rigorous. Weather forecasting, also, would be easier in the absence of an atmosphere.

We must, however, be more general still. The asymmetry of time, the fact of the *dividing present* over whose boundary there occurs that flow of impressions, that continuous gaining of knowledge, which is our conscious being, confronts us with *novelty*, with thoughts which transform our picture of the world. Not the actuality of the experience, but the acceptance of its possibility, the awareness of things beyond the reach of present thought, is what matters for the value-construct. For the paradox of the expectation of things which cannot be envisaged destroys the self-containedness of the world, on which the determinateness of the value-construct depends. We do not know at how much to value this thing in terms of that, because we expect to find out on future days more and more, perpetually, about what these things can do. The value-construct *ignores ignorance*, the ignorance which is continually altered in character, continually renewed by the very passage into the present and the past of part of its former field and the replacement of that field by something again unknown. It is for this overwhelming reason also, besides the needed synchronicity of choices, that the value-construct must be timeless.

22.2 *Rational determinacy excludes involuntary unemployment*

General equilibrium, a fully-informed adjustment of the action of each member of the society to that of every other, in view of his own desires and endowments, evidently cannot include involuntary unemployment. In the general pre-reconciliation of all actions, nothing is 'involuntary'. Keynes's first task, in *The General Theory of Employment, Interest and Money*, was indeed to show in what sense unemployment could be involuntary. The need to answer this prior question, which would be so insistently present to the mind of every economist trained in the value-theory economics of the previous seventy years, stood in poignant contrast to the facts, obvious to every one whatever his preconceptions, that millions of British people in the early 1930s would have eagerly accepted almost any job in their own trade at any wage approximating what had been paid in former years. Massive general unemployment was beyond the power of the suppliers of labour to remedy by any individual or collective action of their own. That theory, then, which asserted that involuntary unemployment was a meaningless expression, must be repudiated as a first step. As an interpretation of reality, value theory was wrong, but as a logical construct it was coherent and self-consistent. Which of its premisses was at fault? 'Full information' was the almost tacit assumption which was so astoundingly at odds with our real human predicament of daily, hourly and momently ignorance of what will happen next, act we never so wisely. Keynes's intricate argument was a patient cutting of the intellectual entanglements which prevented his colleagues from recognizing the implications of our human irremediable un-knowledge of the circumstances in which our actions will take effect.

In the course of clearing a path to that conclusion, he himself was often almost ensnared by the technical *insidiae* of value theory itself, and the very first of all such traps was the difficulty of showing how a man who is free to accept a lower wage can find himself excluded from employment by the unpayability of employing him. Can he not sink his wage demand down to the point where his contribution to the value of a firm's output covers it? Chapter 2 of the *General Theory* is devoted to this problem, and spends the greater part of its length on a trivial consequence of that 'money illusion' which the years since 1945 have shown to be transient. In 1970, people no longer think that a change of money income implies an equi-proportional change in real income. But would this alone account for the experience of a generation of high employment? Chapter 2 of the *General Theory* comes at last to a glimpse of the real theme which Keynes was about to pursue. But that theme is never explicitly linked to the technical problem of showing how unemployment can be 'involuntary'. Keynes never quite attains the heart of this particular matter. He does not say that the incongruity between the desires and intentions of income-disposers in their private capacity as such, and the desires and intentions of business men in their responsibility for directing enterprise, lie in the *composition* of the incomes receivable by the one and payable by the other. Income-disposers sometimes wish for an aggregate income largely composed of retainable and preservable 'wealth' in a general and liquid form, but in order to provide them with such, the enterprisers must order, produce and themselves acquire for their firms, equipment which is highly specialized, expensive, *durable and obsolescence-prone*.

Keynes spared his readers, even in the deliberately provocative *General Theory* of 1936, the ultimate force of his conclusion, that rational conduct is an illusion and unrelated to the realities of business. That final smashing of the idol was reserved for his last version of the theory of unemployment, the *Quarterly Journal* reply to his critics. He nowhere speaks, I believe, of 'rational conduct' in those terms. His summary statement, uttered in speech, was 'Equilibrium is blither'. Thus, then, our argument passes from the fundamentals of time and being to the practical conditions of business. Keynes undertook the destruction of the rational value-theory ideal. In order to be understood, indeed in order to arrive at his goal from his own starting-point of adherence to the traditional view, he spoke the language of his opponents. The *General Theory of Employment, Interest and Money* proceeds in terms of functions, and regards variables as in some sense 'dependent' on each other. But this dependence of many variables upon each other, in a web of mutual determination, is vain for the defence of the traditional standpoint. For *one* variable is left unchained. Investment, the flow of orders for (durable) equipment, is at the mercy, not of other variables, firmly clasping its shoulder in a function-grip, but of the ever-dissolving and re-appearing will-o-the-wisp of expectation; of hopes and fears, of surmise and despondency. Investment is the maverick variable not fully harnessed into the team.

22.3 *Rational determinacy excludes money*

Keynes had pointed to a variable which changed with abrupt, calamitous and unaccountable dislocations, plunging suddenly into chasms unforeseeable in advance. But in the *Treatise on*

Money he had pointed to a phenomenon which, in quality if not in quantitative power, goes further still to undermine the conception of an orderly economic universe. The rate of interest is shown in the *Treatise* to depend on the market inter-play of two camps of speculators holding contradictory views of the impending movement of bond prices. The Bulls and the Bears of the gilt-edged market must be in *disagreement* if any bond price is to remain even momentarily where it is. Thus, in almost any situation, almost any behaviour of bond prices will disappoint one or more of the camps of asset-holders and cause them sooner or later to alter their conduct. Such an 'inherently restless' variable is plainly at odds, in principle, with the notion of a stable equilibrium, though the leverage exerted by the interest-rate on prices, outputs and investment may sometimes be small. If the interest-rate can claim to be an equilibrating price, what it equilibrates is not saving and investment (which, so far as interest is concerned, play only on the fringes of the game), but the speculative notions of the holders of the huge stocks of existing (old) bonds and the huge stocks of money. And speculators have nothing to gain from stability, unless they are 'speculators' purely in defence of their wealth.

It is no mere accident that a book which was begun as a *Treatise on Money* should become the origin of the theory of employment, that is, the theory of output as a whole. For money, a familiar, omnipresent and indispensable feature of our economic society, can have no truck at all with the timeless rational construct of value. Money, in that real society, is an *asset*, that is, a means of storing wealth, of preserving and conveying it through time. Money is also a thing whose desirability, through whatever psychic channels it may run, springs ultimately from a mere convention of exchangeability. Money would be unwanted, were it not counted on to be exchangeable for things which can be eaten, burnt as fuel, worn as garments, or used as tools. It is a mere proxy for such things. Such a thing can have no possible place in the value-construct. In the timeless system with its perfect information for every member, the only aspect of money which is needed is that of a unit of account. Complete pre-reconciliation and simultaneity of all choices means that both sides of all exchanges of goods for goods are decided on in the system's timeless present, there is no place for a *reserve* of purchasing power whose use is postponed. Money is the means of deferring choice and in the timeless system there is no date to which choice can be deferred, nor is there any prospect of subsequent improvement of knowledge as a reason for electing to defer it. In the sole timeless moment of the value-construct, a good which cannot be enjoyed in that moment is not a good.

The theorists of the value-construct, believing that money could not be valued as an enjoyable or as an instrumental good, denied it the standing of a good and deemed it a mere accounting symbol. Thus they left it outside the value system, regarding its quantity as a tide which lifted or lowered all vessels equally and made no difference to their relative positions. They did not recognize their system as timeless, but they treated money in the way that timelessness requires. Their instinct was right. To include asset-money in the essential account of economic affairs is to abandon the value-construct, the rational ideal. Money as an asset serves a world essentially divorced from the demonstrable adequacy of reason. But not money only. Every *asset* lies equally outside the rational field. An asset is something which looks to a future, and the future, denying us knowledge, denies us the grist for the mill of reason. Money in any sense except the de-natured one of a pure unit of account, serving a system where all accounts balance out and leave no residue, dissolves the rational ideal.

22.4 *Rational determinacy excludes imperfect competition*

Money in its full nature is an idea incompatible with that of rational determinacy. Scarcely less so is imperfect competition. Departures from perfect competition fall into two classes. Where a firm is in some degree of competition with a great number of others, though selling a product somewhat distinct from theirs, and is unable to ascribe a loss of customers to the action of identifiable rivals, we speak of monopolistic competition. The effect of this departure is to deprive the value-construct of the power, which under perfect competition is part of its essential nature and unified design, to solve the adding-up problem by demonstrating that the product will be precisely exhausted by payment of the factors of production at the rate of their marginal productivities. The other departure is far more disastrous for the analyst's basic supposition that conduct is based upon well-informed reason. For in duopoly we have the paradox that it is *logically impossible* for both contestants at once to act upon one and the same non-fallacious assumption about each other's conduct.

Perfect competition has a double role in assuring the solution of the adding-up problem. If the production function, associating output in physical terms with the quantities of the factors of production, is of the type which gives constant returns to scale (that is to say, such as can be generated by a straight ray pivoted at the origin and allowed to swing up from lying along one axis and down again to lie along the other) then in physical terms the product will be precisely exhausted by being distributed to the factors of production at the rate of their marginal physical contributions. It will be precisely exhausted also, even when the production function is not of the constant returns to scale type, provided it takes place at a point of tangency between such a surface and the actual production surface. For then there is no relevant difference between the two situations: one and the same tangent plane will, at the point of production, represent the marginal conditions on both surfaces. Now perfect competition is required in either case in order that the market value of the product may be proportional to its physical quantity. For so long as that is so, everything we can say about the production function when the product is measured in physical terms will be true when it is measured in value terms. When an ounce or a litre of the product is worth a shilling, and the price is the same regardless of the size of output to be sold, it does not matter whether we measure the product in ounces, etc., or in shillingsworth. But perfect competition is *also* needed, if the production function is not of the constant returns type, to ensure that production shall take place at a point which is tangent to a 'constant returns' surface.

Duopoly is the situation where a good which has no close substitutes cannot be obtained from any except two firms. The aggregated demand-schedule of all potential buyers of this good being given, the price will depend on the combined output of the two suppliers. Firm 1 must base its choice of its own output on some supposition about the output of firm 2. Let us suppose for example that firm 1 assumes that firm 2 will maintain a given output regardless of the output of firm 1. The demand curve facing firm 1 will on this supposition be the aggregate demand curve less the constant quantity supplied by firm 2, and firm 1 will accordingly choose its own output so as to maximize its own net revenue in these circumstances. Firm 1 is thus adopting, in a situation entirely symmetrical with that of firm 2, conduct different from that which it ascribes to firm 2, on which supposed conduct of firm 2, firm 1's conduct is based. This inconsistency is ineradicable. Firm 1, perceiving that its own intention, and its own supposition about the intentions of firm 2, are inconsistent, may ascribe to firm 2 the belief that firm 1 will maintain a given output while firm 2 maximizes its own net revenue. But if firm 1 ascribes this belief to firm 2, firm 1's action must again be different from that which it is now ascribing to firm 2. However far the *general duopolist* (either of the two indistinguishable firms in their symmetrical situation) carried his steps of ascription of more and more 'sophisticated' conduct to his rival, there can be no attaining consistency between his own action, dependent on that ascription, and that which he ascribes to his rival. So long as the duopolists refuse, or are unable, to combine into a monopolist, reason cannot tell either of them what it is best for him to do.

22.5 *Logical rigour and ineffective compromise*

The value-construct was, of course, understood by its proponents to be an idealized picture of the field of phenomena they were concerned to systematize. When, in the interests of rigid proof and incisive economy of argument, one resorts to abstraction, it is natural and commendable to push that policy to the limit of its power. To give to the untidy, crowding and variegated mass of economic events the austere structural necessity of mathematics was a splendid aim and achievement. Having shown the skeleton which gave form to the whole, they were willing to put some flesh upon it. They did not apprehend correctly the concessions they would have to make. Not recognizing that their system, to fulfil its purpose of making conduct rational, would have to be timeless, they made it instead *stationary*. It was plain that in the world of elapsing time, supplies of goods must be flows, so-and-so many tons or litres per hour or year. But equilibrium as they conceived it was a state of affairs. To make a static picture out of a set of flows is to construct a *stationary state*. This curious monster (dismissed with gentle scorn by Alfred Marshall) has no claim upon our credulity. It is no more than the timeless system repeating itself along a meaningless dimension. Not even the Economic Man could endure to live in such a prison without wrecking it by starting to save or to investigate the other possibilities with which his resources would surround him. But the builders of the rational construct of value did not perceive themselves to be committed to a timeless system. The stationary state was for them the real world constrained as it were to run upon straight rails instead of a curving road, without any essential changes in its mechanism but having the advantage of being much easier to study. The stationary state, nonetheless, is a pointless declension from the purity of argument of the timeless system.

Besides resorting to heroic abstractions, the value-construct casts out some minor features of reality, which can be restored without seriously spoiling its incisiveness. The perfect, instantaneous and synchronous market evidently requires some quasi-instititutional frame as a mechanism or means of organization to show in detail *how* it distils the price-data which it diffuses. Walras proposed *tâtonnements*, Edgeworth envisaged re-contract. The idea of a pooling of schedules of conditional promises* has the same end in view. Markets in reality are not perfect, but their powers are sufficiently remarkable to explain and excuse in large measure the value-theorists' tacit belief in the ability of markets to provide *complete* information. The vast incompleteness which markets can do nothing to cure was recognized by the great realist with a rational training, Alfred Marshall, but not by the rationalists with no 'real' training, the exponents of pure abstract general determinacy.

The value-construct at its most uncompromising level of

---

* G. L. S. Shackle, 'L'equilibre: étude de sa signification et de ses limites', *Cahiers de l'Institut de Science Economique Appliquée*, Suppl. No. 134, 1962. Also *A Scheme of Economic Theory*, Chapter 2 (Cambridge University Press, 1965).

unified simplicity also departs from reality by its exclusion of indivisible goods. If there are goods whose technical purpose can only be served by the intact presence of a complex physical organization, for example, an intricate machine, a telephone system, a railway, then we cannot apply to them the methods of 'small differences' on which the differential calculus depends. Such practical details, however, are far from the question of the nature and meaning of value theory.

Rationalism, the belief that conduct can be understood as part of the determinate order and process of Nature, into which it is assimilated by virtue of the fact that men choose what is best for them in their circumstances, and their circumstances are laid down by Nature, is a paradox. For it claims to confer upon men freedom to choose, yet to be able to predict what they will choose. It speaks of *choice*, and what can this mean, except that a man is confronted with *rival available* actions? All the actions are available, but all except one are forbidden: forbidden by reasoning self-interest. By assuming that men pursue their desires by applying reason to their circumstances, the analyst can tell what their conduct will be, provided he can also assume that not only he, but they, are in possession of full knowledge of those circumstances. Why should a man not know his circumstances? There are the actions of other men, freely chosen by them and constituting part of our individual's circumstances. How can men know each other's concurrent free choices? By pre-reconciliation in a general equilibrium. There is also the future. For the sake of pre-reconciliation of choices, and also for its own unfathomable possibilities, the future must be assumed away. Thus the value-construct describes free, pre-reconciled, determinate choices in a timeless system. It is an arresting triumph of the formal imagination. Beauty, clarity and unity are achieved by a set of axioms as economical as those of classical physical dynamics. Can the real flux of history, personal and public, be approximately understood in terms of this conception? The contrast is such that we have difficulty in achieving any mental collation of the two ideas. Macbeth's despair expresses more nearly the impact of the torrent of events.

22.6 *The fallacy of a general economic explanation*
of economic affairs

The dissolution of belief in the value-theory account of economic affairs was an aspect of the dissolution of Victorian social and international stability. The depressions and business crises of Victorian times could be seen as occasional failures or aberrations of a basically orderly system. British troubles of the 1920s, and world troubles of the 1930s, made this difficult. But they did not overthrow in any lasting way the economists' vested interest in an analysable economic world. The trouble is that the world is not economic. It is political-economic, power-struggle economic, social-discontent economic, it is economic only subject to unappeasable greeds and rivalries and implacable enmities. A general *economic* explanation of economic affairs is an ambition which flies in the face of history and the observable contemporary scene. The economists' only hopeful objective is to provide an account of that shawl of loosely interknotted strands which waves in the wind of the other human influences, political contention, technological invention, explosion of population. He can seek to describe its modes of potential response to each fresh kaleidic shift of the environment, during the time till that shift is superseded by another. But he cannot tell what these shifts will be. Economic affairs are not self-contained or insulated, they cannot have a self-sufficient explanation.

BOOK IV

Statics:
The Rejection of Time

23

The Calculus and the Subjective Ideal

Marginalism was the natural fusing of two ideas perfectly adapted to each other. The result was, in effect, a single idea of such ascendancy that the whole of economic theory depended from it for more than fifty years. One of these ideas was a fact of observation which solved the problem of economic determinacy. The other was the classic mathematical criterion for determining numerical values of the argument of a function which correspond to extreme values of the function. The strands of thought that were here spun together were enough, in numbers, intuitive power and in beauty to support an entire scholarly discipline and give it some aura of the prestige of mathematics itself. We may list those strands: self-contained completeness and determinacy; independence of other disciplines; the establishment of human reason as the determining principle of individual conduct and of the general course of affairs; the establishment of economics as a 'geometry' in the old sense, of a deductive system self-sufficient except for the choice and acceptance of a few axioms; the incisive beauty of mathematical demonstration. Small wonder that value theory, thus proudly caparisoned, was willing to ride on alone, treating even money as an extraneous and subsidiary matter, and all other disciplines than itself as having nothing to contribute to it, save only mathematics.

Production-cost per unit of each of two goods had been regarded as determining the quantities of them which would exchange for each other on the market. But what if the unit cost of production varied according to the number of units weekly or hourly produced? Value would then depend on output, and what determined output? The schedule which associated each output with a unit cost gave only one equation for those two unknowns. The system became complete when another equation was provided, which paired with each other hypothetical prices and weekly numbers of units which would be bought. This second equation expressed desires, needs, tastes, as a quite independent matter from the technology and physical endowments which governed cost of production. Still, the mere presence of as many equations as unknowns did not guarantee that the system was relevantly solvable. Suppose the number of units demanded had been greater, for all prices, than the output which would have carried unit cost up to that price? Suppose, that is to say, that the supply and demand curves had not intersected each other at any positive price and positive output? The *form* of the curves was relevant. And it was here that observation came to the help of reason. For many analysts perceived that weekly quantity demanded, other circumstances given, will be a decreasing function of price. Marshall was puzzled by what would happen if quantity supplied were an even steeper decreasing function of price. But that is another story.

The inverse relation between demand and price was seen as the consequence of a fact of human nature, namely, that the extra satisfaction anticipated from an increment, of a given physical size, in the daily or weekly quantity consumed of some good, was in any given circumstances smaller, the larger the quantity upon which the increment was to be superposed. An increment: a *difference* between two levels of intake; this was the language of the differential calculus. The extra anticipated satisfaction was another difference; and these two differences were mutually corresponding differences, one of them a difference between two values of the argument of a function, the other a difference between two values of the function itself. However, this function was only a part of the whole relevant story. The other side of the matter was the sacrifice involved in buying the good. That sacrifice might well increase by bigger and bigger steps as the quantity bought was conceived successively at larger and larger sizes differing by equal steps. Thus the net total satisfaction, anticipated from buying various conceivable weekly quantities of the good, would increase up to that size of weekly purchase where the gain and loss from one more step were equal. Here was an illustration of the classic problem of extreme values. What size of weekly intake would give the greatest net total satisfaction? That size at which the net difference of satisfaction, due to a small difference of intake, was zero. Rational conduct, in the problem of how much of a good to buy each week, was that conduct which maximized net total satisfaction; and this 'how much' could be answered by reference to a characteristic theorem of the differential calculus. Thus were psychics, mathematics, and the supremacy of reason united in one theme of economics.

In the foregoing we have used repeatedly the expression 'per unit of time', and we have spoken of 'anticipated satisfaction'. Real experience 'takes time'. It finds us at one instant and leaves us at another, the experience having filled an interval of time, however short. Experience of the elapsing, extended moment impels us to hypothesize a succession of moments, to construct extended time. Extended time, in one direction, is available to be filled with content, but content is not available to fill it, except it be invented, even if on suggestions offered by experience. Since all these notions arise from our intuitions of the nature or meaning of experience, we might feel that their explicit presence is essential to any theory in economics which is to shed light and satisfy curiosity. Yet questions can be asked which do not involve any reference to any aspect of time. Logic is about propositions which can be precisely and completely stated. Time by contrast offers us a world half-invisible. We cannot have experience of actuality at two distinct 'moments'. The moment of actuality, the moment in being, 'the present', is *solitary*. Extended time, beyond 'the moment', appears in this light as a figment, a product of thought. Thus if we confine our questions to what may be treated as co-actual with itself, they will be confined to a single moment, to strictly contemporaneous things, to a world which can thus in some sense be called 'timeless'. Economics is said to be about choice. But choice, under its most abstract guise, need not be choice amongst things which have any dimension or location of time. The rival entities amongst which we are free to choose may be pure abstractions, so long as choice is being discussed as a matter of logic only.

Rational choice, choice which can *demonstrate* its own attainment of maximum objectively possible advantage, must be fully informed choice. But there can be no full information except about what is past, or else about what is exempt from the world of time altogether. The paradox of rationality is that it must concern itself with choosing amongst things fully known; but in the world of time, only *that* is fully known which is already beyond the reach of choice, having already become actual and thus knowable. Rational choice, it seems, must be confined to *timeless* matters. But economics seeks to understand conduct by, precisely, deeming it to be rational. Thus economics is best advised, if it confines itself to logic, to discuss a timeless system.

'Static' economics, adopting as its method the proposition that men choose their conduct by applying reason to their circumstances in pursuit of their desires, discards time. It does so necessarily. It still has within its reach a great area of questions. To claim (as the present writer does) that these questions, which can be divorced from considerations of time, are essential to our understanding, and the answers to them necessary for full illumination of the economic field, is to say that that field, of its nature, cannot be served by a completely general, undivided theory springing from one sole set of pre-suppositions. Economics, concerned with thoughts and only secondarily with things, the objects of those thoughts, must be as protean as thought itself. To adopt *one* rigid frame and appeal exclusively to it is bound to be fatal. It is as though we should draw up a plan of exploration of an unknown country, and rule out any change of that plan, even one suggested by what the explorers actually find. But one valid, indispensable model is the static model, the model based on the premiss of the 'rejection of time'.

Economic theory depends upon expressions, meanings and ideas which refer to the world of universal experience. In this sense, it is of course not 'self-contained'. The only strictly self-contained system of thought would be one consisting of relations amongst undefined entities, and of propositions concerning those relations: in short, a pure 'geometry' or deductive system detached from any referend outside itself. It would be a branch of pure mathematics. Moreover, it would need symbols, and there would be some difficulty in preventing these symbols from taking on a kind of objectivity, as points and lines, the symbols of Euclid's geometry, do in his system. Self-contained-ness is relative. But economic value theory achieves self-containedness in one respect. Its terms have referends in real experience, but the relations of the terms with each other are fully stated, and not subject to interference or modification from outside the system. Moreover, economic value theory tolerates no intermediaries between its terms and their 'real experience' referends. It assumes (with some high-handedness) that the link between terms and referends is supplied by convention resting on an extremely frequent handing-about of these terms in ordinary discourse and conversation. *It is safe to assume* (we may hear the economist saying in defence of his position) that everyone knows what is meant by preference, by satisfaction, by indifference. It is by this direct assimilation of what it assumes to be facets of universal human experience, with the otherwise abstract and empty symbols of a pure geometry in the basic sense, that value theory sets up its claim to be invincible in cogency, yet real in content. It is thus, also, that it debars itself from reference to all but a rarified distillation of real experience. The 'subjective ideal' is the life governed by pure reason, able to be completely analysed and understood by the unaided logician.

Marginalism became the ascendant notion of economics through its discovery that a principle of conduct which was natural and intuitive in men's management of their affairs, namely to pay attention to *differences*, to what would be the extra gain of a small extra sacrifice, was in fact the key idea of a formal mathematical procedure for determining that numerical value of the argument of a function, to which there corresponds an extreme value of the function. Intuitive conduct was logically correct and justified conduct, it was mathematically correct conduct, it was conduct which led to making the most of given resources, or getting given effects from the least resources, it was conduct which achieved economy. But this fact opened the tool-box of the differential and integral calculus (it is all one) for the economist's use. However basic and comparatively simple the items from this tool-box that he actually needs, the marginal idea turned out to be at one and the same time the essence of economy and the pass-key to a perfect formal apparatus for tracing the detailed and particular consequences of logical economizing procedure in various contexts and applications. The marginal idea amounted to an assertion that economic principles are simply mathematical principles anchored explicitly to a particular field of phenomena. And such a statement could be made of many branches of physics, and, in later years as it has appeared, of many branches of biology, of communication theory and of fields of science in every direction. By the marginal principle, economics was suddenly given (so it seemed) the full standing of science. Alfred Marshall (the accusation that he relied in his economics on a non-measurable 'utility' must be the most grotesquely and blatantly unjust in the history of our discipline) had pointed out that economics possesses a means of measurement somewhat approaching the public objectivity of physical measurement:

An opening is made for the methods and the tests of science as soon as the force of a person's motives – *not* the motives themselves – can be approximately measured by the sum of money, which he will just give up in order to secure a desired satisfaction; or again by the sum which is just required to induce him to undergo a certain fatigue.*

Marshall's distinction between motives themselves, and their force, might not be accepted today, when the meaning of an idea has been said to reside in our method of measuring it. But Marshall's concept of utility was as 'operational' as any concept can be: the utility anticipated by a purchaser is measured by what he will pay for it. That measure attains public standing and unanimity in the *market*, as the price to which individual members of the market can all adjust their conduct by suitable composition of their shopping-lists. The subjective ideal of reasoned economy, the mathematical ideal of perfectly analysable conduct, appeared, in the 1870s, to be one and the same.

* *Principles of Economics*, eighth edition, Book I, Chapter 2, p. 15.

24

Simultaneous Equations and the Market Ideal

24.1 *The concept of co-valid equations is indispensable to the economist*

Economizing can be idealized and represented in the ultimate degree of formal perfection by means of the calculus. The calculus furnishes for it a ready-made apparatus of thought which is precisely apt, not only to the requirements of expression and manipulation, but to the nature of the intuitive act by which people everywhere, never having heard of the differential calculus, correctly adjust their budgets so as to get the most satisfaction from their means. Indeed, for the analyst, the calculus does much more than this. For his question: What shall I do next to gain insight into the implications of the economizing impulse and its logically necessary manifestations? is answered by his mathematical apparatus itself, which suggests to him with almost the force of natural instinct the procedure for investigating rational conduct. The individual or the firm, or the analyst on their behalf, have only to describe mathematically their circumstances and the hypothesis of the fulfilment of their desires to the utmost degree which those circumstances allow, and then to solve the resulting equation for that unknown which represents the lever under their hand, the adjustable quantity, the variable which is 'independent' in the sense of being choosable at will. In rendering these services, mathematical procedures and conceptions offer an immense gain in efficiency. But they do not provide something actually *indispensable* to the dissection of the maximizing procedure. It is when we come to consider the inter-action of the economizing endeavours of many individuals and many firms, the process in which prices are not *data* but are unknowns whose values must be elicited by the market, that we find economic theory resorting to a mathematical conception which would scarcely be within the reach of 'non-algebraic' thought, namely, the con-

ception of a *system* of equations for which it may be possible, by
formal manipulations, to find a set of values for the unknowns
such as satisfies every equation of the system, and is the only set
of values which does so. This conception, known not very
felicitously as a system of 'simultaneous' equations (their
'simultaneity' has nothing whatever to do with the calendar,
and means *co-validity*) goes distinctly beyond 'common sense',
and places economics under a debt to mathematics which it
could scarcely have escaped.

24.2 *Indeterminacy of Quesnay's* Tableau

The first great inspiration to come to an economist was, perhaps, Quesnay's *Tableau Economique*, in which he saw economic
society as a system of inter-organized activities, a unity in
which each component process sustained and was sustained by
the system as a whole. Quesnay saw the system as a 'steady
state', unchanging from year to year, and he understood that
the power of the system to maintain itself in this constancy
rested on a balance, within each component sector, between
the inputs and the output of the activity proceeding in that
sector. Each sector must be supplied, in each year, with just
those quantities of those services and materials which its continuing activity of supplying other sectors with their necessaries,
likewise determined in quantity, required. The balance thus
determined within each sector was a technological one. It
would have been possible for the proportions amongst *sectors*
in the *Tableau Economique* to be different, and for the constancy
of the resulting system to be nonetheless assured. The *Tableau*,
in short, so long as no more is assumed about it than its self-
sustaining constancy, is indeterminate. Quesnay's conception
implicitly likened the economic society to a living organism.
In referring to it we might speak of organs instead of sectors,
and functions (in the biological sense) instead of activities. But
the 'steady state' which living creatures (for a brief span)
maintain is to be found in countless different orders, genera and
species. Quesnay's *Tableau* does not solve the allocation problem. For example, the Artisans could be omitted from it,
leaving the Farmers and the Proprietors to sustain each other

by doing without manufactures and simply consuming the produce of the soil.

Quesnay contributed two vital insights, the conception of a system of inter-organized activities, and the notion of the role of *intra*-sectoral technological balance. That balance between inputs and outputs of each single sector was a balance of exchange, the inputs were supplied (by other sectors, or by the people who worked in the sector) in exchange for the outputs, and thus inputs in total were counted as of equal value with the resulting output. We must consider this to be the case despite Quesnay's view that only Nature was really productive. In the Farmers' sector, the Farmers and the land together produced a crop, which rewarded the Farmers and the Proprietors of the land, over and above the provision of seed corn for next year. Neither the Farmers nor the Proprietors ate (as they might have done, without destroying the constancy of the system) the whole of their reward as food, but exchanged some of it for manufactures. The artisans received food and raw materials from the other sectors, and gave manufactures of equal value in exchange. The complex circuit was complete and self-maintaining. In Leontief's work two centuries later it was displayed in a far greater complexity, but with the self-same essential meaning. The central purpose of Leontief's analysis is to calculate the changes in the interior proportions of the system, consequent upon a change in the proportions of the final outputs which emerge at its boundary. The need for such an analysis demonstrates the possibility of infinitely many different allocations of the ultimate sources of productive power. How is this allocation determined? Who allocates those resources, who determines what quantities of what factors of production shall be devoted to this or that product, and consequently what respective annual quantities of various products shall be made? The allocation is done, in a 'western' society, by the members of that society taken together. But these component individuals have widely various tastes, interests and endowments. How is a scheme of allocation to be compounded from this diversity? The problem of allocation is the problem of reconciliation.

252 STATICS: THE REJECTION OF TIME

24.3 The criterion, logical possibility, and method, of
ideal allocation of given endowments to lines of production

What conditions must be fulfilled, if we are to claim that the
allocation of a society's means of production, when these are
possessed in a given pattern by the members of the society, has
been ideally performed? What fundamental Scheme of Things
must be assumed, if such an ideal performance of the allocation
is to be logically possible? What, precisely, must the operation
be, which will perform the allocation ideally within that basic
predicament? It is these three strands, intimately involved with
each other, that constitute the problem of ideal allocation. In
answer to the first of these questions, we shall propose one
condition as necessary and sufficient: The *general individual
interest*, that is, an abstraction with which every one of the
member persons or firms of the society can in relevant respects
identify himself, must be able to choose his conduct (course of
action) so that he can *demonstrate* that his choice is the most
advantageous for himself in view of his desires and means. We
shall not require him to be able to demonstrate it to anyone
other than himself. By referring to the general (omni-represen-
tative) individual interest, we require that the choosing of his
demonstrably most advantageous conduct be possible to all
individuals *simultaneously*. Conduct fulfilling this test must be
possible for all of them at once. This in turn means that their
choices must be reconcilable with each other.

This first answer can be re-expressed so as to elicit some
implications. We can define ideally advantageous conduct as
that which satisfies the individual's desires to the highest degree
possible in his circumstances. The demonstration to himself
that this has been achieved will require him to have perfect
knowledge of what those circumstances are. Amongst those
circumstances, and playing, like the rest, an essential and
inescapable part in helping to determine the outcome of some
specified course of conduct of his own, will be the actions chosen
and intended by others. Thus it appears that *every* individual is
required, by our criterion of ideal allocation of productive
effort, to confront a range of rival available courses while
already effectively knowing what others have chosen. This is the

paradox of rational conduct. It has to be resolved, if at all, by our mode of coping with our third question.

The means of resolution, in brief, is that choices must be *pre-reconciled*. This requires that they be expressed, in the first place, as *conditional* intentions, each of them as a variable whose numerical value will depend on the value assigned to some argument-variable. And when the resulting equations have been put into suitable shape, they will have to be treated as a system of co-valid equations and solved *simultaneously*. It is the prime and essential purpose of the market to pool the statements of conditional intentions and to seek a general solution which will prescribe for every individual, A, that action which, in fact, A would choose for himself if he knew that each other individual, X, was going to perform the action prescribed for X. In its ideal and abstract operation, the market solves two problems which are essentially one, the problem of how the individual interest can fully know its circumstances, and the problem of how individual choices of conduct can be reconciled so that each individual is allowed the most advantageous conduct for himself which gives a corresponding opportunity to others. The two problems are a unity. For the circumstances which should be presented to an individual as effectively his, are those which will result from the exercise by every individual, that is, by the general individual, of equal freedom in the light of perfect, and therefore equal, knowledge. In view of the problem of knowledge of circumstances, we can better say that the market *pre-reconciles* the choices. In what conceptual setting can it do so?

24.4 *Only a timeless system can pre-reconcile all choices*

To pre-reconcile the choices of several individuals is to make these choices dependent on each other, as a unity. One such choice will be accepted only on condition that every other of the specific actions, proposed by the pre-reconciling solution, is also accepted. The choices are inter-conditional. Thus they are necessarily logically and formally simultaneous. The prescriptions of individual action composing a general pre-reconciliation or solution, a general equilibrium, are parts of a unity. The meaning of each depends on the whole, this inter-dependence being the entire purpose of the pre-reconciling operation. By offering its prescription to each individual, the solution *in effect* furnishes him with complete relevant knowledge of the choices being made (the prescriptions being agreed to) by all other members of the society. Any choice which was made *earlier* than the act of general inter-commitment cannot have been made in view of that, not-yet-existent, commitment. Any choice made later than that general act cannot have been taken into account in the forming or finding of that general solution. Thus if a *general* pre-reconciliation is to deserve its name, it must, literally, embrace *all choices*. All choices, therefore, must be simultaneous and the system of actions which they represent must be strictly *timeless*. In a pre-reconciled system there can be no earlier and later. The system of actions must be looked on as *exempt from time*. In the notion of general equilibrium the rejection of time imposes itself inexorably.

24.5 *Time and logic are alien to each other*

Time and logic are alien to each other. The one entails ignorance, the other pre-supposes a sufficient axiom system, a system embracing everything relevant. The void of future, but relevant, time destroys the possibility of logic. We can conjecture, imagine and contribute to the future, but we cannot reason about it, save on the basis of figment, in some degree.

The notion of a system of simultaneous equations is a formal abstraction, and when used as the substance of a model of the actions of an economic society, it necessarily reduces that model also to a formal abstraction. This abstraction enforces upon us an insight of vital significance; the inter-dependence of choices as regards their effect and meaning, the inter-dependence of the *nature* of specific acts. Thus we have, yet again, an illustration of the need of economic theory to emancipate itself from the search for perfect *generalness* of its self-representations. The world is such that general, comprehensive, omni-competent models of it do not make sense. The object turns into a series of different objects under inspection. The world which the economic theoretician must study is *protean* in the profoundest sense. It is logically manifold in nature.

24.6 *The need for plural models extra-logically combined*

In order to achieve demonstrative proof, the economic theoretician must reject time. In order to reflect the human predicament, he must consider time as the fact above all facts, conditioning every thought, act and meaning. At first sight, it may seem that he has the choice between double-think and compromise. He can make distinct models, one timeless and rigorously reasoned, the other time-conditioned and deficient in premisses. Or he can try to fuse the two strands. But compromise is not in this context meaningful. Rigour is unique. Many-valued logics can admit the inconclusiveness of a reasoning process. But this is to admit that, in some circumstances, reason does not allow us to say what will happen. Theory in economics must use models which exclude each other. If they are to be combined, it must be by a psychic process which is ultimately extra-logical.

25

Partial Equilibrium

25.1 *The nature of* particular analysis

Economics is the study of conduct and its outcome. If that conduct has its origin in thoughts, these are the thoughts of some individual, and the study of it is evidently obliged to start from a consideration of the situation of such an individual, as to what he desires, what he knows, and what he possesses of personal capacities, organizational links with other people, institutional settings and material resources and purchasing power. It is reasonable and unavoidable, if we take the individual psyche to be the relevant source of conduct, to study its delimited personal field of knowledge and action. That field may include all the powers of the statesman, military commander, trade union leader or head of a great business, or only those of an income-earner and income-disposer. The analyst's point of view will in all cases be the same, so long as he studies conduct as the expression of thoughts. No matter how complex the influences that bear on these thoughts or how intricate a network of interactions with other people embraces them, the analyst's questions to himself will bear on what the individual will do in his circumstances as they are seen by the individual. This method of *partial* or *particular* analysis stands in contrast with the logically subsequent attempt to examine the *inter*-actions, the influence or constraint exerted upon one man's conduct by the actions of another, the suggestions offered to the individual by the conduct of his partners in exchange, his suppliers, customers, employers or employees, and in contrast with the general picture, with its own principles arising from its all-encompassing and general scope, which the inter-actions themselves compose. When the conduct of individuals, studied as such, has been composed into a picture which takes account of the necessary, unavoidable, intentional inter-actions of the individual choices of action, and sees those choices as influenced and shaped by an awareness of each other, we have a *general* analysis. This again may be contrasted with an analysis concerned with aggregates, where individual detail is not preserved even implicitly or by the study of typical agents or firms, but is submerged in a few great summations. There thus arises the need to ask whether particular analysis can be a self-contained end in itself; or, if it is merely a preliminary to a general analysis, whether the passage from particular to general is simple and direct, or whether it gives rise to subtle difficulties and dangers.

Partial analysis recommends itself to the analyst by other things than its natural and logical conformity to his subject matter. When the mass of intricate connections which must, in principle, be studied by a general analysis is removed, the attention thus economized can be spent on considering the individual's situation and reasoning in more detail. Knowledge of the special conditions and technologies of particular industries can be applied, as Alfred Marshall applied such knowledge to great effect in explaining general principles by concrete cases. If the phenomena studied by the economist are to be seen as growing out of the soil of practical business, partial or particular equilibrium analysis is the only way. But we may go much further than this. The value-construct in its unifying simplicity depends on the assumption of perfect competition, and perfect competition is to be seen in action, as it were, at the particular equilibrium level. When we say that perfect competition enjoins upon the firm an output which brings marginal cost up to equality with price, we are evidently invoking the interests and rational conduct of the individual firm, and we are in fact specifying its *particular equilibrium*. It is, as we have seen in Chapter 14, the assumption that each firm in an industry will behave in this way (and will have the knowledge necessary to do so) that enables us to speak of the supply curve of the product of this industry in the sense of a one-to-one correspondence between the number of physical units offered by the industry per unit of time, on one hand, and the price per unit, on the other. And if we are to claim that the whole weekly or annual produce of the economic society will be precisely exhausted by payments to the suppliers of productive services at the rate of their marginal productivities, we must invoke the effect of perfect competition on the individual firm, in enabling it to sell any practicable output of its own at a market price invariant against changes of that particular output. For only thus can the output be measured indifferently in physical and in value terms. Finally the claim that with a given income distribution, perfect competition ensures that society's desired outputs of goods will be produced at minimum cost, also rests on the response of the individual firm to perfectly competitive markets. We ought then, to examine the supposed mechanism of these effects.

25.2 *An inconsistency of particular perfectly competitive equilibrium*

It is an irony in the value-construct that in seeking to picture economic conduct as the perfection of rationality, and in using for this purpose the assumption of perfect competition, it should oblige itself to suppose firms to deceive themselves. For the essence of perfect competition's analytical effectiveness is that the firm supposes itself to be unable to alter the price of its product by changing the weekly (etc.) quantity it puts on the market; unable, because that quantity can at most be only a very minute proportion of the output of identical products by the industry as a whole. Yet when the value-construct is called upon to explain how an equilibrium market price is arrived at, it refers to the mutual confrontation of a south-eastward sloping demand curve and a north-eastward sloping supply curve: the price, it thus supposes, must be lower in order that a larger weekly or annual quantity may be sold. The industry is the sum of its firms, and if one firm increases its output, the smoothly-working market mechanism which the value-construct's perfection of rationality requires must reflect that increase, however small a proportion it may be of total output, in a somewhat lowered price. The value-construct thus seeks to 'have things both ways'. The firm behaves in a way which does not reflect the objective truth. In this last sentence we refer, not to any discrepancy between the value-construct in its ideal abstraction, on one hand, and the world of experience on the other, but to two aspects of the value-construct itself. It contains an internal contradiction. It supposes the perfectly rational firm to deceive itself, or else it supposes the perfectly efficient market to have frictions which give way by perceptible degrees instead of in a mathematically continuous fashion. If market price is a continuous function of output; let us re-inforce the idea by saying even a differentiable function of output; and if that function is monotonically decreasing, then price must give way a little when the firm, by increasing its contribution, increases the industry's output a little.

Does this contradiction matter? Is it not positively advantageous, as bringing the value-construct nearer to realism? At least the recognition of it may discourage our temptation to take too literally, in our theorizing practice, the term *analysis*. Analysis is the intellectual process appropriate to a problem assumed to be already fully stated and ready made. But the economist's task is utterly different. He must begin by posing his own problem, and that is a task of selection and composition, of the scanning of a field of manifold suggestions, a business of design and construction with materials and elements which he himself chooses. The problems of economics, the questions to be attempted, await their setting by the candidate himself. The differential calculus, in its technique of solving an equation where the derivative is supposed equal to zero, in order to locate, in terms of the argument, an extreme value of the function, is implicitly supposing that all the real difficulties have been overcome. The form of the function has somehow been determined, not by the analyst, but by the economic subject whose conduct we are studying. For if he does not know it, it cannot guide his conduct. Or is he supposed to proceed by trial and error? In that case, what purpose is served by introducing the notion of differentiation of a function? Ought not the analyst to follow directly in the footsteps of the economic subject, the exerciser of choice and judgement, the conduct-decider?

25.3 *Analysis cannot reveal the firm's necessary heuristic process*

The value-construct must, however, be recognized, in particular equilibrium of the firm, to fudge its reasoning. On one hand, it declares that each firm treats the market price of its

product as *given*. On the other, it regards this market price as
the outcome of the inter-actions of the exploratory conduct of
firms. The market price *arises* from what firms do. They cannot
know what to do, except by trial and error, by seeing what
addition to total cost is made by some specific addition to
output, and at what price, when output has been thus augmented, its whole output can be sold. The fact that it is selling
in a 'perfectly competitive' market is not announced to the
firm by some independent or public agency, but must be
established by the firm for itself. The gaining of necessary
knowledge is the first task of the individual (as consumer or as
business man) who wishes to make his conduct a rational
response to circumstances.

The internal inconsistency of particular perfectly competitive equilibrium (equilibrium of the firm, consisting in a choice
of output which makes marginal cost equal to price) illustrates
also that it is beside the point to rely unquestioningly on
inferences which depend on the exact and formal fulfilment of
mathematical conditions by the economic subject matter. That
subject matter, as we have argued above, is in the first place a
heuristic process and not a cut-and-dried presentation of
established, unquestioned fact. But secondly, it is coarse-
grained and essentially imprecise. To treat it as conforming to
ideal mathematical conceptions (continuity and differenti-
ability), to attach *economic* meaning to limiting processes and
other such abstractions, in a literal rather than a suggestive
sense, is to invite misconception and fallacy. Economic conduct
must concern itself with, and base itself on, what can be known
and on the degree of accuracy which is practically measurable
and meaningful. Formal reasoning is incisively and vitally
suggestive. The caveats in its use are imperious and equally
vital.

25.4 *The mutual independence of demand and supply curves*

Even these considerations may be overshadowed by the consequences of treating the firm or the individual as a microcosmic
model of the whole economic society, a model merely needing
to be scaled up, and offering propositions, true of itself, which
(it has been incautiously thought) will also be true of the

macrocosm. For as we saw in Chapter 14, the method of confronting with each other supply and demand curves, in the simple manner which so strongly commends this tool, requires us to suppose that nothing which happens to the quantity supplied, and nothing which happens to the price, in any way displaces or transforms the demand curve. Movements *along* the supply curve (we have to assume) leave the demand curve, and the demand conditions which it expresses, unaffected. Those demand conditions are governed by, amongst other things, the incomes of the potential buyers of the commodity in question, and those usually include the suppliers of work and other means for producing the commodity. If the output or the price of the commodity change, so evidently will the incomes of these factors of production. How then can we move along the one curve, in search of an equilibrium or intersection, without being compelled to re-draw the other? The mutual independence of demand and supply conditions is only plausible if we are speaking of a minute portion of the economy; only, that is, for *particular*, or *partial*, equilibrium. But until the 1930s, it was supposed that full employment (the absence of 'involuntary' unemployment) was guaranteed by the freedom of suppliers of work to reduce the wage that they asked. Marshall himself warned his reader of this limitation of partial equilibrium.*

To treat the *labour market* as being amenable to analysis by the apparatus of inter-secting, mutually independent, demand and supply curves, was plainly to abuse the device of particular equilibrium. The labour market is not a 'particular' market, but an essentially general one encompassing all production. This does not, of course, mean that it is a perfect market. It is an assemblage of inter-acting markets. To scale up the method of particular equilibrium as a means of analysing as vast an aspect of things as the labour market is, of course, to be guilty of the 'fallacy of composition'. It may be that the value-construct can defend itself against this charge. For the value-construct, as we have seen, applies to a system of timeless pre-reconciliation, a system where 'money' is a mere unit of account, and a system where unemployment cannot be involuntary. But this was not the line of thought followed by

---

* Alfred Marshall, *Principles of Economics*, Preface to the second edition.

those who resorted to value theory as a means of analysing employment and output as a whole.

For the sake of this chapter's completeness we must return briefly to another aspect of the close inter-relation of partial equilibrium and perfect competition. Mr Sraffa's most startling conclusion, in his famous article of 1926,* is that for a firm whose product and whose factor markets are *all of them* perfectly competitive, both price per unit and cost per unit of product will be invariant against changes of the firm's output, and thus the firm will be quite unable to choose an output which equates its marginal cost and its marginal revenue, each of which are unchanging for all outputs. This is a conclusion apt to *particular* equilibrium. As soon as the firm, in such a position, starts to expand, it will (as Mr Sraffa well recognized) destroy the perfectly competitive conditions in its markets.

25.5 *The essential imprecision of economics*

How did so much weight come to be laid, with such *insouciance*, upon particular equilibrium? We can venture only one suggestion. Those trained to 'neglect the second order of small quantities' were all too ready to see in that perfectly legitimate technique (the limiting process of transition from difference-quotient to derivative) a sanction for neglecting other things, with no less a gain in convenience but with very different implications for logical rigour. And yet, let us at last come full circle. Marshall was the uninhibited user of particular equilibrium; we might say, the inventor of it. Marshall also was the economist who made clear by his bold practice that economics is an *essentially* imprecise subject.

* 'The laws of returns under competitive conditions', *Economic Journal*, vol. XXXVI (1926).

26

The Rejection of Time

26.1 *The dilemmas concerning time*

Time seems almost identifiable with experience or even with being. Thus we might suppose that no dissection of the affairs of men could be of the smallest interest which sought to dispense with it or escape from it. Time has, however, many faces, and it might seem reasonable to argue that there is no presumption that all of them must necessarily play a part together in any discussion of business or life at large. There is time as the moment of experience, the moment in being, the moment of actuality, the solitary present. There is time as the frontier of the void, the edge of the field of imagination of what may become. There is time as co-valid distinct and ordered references of thought, extended time existing only in present thought but giving room for the sequential arrangement of conceived states or transformations. There is time as measurable lapse. There is time as the sense (the psychic counterpart) of the (mathematical) integration of experience, the sense of adding-up the experience of sequential moments, time as the sense of duration.

In order to claim to be general, a theory of human affairs would have to show all these faces of time, if not others also, in combined and inter-active presence in a man's thought, in his experience. They are *faces* of one thing, so we are suggesting. Yet their co-presence seems to confound logic. If the present is solitary, the only locus of being and actuality, how can other moments be real, how can they act upon the present, what validity have they except as figments, mere subject-matters, abstract labels and cells of a filing-system, in a structure of *present* thought? Is, then, the present moment a sole existent thing, not merely isolated but all-inclusive? Against this, the present consists in transformation, each moment's being is the birth of another moment. Sequentiality appears to be inescapable. Duration, of its nature, involves the supposition of other moments than the present, since it is the sense of the summation of their effects. Time seems to lie wholly within the mind's present activity, yet the product of that activity is the conclusion that in several respects the mind can only make sense of its experience by treating time as external to it, as independent of it. It is not surprising that such an array of dilemmas has not been resolved, but rejected, by the theoretician concerned to analyse the *scene*, the *conventional* account of the nature of their affairs which men offer to themselves. Means of escape have lain between two extremes. Time can be totally and rigorously excluded and ignored, so that the elements of theory can be *freely* composed into any pattern, unconstrained by the logical consequences of sequence. Or time can be treated as a space, where one element rests upon another according to certain rules of construction. Between these two there has also naturally been a search for compromise, and it has proceeded by selection, by the inclusion of one or two of what we have called, for want of language to achieve comparison where no comparison can serve, the faces of time.

26.2 *Time and the relegation of reason*

Time as measurable lapse is the one which has seemed most necessary to a theory of conduct, a theory of deliberative action. Does not action 'take time'? But the economist's theory of deliberative action is a theory of deliberation, not of action. Deliberation itself, no doubt, 'takes time', but that is not the point. The theoretician's concern is with the basis, nature and result of the deliberation. His method, in value theory, has been to regard *men as practitioners of reason*, as the exercisers of choice by reason in face of full information, known to be such. But full relevant information for a chooser must include knowledge of what others are choosing. Rational choice must be pre-reconciled choice. Pre-reconcilable choices are simultaneous choices. The act of pre-reconciliation makes them effectively a single and unified choice. Two choices are not pre-reconciled if one is made before the other. Pre-reconciliation means not merely dependence of one choice on another, but their inter-dependence. The world of pre-reconciled choice must therefore be in effect timeless, it must have no 'earlier' and 'later' in respect of choice. But it is choice which turns physical action into conduct. To the analyst concerned with one sole occasion of simultaneous exchanges, the essence of the matter is the purely formal inter-relations of what things and quantities shall be exchanged. To him it will be meaningless to ask whether the quantities exchanged are exchanged per day or per week, or related to any interval. A world, or a system of actions, which is timeless in respect of choice may as well be timeless in respect of everything. The timeless world is the world of one problem, the possibility and meaning of the pre-reconciliation of choices, and for that problem it is the only world. We are saying, then, that in a non-timeless world, a world of earlier and later, there can be no pre-reconciliation of choice, therefore no fully rational choice, therefore no rigorous analysis of conduct as reasoned response to fully-known circumstances. The theoretician is faced with uncompromising alternatives. He can declare that in understanding men's conduct, certainty can come only from assuming it to be rational, and therefore to be part of a world that allows rationality. Then he must abandon everything which cannot be encompassed by a timeless world. Or he can accept the world of time and give reason no greater place in his scheme than that of the drill-book in grand strategy. Value theoreticians for the most part have not acknowledged this dilemma. Either they have not been aware of it, or they have resorted to the meaningless and self-destructive assumption of 'perfect foresight' (by what means and with what logical con-sequences perfect foresight is attainable they do not consider), or they have, with far more commendable judgement, em-barked on a necessarily non-rigorous compromise in which common sense gets the better of logic and allows much insight to be attained by reasonings which do not compose a structure but must be combined with each other by extra-logical pro-cesses of thought, and often invoke arbitrary assumptions with-out much emphasizing their highly special character. The complaint which seems legitimate in this regard is not that economists are content to use rigour when it suits them and discard it when it shows itself obstructive, but on the contrary, that they push elaboration and ostensible precision of argument to heights which are not justified by their foundations.

26.3 *The arbitrariness of assumptions concerning the acquirement of knowledge*

A timeless world would in principle allow pre-reconciliation of choices to be performed by a computer. A 'real' world is perhaps conceivable in which a hand-to-mouth existence proceeded by means of discontinuous general market-days having no mutual influence across the time-intervals separating them, so that each market occasion would be self-contained and a set of prices would be able to be determined on it which would clear the market, leaving no aftermath of unsatisfied demand or supply. Each such market occasion could then in our sense be 'timeless' and permit perfectly rational conduct. In fact, however, prices have to be determined on markets which are in effect always in operation, or whose occasions are linked by the possibility, open to dealers on them, of postponing demand or withholding supply in hope of more favourable prices. Continuous markets, as we may call them, are thus speculative markets in some degree, and we are at once involved in *time as the field of expectation*. Moreover, real markets are not operated by means of time-discrete computer solutions, but by the continuous inflow of orders to buy or sell, continuously collated and resolved into prices from hour to hour or from moment to moment. The market is the means of such pre-reconciliation of choices as the real world achieves, but its solutions respond unpredictably to shifts of the extra-economic setting and to the inherent restlessness of speculation. Some of the arbitrariness which value theory has allowed itself occurs in assumptions about the time-path by which prices, and quantities supplied and demanded, will move towards a market-clearing adjustment when a 'dis-equilibrium' situation has emerged.

The formal transition from a solution of a system of conditionally preferred timeless actions, to a system where the actions are described as the exchange of stated quantities of goods per unit of time, involves and illuminates no problems. It is a purely formal and ineffective change of dimension of the description of the actions from 'exchange of x units of good X' to 'exchange of x units of good X per t units of time', a change from dimension x to dimension xt^{-1}. In itself, it makes no difference to anything. It is only when we suppose these quantities to form parts of *continuing* flows that possibilities and difficulties arise. We can now ask: Suppose a set of flows has been going on which does not satisfy the criterion of being the best that every member of the society can do for himself, given equal freedom with every other member, and perfect relevant knowledge? Attempted adjustments will begin. How are these to be guided? As one member adjusts his action to the existing set of flows, similar initiatives by other members will alter that set and stultify his action. Trial and error may conceivably lead each individual to modify his action in the right direction, until by a miraculous chance all arrive, at the same instant, at what will prove to be a general solution, a general equilibrium. But it is evident that the problem of describing what, in general terms, a solution would be like when found, or even that of computing a specific solution to a particular set of conditional intentions (intentions stated as equations with prices as variables) is different in nature from that of showing whether, how and why such an equilibrium would be attained by realistic market processes from a non-equilibrium. The second involves (while the former takes as solved) the question how individuals will acquire needed knowledge, and what specific policies and actions they will adopt, in its absence, in order to acquire it. Every such a question, applied to each and every individual, is open to an infinity of different answers, amongst which the analyst's choice is perfectly arbitrary.

26.4 *In a non-momentary world prices are* convention

It is, of course, impossible for the individual interest, whether person or firm, to keep continuously under review all the possibilities, existing at any time and changing all the time, of satisfying its needs more cheaply or of adapting its methods and products so that its needs themselves become such as can be more efficiently satisfied. Partly for this reason, and partly for more fundamental reasons, many prices are what they are by convention or by 'accident'. The real business of the market is a continual patching and piecemeal improvement of an always obsolescent set of prices. To speak in this way, however, is itself misleading. It tacitly assumes that some notional set of prices exists at any moment which, if it prevailed, would be 'correct' or 'optimal' by some objective standard. It is this notion of the existence of a meaningfully determinate equilibrium, in any setting except that of the timeless world, that we are calling in question. In any other world, prices are *convention*. They depend upon expectation, which is *originative*. When public prices must be agreed amongst those who are in some respects free to invent the suppositions on which those prices must rest, and who are indeed obliged to invent them since they are not supplied by observation of what is actual, the prices which are agreed are one set out of infinitely many possibilities. Prices thus agreed may properly be called conventional: 'For want of better reason for choosing some other price, let us agree on so-and-so'.

26.5 *Time inseparable from tool-using*

The idea of a process of accumulation involves time both as measurable lapse and as extension, and the latter in two ways. Lapse of time must be present as the necessary condition, the vehicle or at least the reflection of a transformation, the carrying-up of the accumulating pile to a larger size. The amount which is added to the pile between two dates will be a function of the 'distance' between those dates, and this distance can evidently be conceived as measurable on an axis, the 'calendar axis'. And the process of accumulation must evidently be viewed by any participant in it from some one date on that axis, so that he will have either to consider a record of something past or contemplate an intended process having some purpose associated with a future date. That future date will be at some particular 'distance' from his viewpoint date, and thus will again involve the idea of extension. Such ideas are difficult to express without circularity or tautology. We can at any rate say that the appropriate formal expression of accumulation, the integral, evidently incorporates an argument variable to which there must correspond an axis. On this calendar-axis we can mark our dates, one of them the participant's viewpoint, another the date to which his intentions and expectations look forward, a third perhaps the date which 'the record' or 'the books' show to have inaugurated the process of accumulation. Time bulks large in the notion of purposeful human accumulation. But accumulation is inherent in any mode of living other than the purest tool-less hand-to-mouth gathering of food. The use of tools, of an inventory of partly prepared materials, of equipment or produced facilities of any kind, implies that there has been accumulation. The intention to produce or improve tools or productive facilities is the intention to accumulate.

26.6 *Reason must compromise with time*

It is plain that in order to achieve a theory of value applicable to the real human situation, reason must compromise with time. Many different expedients have been harnessed to this purpose. One of them is merely an evasion. We can be content to compare a number of different equilibria, without assigning any meaning to the question how any transition could be made from one to another. Indeed, since the motive power of any such transition could come from sources of the widest diversity, and might be expected in general to influence the path taken by the transition, and to govern the character of the new equilibrium, if any, that was attained, no general theory of movement between equilibria seems practicable. At most we may devise an arbitrary theory, and not one theory but an indefinite number. But a prior question is that of the meaning to be ascribed to the equilibria which are being compared.

If they are conceived as timeless or as time-discrete equilibria, it is evident that no question of the nature of a transition from one to another could arise. We must, instead, regard them as successive states of a continuing economy, where at any one date the members will be choosing their immediate conduct in the light of its assumed effects and of envisaged possible states and transformations of the economy. But since the analyst usually wishes to regard transformations of the economy as governed by autonomous circumstances surrounding it, which by their own changes render one equilibrium obsolete and impose the need for a new one, he will wish to be rid of transformations which would arise otherwise than in response to external circumstance. He will therefore assimilate an *equilibrium* to a *stationary state*. It has very usually been tacitly assumed that this assimilation is legitimate and easy without any need for justification or discussion. It has not been thought necessary to break down the simple assimilation into detailed assumptions. Nonetheless the kinds of assumption which are called for are of some interest. There must plainly be no propensity on the part of the members of the society all taken together to accumulate goods into a stock-pile, or to make durable tools. Such actions would constitute a departure from stationariness. No difficulty need be felt over accepting this. But it will also be necessary for the outfit of equipment and inventories of raw and partly processed materials, possessed by the society at the outset of a calendar-interval of stationariness, to be so composed of this quantity of this item and that quantity of that item, and for all these items to be so orientated, that this outfit of equipment can, and will, be *self-maintaining* in a stationary condition. There must be enough trees ripe for felling to supply just that quantity of timber which is going to be needed to repair the houses and ships which are about to fall to pieces, enough younger trees approaching maturity to replace those which are going to be felled, neither too many nor too few for an exact replacement; and so on and so forth throughout the entire catalogue of kinds and items of equipment. It is needless to add that the members of the society must be devoid of ambitions or inventive powers, they must learn nothing and forget nothing. How, we are bound to ask, can a process of transition from one state to another come about in such a way as to leave no dis-equilibrating traces in the minds or the material possessions of the members? It must be concluded that the notion of *equipment* must be banned from such models. Transitions from one stationary state to another can be studied only in the context of a hand-to-mouth subsistence economy.

26.7 *Kaleidic interpretation*

Comparative statics, the detailed structural comparison of time-less systems, or of stationary states, differing from each other in their internal proportions, is an obvious and essential step in exploiting the economic theoretician's central method, the assumption that economic events are the result of the inter-action of persons (or *individual interests*) guided by reason fully supplied with knowledge. It does not lead us to an under-standing of movement. It seems natural to assume that each of the interests involved in a non-equilibrium situation in a con-tinuing economy will be groping and experimenting in order to bring his own affairs into the best attainable relation to the rest of the economic society *as it is* at any moment. Further, we may perhaps permissibly assume that such efforts of all the members of society will gradually attain a concert or recon-ciliation, and that if tastes, technology and institutions are assumed constant, and speculative and expectational factors somewhat passive, a new equilibrium will be approximately attained. The route to that equilibrium can only be described if we are willing to make a mass of arbitrary assumptions. It is surely better to regard the process as non-determinable and disorderly. The equilibrium which is eventually attained may well depend in its character on that of the route which has led to it. Nonetheless this *kaleidic method* may offer some hope of fusing the variety of strands which the comparative static and other lines of thought suggest. The wish to make such a fusing rigorously logical and demonstrative is an ambition that seems bound either to distort the resulting conception of economic society, or to deny us insights which are not necessarily useless because not strictly, or even tenuously, proven.

26.8 *The limits of* ceteris paribus

It is the method of particular equilibrium, and of *ceteris paribus*, the study of a small simplified and insulated part of the eco-nomic society, a single individual or firm, the making and selling of a single commodity, which allows processes of adjustment to be studied while the question how participants can be sufficiently informed of their circumstances is held at bay. For *ceteris paribus* can allow us to suppose that the individual interest can base its actions on the observation of one price or one weekly or yearly quantity, and can thus proceed by trial and error, by *tâtonnements* or by re-contract. With the further assumption of perfect competition, we can have stable curves of demand and supply intersecting at a price–quantity point which will clear the market, and which can be discovered by the natural procedure of reducing or raising price in face of excess supply or excess demand. But the stability of the curves still depends on our excluding changeable expectation and speculation.

26.9 *Reason or Reality?*

Human nature impels men to apply reason to their affairs, the human situation turns those affairs into problems of policy and action which overwhelm the fragmentary, doubtful, disordered and often seemingly self-contradictory evidence and suggestion which the general scene supplies for their reason to work on. Ought the analyst, then, to abjure problems which do not yield demonstrative solutions? Or ought he to examine the psychic processes, transcending and supplanting reason, which serve for guidance where data are lacking and demonstration at a loss? The disgust with theory which economists express from time to time is partly, we think, due to an awareness of the intimate involvement of the producer with technological matters, with questions on which economic theory has nothing to say, questions which are the field of the engineer, chemist, metallurgist, soil scientist, geneticist. These questions, which occupy, directly or by delegation, an important part of the business man's time, and may even account for the emphasis placed in earlier days on cost of production as the explanation of value, are dismissed by the economic theoretician as no concern of his, save in their broadest outlines and effects. He assumes their answers known. He has lately concerned himself with the cost of getting the answers, but here by a strange irony economics finds itself defeated. The worth of new knowledge cannot begin to be assessed until we have it. By then it is too late to decide how much to spend on breaching the walls to encourage its arrival.

Over against the theoreticians there has often stood a Descriptive (or Historical) School. Such a School will always be able to make a seductive case (we use the term in no pejorative sense) since they need not place any particular boundaries on their field of interest and can describe all details of 'what appears', whether these concern organization, institutions, law, technology, business practice or any detail of life. A descriptive approach wishes to let 'facts' speak for themselves. But the General Scene, the panorama of human affairs, can be described in terms of any one of an infinity of different classifications, that is, of different languages, for a fact is the response of things to ideas, namely, to those pre-shaped and pre-arranged filing cabinets by the filling of which 'facts' come into being. Description is taxonomy, and taxonomy is theory, but theory aspires to be more than taxonomy. For taxonomy is expediency. But ought there not also to be a Principle? It was because theory, the Theory of Value, believed itself to have found a principle, the principle that men act by reason in adapting the conditions of Nature to their needs, that theory was prepared to go to any lengths in preserving this inestimable gift, and assigning to it over-riding prerogatives and rights, even in face of the silent fatality of time.

BOOK V

Diachronism:
The Artefact of Time

27

Diachronism: The Assimilation of Time to Space

27.1 *The calendar-intuition*

Time, when this word appears in the diagrams of economists, is a label affixed to an axis, that is, to the visual presentation of a *space with succession*. A space, in the most general and abstract sense of the word, is simply a class or set of items. These may be numerical values, or locations somehow specified, or mere names. The pegs on a hat-stand constitute a space; so do the names of houses in a directory, or of horses in a race. *Succession* is a super-posed idea. It may be implicit in the character of the class of items. If these are numbers, succession will belong to the nature of this space. But in general, a space is a class, and not a sequence, of items. The calendar is evidently a *class with natural succession*. Yet when we say evidently, what is the evidence?

Let it not be thought that we are here involved in saying what is meant by succession. *Successor* is one of the mathematicians' elemental indefinables. We are supposed to recognize succession, but not to reduce it to anything more basic. How then, do we know that moments follow one another? How do we know that another moment will follow this present one? For if we are prepared at all to speak of *a moment*, we have surely to admit that each present moment is *solitary*. The moment of actuality, the moment in being, the moment of experience, has its unity. There can be no two moments side by side, each claiming to be *present*. However, the nature of the present moment is that of something experienced, and this implies that it is something about which we make discovery, which brings in new knowledge. The present exists by transforming itself into a different present. This transformation is continuous, at any rate nothing in our experience seems to deny such continuity. The present moment thus appears to be paradoxical, something which we feel to have a unity and an exclusive solitariness, yet to be continuously, smoothly transformed, across bounds which continually dissolve, into a different identity. The essential nature of the idea which we name as 'the present moment' is such as to imply and involve a successor-moment, which in turn must have a successor, and so on. Thus the *calendar-intuition*.

27.2 *Time as an axis-label*

The calendar of course involves something beyond 'space' and beyond succession. It implies measurement. But this merely requires us to select some cycle of transformation such as the position of the sun, or other feature of the firmament, in relation to the terrestrial horizon. Measurement of time requires the assumption that some easily recognizable cycle will repeat itself as long as we need it, together with the willingness to define a unit of duration as the lapse of time required for the cycle to complete itself. The quality of being a space in the abstract and general sense; the idea of succession; the possibility of measurement; these are the constituents of the conception which we represent visually in our diagrams as an axis labelled 'time'. The implications and temptations of this proceeding ought to be considered.

27.3 *The actual present. The figment of extensive time*

One character of our notion of 'the present' is better suggested by the spectrum of natural colours. The wave-lengths and their corresponding colours are distinct, yet they dissolve imperceptibly into one another without sharp or uniquely defined bounds. 'The present' is not a *point* representable, let us say, by a number in the continuum of real numbers. For 'the present' is a transformation, an event, an entity with structure or configuration. This is evidently not merely a 'timeless' structure which could find elbow-room in a dimension orthogonal to that of time, for transformation, in our intuitions, implies earlier and later. Within 'the present' there is in some sense a brief span, 'the present' is a binocular conception involving a comparison of stages or of viewpoints. On the calendar-axis, then, 'the present' must occupy a brief segment. But this segment will be exceedingly brief, and to say so is meaningful even if we cannot in any way say how long the present is. The expression *the present moment* must be allowed to express our direct and irreducible intuition.

If, then, the present is solitary, if all thought and experience are compressed into 'a single moment', what does the rest of the calendar-axis mean? To treat the rest of it as in every way comparable and of like significance with the present will be a denial of reality. In the scheme of things which bounds human experience, one moment by itself is present, though it exists only in the act of disappearing into a different moment. The present alone is available for inspection. The knowledge of the *eye-witness* is confined to it. By what warrant shall we fill the rest of a calendar-axis with anything in particular? That part of the calendar which represents 'the past' can be filled with what the visible present suggests or implies about the past, and with what memory tells of it. The record of archaeology, written history and the account-books is part of the visible present. It can be projected on to that part of the calendar to which it refers. Our mode of thought requires us to assimilate *time*, in one of its senses, with *a space with succession*, in order that we may arrange the record appropriately in our thoughts. Part of the calendar-axis, then, can be filled with material provided by the presently visible or memorable record. Does this warrant us in filling the other part, on the other side of the present, with some content from somewhere? From where is such content to come?

27.4 *In what sense do we suppose the future 'faithful to the past'?*

Evidently we can fill it only by supposing that *in some sense* it will be faithful to the past. The essence of our difficulty, as analysts or as enterprisers, is to say what the mode of that faithfulness is, in what ways and degrees it will be qualified or subverted by *novelty*. There are plainly great dangers, and perhaps two in particular, closely linked with each other. In searching the record for evidence of repetition, evidence of

stereotypes, we are likely to treat the field of economic phenomena as self-contained and self-sufficient; and we are likely to
look for large-scale and encompassing repetitions rather than
those which may belong to the fine structure of human affairs.
History may use largely the same building-blocks from age to
age, without by any means producing similar buildings. The
limitless diversity of natural orders and species of living things
depends ultimately, we are told, on a unified basic bio-
chemistry. The structure to be studied is, perhaps, that which
determines what *can* happen.

It may be that the shapes of the building-blocks of human
affairs constrain or bound, without determining, the large-
scale constructions which can exist. If so, what are we to say of
the fact, which seems to be evidenced to us by inference from
what lies before our eyes, that history has in the past taken one
particular course? Only one story has been really lived. If we
suppose that in some sense there are variant possibilities for
what is to come, how do we explain that history took in the
past the particular course that it did, and no other? Such words
offer themselves as *randomness, inspiration.* No clue is known as to
why one particular atom of radium disintegrates at a particular
point of the calendar. This, on the face of it, seems to be something to which 'randomness' applies. But to say so is merely to
acknowledge ignorance of the nature of this phenomenon.
There may be 'random' heritable mutations of living species,
of which a very few confer upon the individuals a decisive
advantage in some environment which has arisen or is available,
so that Nature 'selects' these individuals to propagate their
particular mutation, and the new species with its special
aptitudes (or its general decisive superiority, e.g. of brain-
power) survives. Or a quite different formulation can be found.

Let us concede to the formal analyst of conduct that men
choose according to reason. If the data of the problem are insufficient, they *originate* some hypothesis to take the place of
data. Choice is always amongst thoughts, for it is always too
late to choose amongst facts. Then the problem we are engaged
with is pushed back one stage, and the question becomes: What
determines the thoughts? So we can give up 'randomness' in
favour of 'inspiration'. The point of all this argument is not,
however, to advance an explanation but to ask whether the

uniqueness of the past is a warranty for supposing that a unique future is implicit in that past, or in 'the nature of things' which underlies that history? For if not, we shall be well advised, perhaps, to use models of conduct and of human affairs, which do not pre-suppose a determinable determining structure in the sources and bases of those affairs.

27.5 *The past sufficient to the future: an unwarrantable supposition*

We referred to two dangers. Let us try to justify this suggestion. It does not seem warrantable to suppose that economic affairs are an insulated, separately explicable, part of human affairs in general. The human struggle to survive, to acquire and to expand, expresses itself in forms of action which we call economic or diplomatic or political or warlike. The boundaries are unreal, a mere intellectual convenience. Unless we are pre-pared to build an all-encompassing model of human conduct and society, our model of any aspect of this conduct must be one which seeks, not to show that men are bound to act in this one way or that one way, but to list the ways in which they are capable of responding to this or that set of circumstances external to the special field of conduct (economic, political, etc.) in which we are interested. The model of economic con-duct cannot plausibly seek to be self-contained. If we do treat it, consciously or otherwise, as self-contained and self-sufficient, we shall be the more likely to suppose, not only that purely economic affairs are sufficient to themselves, but also that the past is sufficient to the future. Both suppositions seem to lack evidence in their support, both seem to fly in the face of all experience. Economics has gained powerfully from its posses-sion of a test by which to tell whether given phenomena are 'economic' or not, the test of their involvement in valuation and exchange. But this power to distinguish economic aspects of conduct, of the inter-action of conduct, and of human affairs in general, has often been mistaken for the power to treat these aspects as the whole of something which can be studied by itself in disregard of that deep intricate skein of interests, thoughts and powers in which it is inextricably bound up.

27.6 *Evidence for extensive time not evidence for determinism*

The belief that there will be other moments than the present; that these moments will succeed or flow into one another; that this procession of distinguishable moments may be thought of as a *space with succession*, an axis; this belief as a whole suggests insidiously that not only the axis, the futurity of time, can be thought to exist, but that therefore its cóntent also must in some sense exist. But such a linking of ideas is a non-sequitur. The assimilation of time to the space of our senses, 'space' in the conversational meaning of the word, seems to proceed by a false analogy. What exists is in the present. If we claim or suggest that the situation or events of one date are the outcome or constrained sequel of those of an earlier date, we ought to show in principle, or at least to recognize the need to show, by what *vehicle* the influence of the earlier states or transformations is carried into the later ones. In purely physical matters we need do no more than refer to the observed fact that physical changes are slow, regular and accountable. But does this apply to thoughts?

27.7 *Differential equations and description of human affairs*

The temptation to assimilate time with a physical space may no doubt arise in part from the description of physical movement by means of differential equations. The structure of a differential equation whose argument is time has two faces. It describes in some sense the structure of the *general moment* in some particular defined respect or subject matter; in so doing it describes the structure of the present moment, a specimen of the general moment in respect of the particular subject-matter. But the differential equation, if it can be solved, furnishes an algebraic expression which describes a curve or path in the large, the entire trajectory or *course* of movement. If we examine in this light the tacit pre-supposition that time can be assimilated to an axis, not merely for description of history but for explanation of the engenderment of history, the question to be asked becomes the question whether human affairs are amenable to be described by means of a differential equation. When time appears to us as an axis, and as one axis of a Cartesian frame whose other axes serve the representation of economic variables, there is a strong temptation to ascribe a permanent existence to determinate paths which economic affairs are obliged to follow. We are accustomed to the notion of planetary orbits along which the planets travel in a manner which, for practical purposes, is perfectly predictable. Their doing so can be explained as a consequence of relations of mass, momentum and distance which are in a formal sense essentially simple. It can be said that a planet follows such an orbit because of two things: the nature of the universe, manifested in the laws of physics; and the past history of its own motion. Both circumstances are implicitly combined in the differential equation of planetary motion. If, then, the large features of the universe work by mechanism, by a mechanism which so pre-destines their behaviour that we can literally describe it by a curve drawn on paper, a curve which we are thus led to think of as resembling the track prescribed for a race, existing in its own right and as a whole no matter whether the runners are at this point of it or that, it will be natural to transfer, consciously or otherwise, some parallel of this conception to human affairs. Yet it is at least plain that if there is a mechanism of those affairs, it does not share the basic simplicity of celestial mechanics. And it must surely be an open question whether 'mechanism' is a term that can properly be applied to an engenderment of events which involves the continued acquisition of knowledge, the endless composing of imaginative figments concerning what those events will be, and the, at least ostensible, shaping of the events themselves by human decisions or choices resting on those products of imagination. There is a great divorce between the view we take of our affairs in our capacity as *participants*, players of a game whose course we feel ourselves to be helping to shape, and the view we take as scholars, spectators of a stage play whose script we think we ought to be able, with a little more attention to previous scenes and a little more extensive knowledge of the business of the dramaturge, to read and to foresee. In the scholar's paradoxical view, all history has a real existence, all its moments, though their meaning depends upon their possessing sequence in time, none the less co-exist at every present moment. The real co-existence of the stages of history is in the scholar's mind, and this he would doubtless acknowledge. Yet the sequential *meaning* of those stages must tend to establish history in his intuitive view as something other than mere thought. When we compel ourselves to take the stance of pure observers, when we banish from thought everything that does not lie before our eyes, we are obliged to say that from this viewpoint, time as an axis, as a space, is an artefact of thought.

27.8 *The cyclical temporal frame and the spatial intuition of time*

The spatial intuition of time, time as room for something, is strongly suggested and supported by the insistent, inescapable natural repetitive frame of life. The cycles of the hours and seasons are in a sense a landscape which can be revisited. It is said that with certain peoples whose way of life is simple and 'unprogressive' this is the dominant view of the matter: existence itself is cyclical, and brings us back constantly to the same sunrise and the same summer. People who suffer a more varied history are conscious that today is not the same day as yesterday, and that whether or not history in terms of aeons is cyclical, it is not cyclical in terms of the centuries. Yet even with this awareness our common speech betrays the desire for return, for continual recognition of things which do not change. We speak, with satisfaction and moral comfort, of tea-time, of harvest-time, of 'the' week-end, of proper-named days of the week or months. We 'come round again' to the beginning of the academic year. The proper names, Thursday or April or Michaelmas Term, the word 'the', implies identity in some sense. In a landscape we can move about at will, in time we cannot do so in the same sense. Yet in so far as life is repetitive and cyclical, we can do so by merely waiting. It is the cyclical aspects of nature that enable us to measure the lapse of time. What can be *measured* is surely real? The cyclical temporal frame gives us locations in which to place remembered, re-corded or 'expected' events. This effect is strengthened by the mutual consistency and unvarying pace of the natural cycles when measured in terms of each other. There is a *context* of cyclical processes, a 'flow of time'. By a certain paradox, it is the cyclical character of some phenomena which makes possible the temporal location of those events which are singular and non-repetitive.

27.9 *Stereotypes of experience and time as a* space with succession

Theory in many disciplines is of course the study of temporal sequence, the study of transformations. The elemental basis of systematic *knowledge by experience* is that things of certain kinds happen in a fixed configuration which can be described only by saying that two specified phenomena were concomitant, or else that they were sequential. Induction may be insecurely based in logic, but it is the means of our learning to cope with practical life. The fixed configurations, the stereotypes, serve a three-fold but unified purpose. They tell us what to expect, for when the 'early' part of such a pattern is seen to be present, the rest is counted on to follow. The stereotype tells us, as it were, not to be disturbed when something which forms the later part of such a pattern occurs unexpectedly. For search may reveal traces of the earlier parts having, after all, occurred in their right place, though they escaped notice. The finding of these traces is *explanation*. And the stereotype provides us with technology. It tells us what state of affairs must precede, if a specified desired state is to follow. Whether we use or eschew the term 'cause and effect' seems to have no practical bearing. If we have gained an assurance that the stereotype in question is robust, has a power of survival, that is all that matters. If we believe ourselves free, in some sense, to select this situation rather than that, and if we know that this selected situation has regularly been *followed in time* by the situation which we desire, we may claim if we like that we have 'caused' the desired transformation. Or we may deem such a phrase to be a pointless gloss, neither justified nor refutable. But sequence in time comes into the matter of description of configurations or stereotypes, and these are the building-blocks of explanation, of scientific (i.e. conditional) prediction, and of technology. Time as a *space with succession* is perhaps an artefact of thought, but an indispensable one.

28

Marshall's Accommodation of Time

28.1 *Permanence at the heart of change*

'The element of time is the centre of the chief difficulty of almost every economic problem.'* Marshall's statement places him far along the road of realism, yet still in some sense turning aside from the full strength of the matter. For we might object that time is not only a source of the difficulty which the analyst of value encounters, but is the very nature and being of his subject matter. Thought, action and event, history and novelty are the face of time. It must be questionable whether in any attempt to describe our world, meaningful withdrawal and abstraction from time is possible. Yet value theory in its rigorous form must deny it any mention. Value theory thus appears as a branch of mathematics, whose nature of pure logical construction, independent of any observational reference, absolves it from considering time and, indeed, allows it only to import into its fabric a suitably de-natured concept, time as a *space* in the abstract sense, a range of variation of a variable. Marshall's statement may be deemed to convey just a hint of regret that the problem of economic conduct and events cannot be freed from the necessity of considering succession, the fact that things happen one after another. Yet to say so is querulous. For the *Principles* is a relentless effort to bring into one fabric of argument the two incompatibles, the analysis of conduct by virtue of its being reasonable, and the denial to reason of the means of its full exercise, the denial to it of knowledge of that part of the succession of circumstances which is still to come into being. Marshall speaks consistently of business men as being motivated by what they expect. His curious elliptical, or telescopic, conception of the long-period supply curve is expressly designed to bring into the picture of

* *Principles of Economics*, first edition, Preface, p. vii.

[286]

the business man's policy problem the latter's awareness that a step-by-step expansion of his scale of operations will bring into view the practical detail of possible economies of large scale. The long-period supply curve is (among other things) an envisagement *ex ante* of possibilities confidently foreseen in general effect but awaiting a careful and gradual exploration in order to come fully within reach. Marshall was no timeless abstractionist. Yet he was a mathematically trained analyst seeking to understand what he saw men doing by considering what they ought reasonably to be attempting. He sought, with limitless patience, high practical wisdom, resolute realism and subtle innovation to spin together into a serviceable thread of thought, the mutually repellent strands of rationality and novelty.

Marshall saw that a basic dilemma faces the economist. His aim is to construct a science, a body of principles giving insight into economic conduct, organization and events at every time and place; yet 'The central idea of economics, even when its Foundations are under discussion, must be that of living force and movement', and 'The main concern of economics is thus with human beings who are impelled, for good or evil, to change and progress.'* Science is the seeking for, and the attempt to represent by words or other symbols, something permanent and *un*-changing at the heart of things. Can the basic stuff and essence of the world be such as to explain its perpetually evolving life-forms and the endless flux of human history and affairs? Marshall worked in the immediate glow of the Darwinian revolution of thought, and at a time when Britain led the world in technological advance. He was convinced that the economist must study change. Yet he must be a seeker of principles and not a mere chronicler of the superficial. How was this contradiction to be resolved? An attentive and reflective reader of Marshall must surely come to recognize that the *Principles* is, in the main, an intense and unremitting struggle with this central theme. The pre-occupation with it gripped Marshall's mind and shaped his thought. His style, so placid and relaxed in some of its aspects, disguises the single-minded concentration which this problem exacted from him. His most

* *Principles*, Preface to the eighth edition, p. xv.

difficult passages of converging suggestion, his central innovations, his most vivid concrete examples, are all concerned with it.

28.2 *'Continuity', 'the Normal' and the landslide technique*

One idea to which Marshall had recourse was that if change
was continuous in the sense of proceeding by such small steps
and in such varying respects as to be only perceptible over long
intervals, the principles which generated change at one date
would still be recognizably at work, even if they had themselves
meanwhile been modified, at later dates, the sources of whose
events would again be reflected later on, so that the analyst
when considering each date and stage would feel that the
system he was studying had not lost touch with its earlier nature
and that the insight he gained into one stage had some relevance
to other stages. What distinct and clear case can be made for
deeming this argument valuable and useful? It means that if
the object under study was the mode of operation of an
economic society during, perhaps, one generation, one observer's active lifetime, it could be regarded as having unity and
identity in the same way as the biography of an individual can
be seen to deal with a unified whole despite the maturing and
ageing of the person concerned. In his Preface, Marshall
devotes some paragraphs to what he calls the Principle of
Continuity. This term seems to stand for something which
many aspects of our experience have in common. It is summed
up on the title-page as *Natura non facit saltum*. It is this term and
this phrase which I have sought to gloss as an appeal to the
gradualness of change as a means of ascribing to it permanent
and discoverable causes. For in the body of his book Marshall
gradually makes clear a more distinct technique. He supposes
some shift of circumstances to occur in matters which are not
the direct concern of the economist, some shift of taste, technology or natural conditions, and then traces its successive
consequences on the supposition that this shift is a single,
isolated and once-for-all occurrence which leaves people to
work out stage by stage their economic response to it. Within
this frame he speaks of the 'Normal'. The Normal, in the
matter of price, daily or yearly quantity supplied, quantity of

resources employed in a given industry and so on, is the response for which time in two respects is sufficient. There must be time enough for the technological process of adaptation to occur, and there must be the prospect of the altered circumstances of demand or supply continuing long enough to make the response worth while. If both these pre-conditions are fulfilled in the ultimate degree, we have the Long Period, allowing adaptation to go the full length which the participant business man, or perhaps the analyst himself, can reasonably discern. The Normal is what *would* come about, given the 'experimental' or *ceteris paribus* conditions which, in fact, cannot be preserved. If time for adaptation is prescribed by the analyst as shorter than might be eventually needed, or if the duration of the new circumstances is assumed to be limited, then there will be a 'normal' adaptation in respect of these restricted opportunities. The Normal is relative to the opportunities. Insisting on the continuity of change, Marshall shows how it can be dissected into stages each having its own unity and rationale.

28.3 *The long-period supply curve*

Marshall shows us the long period from two viewpoints, that of the business man who stands, as it were, upon the calendar axis and looks, by imaginative construction based on suggestions offered by the past and the present, *along* it to future dates, and that of the detached and knowledgeable observer who stands outside the participant's axis and can view all its distinct dates as co-valid. In a more modern idiom than Marshall's we might say that the participant business man takes necessarily an *ex ante* view of the stretch of time in which his present decisions will take their effect, while the analyst can take an *ex post* view of what to the (imaginary or hypothetical) participant still lies ahead. The participant at each location of his 'present moment' is concerned to make or modify a policy or a plan. The analyst can ask himself what features will be typical of the experience of the business man as his 'present moment' takes up successive locations. The reader familiar with Marshall will know that he does not articulate his thought in this way or make any express distinction of the viewpoints. Yet it is, upon reflection, *essential* to the economist's task that he should see himself in the two capacities, first as participant, the *prisoner of the present*, able to escape from the instant of existence only in imagination and figment; and secondly as disembodied surveyor of history, able to move at will through its successive epochs and to record, not this super-human reproducing or pre-producing of events, but the illumination it can throw on the real participant's predicament, the unforgiving compulsion to decide and act or else to suffer events to decide for him by default. Perhaps it is not unjust to Marshall's profound insight to say that he made this vital distinction by instinct rather than by express steps of reasoning, and in consequence did not fully unravel his complex skein of thought for the benefit of his reader. He, in fact, gave it a very elliptical expression which the reader would often prefer to have had in a fully spelled-out form. For the long-period supply curve combines both viewpoints into one statement and one diagram. The curve is an expression of what the participant broadly and imprecisely expects, necessarily in general terms. In this aspect it need not, and cannot, be a picture, accurate or even approximate in detail, of what it alternatively stands for, the path followed by the firm as time passes. That path, as a portion of real history, can only be known by waiting until the stretch of time in question has elapsed; by waiting until the *ex post* viewpoint, for that proper-named interval or segment of the calendar, has been attained. In a theoretical context it is open to the analyst to provide himself with sufficient assumptions to show what path will be followed by the abstract firm in its abstract circumstances. Marshall's most concise and satisfactory account of the long-period supply curve is to be found in his Appendix H, 'Limitations of the use of statical assumptions in regard to increasing return', footnote 2 to page 809 of the eighth edition:

One difficulty arises from the fact that a suitable time to allow for the introduction of the economies appertaining to one increase in the scale of production is not long enough for another and larger increase, so we must fix on some fairly long time ahead, which is likely to be indicated by the special problem in hand, and adjust the whole series of supply prices to it. We could get much nearer to nature if we allowed ourselves a more complex illustration. We might take a series of curves, of which the first allowed for the economies likely to be introduced as the result of each increase in the scale of production during one year, a second curve doing the same for two years, a third for three years, and so on. Cutting them out of cardboard and standing them up side by side, we should obtain a surface, of which the three dimensions represented amount, price and time respectively. If we had marked on each curve the point corresponding to that amount which, so far as can be foreseen, seems likely to be the normal amount for the year to which that curve related, then these points would form a curve on the surface, and that curve would be a fairly true long period normal supply curve for a commodity obeying the law of increasing return.

Here as everywhere, Marshall wants the mutual confrontation of the demand and supply conditions of a commodity to be described by means of curves, each a relation between price per unit measured on one axis and (daily or annual) quantity measured on the other. But in order to treat price as a function only of daily or annual quantity supplied, and to take all other circumstances as given, we must specify the number of years available to the business man, between his present moment and the date when supply is to flow at a named scale, for introducing the economies which that scale makes possible. Once that available preparation time is specified, any one scale will, in Marshall's conception which our quoted passage describes, allow certain economies in production to be applied, and it is the particular character of those economies which will determine the supply price per unit at any hypothetical scale. In the end, therefore, supply price has to be looked on as a function of both scale of production and time available for preparation. If, despite this, we insist with Marshall on a curve and not a surface, one curve and not a family of curves, what is to be done? In the first sentence of our quoted passage, he proposes simply to select a particular length of preparation-time according to the problem in hand. But in the rest of the passage, he is proposing by implication to call in aid an estimate of demand conditions for each future date so as to find, for each such date, its equilibrium price–quantity point, whereupon the locus of these points, which will be a 'twisted curve' or 'space-curve' whose points are located in three dimensions, will be regarded as the *long-period supply curve*.

This is a strange procedure, and hard to justify. The purpose of confronting with each other a demand curve and a supply curve is to exhibit the mode of determination of that price–quantity pair which can represent both demand conditions and supply conditions simultaneously, and is therefore the market-clearing equilibrium. But Marshall's long-period supply curve cannot serve this purpose, since it must call upon a forecast of demand conditions in order that its own shape may be known. In fact, Marshall's long-period supply curve is useful only *ex post*, as a record and statement of the path of expansion which some firm has actually followed. In our quoted passage, Marshall's wording explicitly adopts an *ex ante* view: 'so far as can be foreseen, seems likely to be the normal amount for the [particular] year...' It is more difficult to tell whether this is the view of the participant or of the analyst. In either case, it seems impossible to accept the long-period supply curve, thus arrived at, as an analytical device. It can express a forecast or a piece of history, but it does not preserve the mutual independence of the two sides of the market, in the way which the simple scissors-diagram requires. We ought to notice the presence here of the word *normal*. Is this the means by which Marshall hopes to give back to the long-period supply curve its analytical capacity? Does the reservoir of potential economies of large scale confer upon the firm an inherent law of its own expansion? In a letter to Edgeworth dated 26 April 1892, Marshall refers to Sir Henry Cunynghame's proposal to assign to each of a succession of dates its own pair of mutually intersecting demand and cost curves, a proposal which Marshall was in fact recalling in the passage we quoted above. These were referred to by Sir Henry Cunynghame as 'successive' demand and cost curves, and Marshall notes in parenthesis: '"Successive" may imply a regular correlation of sequences, which there is *not*.'* In repudiating 'a regular correlation of sequences' Marshall seems to be implicitly rejecting any notion of a path of expansion inherent in the nature of a particular firm or in that of firms and their situation in general.

We referred above to the two viewpoints from which Marshall seems to consider the long-period supply curve. In the

---

* Marshall's italics. Letter quoted by Mr Guillebaud in *Principles of Economics*, ninth edition, vol. 2, p. 808 (Editorial Appendix to Appendix H).

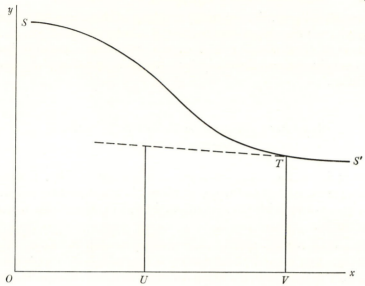

Fig. 28.1. This reproduces the relevant parts of Marshall's Fig. 38 (*Principles*, eighth edition, p. 807). 'Scale of production' is measured on the *Ox*-axis, expenses of production per unit on the *Oy*-axis, *SS'* is the supply curve for expansion, and the curve shown in dashes is the curve for subsequent contraction.

second of these views, the curve seems to stand for a history of the successive attainment of various scales of production, rather than a range of alternatively choosable, mutually exclusive positions. Marshall refers in Appendix H, for example, to what would happen in case an expansion of output was followed by a contraction:

The shape of the supply curve of Fig. 38 [*Principles*, eighth edition, p. 806; see our Fig. 28.1] implies that if the ware in question were produced on the scale *OV* annually, the economies introduced into its production would be so extensive as to enable it to be sold at a price *TV*. If these economies were once effected the shape of the curve *SS'* would probably cease to represent accurately the circumstances of supply. The expenses of production, for instance, of an amount *OU* would no longer be much greater proportionately than those of an amount *OV*. Then in order that the curve might again represent the circumstances of supply it would be necessary to draw it lower down, as the dotted curve in the figure.

Marshall is here quite evidently thinking of the curve SS' of his Fig. 38 (our Fig. 28.1) as a tracing of events, a record, not as a statement of alternative and mutually exclusive possibilities, all conceived simultaneously by a business man at some one moment.

28.4 'Every plain and simple doctrine [of value] is necessarily false'

Economics is the study of a sector of human affairs, human affairs are a part of history, and history is transformation without pause and without repetition. Marshall drove this home untiringly:

The present volume is concerned throughout with the forces that cause movement: and its key-note is that of dynamics, rather than statics. The main concern of economics is thus with human beings who are impelled, for good or evil, to change and progress. Fragmentary statical hypotheses are used as temporary auxiliaries to dynamical – or rather biological – conceptions, but the central idea of economics, even when its Foundations alone are under discussion, must be that of living force and movement.*

'The *forces that cause* movement.' A force is something generalized and abstract. If there were as many 'forces' as there are movements each uniquely identifiable by its form or circumstances, the 'forces' would be mere casual and diverse concomitants with nothing in common: they would provide no explanation, they would do nothing to give insight or bind events into a system. Forces belong to theory, and theory aspires to be universal, to give a meaning to events at all times and places. If, then, the world which we seek to explain is not the same world on any two occasions, how can it be appropriate to speak of 'forces' and 'causation'? Marshall recognized this dilemma:

It is only recently, and to a great extent through the wholesome influence of the criticisms of the historical school, that prominence has been given to that distinction in economics which corresponds to the distinction between strategy and tactics in warfare. Correspond-

---

* *Principles*, Preface to the eighth edition, pp. xiv–xv.

ing to tactics are those outward forms and accidents of economic organization which depend on temporary or local aptitudes, customs and relations of classes; on the influence of individuals; or on the changing appliances and needs of production. While to strategy corresponds that more fundamental substance of economic organization, which depends mainly on such wants and activities, such preferences and aversions as are found in man everywhere. They have a sufficient element of permanence and universality to enable them to be brought in some measure under general statements, whereby the experience of one time and age may throw light on the difficulties of another.*

Commentators of Marshall have been less myopic than those of Maynard Keynes, yet they also have on the whole been interested far more in the detailed arguments of Book v than in the philosophy of the *Principles* as a whole.† The ascendancy of that book, however, is natural and inevitable, since it contains the core of Marshall's technical apparatus and the part which can best be tested by reason. The unifying theme which runs through those chapters is the study of how time-relations govern economic results. Marshall has insisted everywhere that any cutting-up of the stream of history into parcels and stages is arbitrary and unreal. Yet dissection is unavoidable if the structure of circumstance and influence is to be exposed. It is in Book v that the famous apparatus of short and long periods, which has long since become part of the fabric of thought in economics, is developed. It is here that concrete and abstract are blended in the notion, found elusive by so many commentators, of the Representative Firm. And here Marshall shows how the detailed content of the notion of cost and of supply-price depends on the circumstances of the intended production in its aspects of time: whether preparation is being made to fill a single order or to meet a demand expected to

---

* *Principles*, eighth edition, Appendix C, p. 777.
† However, a very distinguished member of the London School of Economics told the author that when, as an undergraduate, she was set to write an essay on the *Principles*, she declared Book v to be 'a digression'. This judgement was, in my view, evidence of a deep insight into the nature of Marshall's basic problem of method: how to make the equilibrium tool serve the analysis of some part of the historical process. Tensions between method and meaning are more evident in Book v, because the equilibrium apparatus there imposes its logical rigours on the argument.

continue for many years. In the midst of Book v Marshall glances briefly at the Stationary State. His view can be seen in two of those marginal summaries which so greatly help the reader to find his way back and forth in the *Principles*: 'In a stationary state the doctrine of value would be simple' (p. 367). 'But in the real world a simple doctrine of value is worse than none' (p. 368, both pages in the eighth edition). On this latter page, Marshall's theme concerning time, cost, demand and value is summed up with an incisive force unusual for him:

In the world in which we live, every economic force is constantly changing its action, under the influence of other forces which are acting around it. Here changes in the volume of production, in its methods, and in its cost are ever mutually modifying one another; they are always affecting and being affected by the character and the extent of demand. Further all these mutual influences take time to work themselves out, and, as a rule, no two influences move at equal pace. In this world therefore every plain and simple doctrine as to the relations between cost of production, demand and value is necessarily false: and the greater the appearance of lucidity which is given to it by a skilful expositor, the more mischievous it is. A man is likely to be a better economist if he trusts to his common sense, and practical instincts, than if he professes to study the theory of value and is resolved to find it easy.

29

Capital, or the Time-Net of Production

29.1 *The* technological structure, *and the* time structure, *of production*

In Fig. 29.1, both axes are scaled in intervals of time. On the west–east axis, an eastward succession of points represents the technological sequence of phases in the production of some object, these phases being spaced according to the lapse of time required for the performance of each phase. On the south–north axis, successive northward points represent sequential dates in the real historical calendar. At any randomly-selected calendar date all the phases in the production of an object of the kind in question will be simultaneously proceeding, and each will be represented by some partly-finished embryo of such an object. Thus at any moment there will be in simultaneous existence a collection of embryonic products, each at a different stage of development towards the complete and perfect object. This collection represents the essence of the notion of the capital involved in the production of objects of the kind in question. If we wish we can trace on such a diagram the (as it were) personal history of an individual, identified or proper-named, embryonic product. At some historical date this proper-named embryonic product will be at the most primitive of its technological stages, perhaps existing as an unshaped mass of native rock or timber. At later dates it will have taken on shape, structure and the accretion of initially separate parts in a growing complexity. At some date it will be complete and finished. Such a life-history will appear on our diagram as a diagonal path running north-eastwards through the points in each of which a technological stage is paired with a calendar date. Lastly, a north–south line erected at any point on the east–west axis will express the notion that at each and every calendar date there has existed or will exist a tangible representation of the particular technological phase which that particular east–west position stands for. At the most primitive stage, for example, a north–south line will express the idea that every day a new block of stone will be carved from the quarry-face or a new length of yarn will be spun from the natural fibres. This, then, is the first of our pictures. But there is a second degree of complexity.

Each momentary phase in that course of events leading to an item of product finished and ready for use will itself consist of many distinguishable operations occurring in different places and affecting separate physical objects, which at subsequent phases will be assembled in order to operate further on each other or to constitute a physical unity. At any one such moment, a variety of materials, ultimately to be incorporated in the finished object, will be being fabricated and fashioned in various work places. Some of the products emerging complete at such a moment will be tools intended for use in later productive activities. Thus the productive organism as a whole, embracing all the work of the society, will consist of a network of channels converging on, and diverging from, nodal points where many contributory embryonic items or *intermediate products* are assembled into the objects representing a further stage, which will then be distributed to many different work places in order to contribute to the activities going on in them. Only at the fringe of this net will some complete products emerge ready for the use and enjoyment of consumers or *final users*.

The appropriate picture of this second aspect of complexity in the general productive scene is the input–output matrix. The scene is divided, in a manner partly arbitrary, partly dictated by technology and partly constrained by convenience of computation, into *sectors* or *activities*, terms for which the word 'industries' can be quite respectably substituted for common-sense purposes. Sectors and products are to be so specified that they can be placed in one–one correspondence. Then in general each sector will supply its product to other (in principle, all) sectors and each will buy supplies of materials, power or durable tools from other sectors. The sectors into which the productive scene is divided are numbered 1, 2, 3, ..., n. In its capacity as a supplier of its product to other sectors, the general or representative sector will be labelled i, and in its capacity as a purchaser of their products from other sectors, it will be

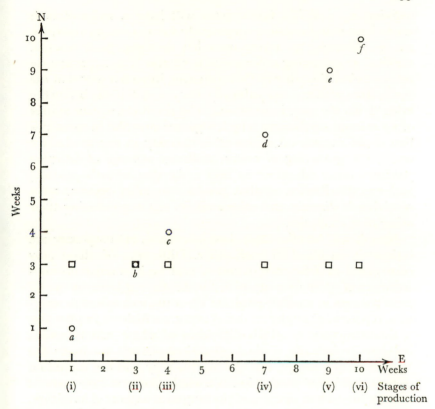

Fig. 29.1. The northward axis represents the calendar, the eastward axis represents the technological stages of the production
process, distributed according to the time required for each stage.
The NE diagonal represents the production history of a particular
parcel, with stages a, b, ..., f. The squares represent co-existing
embryonic parcels.

labelled j. In speaking here of the product of a sector, we mean
the intermediate product or embryonic item which emerges
from the activity of that sector, the goods emerging from its
gates and not merely its *value added*. The value, at given prices,
of the product of sector i annually (or weekly, etc.) bought by
sector j may be written X_{ij}. When this is divided by the value
Z_j, at consistent prices, of the goods annually emerging, as it
were, from the factory gates of sector j, we have an *input*

coefficient $a_{ij} = X_{ij}/Z_j$. Each sector will have a series of such coefficients with j standing respectively for $1, 2, \ldots, n$, and these can be arranged in a row from left to right. Such rows of coefficients belonging successively to sectors $1, 2, \ldots, n$, can be set one below the other in that sequence, in such a way that the coefficients with any one value of j, say $j = 3$, fall one below the other down the page in a column. The result is a square matrix of $n \times n$ input coefficients which together describe in quantitative detail the second aspect of complexity in our productive scene, the gathering of many confluent streams of different products into each sector to help make that sector's product, and the distribution of that product to other sectors, some receiving it directly and others via its aid in producing their other direct supplies.

Now it will be clear that these two kinds of complexity are intimately involved in each other. Difference of phase may correspond to difference of sector, and be in a sense the consequence of it: an item must itself be fabricated before it can be incorporated in another product. Thus the technological structure represented by the matrix of input coefficients implies also a time-structure in which difference of phase can intervene between technically distinct operations. When we study the texture or physiology, and the morphology and the evolution, of the organism of production as a whole, we must take account of both the technological and the temporal aspects of its nature. This is why the title of this chapter refers to *the time-net of production*.

29.2 *Equipment items use-directed and time-directed: the concept of orientation*

The *time-net of production*, or the *capital scene*: by these expressions we mean not only the entire compass of all production-goods existing at some one moment, but the orientation of each item of the list towards other *items* with which they will be combined or to which they will be applied, and also towards other *moments* when they will pass through these intended moves or stages. The capital-complex is not merely a list of items, not merely a list of fields, forests, mines, wells and quarries, of plants, systems, machines, tools, stockpiles, goods awaiting process, transport or sale. It is a list of such items, each of them use-directed and time-directed, possibly to be divided and despatched down many divergent channels, but together exhibiting the momentary, still-picture phase of an intricate dance or drill, the conception of which exists in some sense entire at each such moment, like the score of the music to which the dance is responding. We have to ask in whose mind this conception does exist, how it came into being, what assurance there is that it will ever be actualized, and what influences can deform or disrupt it.

It is obvious that no one mind conceives the whole at any moment, still less accompanies it at all moments. Millions of minds are required to assign at some moment to each item its technological and its temporal orientation. In each mind there can exist in detail a small part only of the whole picture, though perhaps also successively more-inclusive partial pictures with successively less detail. It is apparent that given items in the capital list or capital complex will be included in the pictures conceived by many different minds, and that these pictures need by no means assign to a given item the same, or even compatible, orientations. It is plain, too, that the orientation of any item or class of items need not stay the same in the mind chiefly concerned with it. Intended purpose and application, intended technological or market career, can be adapted to changes of data or of their interpretation.

The orientation of a capital item will be determined by its owner with a view to maximise its value, namely, the exchange-value of it or its services or potentialities on the market, discounted to the present at the market interest-rate prevailing for loans of the term in question. Such is the ideal. The problem of finding the demonstrably most valuable orientation of an item, or the most valuable directions for parts into which it can be divided, is plainly unsolvable in practice and even in logic. This conclusion does not rest on the unthinkable multiplicity of possible time-nets, possible patterns of orientation of all the items existing at some moment. For such multiplicity is present in any market charged with pre-reconciling the choices of great numbers of people with diverse tastes in regard to a rich variety of goods. Provided each member of such a market can list his mutually exclusive conditional preferred actions, one for each of the possible combinations of actions promised by others, it may in principle, by means of a sufficiently powerful computer, or in practice, by the ordinary procedure of the market, refined to a greater or less degree by some such device as re-contract, be possible to find a general solution such as to prescribe for each member the action he would prefer, given the acceptance by all other members of the actions respectively prescribed for them. Multiplicity is then overcome by the publication of tentative prices which are themselves both the guide and the consequence of the actions of all the individuals. The problem of multiplicity is solvable. The problem of novelty is not.

The orientation, at some moment, of the items then composing the capital complex will be such as to imply that this composition will evolve. The destiny of some items, according to their owners' intentions and those of potential purchasers, will be to contribute to the making of durable tools to augment and improve the existing outfit. The orientation will imply positive net investment by the society as a whole. This investment orientation will be partly determined by knowledge which has been gained and technology which has been invented since some of the existing durable equipment was designed. The orientation will have been evolutionary at all previous times for many decades and centuries. It is evident that the existing technological composition of the capital complex is the result of the particular state of knowledge and of expectation which prevailed at each previous date. It is a palimpsest of earlier orientations. We may sum up the whole matter: orientation at any moment is governed by the then state of expectation. Composition at future moments will be partly the consequence of orientation prevailing now. Thus composition depends on past states of expectation, while orientation depends on the present state of expectation. The total value now assigned to the existing capital complex will depend on both composition and orientation, since composition determines what there is to be valued, and orientation defines the uses, directions and destinies (as seen at present) from which the values arise. The chief vehicle which carries the expectations of one age into the equipment of another is evidently the durable part of the capital complex of the former age. The railways of the 1840s provide a frame of transport in the 1970s. Forests must be planted by one generation for the benefit of another. But there is also a strong heredity, if shorter in its effects, amongst non-durable items. What can be made today with least cost for given usefulness depends on what materials exist and what technique has been organized and laid out in the recent past.

29.3 *The bearing of capital theory*

The role of a theory of capital within the general body of economic doctrine has been a peculiar and inconstant one. It was originally designed to explain the nature and justification of an income derived from the possession of a stock of goods which had themselves been produced, as distinct from income derived from work or from the ownership of the soil with its life-giving powers. But since products and money could be exchanged for each other, it seemed plain that some natural balance would come about between the income-yielding power of a stock of products and that of the sum of money for which this stock could be exchanged on the market. Need there be any distinction between a sum of wealth embodied in products and the same sum embodied in money? The income derived from a stock of wealth came, in continental theories, to be treated as one and the same regardless of the form which that wealth happened to take in some hands at some moment. Money, however, can be borrowed and lent. There is no institutional principle or law which forbids it to be lent at a different ratio of income-to-wealth than that currently prevailing for concrete products. Thus disturbances could occur in the asset-market. The general price level of goods of all sorts could be impelled up or down, with consequences on the level of employment and the size of general output. Capital theory thus became en-meshed with the theory of money and both of those theories became involved in theories of the cumulative process of price increases and of the business cycle. Capital theory became, in fact, one of the tributary streams which suddenly coalesced into the great macro-economic river. What were its methods and assumptions in seeking to serve those purposes?

29.4 *Capital requires, and rewards, deferment of the fruits_of effort*

Two gains were scored at one blow by a single arresting and suggestive idea. The very meaning of capital involves the looking forward to results at a later date. Capital is *potential* service and usefulness, what is potential is, at best, in the future. Capital is intermediate products, embryonic items *not yet* ready for application or consumption. To make a tool for productive purposes is to take an indirect but ultimately more fruitful route to that production, a route which many would exploit if there were not some corresponding and ultimately unavoidable disadvantages, a route which means delay for the immediate future in hope of great reward. In short, *capital is time*. This, of course, is too condensed a statement. It means that capital is the manifestation of the role of time lapse in the productive process. But if capital is time, we can measure capital by means of some measure of time. And if so, we can solve the impossible problem of adding together the physical or technological quantities of a vast diversity of items, the items of what we have in this chapter called 'the capital list' or 'the capital complex'. But this is not all. If capital is time, if capital is a looking to the future, then capital is delay. But delay is an inconvenience, a disutility, a discomfort, something which will not be borne except for a reward. Can production by means of capital offer and furnish a reward? It can offer the extra fruitfulness of production by means of tools, of powerful artificial aids to human muscle, human dexterity, human stamina and human manipulative reach; in our own day, even to human power oi calculation. Thus capital seems to demand, and to offer a prize for, the endurance of delay. It can provide, and justify, an income. What will determine that income? It will be such, the theory says, that to increase it by a further extension of the capital stock, and thus a further extension of delay, would entail an extra discomfort not able to be compensated by the extra income: there will be, here as elsewhere, a marginal balance.

29.5 *Questions on meaning and method*

In thus condensing the theory to a few lines, we are able to avoid or elide the difficulties that arise when distinct meanings and explicit assumptions are asked for. What precisely is the mode of expressing a given capital list as a quantity of time lapse? In what sense exactly does an extension of the capital stock entail an extension of delay? What is the *technological* explanation of the power of the capital stock to reward the patience which enables it to be accumulated and maintained? Why is it that this power diminishes as the capital stock is progressively extended, as the theory seems to suggest is the case when referring to a balance, at the margin, between extra reward and extra discomfort? What happens to the time measure of a capital list of specific technological composition, when the orientation of that list changes? Or is the notion of time measure dependent for its meaning on a particular orientation? How does the theory accommodate the contrast between the passive role of those capital items which are intended to become the substance of finished products, and the part played by power-driven and self-regulating tools or systems, which render productive *service* in a manner which closely imitates human labour? In seeking to answer these questions, we shall bear in mind the ultimate purpose of this exercise, which is to judge whether, despite difficulties of detail, the central idea, that a capital stock manifests the role of time lapse in production, can be maintained and applied.

The brief argument of the preceding section is not to be thought of as the 'Austrian theory of capital'. The double connection of time with the capital stock, as both a measure of the size of that stock and an explanation of its being a resource, is to be found in the literature of the Austrian theory. We have taken that powerful suggestion and have sought to give it a form abstract and unencumbered enough for its essence to appear. For the task of spelling it out as a precise and detailed construct has proved baffling and elusive ever since its origination in the 1880s. Its chief disabilities are on the one hand its difficulty of escaping from the framework of the stationary state and the 'comparative static' method; and on the other, the ironic reluctance of *durability*, which far more than any other factor brings long time lapse into a process of production, to fit easily into its formula.

At the outset, there is a crucial difficulty. The Austrian theory distinguishes 'original means of production', natural forces and human services, which it is the object of a productive method to economize, from 'produced means of production' which are the passive vehicles carrying through time the effect of inputs of original means to the date of the final consumable product. The 'produced means of production' or 'intermediate products', are scarce only because they represent delay in the emergence of the usable and enjoyable result of original inputs; and these produced means do not themselves yield dated services which can be 'put in' at a longer or shorter time-distance before the emergence of the final product. Yet it is plain that this is not an appropriate way of looking at durable tools. Once a tool exists, it is a source of services not essentially different, in that capacity, from a human source. Why should it be differently treated? However, we shall try to present the Austrian theory in its own terms as a basis for examining in detail its powers and limitations.

29.6 *The Austrian theory of capital*

Let us suppose that a unit parcel of a specified good ready for the consumer's use can be produced by the work of one man on one acre of land during one hundred successive days. At the end of the first such day the embryonic parcel will contain, as it were, one *factor-day* of the original means of production, labour and land combined in those proportions. At the end of the second day, the embryonic item will be the repository of two factor-days, and so on until at its completion and sale to a consumer it represents 100 factor-days. This life-history of one particular parcel will be represented on Fig. 29.1 as a diagonal running north-eastwards from the origin, which latter stands in such a diagram for the present moment on the south–north axis and for the technical start of the productive process on the west–east axis. Suppose that one such parcel is started every day until 100 men and acres of land are engaged in producing this kind of product. At any moment randomly chosen after that there will co-exist 100 embryonic parcels, one at each of the 100 stages of the productive process. The total of factor-days represented by this collection will be $1 + 2 + \ldots + n = \frac{1}{2}n(n+1)$ where $n = 100$, that is, 5050 embodied factor-days. Let us now suppose instead that each of the 100 factor-days of productive input which are each day available is spread over two parcels instead of one, and that conformably to this, the productive history of any one identified parcel lasts for 200 successive days, during each of which one new parcel is started. Since there will now be 200, instead of 100, concomitantly existing parcels but still only 100 men and 100 acres, each man–acre will have to devote its effort to parcels at two different stages. On any random day there will be, amongst the 200 parcels, one parcel which needs half a factor-day to complete it ready for sale, and one which needs a whole factor-day to complete it. Since only one man–acre is available to work on these two parcels, only the one which is within half a factor-day of completion will be able to be completed, while the other will be brought to the stage where it can be completed by one more half factor-day on the morrow. Thus on each and any random day, one parcel will be completed and sold to a consumer. Since the total force of man–acres is unchanged between our two cases, and since we have said nothing about any essential change of technology, this equality of the two outputs is what we should expect. But the number of factor-days *contained* in the stock or list of co-existing embryonic parcels will not be the same. If for simplicity we at first change our unit to one-half of a factor-day, the total of embodied half factor-days will be $\frac{1}{2}n(n+1)$ with $n = 200$, that is, 20,100 half factor-days or 10,050 full factor-days. It then appears that the lengthening of the time taken by one parcel to pass from inception to completion through all embryonic stages has the effect of increasing the total stock of embodied factor-days in all the co-existing parcels taken together. The doubling of the total time for each parcel, in fact, in our example roughly doubles the total stock, taking it from 5050 to 10,050. These totals have an alternative interpretation.

A factor-day is a quantity of productive services, namely, the service rendered by one man working with one acre during one day. This packet of productive service can be applied to an embryonic parcel at any stage, earlier or later, of the process of producing that parcel, and can accordingly remain embodied in it for a longer or shorter time up to the moment of completion and sale. A factor-day which performs the very first stage of production of some one parcel will, in the first of our two cases, remain embodied for 100 days. A ciné-film having one frame per day, and showing in its 100 frames the entire production history of one particular parcel, would include that earliest factor-day in *every one* of those 100 frames, for the effect produced by that earliest factor-day would remain embodied in, or impressed on, the parcel throughout all the subsequent stages of production. The factor-day applied on the second day of the parcel's production life would remain embodied for 99 days, the packet of service applied on the third day would remain for 98 days, and so on. When the strip of film was complete, we could count up the total of *factor-day embodied days* pictured by it. The total, in our first case, would be $100 + 99 + 98 + \ldots + 1$, or $1 + 2 + \ldots + 100$, that is $\frac{1}{2}n(n+1)$ for $n + 100$, or 5050. In our second case it would similarly be 10,050. In fact, the film-strip biography would present to us all three of the aspects of the productive scene included in Fig. 29.1. It would picture side by side, in our first case, the 100 technical stages of production, able to be interpreted either as 100 co-existing parcels each at a different stage, as shown on the west–east axis; or as 100 phases in the life of a single parcel, as shown on the north-eastward diagonal: or on the 100-day segment of the calendar required for the complete process of production of one parcel, as shown on the south–north axis.

The number of factor-days represented by the entire list of co-existing embryonic parcels, one at each daily stage, is in fact the same as what we have called the number of *factor-day embodied days* in one completed parcel. If the former is a measure of the size of the capital stock represented by the list of parcels, so then is the latter. Thus if other things are the same for both cases, we can compare the size of the capital stock in the respective cases of a 100-day process and a 200-day process by comparing the number of factor-day embodied-days in the respective specimen parcels which they produce. The 100-day process needs, in our example, a capital stock of 5050 factor-day embodied-days. The 200-day process needs a stock of 10,050 factor-day embodied-days. But if other things are not the same; if, for example, one process employs 50 man–acres always at work, while the other employs 100 man–acres always at work, we shall expect the latter to involve a larger capital stock even if the production history of one parcel takes the same total length of time in each case. We must therefore divide the number of factor-day embodied-days by the number of man–acres employed, and so obtain an *average period of production*. In our example, the average period in the first type of process will be 50.5 days, and in the second 100.5 days.

The average period of production, in terms of the highly abstracted and artificial model which we have set up, measures the average delay between the date of input of a factor-day and the date when the consumable results of this work become available. It thus gives an operational meaning to the conception that *capital is time*. It shows also why a larger capital stock involves a psychic cost or disutility, namely, the impatience which it supposes to be felt by the members of a society to secure and consume the fruits of any and each particular day's labour. Our model has so far made no suggestion as to why a process of production which involves a larger capital stock can offer some compensation, in the form of a larger product per man–acre, for the disutility arising from the longer average period of production which the larger capital stock implies. But first the notion of the average period of production can be clarified in some respects.

29.7 *The average period of production*

Our very simple arithmetic has yielded some rather untidy answers, 50.5 days and 100.5 days instead of a round 50 or 100. The reason for this is the method we have adopted by which we count a series of discrete factor-days instead of considering a flow of input continuous in time. The notion of a 'day' comes in twice: it is needed as one dimension of a 'packet' of input, since one man on one acre can only achieve something if given a lapse of time in which to do it; and it is needed as the unit in which we measure the lapse of time during which any particular packet of input remains embodied in a particular parcel during the completion of that parcel. There is no reason, however, why our packet of input of productive services should consist of a whole day's work of one man on one acre. We could instead define the factor-hour or the factor-minute. Indeed the series of steps, by each of which we make our time-interval shorter and shorter, can be formally conceived as endless, so that we envisage the notion of an intensity of input at an instant. That intensity may be such, for example, that *if* continued for a whole day it would produce the effect of what we have been calling a factor-day. Or the man might work only at half pressure, so that the intensity or rate of input at some instant would be described as half a factor-day per day. If we suppose the entity of one man on one acre to be technologically or constitutionally constrained to work at some one intensity, never departing from it, then a man–acre becomes itself the name of a definite intensity, and can serve as a *unit* of intensity. The intensity of application of productive service to a particular embryonic parcel of product need not be one unit, but could be several units or a fraction of a unit. Nor need it, of course, be the same at different instants. Let x be the number of time-units which have elapsed since some fixed instant $x = 0$, so that numerical values of x correspond to named calendar instants. Let z units of intensity measure the rate of input of productive service to some parcel. If between two instants x_1 and x_2, input proceeds at an intensity z_1, the packet of input thus applied can be written $z_1(x_2 - x_1)$, or $z_1 \Delta x_1$. The general packet representing any and all such packets can be expressed $z_i \Delta x_i$, and the total of all input needed to carry one parcel from start to completion will then be $\Sigma z_i \Delta x_i$. If now we deem the number of such packets to increase beyond all bounds as their durations get shorter than any pre-assigned non-zero length, we can write the total input into one parcel as

$$ S = \int_t^T z(x)\, dx, $$

where we suppose the parcel to be started at an instant $x = t$ and completed at an instant $x = T$, and where we suppose the intensity of input to be a function of the stage of production which has been reached at any instant x, or to be simply a function of x.

In this formula, the letter S stands for the accumulated input which has been stored up in a completed parcel by applying input to that parcel from the date $x = t$, when its production was begun, to the date $x = T$, when its production was completed, the input having been applied at an intensity $z = z(x)$ dependent on x. Now instead of confining the meaning of S to the state of a completed parcel, let us give S the meaning of the accumulated input which has been stored in a parcel at any stage of its production, so that S will depend on the lapse of time T, now regarded as a variable, which has taken place since the moment $x = t$ when the parcel was started. If, during a past interval, C, sufficient to complete a parcel from start to finish, the starting of new parcels has gone on continuously, one such having been started at 'each instant', the total input stored up in all the co-existing embryonic parcels will now be

$$Q = \int_t^C S(T)\, \mathrm{d}T.$$

If the flow of input into all these embryonic parcels taken together (their number being deemed to increase beyond all bounds while the intensity of input into a random parcel becomes smaller than any pre-assigned size) is Z, the average period, y, of production will be expressed as

$$y = \frac{Q}{Z} = \frac{\int_t^C S(T)\, \mathrm{d}T}{Z}.$$

The principle of this 'continuous' expression of the average period is the same as that involved in our discontinuous expression where we counted the finite number of discrete factor-days.

29.8 *Fineness of the production net and length of the average period*

In what we have so far said of the relation between time and capital stock, one feature is conspicuous. It is the entire absence of any suggested reason why a longer average period of production, a larger capital stock, should be advantageous. The number of completed parcels emerging daily for sale to consumers from the process with an average period of production of 100 days is the same as the number produced by the process of 50 days. The motive and the reason for this feature are plain. The essence of the Austrian theory is hard to make clear even with a model abstracted to the last degree; and this abstraction has consisted in reckoning input, output and capital stock all in terms of factor-days. Output in each process is measured by the number of factor-days of input it absorbs, and since this number is the same in both processes, output as thus measured is also the same. The paradox of the Austrian theory is the contrast between the arresting simplicity of its basic proposition, that a capital stock is the physical manifestation, existing from moment to moment, of the fact that a devious but thereby more efficient method of production is being employed; and the great difficulty of translating this broad notion into the details of working mechanism.

The notion that capital is time expresses an aspect of the efficacy of the division of labour. We return to the time-net of production. A finer and finer sub-division of products and of tasks or operations enables each effect to be produced by a more subtle and apt assembly of parts and contributory processes. Each operation, each tool, each physical manifestation can be used as a tributary thread in a thousand or a million different weaves. Those products can then be designed from a precisely chosen blend of ingredients and forms so as to fulfil some precisely defined purpose. A great diversity of activities can be brought directly or indirectly to converge on some one task. Why should such enrichment of produced resources of production entail a *greater average delay* between the application of human efforts and the availability of the results ascribable to those efforts? Interpretations of the Austrian theory could easily mislead us on this point. It is not true that if we compare two systems of production, the one offering greater division of labour necessarily entails more delay. What is true is that if we compare two average periods of production, the longer one will often permit some systems of production whose degree of division of labour is greater than the greatest permitted by the shorter average period. Thus by extending the period of production we may render accessible some degrees of division of labour that were not accessible before. Of two production nets, the more intricate and more highly sub-divided need not involve a longer average period of production, but if we allow a longer average period we shall be able to find a production-net whose greater sub-division and intricacy results in an economy of the productive efforts of men and Nature.

29.9 *Growth of value of embryonic products with passage of time*

So long as we define a unit of output simply as what results from the input of, say, one hundred factor-days, it is evident that we cannot express the superiority of one method of production, involving a long average period, over another method using a shorter average period, as a larger number of units of output. That comparison requires a unit of value in which to measure output. The Austrian theory, in fact, conceives the value of each embryonic parcel to grow, during its production history, not only by the input to it of successive factor days but also by the mere passage of time. The traditional efforts to give such an idea some realistic illustrative content are not convincing. They have referred to the increase in the weight of timber in a growing tree, or to the improvement in the quality of wine as it matures. It is plain that unless the ground on which the tree grows is valueless for any other purpose, its growth is due to natural forces which require indeed, but do not merely consist in, the passage of time, and which have a market value. Even the maturing of wine requires the use of storage space. But such objections are beside the point. The longer period of production allows the deployment of finer, more subtle, complex and specialized technical methods. The effect must still be expressed in the growth of value of each parcel at a faster pace than what is accounted for by the mere input of factor-days. If, then, we measure output in terms of value, ought we not to measure in that way the size of the capital stock?

Modern versions of the Austrian theory regard the value of each factor-day which has been applied to an embryonic parcel as growing in value during the whole time from that application until the completion and sale of the parcel. The percentage per time unit at which that growth occurs is deemed to be uniform, for any one method of production, from start to finish of a parcel, and this uniformity is explained as a necessary condition for the most economical use of means of production, for if the value of a factor-day applied to the process at one stage was able to grow faster than that applied at another stage, it would be advantageous to re-arrange the method of production so that more input was applied at the faster growth stages and less at slower growth stages. The final purpose of the Austrian theory is to show by what interplay of forces the uniform proportionate pace of growth is determined.

29.10 *Determination of the pace of proportionate growth*

We have spoken above of 'comparing two systems' or 'two average periods of production', and also of 'extending' the average period of production. This latter expression is dangerous at the present stage of our argument. An examination of the Austrian theory, and of its possible relations with a theory of the production net, must rest at first on a comparative-static method. We must be content to compare two methods of production which are fully in being, each in a stationary condition. When we do that, we can suppose the members of a society to be asked to make a choice amongst a number of rival situations open to them. They can begin by rejecting all those methods which involve a longer average period, calculated as in our 'parcels' model, but do not yield parcels, in exchange for a *given* steady input of factor-days, which are more desirable and valuable than some shorter method gives. Thus their range of choice will be reduced to those methods which, if longer, give better parcels, and if they give better parcels, are longer. If the differences, in each of these respects, between 'neighbouring' methods is small enough throughout the range, there will be some one method which is preferred above all others, and is preferred because the next longer method does not quite compensate its extra length by the extra value of its parcels, and the next shorter method does not quite compensate its inferiority of value of its parcels by its lesser length. It is plain that the character of the methods composing the range, in all technological respects, that is, their respective lengths and the size and technical quality and character of their parcels, will be determined by the state of the industrial arts. It will not be a matter of taste, though it will be a matter of what knowledge is possessed by the engineers and managers. But the value put by members of the society on any particular combination of length of process and quantity and quality of product will, by contrast, be a matter of taste. Taste and technology together will select one method, of one determinate average period of production. In so far as this determination is part of a general equilibrium, in which all available alternatives of use of resources and forms of consumption have been passed in review by all the members of the society and their choices have been pre-reconciled, the value placed on the parcels, in comparison with that placed on factor-days, will properly reflect the response of society's tastes to its technological environment, and we can claim that tastes and technology together have determined the percentage per time unit of growth of value of a parcel as it traverses the sequence of stages of production.

29.11 *The Austrian theory excludes changeable orientation, uncertainty and novelty*

If our gloss on the Austrian theory of capital does it justice (despite some changes, at least in presentation, which we find necessary for its effective defence) it is plain that this theory belongs unreservedly to that Theory of Value which assumes perfect knowledge, for all participants, of an unchanging economic world. This is evident from several points of view. The Austrian theory totally ignores what we called, in the early pages of this chapter, the changeable *orientation* of capital items. It tacitly assumes, not merely that the capital items co-existing at some moment are, in terms of Fig. 29.1, a projection, on the west–east axis, of a stationary or repeatable production history pictured on the north-eastern diagonal, so that they can belong to, and maintain continuously, a stationary state, but that this stationary state is understood, accepted and intended by all the members of the society, so that no practical or even conceptual distinction need be made between the notion of the co-existing items of the capital list, the items representing, between them,

all stages of the production process, but destined individually
for incorporation in different 'parcels' which will be available
at different dates, on the one hand, and on the other, the
abstract notion of the production history of some one parcel;
abstract, because there is never any moment when that production history tangibly or visibly exists as a material actuality. It
exists only in the mental eye of the detached observer, using
the historian's diachronic faculty of treating different historical
moments as a co-existing intellectual reality. The Austrian
theory thus ignores any *process of change*. If change is to be
studied, this must be done by the comparative-static collation
of two 'stationary states', two economies each in itself unchanging, with no study or explanation of any path leading
from one to the other, but a simple contrasting of their characteristics. It also excludes any awareness, on the part of the
members of the society, of multiple possibilities of the future
course of events; it ignores uncertainty. Above all it excludes
any awareness of the possibility of new knowledge, it excludes
the recognition, by the participants, of novelty.

29.12 *The theory of capital and the stationary state*

We saw in the preceding chapter how extreme the assumptions
are which the stationary state requires. The material composition of the capital list or capital stock are required to be such
that there is an item ready at every stage to be carried into the
next stage and fill the place at that next stage which will be
vacated by the item at present occupying it. The relative
quantities of the intermediate products, the embryonic goods,
existing at each stage at every moment must be right and
adequate for this replacement. How can such balance be
attained? If goods at an earlier stage are necessities for the
production of goods at the next and subsequent stages, the
capital stock can be built up only 'from beginning to end'.
Products representing earlier stages must be produced first in
order to serve in the production of the goods belonging to subsequent stages. But while this build-up is going on, the capital
stock will of course be quite unbalanced and greatly distorted
in comparison with its eventual stationary composition. Many

people will be earning incomes in producing goods at the earlier stages, which they will wish to spend as consumers. But if the final stage of the process has not yet been reached, or not enough goods ready for consumption are yet coming off the production line, the prices of goods at the late stages of the production history will tend to rise in relation to those at earlier stages, in the manner and with the effect envisaged by Professor F. A. Hayek in a book once famous and provocative of intense discussion, *Prices and Production*. 'Original means of production', our *factor-days*, will be drawn away from the earlier stages to give an artificial or emergency impetus to the production of ready consumables. Thus a fresh imbalance will be provoked and the attainment of the ultimate stationary balance further interrupted.

Such technological difficulties are an obstacle to the attainment of the stationary state, but they are overshadowed by those of expectation. What is to prevent people, whose capital stock is in a state which makes stationariness immediately *possible*, from planning not to use it in that way? What is to guarantee a stationary orientation of the items of a capital list merely because this list is technologically capable of being so oriented? To be content with stationariness, the members of the society must be insulated from changes of knowledge and undesirous of accumulating wealth. However, the stationary state is not meant as a stylized model of reality but as a mere extension of a purely formal and abstract logical construction, that of a general timeless equilibrium. *General equilibrium* makes it possible to conceive of strictly rational action by all the interacting members of a society. It does so by recognizing all such actions to be effectively synchronous, and thus it abolishes any role for a *sequence* of moments and confines all actions to one and the same moment. General equilibrium refers to a *timeless* system. But capital theory by the nature of its subject matter cannot be fitted into a purely timeless system. How can the Austrian theory, which declares that capital is the physical reflection of the role of time in production, conceivably have meaning in a momentary system?

It needs only to realize the stationary state by means of the notion which we have called orientation. The stationary state, in its capital stock aspect, is merely a technologically suitable

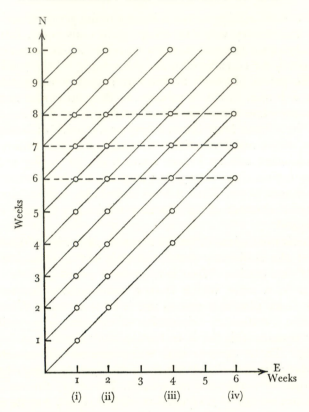

Fig. 29.2. Each north–eastward diagonal represents the production history of some one identified parcel. At each dot on its diagonal the parcel has reached a particular (eastward) technological stage at a particular (northward) date.

Each east–west line of dots represents the collection of embryonic parcels co-existing at the date (northward position) of that line.

collection of capital stock items each with a suitable orientation. The items must constitute and represent a complete series of stages in the production of one parcel of product. But they must, of course, not belong to one and the same parcel, but to as many different parcels as there are stages. The design of every parcel will be the same as that of every other, and each embryonic parcel, at its own stage, will be technologically capable, and orientationally intended, to replace the next parcel when every parcel moves one stage. It is the purpose of Fig. 29.2, which is essentially the same as Fig. 29.1, to illustrate this conception. Let us imagine a straight line parallel to the west–east axis translated bodily northward while continuing to lie due east and west. At successive northward positions it will represent the state of affairs at successive calendar dates. Each of these states of affairs will be technologically identical with every other, and each will consist of the capital list of items representing all the technological stages of production. The series of north-eastward diagonals, with successively more northward points of intersection with the south–north axis, represent the production histories of different parcels. The stage which any one parcel has reached at any calendar date is that one represented by the eastward position of the point of intersection of the diagonal belonging to this parcel with the west–east line belonging to that calendar date.

29.13 *Determinacy of the size of the capital stock in value terms*

We have sought in the foregoing pages to give an account of the Austrian theory of capital which avoids some of the unnecessary complications of that theory in the form which its chief originators and modern exponents have sometimes given it. In this way we have tried to give to the essence of that theory a form which shows to best advantage the insights which it offers and the structure of assumptions and methods of reasoning on which it rests. Amongst the supposed difficulties which we have rejected is that arising from the notion, correct in itself, that when the size of a capital stock, or the length of the average period of production, is reckoned in value terms, that size or length will depend on the percentage per time-unit at which the value of embodied factor-days are taken to grow, and that since the determination of this percentage is one of the objects of the construction, it cannot be taken as known. To regard this as a fatal obstacle, however, is like arguing that because price and quantity demanded of some commodity are inter-dependent, neither can be determined until after we have determined the other, and so neither can be determined. By considering a physically defined product which follows an isolated path of production, in the way we have supposed our 'parcels' to do, we can show that the terms of exchange between greater (physical) output from a given steady input of 'original' means of production, and greater delay between date of input and date of related output, are set, at each point of a schedule, by technology, and that the choice of a marginal rate of exchange, and thus of the corresponding point of the schedule, is made by the tastes of the members of society. In a model thus simplified and reduced to the study of a single product measurable in physical terms, it seems possible, granted one assumption, to show that there is determinacy of the method of production that will be chosen and of the corresponding size of capital stock and of output. The required assumption is that 'impatience' to have the consumable results of input of productive service can really be supposed to operate in a comparative static model of our sort in the way the theory suggests.

29.14 *The brilliant Austrian result and its high cost in abstractness*

By its claim to measure a heterogeneous capital stock as a scalar quantity, and to do so by means of a technological and wholly objective characteristic, and, having done so, to base upon the result a demonstration of how the income from ownership of such a stock is determined, the Austrian theory appears to perform a *tour de force* of great brilliance and effect. That impression is not, I think, erased by the formidable difficulties which appear when we try to spell the theory out in detail. The effect of those difficulties is that the logical structure which they leave intact when account has been taken of them is confined to such highly artificial and abstract conditions. We turn now, therefore, to examine the chief objections and see how much of the essential Austrian structure can be regarded as merely obscured, and not abolished, when the assumptions are made more general.

The essential questions seem to be the following:

1. When we relax the extreme simplification of our 'parcels' model, is it still possible to define operationally or even formally the notion of an *average period of production?*

2. Does the difficulty of relaxing that model arise principally from the need to replace an isolated process of production, in which only 'original means of production', labour and natural forces, are applied to the embryonic parcel as it traverses successive stages, by the notion of a *net* in which streams of different intermediate products converge upon each sector (plant or industry) and the product of that sector is distributed to many other sectors?

3. Or does it arise chiefly from the presence of durable tools which, having themselves been constructed by a process which takes time, are then used for many years in contributing services to the production of parcels of goods sold to the consumer at many different dates?

4. Or is the ultimate trouble the fact that when we abandon the stationary state and the comparative static method, and consider an evolutionary process in which the capital complex is growing and is changing in composition, there is no necessary or identifiable termination of the history of any particular packet of input, which might then be deemed to go on helping to produce instruments or embryonic goods which help to produce further goods and so on indefinitely?

5. Is the 'impatience', to which the theory appeals in order to show that a capital stock is a scarce resource, a reality which could in fact lead to the dissipation of that stock, or to the failure to build one up?

29.15 *Orientation of presently existing objects alone contains the 'period of production'*

The human mind is sorely tempted to assimilate history and the calendar with a landscape in which fixed objects can be visited and revisited, to whose parts they assign, paradoxically, a simultaneous and permanent co-existence despite their origin of sequential events in time. To exist, however, is to be present in the present, in a single moment, and what exists of history is, at any moment, its traces in the material world and in memory. What we have called the capital list or the capital stock is a collection of material objects or of forms which we have impressed upon the environment, and its aspect of *sequence in time* is a matter purely of our thoughts. The record may show that these objects and forms were arrived at in a certain way, by a certain sequence of operations and events, and that thus the production history of a given object was such-and-such. But this is not directly relevant to the mutual relations and intended purposes of things which exist now. It is this *orientation* of the presently co-existing objects which solely contains what we are measuring when we examine the 'period of production'. Orientation is thought, design, intention, expectation. Thought is mutable and elusive, thoughts in different minds about 'the same' objects need have little in common. If an average period of production is to be conceived as discernible in principle in the complex net of activities and channels of supply of products between sectors, its meaning will be that of a plan or policy accepted for the time being as a basis of immediate action, but by no means guaranteed, or even at all likely, to be realized through the events of future years. Such a plan or policy would have of course to be elicited by enquiry or observation at thousands or millions of different points in the net. Technology which dictates what ingredients and tools are needed for what purposes and products would give it stability in some 'short period'. The length of that period of stability would perhaps be decreasing through accelerating discovery and invention, but the pace of innovation would itself be limited by economic considerations, by commercial organization and habits and by contracts. To some degree, allowance could be made, by an investigator of the average period of production, for tech- nological innovation already visibly heralded by invention. But invention itself, new knowledge, by its nature cannot be fore- seen. Such an investigator might try to discover the length, at each historical epoch, of that 'short period' during which the average period of production changed only by, say, one- twentieth of its initial length. However, the tedious and expen- sive difficulty of such investigations seem to make them mere fantasies. The point to be made is that the average period of production is, at best, a plan conceived at some one date, but destined never to be realized because the full deployment of events which it envisages would take longer than the changes of technology, taste, population and markets which would render it obsolete. What accounts for the protracted time of that deployment, however, is not only the complexity of the production net but the presence in it of durable equipment.

29.16 *Durability of tools and inter-contributory production defeat the calculation of the period*

We have referred to the idea that a tool which takes both time to build and time to yield up its store of useful service defeats the attempt to calculate the average period of production of that service and of other goods which that service helps to produce. To see this, let us suppose in our 'parcels' model that the factor-day comprises the work of one man on one acre with one tool (of a given specification) for one day. The tool is durable, and only has to be replaced after helping to produce n parcels. Then if, alongside the processes of production of the parcels themselves (let us again suppose that one parcel is started and one completed each day, while each parcel takes 100 factor-days to complete) there is another set of processes in which a tool is started and completed every nth day, each tool requiring for its making from start to finish 100 factor days of man–acre and tool but not wearing out the tool thus used. Then a stationary flow of production will again be possible. Each man employed on parcels will only require a new tool every $100n$ days, but since there are 100 men so employed, one new tool will be required every n days, and one tool will be forthcoming every n days. The factor-days applied to producing tools will remain embodied in an embryonic tool for an average of approximately 50 days up to the moment of its completion. Thereafter $1/100n$ of the tool's total capacity for service may be deemed to be used up each day, so that if the tool contains 100 factor-days, the average time that a factor-day remains embodied in it, from its completion to the end of its useful life, will be

$$\tfrac{1}{2}(100n+1)100n/100 = n(100n+1)/2.$$

We thus have an 'average period of production' for factor-days applied to the production of each tool, taking account both of the time taken to build the tool and the time taken to wear it out in use, of $5050 + n(100n+1)/2$. For $n = 10$, this would be

10,055. The source of the difficulty with durable tools now emerges. In order to combine the contribution which we have just reckoned to be made to the average period of production of one parcel of *product* by the use of durable tools in the production of such parcels, with the contribution made by the application of man–acres to the parcel itself, we need to *value* the services of the tools in terms of man–acres. For we have already taken account, in considering the durable tools, of that part of each factor-day indirectly applied to a parcel, and what we have then to take account of is the man–acres directly applied to the parcel. The effect of the introduction of durable tools is to compel us to resort to valuation.

In the foregoing paragraph, a rather intricate argument has suggested that durability of some intermediate products is sufficient to compel a resort to valuation. This may seem puzzling. Are not men, and still more certainly, acres of land, durable? The difference is that tools are made by the application of man–acre services, while men are not regarded as a product with a cost of production, and land by definition is the factor which is permanently maintained by Nature. The making and using of tools is a different mode of application of man–acre services to the making of 'parcels' of consumable product, from their direct application. In order to combine these two modes into a calculable average period during which a man–acre day remains embodied in the productive process, we must value them in terms of each other.

Valuation is necessitated in an overwhelmingly more unmistakable way, when we altogether abandon our 'parcels' model, with its isolated progression of an embryonic product from one stage to another without any contributory streams of other intermediate products, and turn to consider the production net.

When durable facilities of production at some point of the net help to produce intermediate products or services which are distributed directly to scores or thousands of other plants and sectors, as with a telephone system, electric energy or packaging materials, it is logically as well as practically impossible to say what proportions of the services of the durable tool are going in what directions, without valuing the products they help other sectors to produce. If we must resort to valuation of the items of the capital complex or capital stock, as a step on the road to discovering the average period of production implicit in that capital stock, we shall have as part of that step to apply some proportionate pace of growth, some 'interest-rate', in order to take account of that very effect of the passage of time to which we are ascribing the advantage of a long period of production. But if so, we are introducing the proportionate pace of growth twice over, as a datum and as an unknown, and we are in danger of having too many unknowns for our equations. Durability considered by itself, and the fact, considered by itself, that products help to produce products not merely in the sense of a simple isolated series of embryonic stages, but in a complex and intricate net of converging and diverging channels of supply, are each sufficient to render unworkable the notion of a technologically determined 'average period of production' confronting the impatience of the members of the society to have the consumable products of their work. In combination, these difficulties re-inforce each other.

29.17 *The meaning of 'impatience to consume'*

We come then to the questions, intimately related to each other, on one hand of the nature or rationale of that impatience and its effect, and on the other of the status of the concept of an average period of production in an economic society which intends to augment continually its capital stock, using part of its general output for net investment in productive facilities. Why should the prospect of a lapse of time between the date of applying factor-days to embryonic products, and the date of enjoying the fruits of that input, engender impatience? What desire, precisely, would underlie that impatience, what action would suggest itself as a means of relieving the impatience? There are two kinds of situation in which these questions might be asked. They could be concerned with a proposal to build up a capital stock which did not yet exist, or to maintain one which did already exist in a balanced condition such as to make possible a 'stationary state'. If, in the first case, all available men and acres were already engaged in production, the decision to build up a capital stock would mean that the flow of consumable goods which could be looked forward to for the near future would be less than it could have been, and that in a further future, when the capital stock had been brought to a state of balance where a new stationary state, with a longer average period of production, had been established, the flow of consumables from an unchanged input of man–acres would be larger, and able to be permanently larger, than before the capital build-up was begun. Here, impatience has an evident and natural role, in presenting an obstacle which the hope of an eventual larger income of consumables will overcome to some degree.

We can bring out the essentials of the matter by our parcels model. If, initially, N man–acres are engaged at each of the 100 stages of production which compose the present technology, a stationary state can proceed in which N parcels are completed and N new parcels are started each day. One day, the number of parcels started in the present technology is reduced to $\frac{3}{4}N$. The $\frac{1}{4}N$ man–acres thus released are applied to the first stage of $\frac{1}{4}N$ parcels in a different technology which can complete a parcel in 200 days by the steady daily work of $\frac{1}{2}$ man–acre. On the next day, a further $\frac{1}{4}N$ man–acres become available for the new-style parcels because $\frac{1}{4}N$ fewer old-style parcels than before reach the second stage of the old technology. Thus the $\frac{1}{2}N$ new-style parcels which on this second day reach the second of their 200 prospective stages can each be supplied with its necessary $\frac{1}{2}$ factor-day. So the daily transfer of $\frac{1}{4}N$ man–acres from the old- to the new-style parcels goes on, until after 100 days the old technology produces its last daily batch of N parcels and on the morrow will produce only $\frac{3}{4}N$ parcels. Thus, during days 101 through 200, the daily output of parcels is only $\frac{3}{4}N$, all of them coming from the old technology. During all these days from 101 through 200, $\frac{1}{4}N$ man–acres are being daily transferred to the new-style parcels in order to carry them through the second half of their 200-day productive life, and all the while the first batch of new-style parcels are of course being followed up by other batches of embryonic new-style parcels which are daily started by the man–acres who have been transferred to, and remain in, the new-style technology. On the 201st day, the first batch of completed new-style parcels will emerge. There will be $\frac{1}{2}N$ of them, precisely replacing in number the $\frac{1}{2}N$

parcels by which the daily output of the old technology will, by this 201st day, have dropped. Thus on the 201st day a new stationary state comes potentially into being. As in the old one, each day, so long as the new dispensation continues, will yield N parcels, half of them from the old and half from the new technology. Half of the 100N man–acres will be working in the old technology, half of them in the new. In the old technology, one man–acre day (one factor-day) will be daily applied to each of the 100 times $\frac{1}{2}N$ embryonic parcels, while in the new technology, one-*half* a factor-day will be daily applied to each of the 200 times $\frac{1}{2}N$ embryonic parcels. Thus in the new stationary state the *number* of parcels daily emerging will be the same as in the old. They can, of course, reflect a more powerful 'division of labour' in the new technology by being bigger or better.

In speaking of 'new-' and 'old-' style parcels, and of the 'new' technology, we do not in this context by any means refer to newly *invented* technology. We exclude changes of knowledge from this argument in order to study in isolation the balance between impatience for immediate fruits of labour, on the one hand, and the prospect of the greater fruits of *given* quantities of labour which can be had by overcoming that impatience, on the other. The more powerful division of labour, we are supposing, is known to be available in varying degrees according to the length of the average period of production that the society is willing to tolerate. Will they not push their exploitation of the technological advantage to the point where a further small extension of the period is, in prospect, too distasteful to be overcome by the prospective increase in *maintainable output?* For the exchange which the society is proposing to itself is a once-over sacrifice for the sake of a permanent increase in the flow of consumables which its supposedly given endowment of man–acres can provide.

In our parcels model, and in any model or real society whose essentials it reflects, the promise of a larger flow of consumables in a new, maintainable stationary state, from an unchanged quantity of men and acres, would be required in order to overcome the 'impatience' to consume, the reluctance to accept for a short time a *reduced* real income for the sake of a larger income able to be maintained indefinitely. On the most classical lines of balance at a subjective margin, we can see how the attainable size of capital-stock, the attainable length of the average period of production, might be determined, and even by what sort of actual process of transition it might be attained. On these lines it seems that we might fairly describe a capital stock as a scarce good, and claim that this scarcity justified the drawing of an income by its possessors. But there is a different question. When such a stock exists, let us suppose in a state oriented to stationariness, will this stock be capable of being dissipated, of being disinvested, in such a way that its possessors could threaten to cease maintaining it if they were not permitted to draw an income from it? In our parcels model, we could describe a reverse process to that of the building-up of the stock. But in that model we have quite omitted to give any indication of technological details in the claim that a larger stock makes possible a more powerful division of labour. In describing the build-up process, we reverted to a model which makes no explicit provision for durable tools, and which uses the single-track, isolated process of production without contributory streams or any hint of the complexity of the production net. It is these aspects of production which we have shown to be most difficult to accommodate in any version of the Austrian theory, and it is these which cast doubt on the notion of a systematic and orderly general dismantling of the productive apparatus of a modern industrial society.

29.18 *General disinvestment as an orderly process is impossible*

The production net is organic. It is a system of *inter-necessary* activities, using huge and complex blocks of plant each functioning as an indivisible whole. There have been experiments in large-scale dismantling of systems, as in the British railway network and coal industry. But these have been mere displacements of one technology by another, the railways by roads and aircraft, the coal mines by oil, natural gas and nuclear power. They have not been part of an endeavour to consume the capital stock and dissipate the stored-up wealth. In what sense would that be possible? How much of the invested work which has built up the material embodiment of the production net

can be got out of it again by a process involving its disappearance rather than its use and maintenance?

Modern production depends upon vast systems which function as wholes. Railways and telephone networks depend in
some measure on their *universal* accessibility. We cannot melt
down the copper in our electric power systems and use it for
cooking pots, for the production net would perish long before
any use could be made of the salvage from its wreck, and we
with it. The threat of the owner of the capital stock to dissipate
it would be an idle one. The effective threat is to cease to renew
it continually in ever-new forms and technologies, with new
products and new tools. The picture of a technologically
stationary capital complex is a mere abstraction, and emphasis
upon it illustrates again the bias of economics towards quantity
and proportion to the neglect of form.

29.19 *Marginal balance and inter-temporal alternatives*

The theory which ascribes value to the balance of preferences
at a margin, and which took command of economic theorizing
in the last third of the nineteenth century, was a highly specialized doctrine directed at quite abstract and narrow questions
in a peculiar context of thought. In other chapters we have
sought to suggest some of the aspects of this specialness. The
theory of value was able to be constructed by purely deductive
methods, since it sought only to show that certain consequences
followed logically from certain premisses. Its sole content being
a structure of reason, its method also needed nothing but
reason. In supposing that reason, and a consultation of their
own desires, would provide men with all necessary guidance for
their economic choices, the theory tacitly assumed that the
basic knowledge, on which reason could operate, was available
to them. The *effect* of specified actions was assumed to be known,
both in matters of physical technology, of market response, and
of their own feelings. All that was needed was a careful search
amongst attainable results and a logical tracing back to find the
appropriate action. The answers provided by such a theory are
narrowly confined in their application to questions where it can
be assumed that men do possess the facts. They thus *excluded* all

questions where it is impossible, in the nature of human affairs as we experience them, to have such knowledge. Since the necessary knowledge included knowledge of other men's intentions, it was needful that the intentions of all members of the society should be pre-reconciled, should logically co-exist and exhibit mutual and systematic coherence. But such *logical* co-validity, in the nature of things, implies and requires in effect simultaneity in time as well as simultaneity in logic. The general equilibrium system is in essence a single-moment system, extension in time is alien to its nature. Yet men know that they have experienced and will experience other moments than the present. They can and do 'look forward'. They are conscious of a future in which they will need consumables, and of the possibility of increasing the fruitfulness of their own labour by deploying it over 'a stretch of time'. How far should they sacrifice the near future, seen in expectation, in order to make the income of an expected further future more assured and greater? The analysis of this choice is a typical and inviting application for subjective marginalism. To extend the theory of value so as to include it seems a natural and inevitable thing. Yet such a move means abandoning the timelessness which is of the essence of general equilibrium. How can such a contradiction be patched up? One method, the method which evades all the insoluble difficulties of expectation and uncertainty which we have summed up in the word 'orientation', is to resort to the stationary state. The stationary state is a fudge. Do we mean by a stationary state a self-repetitive process of production and consumption which *has* gone on for long enough for at least one 'parcel' in our model to have completed its production history? If, by some extraordinary conjuncture of influences, such a thing has happened, what is the relevance of this for the destiny of the items which now make up the momentary capital list? The orientation of this list is far from being determined by such a history. The continuance of the stationary state in the future does indeed require a particular balance of composition of the capital list, or at least, of those items in it which will figure actively in such a steady-state production process. But the fact that the capital list is in such balance does nothing to guarantee the persistence of a stationary production process. The conception of the stationary state is a pretence that time is space, that events can be both sequential and co-existent, that somehow a segment of history can be divorced from the fact of the momentary and moving present, that we can avoid the question of whether such a segment is past or future, and, if it is future, can avoid the question of how it can have objective existence other than in some system of expectations. A theory of capital is compelled by the frame of experience, 'the scheme of things entire', to be expectational, to study the question of the orientation, the technological and temporal destiny or intended use of the co-existent items of the capital list. The Austrian theory does not live in this conceptual world but in the unreal one of an *arbitrarily* stationary process.

29.20 *The Austrian theory and Leontief's input–output analysis*

But the Austrian theory is not futile and unilluminating. If it does not map and clarify a landscape of theoretical problems, it reveals the existence of such a landscape. The practical question is how that mapping can be done. The Austrian theory proposes to draw a static picture of what in this chapter we have called the orientation of items of the capital list, in respect of the lengths of time which, in some fixed and maintainable orientation, will elapse before these 'parcels' have become completed consumers' goods. The Austrian theory concerns itself, therefore, exclusively with time. But orientation has another aspect, that of the technological net of intersecting channels of supply between sectors. There is thus another approach to the analysis of the capital stock, a direct investigation of the production net as such, in its technological aspect. The pure technological aspect of orientation is implicitly mapped by Leontief's input–output analysis as a means to answering quite different questions from those of the Austrian theory. Leontief is not concerned to justify an income derived from the possession of intermediate products but to consider how the flows of these products must change in size and technological direction when the composition of general finished consumable output is changed. Evidently there is implicit in a Leontief input–output table a time-orientation of the capital items of each sector, and if some method could be found of getting a quick approximate

picture of this before it had dissolved into a different orientation, the Austrian and Leontief models might be unified.

There is another set of questions. If we are not satisfied with
the notion of a marginal balance between 'impatience' and the
productivity of 'original means of production', what determines
the size and the pace of growth of the capital stock and the
income drawn from it as a proportion of its total value? What,
indeed, determines that value? These questions carry us into
the theory of interest as a monetary phenomenon.

30

Business Cycle Engines

30.1 *Theories of Natural Success, Theories of Capability of Error*

Economic society in the large has elicited two kinds of theory. One kind regards the society's organization as being the result of the inter-action of the endeavours of individual interests each to promote its own advantage. Thus there has arisen the conception which embraces in a single whole the *Tableau Economique* and the General Equilibrium. Unenforced free conduct, subject to the constraint only of the equal freedom of all others, together with the principle that this conduct on the part of each interest is to be demonstrably the best which the condition of universal freedom allows to that interest, leads to the idea of pre-reconciliation as the only scheme of things in which the knowledge necessary for such rationality can be conceived to be available. The accounting principle, that what we start with must all be shown to be absorbed in some transformation which justifies itself by its results, implies that the system of actions must be closed, and the individual actions, or their groups, mutually self-sustaining, so that each activity or sector draws its necessary supplies from identifiable sources. In this conception, reason mediates the operation of Nature. The circumstances of men and their natural needs, an integral part of their inborn constitution, are interpreted by reason as leaving open only one path, any other course representing merely chaos and self-deprivation. Reason thus has a part to play in Nature, even if only as a somewhat less sure and less direct substitute for the instinct which serves other parts of the animal creation. The other kind of theories are not essentially concerned as to whether men's conduct is guided by reason or some more direct mechanism of response. They consider society as a machine, and its performance as the result of its design or conformation. It is the character and form of its built-in behaviour, not the source or the mode of genesis of that behaviour, that concerns these theories in most of their examples. Thought and mind are admitted to some of them, but in a way which contrasts with the duty performed by reason in the General Equilibrium theories. For in this other class of theories of society as a whole, conduct is capable of being unsuccessful. Thus the two kinds of encompassing theory of economic society could be called the Theories of Natural Success and the Theories of Capability of Error. Micro-economic theory, the theory of value, whether in its particular equilibrium or its general equilibrium guise, is the theory of ensured success. Macro-economic theory regards success as merely one possible, and temporary, outcome of a human predicament whose quality is manifested and visible in the real course of history. Macro-economic theories are concerned with the tides which sweep human affairs to and fro.

30.2 *Money and the theory of value*

Macro-economics can be seen as a necessary completion of micro-economics. For the theory of value explained only relative prices, the mutual exchange rates of goods wanted for their own sake. What of money, whose exchange value could not, it seemed, be explained by reference to any technical, physical qualities of its own? Money prices tended all to move together in the same direction. Must there not be some principle which governed money prices as a class independently of that which settled the mutual exchange values of real goods? From this question rose theories of money, dependent, in their Quantity Theory form, on some supposition concerning the size of the flow of real goods which was coming forward to be exchanged for money. Was not the size of this flow determined by equilibrium at the margin between the disutility of labour, as well as that of provision of other means of production, on one hand, and the utility of the goods produced, on the other? In other words, was not the flow of goods determined, naturally and automatically, at full employment level? If such determination of the flow of general output at a level which changed only with the gradual expansion of productive means and capacity could be assumed, the short-term rapid changes, up or down, in the general level of prices could be ascribed to influences 'on the side of money'. Thus monetary theory took a form which did not assign to money any influence on the size of the flow of output of real goods in general, but left that flow as a variable belonging to the theory of value, the theory of natural success including that kind of success represented by full employment. Yet this complete divorce of monetary affairs from those of the production and exchange of real goods, including productive services, for each other, was felt to be unsatisfactory. Was it, for that matter, in fact true that employment was always full? Throughout the nineteenth century and up to the beginning of the second world war, there had appeared to be in industrial nations a cycle of boom and slump with a period of between seven and eleven years, manifesting itself in the general price-level, in employment, and, so far as figures exist, in the national income or general output. It was thus clear that employment could fail, in industrial countries, to be at all times full. Moreover, not all economists were content to leave the theory of money and the theory of value as mutually independent and unrelated matters. Knut Wicksell in *Geldzins und Güterpreise* in 1898, Maynard Keynes (in some degree) in his *Treatise on Money* in 1930, and in a much fuller degree in his *General Theory of Employment, Interest and Money* in 1936, and Sir John Hicks in his article 'A suggestion for simplifying the theory of money' in 1935, all sought to unify the account given by economics of the prices of goods in terms of each other, and the prices of goods in terms of money. In the course of some of these explorations, important steps were taken towards a theory of the business cycle.

30.3 *Wicksell's cumulative process*

Wicksell's idea, the cumulative process, shows how the conditions which give rise to a certain kind of action, intended to take advantage of them or give protection against them, are freshly engendered or re-inforced by those very actions, which themselves are therefore repeated in perhaps a strengthened form; and so on. Wicksell distinguishes from each other the *natural rate of interest*, which in English would be more suitably called the rate of profit or rate of trading revenue, and the *money rate of interest*, at which money can be borrowed from the banking system. When the natural rate exceeds the money rate, money can be employed in business so as to earn more than has to be paid to borrow it. If this circumstance presents itself to many business men at the same time, their endeavours to expand their scale of operations, in order to take advantage of it, will drive up the prices of the means of production, and in so far as these means are goods produced by some of the business men, the expansion will make business appear even more profitable than it did before, so that still more money will be borrowed and still higher prices engendered. In so far as the means of production are human services, their pay will be competitively increased and their resulting higher expenditure will also tend to raise the prices of goods. How long and how far will this escalation proceed? As long, Wicksell points out, as the natural rate is higher than the money rate. For in that situation, every extra unit of goods that can be produced in each week or year will still seem capable of contributing something extra to the total flow of net revenue (the total weekly or annual excess of sale-proceeds of product over expenses of its production). The cost of production per physical unit of goods will be rising month by month, but the price of goods per unit will be rising as fast, will be keeping ahead, and the persisting gap per unit will invite an ever-larger output.

30.4 *The natural rate of interest and the marginal efficiency of capital as 'black boxes'*

We ought, I think, to pay attention to the deep cleavage of meaning and epistemic character between such a conception as the cumulative process and the conception of general pre-reconciled equilibrium in a timeless system. The General Equilibrium deals at one stroke with all the complications of temporal sequence and delay, by abolishing the consideration of time. It has one sole principle: to find a solution in which equal freedom and equal and perfect knowledge, possessed by every participant, is used by him to obtain the greatest advantage which his circumstances, including *these* circumstances, make accessible to him. The analysis of this problem is intricate, but it does not give rise to the need for an indefinite number of arbitrary further assumptions. The general character of the solution arises directly from the essential statement of the problem. With the cumulative process, or any conception involving the engenderment of one situation by another in temporal sequence, we are obliged to answer a series of questions to which the number of non-excludable answers is endless. We have to say, regarding the successive transformations of situations one into another, how fast each variable changes in comparison with others. To express the matter in a convenient formal language, we have to specify the numerical values of a matrix which carries the vector describing the situation of one date into the situation of a subsequent date. But such specification is either arbitrary, or special to each particular historical or social context. In Wicksell's process, the persistence of 'supernormal' profitability may depend on the relative speed of wage rises compared with price rises. Wicksell has encapsulated all such considerations in the expression the *natural rate of interest*. But this phrase dismisses the whole essence of the matter. What the natural rate, as an effective summary of thousands of individual judgements and conjectures, will be, depends on the interpretations which the individuals put, each in the light of his personal and unique experience, on each item of 'the news'. The natural rate is a composite of *expectations*, *original thoughts* merely suggested by the streams of impressions variously received by different individuals. It is this very nature of expectations, elusive and subtle beyond conception, which has compelled the economic theoretician in his task of simplification by abstraction, to exclude them altogether or conceal them in a 'black box' such as the natural rate of interest or the marginal efficiency of capital. The treatment they receive is *arbitrary*. It cannot rest on the logic by which general equilibrium, the image of rationality, is rigidly determined.

The term *natural rate* suggests a technologically determined productivity measured, perhaps, as in the Austrian theory of capital which Wicksell had studied. Myrdal (as a result of a heuristic process which, very much to our instruction, he records in his book*) discarded this notion in favour of a comparison of

* Gunnar Myrdal, *Monetary Equilibrium* (Hodge, 1939).

the total discounted expected net earnings of capital goods, in all of their expected years of use, with their construction cost. This measure, attained by a suitably weighted average, took account, he explained, of the value-oriented concern of business men (in contrast with merely physical measures); of the dependence of the worth of capital goods on expectations concerning their whole-life performance; of the variety of the interest-rates which might need to be applied for discounting future supposed earnings of different deferments; and of the diversity of business men's individual conceptions of the future. It naturally and automatically included in its determining factors the uncertainty inseparable from expectation. Myrdal did not refer explicitly to the mutability which must also inhere in any variable or schedule dependent on expectation. But his frame of thought, being the same as that later adopted by Keynes in the *General Theory*, provided formally for this character also. In Wicksell, however, it was the money rate which was most prone to vary, since it was affected by the changing circumstances and responses of the banking system.

30.5 *The paradox of unity and diversity in the notion of a cycle of phases*

The picture which theory presents to us of the cumulative process, or of the business cycle as a whole, necessarily contains another feature which radically distinguishes it from general equilibrium. Equilibrium is universal, complete, all-inclusive, unique and therefore necessarily pre-reconciled adjustment. A *cycle* is in its nature a multiplicity of situations, each one prone to change into one of the others because it is *not* an equilibrium. Each such situation consists of one numerical value of every one of the variables which compose our picture of the economic society. Each such situation describes the entire society at a particular moment, and a different situation describes it at a necessarily different moment. Thus there enters into any picture of any kind of cycle the notion of a *gap of time* between different states of the system, the notion of a *time-lag* separating one phase of the pattern of transformations from another. The notion of time-lags refers to something which evidently belongs to the essence of the phenomenon of a cycle. Unless there are uneliminable time-lags, why do we not have the instantaneous arrival at a pre-reconciled equilibrium? The question is tautologous. But if there are time-lags, what vehicle conveys through time the influence of the events or situation of one moment to shape those of another? It is this last question which has been neglected in greater or less degree by business cycle theorists, but which typifies a kind of question whose neglect may be destructive to economics.

The mechanism of cumulative change of a general price level or of general output does not by itself account for a complete cycle of boom and slump. We have also to explain how boom is turned into slump and vice versa. If we are to think of any one instance of a sequence of boom, slow-down, reversal, slump, and recovery to a fresh boom, or the type of such sequences, as an organic unity, a phenomenon in its own right springing from the organization of economic society or from the ultimate human predicament and the fundamental nature of things, then we must show that each phase is somehow engendered by preceding phases, or else that all phases are indissolubly unified as a manifestation of one and the same aspect of Nature. Such unity of the business cycle phenomenon implies of necessity some diachronic fibre in history and the course of events. Needless to say, this idea is a commonplace. We take it as an unquestioned axiom of life that what *is* at our present moment is part of a structure embracing past and in some sense future situations. There is, we instinctively hold, either complete determinism, or else a penetration of history by threads of constraint, whereby the *potentiae* of an impending time-interval are not able to be anything whatever, but must fall within some range whose bounds are imposed by what at present exists. Yet Zeno's paradox of the arrow is still with us: What has one moment to do with another? What is movement, if *the present* embraces all that *is*?

In the notion of a cycle, whether in natural or in human affairs, we have two ostensibly contradictory aspects. On one hand there are the phases. These are evidently different from each other and therefore plural. On the other hand, the essence of cyclicality, the ground for referring to the phases as constituting a cycle, is an assumption that this collection of plural appearances is a unity. If we then accept the notion of a solitary, all-inclusive present, transforming itself continuously into another present but not co-existing with any other moment, we are obliged to regard the plurality and diversity of the phases as implicit in the content, nature or 'design' of the general moment, the solitary moment of actuality. So far as the concept of the cycle is justified, its explanation must be discoverable, if at all, by dissection of 'the present'. If the term cycle is justified, everything essential to the cycle must be present in any 'present moment'. Then the problem is, why do not all these composing elements resolve themselves at once, why does not 'the cycle' disappear through a single, comprehensive and immediate adjustment?

In this chapter we have suggested, on one hand that the notion of *time-lags* is indispensable to theories of the business cycle; on the other, that all the working parts of the business cycle, every operative element indispensable to it, must *co-exist* if the notion of cycle is to mean something. Existence is existence in the present, the universal and general present moment. If we do not regard all the operative and essential elements of the cycle as co-existing, we are then obliged to invoke some means of explanation for each separate phase, some means arising from special 'accidental' circumstances peculiar, not only to the phase in question but to the particular instance of the cycle that we are examining. Or else we must suppose that some such means of explanation of each phase arises *ex nihilo* as it is needed. These seem to be the formal alternatives: co-existence of all ingredients of the cyclical phenomenon, or the complete absense of any unity and coherence in any appearances which suggest, but are denied, the character of a cycle. Now it will be justly said that much is made in this volume of the possibility of essential novelty, the occurrence of thoughts which cannot be traced to distinct antecedents and dissected into currents already flowing in the mind of the individual: thoughts which are original, which *start something new*. We do put great weight on this possibility, believing it to be interpretable so as to allow us to conceive conduct and choice as at once free and reasoned. But these considerations are beside our present point. To invoke novelty is to banish the notion of the cycle: the cycle is *repetitive*, what is novel can, as such, only occur once. A theory (if indeed it can even justify that name) will not be a theory of a *cycle* unless it refers to the co-existence of all indispensable elements of that entity in the *general present*. This co-existence does not mean the co-visibility of all such elements to the individual business man who is a participant in the business cycle. What, then, of time-lags? They are the lapses of time which the written record, the material traces, or the personal and living memories, *consultable in the present* (for 'the past' exists for us only in the present, in the marks it has left upon the present), show to have separated the *manifestation* of different elements.

30.6 *The conception of an epistemic cycle*

Action can be suggested by, and respond to, events outside the mind, only if these events are perceived. But action can itself bring into view what was hitherto latent. If, then, the elements which make up the business world include some which will be brought above the threshold of the business men's perception by the action on their part induced by other elements, and if these latter will then be superseded in their influence by the newly visible ones, which will in turn induce their own eclipse by the further action which they stimulate, we may have an epistemic cycle which operates by the successive recognition of elements always existing in the system (the business world) but suffering each in turn a phase of eclipse by the ascendancy of some of the others. An example of such a cycle can be proposed as follows.

Investment is the production of improvements in the circumstances of the society, such as can yield up very little of their value in immediate enjoyment or sustenance. Those who receive pay for making these improvements will nonetheless try to spend part or the whole of this pay on consumption. The demand for consumption goods will thus be strengthened (the schedule or curve of demand will be bodily shifted and deformed so as to represent larger quantities demanded at given prices) in a manner perhaps *unexpected* by the business men who have ordered the investment. Their own action will thus have brought into play a principle which, at first unsuspected and now misunderstood by them, will induce a further increase of the investment-flow with a consequent further unexpected strengthening of consumer demand. Such a 'cumulative process' may at length generate a belief in the indefinite continuance of its symptoms, namely, the progressive increase in physical quantities of goods sold per time-unit and the progressive rise of their prices. The general seizure of business minds by such a belief will give an extra, but last, thrust to the investment-flow. For now the strengthening of general demand which flows from this latest acceleration of the pace of spending on improvements to equipment will have been *expected*. Its occurrence will be seen, not as further improving but as confirming the business prospect. The inducement to increase the investment-flow still further will be lacking. So, therefore, will the now-anticipated strengthening of demand. Expectations will have been disappointed. The inducement to invest will then suffer a weakening leading to weakening of general demand, again, perhaps, contrary to expectation. A downward cumulative process can thus be engendered and, by a train of reappraisals like that of the down-turn but in reverse, may be itself arrested and turned into a recovery.

30.7 *The arbitrary separatism of economic theory*

Such a sketch is designedly a mere stringing together of hypotheses and possibilities. Would its suggestions be rendered more acceptable or more likely to be fruitful by its replacement by a formal mathematical expression of such of its character as could be given any precise form? We think they would not. The reader will say, with entire and unquestioned justice, that by such a sketch no remotest approach to demonstration is achieved. Proof, as the mathematician understands it, is very seldom attained in the kind of reasonings with which economists (rightly) content themselves. A rigorous proof is necessarily about abstractions. Proof exists in thought, and can be composed only of thought-entities designed for its purpose. The impressions gained from the world, in some regions of knowledge, may seem to lend themselves readily enough to impersonation by such inventions of the theorem-constructing mind. But economics is at the furthest extreme from that case. In physics, chemistry, astronomy and perhaps genetics, experimental isolation of a few factors can be arranged by men or Nature. The 'factors' themselves, invented concepts, nonetheless may seem to spring into relief by Nature's own prompting, or to crowd spontaneously in the wake of a single inspired hypothesis. But in economics there is no segregating of influences, no inoculating the situations and their transformations against infection from outside the particular group of elements that we wish to study. History is one whole. The master historians have scarcely contrived to present it as determined uniquely by an internal but exhibitable logic. Abstraction is arbitrary. Any one abstract system is one out of a boundless field of possible selections or inventions. Rigorous proof is worth-while when the abstract system conforms to some great principle or idea which, perhaps, can be encompassed in no other way than by this particular abstraction. The value-construct may be the only way in which we can conceive the actions of all individuals to be chosen in equal freedom and determined by fully-informed reason. The statement of this conception is itself paradoxical, for choice and determinacy seem ill-assorted words. A meaning can nonetheless be found for 'determinate choice' and we have discussed it in Chapter 13. The value-construct thus is in a special position. There is scarcely another context in the whole economic field where it can be said that rigorous proof of theorems derived from an arbitrary choice of premisses has much merit in itself.

The cyclical surge and recession of prices and employment, with a nine-year period, which seemed to prevail from the early years of industrialization until the second world war, gathered a literature which now, perhaps, seems disproportionate to its importance, except for the great catastrophe of the 1930s, which was out of scale with anything that went before. It might be equally possible to discern a political cycle of reform and conservation, or a diplomatic cycle of war and peace. The search for some supposed mechanism inherent in the nature of industrial society may have been gratuitous, when it conceived the phenomenon as something distinctively economic rather than an aspect of the general ebb and flow of human struggles to survive and to acquire. Even in the business cycle field, economics has set itself apart. The nine-year cycle seemed to reflect an aspect of history. But can it be right to treat one aspect of history as self-contained and capable of explanation on its own? There are vaster problems. The problem of how industrialization began, after the millenia of widely-organized but non-mechanical life, seems a more interesting one. We have argued (in Chapter 3) that economics is a non-self-sufficient discipline, since its field is encompassed in the general field of human affairs, activities and ambitions as a whole, and is a discipline with no orientation towards any basic, unifying principle. What we classify as economic phenomena, and endow with special principles peculiar to that class, are threads in a vast supporting fabric without which they would have no location, bearing, meaning or possible existence. In the gigantic scene of the history and pre-history of mankind, infinitely complex and rich in intricate detail beyond conception, economic principles can serve to relate this detail to that detail, can serve to construct stereotypes or recurrent patterns each appearing to have some unity and self-contained robustness of its own, though all capable of being themselves assembled in a more-than-infinity of wider arrangements; can serve to trace threads of influence of one person, party, institution, vision, situation or event upon others; can serve as some of the mortar of the edifice. Yet even so, it is not obvious why some of the principles of men's dealings with each other should be abstracted from the general stream of life and made into a separate discipline. There are dangers in this separatism. It is certain that in the mind of the politician, the jurist, the civil administrator, the diplomat, the historian, the individual in his private and personal life, there is no such separation in any prime and basic sense. What, then, is the role of economics as a tool of the historian?

31

History, Theory and World-Picture

31.1 *Dissimilarity of explanation and prediction*

It is often argued, as by Marshall, that explanation and prediction are merely two aspects of one operation, two reflections
of identical theory:

> The function then of analysis and deduction in economics is not to
> forge a few long chains of reasoning, but to forge rightly many short
> chains and single connecting links...select the right facts, group
> them rightly, and make them serviceable for suggestions in thought
> and guidance in practice. The explanation of the past and the
> prediction of the future are not different operations, but the same
> worked in opposite directions, the one from effect to cause, the other
> from cause to effect.

This passage casts many rays on the nature of Marshall's outlook and method, to which we will return. But we shall not
entirely agree with its conclusion. Marshall speaks of *selecting*
the facts, and this is the difficulty. For prediction, if it is to claim
any scientific standing and not that of mere sooth-saying, must
be conditional, must start with the words *If* or *Provided that*.
And the whole question is: What conditions can the theorist
find, that will both validate his theory and stand some chance
of themselves proving not only to be fulfilled in fact but of
covering all the circumstances? How can he make his list of
assumed circumstances relevantly complete? How can he be
sure that his statements of the conditions pre-supposed in his
predictions are water-tight, inclusive enough, and do not allow
Nature to interpret them so as to slip in some unthought-of
element, which has not been barred by the careful protocol, but
nevertheless upsets the whole apple-cart? When we turn to
explanation, however, there is no denying that we are given
great help in the task of selection. The record of any passage of
history or sequence of situations will seem to exemplify *stereo-*

types, sets of impressions associated in fixed patterns of sequence or simultaneity. Once such a stereotype has established itself in history and experience at large as something recurrent and recognizable, it will itself constitute the basis of 'explanation'. If *A* seems invariably to be accompanied or followed by *B*, we have done something to 'explain' *B* as soon as we have established the presence of *A*. In such a thought-process, or manifestation of a conditioning of our minds, the selection of features or influences which are to be invoked as 'explaining' something is ready-made. The proposition is essentially: If you find *A*, you can be happy about *B*, you can regard the presence of *B* as 'normal' in view of the presence of *A*. The argument does not go beyond the minimum need of the mind for evidence of a familiar state of affairs. There is no assertion that *B* cannot occur without *A* (or even that *A cannot* occur without *B*). But their co-presence is regarded as a natural and often-observed thing, reflecting a facet of the natural order which we can be glad to know even if we can go no deeper into it. The utter lack of rigour in such reactions is beside the point. The mind gropes for the familiar, and in the sea of confusing cross-currents and eddies which human affairs present, any hint of permanence, repetition and obedience to rule will be seized upon. Like a painter studying his landscape in its shifting light and shade, we can discern in any era of history ten thousand possible compositions, but there will appear within the scene a number of self-subsisting sub-compositions. The painter will pick out the dark border of a wood, the group of buildings typical of a farm, the field of a size convenient for a herd, or a stream with the meanders natural to a flat country, and these will necessarily be found contributing to his ultimate picture. The brain of the observer has learnt to interpret certain configurations of light and shade, of patches of colour, as natural features of the kind that we regard as 'things in themselves': farms, rivers, woods. The brain of the historian finds corresponding ready-made assemblies of impressions. Marshall's *selective* stage can thus proceed some way before his stage of analysis and logic need be invoked.

We may even venture to claim that Marshall had some such preparatory process in mind. He speaks in our quoted passage of 'selecting the right facts, grouping them rightly, and making them serviceable for *suggestions'* (our italics). We ought by no means to think of such a procedure as arbitrary. It is *art*, not caprice, which is at work. But there is in all this a plain admission that the art of explanation of the course of history has much freedom. If we stand back from the claim that explanation and prediction are one, in practice and not merely in principle, we shall surely be impressed with their contrasting nature. To be allowed to taste a cake and be asked what were the ingredients is not the same thing as to be given some ingredients and be asked what can be made of them. In practice, history can be 'explained', after a certain style, without any acceptance of determinism, and without insuperable difficulties in finding sets of materials which will compose into an ordered structure. But prediction, obliged to select its own materials and assumptions, is hardly more than theorizing in a vacuum. To ask: How did that traveller get here? is *not* the same as to ask: Where may that traveller go from here? The former has a setting in which clues may readily offer themselves, the latter is not likely to be so well provided with *ancillary questions* whose answers may suggest themselves, and may themselves suggest clues to the intentions or the circumstances of the traveller into the void.

31.2 *Marshall's pragmatism*

In the passage we have quoted, there appears again Marshall's settled dependence on the 'particular equilibrium' method, the method which isolates the market for a single commodity, the industry making that commodity, or the workers in a particular trade, and studies this separated small part of economic society on the assumption that no effects which its own changes have on the rest of society are reflected back to have effects upon itself. For Marshall speaks of 'short chains and single connecting links' of reasoning. These can hardly lead us to an encompassing *system*. They are typical of 'particular' analysis, whose attraction consists in this very manageability, the directness of the steps of inference by which their essential structure is revealed and the uncomplicated manipulation to which its elements lend themselves. This approach seems to preclude any attempt to explain history as a whole on some general, all-pervasive and omni-competent principle. Marshall's endeavour was to explain the typical modes of *contemporary industrial history in the small*. No doubt he saw his procedure as giving insight into the great drift of things in the business aspect of life and the life of society in its battle to survive. He was able to explain how men's material lives were improving through technology, thrift and education, and the social movements of the time. What he was thus able to see, however, was the *texture* of economic history rather than its shape or outline.

What claim, then, was Marshall making for his kind of analysis? It was to be serviceable 'for suggestions in thought and guidance in practice'. A theory which claimed to answer all questions legitimately put to it, all questions properly belonging to some exactly defined field or subject-matter, would *prescribe*, not offer 'suggestions' or 'guidance'. It seems plain that Marshall thought of his constructions as tools for manipulating material whose precise character could not be foreseen, material from which he would select and interpret the ingredients of an argument. Illumination is generated when a recognizable starting-point leads to a recognizable conclusion, when two situations are shown to be facets of the same reality. Marshall's method does not promise, or require, that the starting-point shall be in every respect the one that the enquirer at first proposed (even when that enquirer was himself) nor that it shall give an answer in terms limited in advance. There is freedom. But freedom to devise constructions is not compatible with the existence of an omni-competent, all-inclusive general theory. Marshall does not subscribe to a determinism of thought. His pragmatic, short-range, non-determinist attitude implies that if explanation and prediction are indeed the same, then *prediction as well as explanation* must be free to select and interpret the set of 'facts' which it will use. Theory, in this view, can give unity and structure to small portions of history, each on its own, but not to the vast, intricate flow of things taken as a whole. The unity of explanation and prediction, in this view, resides partly in the limited task which each accepts. Explanation does not claim to show that what happened was the determinate and uniquely possible happening; prediction does not claim to give the only possible account of what must follow the existing situation. Explanation and prediction are unified in a somewhat different sense from the formal and rigorous one. Each is an attempt to describe the texture and feel of reality, to describe the way things typically happen, without being essentially concerned as to whether the questioner wishes to understand a record of past events or the possibilities inherent in a present situation. In its modest and pragmatic aims, Marshall's method evidently differs totally from the great determinist systems. But it would be well for all theoreticians to ask themselves sometimes what is the kind of world-picture which their particular constructions pre-suppose.

31.3 *Scholars are not as ready to predict as to explain*

We have been suggesting that explanation and 'prediction' can be unified in nature and method by allowing prediction to avail itself of a selective process somewhat equivalent to the one which is automatically available to explanation. History places certain goods in the front of its shop-window, and it is out of these that we are naturally tempted to compose our explanatory pattern. Men in influential positions, parties with a weight of votes, the 'accidents' which (so evidently) can divert the outcome of enterprises, campaigns, crusades and conflicts, have in the record already declared themselves. But when they are the elements in a *present* situation, they are potential, not declared, forces and factors. Prediction is at an unfair disadvantage. The symmetry of prediction and explanation is true only in an abstract world, where the data on which reason is to work are complete and certain for both purposes. This symmetry assumes *that the selection of data has already been performed*, in a manner which is guaranteed (whence and by whom?) to be correct. Marshall, by contrast, is explicit that the selection of facts is part of the analyst's task. Now in spite of the symmetry of explanation and prediction which many assert, we see in the practice of scholars a double contrast between their attitudes to the respective tasks. On one hand, while the great majority of historians are willing and eager to explain the past, very few are anxious to prophesy the future. Those bold spirits who do so have a radically different aim and method from the searchers for the detailed background of recorded events. Karl Marx and Oswald

Spengler sought to scrutinize the features of Destiny. Human society and civilization, they supposed, had its own necessity, its fate. There might be room for human individuals to make some small splash of their own, but they were mere swimmers in a tide-race. Those who believe in cyclical history can in some degree apply the scientific procedure of seeking repetitive patterns, but theirs is nonetheless a macro- and not a micro-history. The meticulous collation and scrutiny of documents, Acton's belief that a full documentation would establish, once for all, the motives as well as the actions of history, show a different outlook. They made sense of a sort out of the record which they brought to light, but if what they produced was a 'theory' of the period or events in question, it was by no means a theory of the kind which could be applied to prediction. It appealed, at every step, to ostensible *initiatives*, thoughts, actions and *démarches* which seem to start a new train of events, and which, at most, can only be shown to be a natural or not incongruous sequel to the circumstances which prevailed, but cannot be shown to be the uniquely possible sequel. Prediction, however, as mostly understood, requires us, after stipulating the circumstances and the principles that we assume, to state a unique and necessary evolution of events.

31.4 *Historical determinism*

There is a paradox and a dilemma in the historian's world of ideas. He can claim that history, the objective sequence of states or of transformations,* is uniquely determinate. He can then seek to show the fitting-together of the pieces of this struc-ture, which he could liken to a jig-saw puzzle where only one mode of assembly was allowed by the shape of the pieces. To do this would be to go behind the mere assumption or assertion of determinism to show, in a doubtless rather crude way, how it worked. It is doubtful whether, on these lines, he could speak of *cause and effect*, since the structure would have to be regarded as a unity, each feature and detail of which was determined by the whole. The only 'cause' of historical events, in such a view,

* The case for regarding these as formally mutually equivalent is set out in my *Decision, Order and Time*, pp. 5–6.

would be the Scheme of Things Entire. He could of course point to 'proximate' causes, the more immediate circumstances out of which some event directly sprang. But this would give to the word 'cause' a lesser meaning than we wish sometimes to give it. As we have tried to show in Chapter 13, a world-picture of this kind does not exclude a role for reason. The question whether or not, or in what sense, it excludes 'freedom' seems a rarefied one. There are, as we have also tried to suggest, other schemes by which 'freedom' can be assigned to men who none the less live by reason.

31.5 *Origination, reason and freedom*

Or the historian can adopt instead the notion of a *loose texture* of history. According to such a view, there are constraints on the course which things can take as a sequel to any given state of affairs, constraints imposed by natural physical laws and the time required for ideas to be absorbed and diffused. In any situation, the things that could happen, the situations which could ensue within a given time, would be bounded but not determinate. In this frame we can even suppose that individuals can originate ideas, that thoughts can arise which are not the uniquely possible sequel to previous thoughts or given impressions; that thoughts can arise which have some element of inception, of essential novelty. Then there can be freedom in the sense of freedom of invention, of imagination, without the need to say that freedom means freedom from the constraints of reason. A man can be supposed to act always in rational response to his 'circumstances': but those 'circumstances' can, *and must*, be in part the creation of his own mind; must be, because it is impossible for mortal man, in the life-span he is allowed, ever to have eye-witness knowledge of all his objective relevant circumstances.

In this loose-textured history, men's choices of action being choices amongst thoughts which spring indeterminately in their minds, we can deem them to *initiate* trains of events in some real sense. *Cause* then takes on a different meaning from that of the grip which a rigid determinacy has on each of its component events. Events at the human level will be 'caused' by the original thoughts which give sudden shape to the general pressure of an individual's motives. From such an original, genuinely inceptive cause, we can suppose ourselves able in principle to trace the spreading sequels in many directions. Given a defined 'event', the transformation of one specified situation into another, the historian may suppose himself able in principle to trace its antecedents back by stages to one or several such initiating, original thoughts. This kind of frame or world-picture gives a far more interesting meaning to the kind of analysis which Marshall seems to have in mind. In 'loose-textured' history (if this expression is acceptable) the economist's short-range explanations will correspond in some sense to what he is supposing to be the basic nature of the origins of history itself.

31.6 *The theoretician's need of a world-picture*

The economic theoretician ought to be concerned as to the general nature of the world he is, consciously or unconsciously, assuming as the field of his theorizing. From Herodotus onwards, historians have been consciously and deeply concerned with the 'philosophy of history', the nature and genesis of the stream of events itself and the proper practice and assumptions to be applied in historiography. The question of the meaning and nature of their explanations of what they describe has been important to them. But history is the manifestation of the conduct which the economist seeks to understand. There can be no justified divorce between his theories and his world-picture. It may be that no single and general world-picture will serve as the frame for every question he wishes to ask. But if so, it is all the more necessary to face consciously the question what basic assumptions about the 'receptacle' of human affairs are being made for the purpose of each question. In the end, logic may have to be left behind, and insight sought in an extra-logical fusing of strands of thought which strictly are incompatible. The grinding rules of the grammarians must, in the last resort, be denied their ultimate tyranny.

32

The Sovereignty of Theory

It has been the posture of science that there is truth to be found. Truth is unique. But to be unique it must be complete, since otherwise there will be freedom to complete it in any number of different ways. But there is no knowing that we can ever arrive at the whole truth. In human terms the truth must be something adapted to the mind's capacity and nature. But what presumption is there that the 'objective' truth, and a truth which can be humanly conceived, can be matched and identified with each other? J. B. S. Haldane said: 'The universe is not merely stranger than you imagine, it is stranger than you *can* imagine.' If the unique and complete truth must therefore eternally elude us, there is reason and necessity to accept other insights into the nature of science. Science acquires a freedom, an existence in its own right, it becomes an artefact. Truth may then be seen as plural, choosable, capable of being invented. Its ultimate and essential purpose, that technologies cannot perform, is to console the human mind. It is an ancient view that truth is attained by the poet. A poem is something *made*, originated. History, in the view of its first practitioners, was a personal art. Shape was given to the suggestions and sources available, by the historian in his right and capacity as an *author*. Theory, the conceived Scheme of Things, need not take an earth-bound view. It is constrained, for we shall not be consoled by fantasy. But it can take the suggestions, the impressions, the phenomena, and use them for composition.

When the impressions have been classified into regions of investigation, there will be no knowing whether or not the boundaries which have thus been chosen leave open the paths of illuminating and suggestive connections of ideas. When the compass of potential knowledge as a whole has been split up into superficially convenient sectors, there will be no knowing whether each sector has a natural self-sufficiency. For some sectors it will be plainly reckless to presume it. Human conduct must surely be formed by a confluence of all the needs, interests, institutions and intellectual speculations of the human being. To treat some sub-set of these influences as a separate subject of enquiry is to compound the basic autonomy of theory-making by a further freedom to select the influences. Whatever theory is then devised will exist by sufferance of the things which it has excluded. Such is the position of economic theories. But since it is the position of all economic theories, none can in general claim superiority on these grounds.

Science has made it a virtue to be concerned only with impressions which, supposedly, can be shared and are public. Economics has followed in this track. Its phenomena are those of the market place. Informally describing for its own purposes the source of those phenomena, it has simplified and rendered abstract to the last degree the human concerns and characteristics to which it appeals. They are 'tastes' ('given') which place in order of preference available collections of goods, or the experiences to be derived from them. The character of each of these goods and experiences is also given. The world is divided into the part which lies inside the human mind and the part which provides the mind with a stream or field of impressions from outside itself. To examine the individual mind with the aid of the only person who can directly inspect it is regarded as unscientific to the last degree. Science must rest upon the account of the eye-witness, but only of the eye-witness who looks outward, not inward. Each observer, each eye-witness is an individual, a particular, proper-named, identified and unique individual, but his field of observation must be strictly controlled. Half of what he might wish to examine is forbidden. From heart-searching and self-knowledge, science withdraws the skirts of its garment.

The objective and the subjective. The former to be embraced, the latter to be suppressed and eliminated. It is strange that Science, that vast work of original thought, should be so contemptuous of its origins. In many passages of this volume we have sought to show that the entities amongst which men *choose* are necessarily *thoughts, things conceived*, existent only in their minds, since things existent in the present outside the mind are unique portions of a unity. Choice is made amongst the invented, subjective creations of thought. Is economics, 'the logic of choice', unconcerned with the mode and sources of such invention?

If thought is sterile and illusory, with no more influence on the course of things than is exerted on the sweep of the tide by the sunlight which glints upon its waters, then the psychic link between circumstance and action can be ignored and action and history can be treated as visibly, *publicly* determinate. If choice is the mere registering of the superior objective character of one set of attainable circumstances over another, its greater aptness to serve the *given* needs of the individual chooser or the members of the market, then 'choice' is a mere part of the machine of determinate conduct. But if thoughts can be original in some profounder sense than the unforeseen but determinate response to impressions; if, of necessity, the impressions available to compose the imagined Scheme of Things are the mere skimming of an ocean, so that the freedom to select and the freedom to compose are virtually limitless; then it will be hard for any one composition to claim to be the unique 'truth'. To deny to the theoretician his creative freedom is to say that the landscape painter must paint only the earth and the trees, and leave out the effects of cloud and shifting, flowing illumination; to deny to him his selection of viewpoint and particular moment of sight. Those who test theories for conformity to a pre-assigned frame of demands and suppositions have a duty to consider whether this frame belongs to the same world of originated concepts and questions as that which enveloped the mind of the theoretician; whether their level of abstraction is the same as his; whether the weight they give to incisive simplicity, to inclusive unification, is the same as his.

The claim of theory to a sovereignty, a right to envisage its own questions and to seek, not some ultimate unique truth, but insight, a light on things and a scheme for that restricted class of impressions which it has creatively or arbitrarily defined, rests on the more-than-infinite plurality (cardinality) of the sets of impressions themselves that can be drawn even from a supposedly defined field, the more-than-infinite number of ways of arranging in patterns any given set of impressions, the inexhaustible freedom of thought. Theory, let us boldly say, is not right or wrong but less or more powerful in affording 'a good state of mind' to men confronted with an unfathomable universe.

BOOK VI

Epistemics versus Axiomatics

33

The Science of Imprecision

Economics is rent by the opposite pulls of its subject matter and its intellectual environment. Its field is that of human affairs. Its special part of that field has not, I think, been marked out after a survey of the whole, but rather has been gradually gathered as the appropriate demesne of a compact nucleus, namely, the activity of exchange. The buying and selling of things is a special and unique activity, likely to excite curiosity and sufficiently definite in its nature and restricted in its bounds to offer a seemingly manageable problem. The wonder is that an explicit science of commerce was not founded several millenia before Cantillon's day. Buying and selling is the natural seed-bed of a thousand questions. What is the money which appears in each transaction, what are its properties, its source, its rules? What is the source of the things for which money is given? They are produced. In the ancient world, this might not have appeared an interesting facet of life, since production was done either by Nature when she multiplied the flocks, or by slaves where human effort was required. The scholarly man was not a producer of saleable wares, only a consumer. But suddenly, in the middle of the eighteenth century, Commerce became conscious of its place in the world, and exhibited itself in the work of Quesnay as the life-process of society, composed of the inter-contributory, mutually sustaining activities of Nature, artisans and farmers. The *Tableau Economique* exhibited a self-sustaining, self-contained and self-sufficient system. This system, taken as a whole, was the enclosed and defensible field of economics. But this field differed distinctly from the rest of the field of human affairs. It offered the possibility of arithmetic, of accountancy, of measurement, of adding-up, of tabulation and neat balance-sheets. And measurement and arithmetic were the marks of that Natural Science which was now in full sail. The outer dress of commerce, the fact that weighable goods were exchanged for countable money, could fill the observer's eye to the exclusion of all such questions as motive, judgement, conduct, policy, thought. The ideas that lay in the foreground of human affairs, when these were viewed from the standpoint of History, lay in the background when these affairs were viewed from the standpoint of Statistics. Human affairs *as such* would not have seemed readily assimilable to natural science, readily quantifiable in any essential sense, though kings were doubtless always concerned for their revenues, as the nursery rhyme tells us. But the part of human affairs which was Commerce had not waited to consult the more elevated or dramatic parts, politics, diplomacy, art, religion, before allowing itself to be lured along the road of number and accountancy. Thus a science which is concerned with goods of unlistable diversity has to pretend that the quantity of these goods, considered as one heap, can be measured on a one-dimensional scale, and that the price of the 'typical' item of this heap, or of the 'typical' basket of such items, can be stated. Economics is the science which, of all scholarly disciplines, most recklessly oversteps the gulf between the humanities and the physical sciences. Making a virtue of the imprecision which its double face imposes on it, it has developed the technique of index-numbers into an engrossing and subtle branch of practical mathematics. Seizing on the peculiar character of markets, which draw men of widely different tastes into apparent unanimity concerning the proper mutual exchange values of goods, it has declared these public values to have the force and meaning of such physical attributes as length or mass, and to be able to support a vast structure of aggregative calculations. Economics has veritably turned imprecision itself into a science: economics, the science of the quantification of the unquantifiable and the aggregation of the incompatible. It has followed this road at so violent a gallop, that much which is of significance and influence has been trampled on, much territory has been claimed which cannot be held.

In commerce, the foreground is occupied often by things visible and tangible, possessing physical attributes which inhere in them independently of human desires, assessments or interpretations. This prominence of physical objects with intrinsic qualities and properties has inevitably offered the suggestion that economics can concern itself largely with these intrinsic properties; can assume that the objects have the same permanence of nature, and of significance to their owners and users, when they are seen as economic entities as when they are seen as physical things. When, further, their economic significance has appeared to be unequivocally established on a pre-reconciling market where unanimity prevails concerning the ratios of exchange which are to constitute a timeless or a long-period equilibrium, the assimilation of economics to a natural science has seemed easy. Scalar quantification, mechanism, description of the structure and life of economic society in terms of stable mathematical functions and a closed system of accounts have seemed easy and tempting. The methods of physical science, ready to hand in the eighteenth century, were adopted and have taken over the field. The face of things which has thus been concealed and undervalued consists, among other matters, in the inconstancy of any system whose elements, in fact, are thoughts actual or potential, and not things. Economic values depend not only on judgements of the capacity of objects to satisfy immediate need. They rest on judgements of what other people's judgements will be; on the entire web of technology which in the modern world binds together all conceivable materials, tools, circumstances, skills and knowledge so that everything appears as a skein of endless potential relationships; they rest on speculation, where profit depends wholly on the supposition that prices will *change* in a way contrary to the present beliefs of many participants in the market; speculation in whose very nature there inheres a mutual contradiction of the expectations and hopes of different individuals. They rest also on bargaining, where success depends, not on the co-operative establishment of 'objective truth', but on concealment and deception. Economic values exist under the ever-present threat of novelty which can at any moment render methods and their embodying equipment obsolete. They rest on great tides of social assumption, such as the conviction, which in the early 1970s seems to have seized the entire industrialized world, that money prices in general will continue for ever to rise continuously and rapidly. Because of its superficial facility of measurement, economics has allowed its modes of thought to become in some degree divorced from its subject-

matter. It has tried for a precision, certainty and reach of prediction whose basis is not there.

The divided counsels of economics arise from another source
besides the incongruity of subject-matter and method. Our
discipline seeks to serve two masters. On the one hand it is the
scholar's attempt to penetrate the mystery of human nature and
human ambitions from one special direction; on the other it is
the administrator's means of manipulation of mass reactions.
Government policy is in its basic nature *statistical*, whether or
not it has supplied itself with data. It cannot itself directly care
for the individual but only for the mass and the average of
society. The individual soldier must take his chance, so long as
the army wins the battle. This is the necessary, irremediable
philosophy of government. From this viewpoint, in this service,
economics is not concerned with the sources of the conduct
whose broad effects it uses. In aiming to control the average and
the mass, it wishes only to know about the average and the
mass. It is statistical in its measurements as well as in its aims.
We might describe the contrast between the two vistas of
economic theory in the same terms as those sometimes used by
physicians, some of whom declare that they do not pay attention
to statistical experience but only to clinical experience. Those
who speak so are accused by others of merely basing their procedures on small samples instead of large. However, this misses
the point. The clinician studies in detail and depth the tangible
and concrete realities of his field, the medical statistician,
indispensable though his data are, sweeps the field with his spy
glass at long range. Aggregates, averages, index numbers, are
the only kinds of data that the Civil Servant can put in the
State Papers. The danger is of supposing that these figures tell
of direct contacts with reality, when in fact they are its de-
natured remnants. It is not for nothing that statisticians speak
of their 'kitchen'.

But a science of imprecision is necessary and indispensable.
Government must aim at some formulated results. They can be
formulated only in the broadest terms. The heads and categories of a comprehensible budget cannot be many. Aggregation, the trampling-under of detail and distinctions, the reifying
of 'consumption', 'investment', 'capital', 'general output',
'gross national product', 'the capital-to-output ratio' and a

dozen or so other vast and looming phantoms, are the only means to construct a language of policy. But when they have been constructed, these unrealities are treated as objects of worship. Their precise meaning is believed in. The proportion of 'national income' which some nation is devoting to 'net investment' in order to promote 'growth', is taken to be an unarguable basis for pride or condemnation. We might do well to take more (very justifiable) pride in the ingenuity and audacity with which our science has devised its language of imprecision, and thus keep the real nature and purpose of its procedures more vividly in mind.

34

Languages for Expectation

34.1 Choice *is amongst mutually exclusive co-existents, namely, thoughts*

A theme can be conceived and pursued in its own right and for its own sake; or it can be taken up as a minor qualification of a different line of thought. The theme of expectation, the act of the invention of possibilities and of their assessment as to their capacity to come true (as a sequel to appropriate policies) and as to their attractiveness in their formal character regardless of realism, is an illustration deeply significant for economists. Some writers have been aware of the central, not peripheral, concern of economics with the theme of expectation: Cantillon knew that the merchant's role and resource was to bear uncertainty and accept the results of doing so; Marshall knew that the business man in his choice of action is moved by what he expects; Frank Knight had contrasted risk (which is not risky) with uncertainty (which is); Keynes ended by breaking through the encrusted rationalism of value theory to the notion of investment decision based on the fragmentary suggestions of 'the news'; and Myrdal suggested the elementally brilliant device of contrasting the expectation of a coming interval with the record of that same interval when it is past. For such writers, expectation, we may say, was the electric current which ran through the organizational circuits of the economy; or at least, they had some glimpse of that idea. But these writers were exceptional. The body of orthodox economic doctrine in the main has not dreamt of regarding economic policy-making (for the private or the public interest) as an *originative and imaginative art*. Yet how can choice be other than amongst products of imagination and invention? We cannot choose what we are now experiencing, it is too late for that. The act that we *perform* has already been chosen. Choice is amongst rivals; and rivals, of their nature, must be both mutually exclusive and co-existent. This is only possible to *thoughts*. Choice is amongst things which do not yet exist except in thought. What must be the character of a language, a symbolism and a formal notation which can allow for the far-reaching, surprising and unanticipable implications of this starting-point for analysis?

34.2 *The conceivable sequels to a specific course of action are not* listable

Expectation is the search for answers to the question: What will be the sequel if I take such-and-such a course of conduct? To suppose that a man will ask himself such a question is to suppose certain circumstances. To be free to take some course, rather than obey some necessity, is to be confronted with a number of rival available courses. He can take this course, or not. There must then be another, or others. The same must be true of other men, why should their essential predicament differ from his? But the sequel to the course he takes will be shaped in part by the particular respective courses that they take. To be free to choose one's action implies that its sequel cannot be known. For the choice is made in a world of choice, and the freedom of men to choose destroys their power to know. Choices made by different men simultaneously can indeed, by careful organization, be pre-reconciled. But choices which will subsequently be made cannot, in the nature of things, be pre-reconciled now, at the moment of making the present choice. If they could be pre-reconciled now, they would be made now, and would not be subsequent choices. To envisage the making of choices through time to come is to acknowledge that the sequel to today's, this moment's, choice by any man cannot be known. Thus expectation must be the search for answers, not *the* answer. There are, in principle, rival answers to each such question. Whence then can come the list of these answers, and how can this list be known? It can be known only in special, artificial and highly restrictive circumstances, such as those of a game with rules, or a race for which there exists a list of competitors known and guaranteed to be complete. The *sequel* to a course of conduct means evidently, in practical life, the sequel in certain regards, the *relevant* sequel. No man can be aware, or can care, about the sequel in 'all' respects. Thus if the game is drawing cards from a pack, there can at the outset be only fifty-two answers, each of them exactly specified as 'ace of clubs', etc. In general, in life at large, in history, business, politics, diplomacy and public affairs, where can any list be found, of detailed answers giving all relevant particulars? There is no source of such a list, except what the expectation-former can conceive in his own mind. The list, if we allow ourselves to call it such, is the work of his own thought, unbounded in its scope except by what experience or formal instruction or logic tell him is outside the principles of Nature or the Scheme of Things. Since there is nothing in principle to limit the length of future time whose situations or events may seem relevant, the diversity of the sequels he is free to conceive of seems on this ground to be beyond all reckoning. But we may go further, and appeal to the notion that the course of history (let alone the question of the number of its dimensions) can be regarded as a function of a real variable, that is to say, a function of time-lapse or the calendar; and to the proposition that the cardinality of the functions of a real variable exceeds that of the real number continuum, and is an infinity several orders greater than the natural numbers, the merely countable infinity. Since life is limited, since choice of conduct for the *present* occasion must be made 'now', there can plainly be no possibility of passing indefinitely in review the beginnings of an infinite list of conceivable sequels. The word 'list' itself is, moreover, inappropriate. The expectation-former is provided with no given and ready-made list of relevant sequels to any one of the rival courses open to him. Such sequels are for him to conceive, to invent. He has no grounds for supposing that the process of conceiving ever-different sequels will be brought to an end by their exhaustion. May not the process of inventive thought be inexhaustible? Expectation is not a passive, finished and settled state of thought but an activity of mind which can at no time say that it has completed the imaginative exploitation of its data; for these data are mere fragmentary suggestions in a paradoxically fertile void. It is the unending capacity of the list of answers to be added to, and especially it is the expectation-former's awareness of this unendingness, that imposes upon us a special requirement in our choice of a language for the analysis of expectation. For a language will not do, which supposes the answers to the expectation-former's question: What will follow such-and-such an action of mine? to be given as a specified, finite and known set. Expectation is origination in process. The nature and number of its potential products are, at any moment, unknowable.

34.3 *A language for expectation must express each sequel in terms of hypotheses*

Let us begin the attempt to outline such a language, by deciding to speak of answers or hypotheses as the elements composing a man's conception of what may follow his choice of a particular course of conduct. We could speak of outcomes, results, etc. But the word 'answers' points to the essence of the situation, that a question has been formulated in a specific set of epistemic circumstances, a specific knowledge-situation, and that the questioner is engaged in proposing answers to it, which he will then have to evaluate in certain respects. An answer for us means an hypothesis proposed in response to some more or less definite question, a question of the general form: What will follow *if* I do so-and-so?

34.4 Desiredness *and* Standing *as the orderings of hypotheses concerning one action*

The product of the activity of expectation will doubtless deserve in some sense to be called a system. The process of invention of hypotheses may itself have some orderliness and method about it. But there is more. The answers will be compared with each other in at least two respects. Since the whole business of expectation-forming is meant to subserve some purpose, the rival hypothetical sequels to a specific action will seem more, or less, to be desired according as they represent greater or less success in that purpose or in a stage of its attainment. The answers will be compared as to their *desiredness*. It may be possible for them to be ordered in respect of desiredness, and, in special cases, for the desiredness to be even measured on a scale. There is a more elusive yet equally important attribute of the answers. Regardless of the degree of success that a given answer would represent if it were to come true, there is the question of its 'nearness to truth', the strength of its claim *ex ante facto* to be able to come true. In order to provide a quite neutral term for this second ground of comparison, a term which shall carry no aura of suggestion as to the nature and basis of such an attribute, we shall call it *standing*. Hypotheses about the sequel to a contemplated action will invite comparison as to their standing, and again it may be possible to order them in this respect. Let us say, then, that hypotheses will be compared, and perhaps ordered, in two respects: desiredness and standing. The need for these two orderings, which seem to belong naturally to the business of expectation in its essence and purpose, is our ground for claiming that the products of this activity compose a system. The notion of system suggests that of coherence. One question to be asked, therefore, is about the character and the degree of the coherence which an expectation-former should seek in his pictured future situations and events.

34.5 *Each hypothesis will be an* inclusive *picture of relevant future history*

The basic entities of which such a system is composed must be deemed to be mutually distinct descriptions each encompassing the relevant course of future history as a whole. By relevant we mean that each such description of a hypothetical history will be an abstraction which mentions only salient features that seem important for the expectation-former's interests. This implies that some horizon will be imposed at a date or time-distance beyond which the individual's concern does not extend. Each distinct hypothetical description, however, is to be regarded as covering the whole stretch of the calendar between the moment of forming the description and the moment of the horizon. From this it follows that there can be no question of repeated trials. The expectation-former is not concerned with a *type* of action, of which he can perform as many instances as he likes. His need is to choose conduct now which will lead his affairs into one path or another, and will in some degree affect the whole of that path up to the horizon. Such hypothetical histories, or paths, are thus *rivals* of each other. Two such paths may co-incide over part of their course, but if they differ over part, they are distinct and mutually exclusive. The first proposition we must make, therefore, about coherence in a 'system' of expectations formed or entertained by a particular individual at a particular moment, is that its component parts in some degree deny each other. They are not contributory chapters or incidents in a unified or consistent story. They are rivals.

34.6 *The rivalry of the hypotheses cannot be deemed a* sharing

They are rivals in the sense that the claim of each is a denial of the claims of all the others. At the end of all, when the account is closed and the record finished, it is not possible in logic that more than one hypothesis will match the record and appear as the truth, though evidently it is possible in logic that none will do so. But in what other sense are they rivals? In the present moment of expectation-forming, before the test begins, what is it that they claim in opposition, as it were, to each other? Is their rivalry a matter of *sharing*, or only of comparison? The answer plainly depends on whether the hypotheses are treated as a completed list with nothing to be added, or as a *list in process* which can in principle and in its nature continue to grow, perhaps 'forever'. For without asking ourselves *what* it may be that could be shared, we may say that sharing amongst the members of a list recognized to be incomplete will be in some sense a distortion and give a misleading picture. On what basis of reason are the yet-invisible members of the list to be excluded? Are unborn children to be deprived of the rights of man because they have neglected to be born in good time?

34.7 *Does expectation assess the members of a completed or an uncompletable list?*

By these questions we are led, I think, to the fundamental choice in the matter of languages for the description and dissection of expectation. Is such a language to treat expectation as the business of assessing the members of a list of hypotheses given ready-made, and guaranteed to be complete, and assigning to them their respective degrees of standing on these terms; or is it to treat expectation as potentially endless *origination*, as the open-ended business of inventing hypotheses always, in principle, with more to follow? Established orthodoxy takes the former view, and we may examine it briefly.

34.8 Probability, *the language for a list taken to be* complete

Probability names a collection of reasonings so various that the use of one term to include them all is highly misleading. Its only justification lies in regarding this term as naming a question rather than the attempted answers. It asks: Is there something between perfect and demonstrably justifiable certainty, on one hand, and acknowledged complete ignorance, on the other? If so, what?

It seems evident from introspection, observation and intuition, that there is something between. We are willing to answer questions when we are not sure of the answer. We are willing to offer *suggestions* as to what the answer may be. We do not offer them at random. We stipulate, and try to ensure, some affinity between the conditions apparently envisaged by the question, and those envisaged by our suggested answer. For if it were not so, by what process could we select, as worthy of utterance, one out of the endless possible forms of words that are available? Some thought-process selects and pushes forward some formula as a response or reaction to the question. Why this formula and no other? Or why a few formulae and not an infinity?

If we speak of affinity or congruence between the circumstances described in the question and those described in the suggested answer, can the degree of this relationship be compared for different answers? Can this degree be compared for the answers to different questions? What if the character and context of the two cases, the nature of the details referred to, have nothing in common, and are unlike both formally and in substance? Again, are the comparisons to be thought of as one-dimensional, or does there not arise the question of the number of respects in which affinity can be discerned? Are there classes of special contexts in which comparability is more easily argued for? Can the basis and meaning of judgements and comparisons of the degree of congruence of question and hypothesis be of many different kinds? What are these meanings and bases?

34.9 *A scheme of treatments of probability*

In the scheme of Fig. 34.1, treatments of probability are divided first into those which do, and those which do not, concern themselves explicitly with the nature, and the basis of ascription, of something which, under their own respective meanings, they call probability. Secondly, those treatments which do thus concern themselves are divided into those which do, and those which do not, specify in some exact manner the nature of the evidence on which ascriptions of 'probability' are to be based, and the mode of gathering this evidence. Thirdly, those which do seek to specify in detail the basis of ascription are divided into those which rely on an *a priori* examination of a structure, and those which observe the results of an experiment.

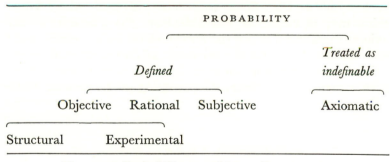

Fig. 34.1. Probability: a tableau of treatments.

34.10 *Axiomatic treatment of probability as an* indefinable

At the outset, then, we see two kinds of discussion which, in both purpose and procedure, virtually turn their backs on each other. One of these is a branch of pure logic or pure mathematics in which probability is an *indefinable*. This treatment is prepared, like a geometry or any system of pure reasoning, to define (freely or arbitrarily) relations amongst otherwise undefined elements, to invent propositions connecting the resulting constructs, and to call these invented propositions, axioms. From the set of axioms thus created, logical consequences are then deduced. The resulting structure is not in its own nature related to any observed or experienced aspect of anything outside the mind. It exists *in vacuo* in its own right of logic. When other treatments have provided suggestions as to the realistic nature of a probability concept, one of these suggestions may be found perfectly conformable to the axioms of the pure system, thus serving to anchor that system to some real class of phenomena. The developed axiomatic system is then ready-made to exhibit a great array of detailed features which will apply to any subject-matter to which a 'probability' of the suggested kind seems appropriate. The axiomatic treatment does not concern itself with the nature or basis of any concept of probability, but only with the elaboration of a structure of theorems about an undefined entity. Such theorems are to be the logical consequences of a set of axioms, that is to say, of a set of propositions exempted *ad hoc* from dispute, which can be freely invented subject only to their being consistent with each other. Something may of course be inferable from the character of the axioms themselves, about the nature of the entity which could serve as their basis. But the axiomatic treatment starts from the axioms, not from the study of human nature, the human predicament, or the observable structure of the cosmos. Logic is its only test.

34.11 *Probability as a means of describing the observable world*

In the axiomatic treatment, the meaning of probability is internal to the system of propositions. It can be seen only in their light, and exists only as the subject of a system of relations. By contrast, there are theories of probability which regard it as a means of describing aspects of portions of the observable world. In the tableau of Fig. 34.1 these are labelled objective. These theories fall into two kinds again sharply distinct from each other. Each kind defines a physical apparatus and some type of performance which can be executed with it, and each assigns probability to the answers to the question: What will be the sequel when this performance is executed? One kind, however, examines the apparatus itself and draws inferences from its structure. The other kind executes the performance and draws inferences from the results. We shall refer to these two types as structural and experimental theories.

34.12 *Structure, symmetry, equiprobability*

The structural theory is confined to a narrower category of situations than the experimental theory. The structural theory depends on finding *insufficient reason*, amongst the members of a logically exhaustive list of answers, for regarding any one of these answers as 'nearer to certainty' than another. Such insufficiency of reason itself, where it is present, depends on the answers being each related in identically the same way to the structure of the apparatus, so that in this respect the structure has *symmetry*. Structural symmetry and insufficiency of reason are the steps of reasoning which enable the structural theory to declare that the answers are *equi-probable*. It is evident that a structural theory has nothing to say, except in the case of an apparatus where relevant symmetry can be discerned or treated as present.

In one set of meanings, then, probability names a consequence of a set of circumstances or a set of conditions, a consequence of the particular design of a structure, mechanism or apparatus, a consequence of a configuration with fixed and given proportions amongst its parts. Amongst this set of meanings we can distinguish one which depends not only on fixity but on symmetry, in some sense and aspect, amongst these proportions. This symmetry is what allows the analyst to say that he can discern no sufficient reason for discriminating amongst a set of classes of answers to the question: What will be the sequel when a specified kind of performance is executed with this apparatus? Symmetry allows him to say that all these classes of answers are equi-probable, that there is no ground for regarding any one such class as 'nearer to certainty' than any other. Thus probability names a consequence of the die being a cube of uniform density and given elastic or 'bouncing' properties, and of its being thrown, during play, on to a plane surface also of fixed and uniform physical resilience, in the atmosphere of an ordinary room. When the die is thrown, this set-up is a notional receptacle able to contain each and every one of an indefinite number of distinct conceived events, that is to say, different trajectories and twisting rotations of the die as it falls and bounces through the air. These distinct phases, making up the phase-space, can be gathered into classes according to which face of the die, from 1 up to 6, lies upper-most when the die has come to rest. We then argue as follows. Nothing is known to the thrower of the die which can lead him to distinguish between one and another of these classes regarding its power to include the result of his next throw. This situation, involving the physical set-up and his own state of knowledge-and-ignorance concerning it (let us say, the technical and epistemic situation) is described as making each of the six classes of phases equi-probable.

34.13 *Ignorance as a basis of assignment of probability*

It is somewhat paradoxical that an explanation should rest upon an appeal to ignorance. For this is ultimately the nature of what we have called the structural account of probability. Two ideas here deserve attention. First, it seems plain that equi-probability is necessary to the structural account as a step of thought and not as a feature of the physical system involved. For an asymmetric die would yield probabilities to the experimental method, despite their being, in general, inscrutable to the structural method. Secondly, there is this latter idea, namely, that probabilities can emerge as an interpretation of the behaviour of a physical system, even if they do not lend themselves to formulation as equi-probabilities. Thus we have to distinguish between two groups of ideas: on the one hand, symmetry with its consequent equi-probability, and on the other, constancy or permanence of structure which may make possible the actual execution of a long series of performances with a physical system without deforming it or wearing it out.

34.14 *Necessity of a dynamic element to elicit the potential of the phase-space*

No paradox, in the sense of a genuine breakdown of logic, is really involved when we appeal to ignorance to explain conduct or to explain the path and product of thought. For any human action, whose results were hurtful to the person taking it, would have been avoided, had he not been ignorant of what those results would be like. Nonetheless, such an account leaves us with great and essential questions demanding an answer, or at least pressing for acknowledgement as unsolved riddles. One of these questions may be expressed by means of an analogy as follows. A given stretch of countryside can provide innumerable landscapes as it is viewed from this or that vantage point. To say this is much like saying, as we did just now, that the technical set-up of die, table surface and atmosphere has within its scope an indefinitely large number of distinct phases. But whether we are considering landscapes or phases, only one of these will be seen in fact if the viewpoint, or the particulars of successive throws, continue identical. There must be some persistent source of a shifting of viewpoint or a shifting of the particulars of the throws of the die, if there is to be any scanning or sampling of the potentiality of the countryside or of the phase-space. The keyboard will not yield a melody, or even a scale or a jangle of notes, unless there are shifting fingers to play upon the keys. It is not sufficient to say that each and every one of the phases is implicit and latent in the technical set-up. *Why should it be elicited?* Some current in the affair, some breeze or moving finger, some pulse in the blood-stream or the brain of the human thrower of the die, something that makes him crook his fingers or jerk his wrist differently from one occasion to the next, must be available and operative to bring out into realization and visible reality the potential phases latent in the technical set-up. There must be some dynamic element. The landscapes will reveal themselves only to one who moves over the countryside.

34.15 *Symmetry is vacuous* without an active random life

It seems, then, that besides symmetry something further is required in any apparatus or set-up to which the structural conception of probability is to apply. The pure presence of phases which, because innumerable details of them are invisible to us, fall into classes which we are obliged to regard as equiprobable, is not by itself enough to ensure, or offer some presumption, that this apparatus will behave in the manner envisaged by the term equi-probable. What is that manner? Can it be other than a *manifested* tendency for the 'equiprobable' classes to appear with some approximation to equal frequency in the course of an active life of the apparatus in question? It may be objected that the claim of the structural theory can be couched in language which makes no mention of performances with the apparatus, no mention of an 'active life' which it will be observed to go through. But this objection would mean that the structural theory was a theory concerning a pure vacuum or lifeless world. What can probability mean, as applied to the answers to a question, if that question is forbidden to take the form 'What *will happen*...?' The extra element which must complement the symmetry of the apparatus, if that apparatus is to *justify* the claim that its phase-classes are equi-probable, is some source of persistent movement or slight re-alignment of the minute component details of the apparatus. The vast majority of alterations from the precise circumstances of one throw of the die to those of another will be invisible. Even when the presence of a shift is obvious (as when the die is shaken for a shorter or longer time in its box, or thrown from a different height above the table) its relevant character and effect will usually be invisible and unassessable. In order that its symmetry may take effect, the apparatus must besides have a principle of life, its fronds must be fluttered or eddied by some breeze or current, it must not be a dead structure simply, but must have within it some source of living and active 'randomness'. Symmetry, then, is not only insufficient of itself, but, in some sense and some degree, it is by itself illusory.

34.16 *The search-element deliberately exploited*

If we may justly argue that an apparatus does not exhibit equi-probability among some definable phase-classes unless it has the power to scan or sample its own potential phases; if there must be, besides potential equi-probability, also actual performance, why do we not examine this performance from the outset? Experimental theories of probability are those which examine the record of performance, and regard it as sketching or loosely indicating some underlying character of the apparatus which can be called its probability-distribution of defined results. That character need not be one which reflects symmetry or approximates a set of equi-probable results. We can consider a die of irregular shape or of non-uniform density. Provided its shape and mass-distribution are *constant*, its behaviour may well unmistakeably sketch a pattern. It will at no stage be possible to say precisely what that pattern is. The record, at each successive throw, may move in this direction or that. It will, so far as actual and recorded tests have suggested, not veer steadily away from the mass of its previous results, but will seem to fluctuate irregularly, but with some sort of stability, about that mass. All this, however, again supposes that there is some *inquisitive* element in the procedure or circumstances of making the throws. There must, whether the die is symmetrical or not, be a *search-element*, an *irregularity*, in the manner of throwing. For, as with a symmetrical die, if every circumstance of one throw was identically reproduced in every throw, it is hard to argue against the notion that the result of every throw would be the same.

34.17 *Jacques Bernoulli's relation between the two methods*

When, as with a regular die, a set of ostensibly symmetrical phase-classes readily suggests itself, and when the physical apparatus is of a kind which will not be affected in its relevant properties by repeated performances, we can of course apply both methods. A distinct relation between the respective pronouncements of the two methods was proposed by Jacques

Bernoulli in his *Ars Conjectandi*, published posthumously in 1713:

In a series of n trials an event which in each of them has the constant probability p occurs ν times; the probability that the difference $(\nu/n) - p$ is numerically less than a given number, tends towards certainty as the number n of trials increases. That is, the probability that $|\nu/n - p| < \epsilon$ [where ϵ can be chosen arbitrarily small in advance of making any trials] tends to unity as n tends to infinity.

Here it is evident that the words 'the constant probability p' mean the result of an examination, made in advance of any trials, of the structure of a system deemed to be 'constant', that is, capable of withstanding the effect of repeated trials without alteration of its relevant character. Jacques Bernoulli is proposing here to study one probability in terms of another. The probability p of an event E is to be given operational meaning (in the 1927 language of P. W. Bridgman) by means of the probability of a different event E', namely, the event that the numerical difference $|\nu/n - p|$ between the recorded relative frequency ν/n of E, and the *a priori* probability p of that same E, shall prove to be less than an arbitrarily small number ϵ chosen before any trials are made. Two meanings of probability are to be brought into relation by a formula which itself involves one of these meanings. Is this the circular argument that it appears at first sight to be? Two things may be said in this regard. First, the notion of certainty can claim to have a public and universal meaning. Some force must doubtless be conceded to this claim. Thus a probability which is said to approach certainty can perhaps be said to have a clear meaning reflected upon it by its goal. Secondly, we are obliged to recognize that provided an *a priori* probability p is attainable for the event E, the question whether in fact $|\nu/n - p|$ for some particular n is less than some pre-selected ϵ can be experimentally examined. It can be experimentally examined by any number of separate series of trials. (What if their answers contradict one another?) But such examination is far from being a method of establishing Bernoulli's proposition inductively, since it suffers from the inevitable logical disability of all induction.

34.18 *Fluctuation of frequency ratio inherent in the experimental method*

The experimental method, then, consists in choosing or de-signing some technical set-up which we have reason to regard as robust and able to remain unchanging in essentials despite any practicable number of performances. If this apparatus is a die, dice-box, table top and human wrist, we throw the die casually and note which face lies uppermost, and we continue to do so as long as we can. At various stages of this process we note the ratios of individual phase-classes to the number of throws which have been made. A picture of some sort emerges, and this is all the evidence which the experimental method can provide us with regarding the probabilities of the system. With-in the terms of the experimental method, 'probability' names a fiction and a phantom, a mere summary of a hypothesis con-cerning the broad character which a record of actual trials with the apparatus will reveal. Are we to conclude that 'probability' has no real existence and no precise meaning? Are we to judge it no more nor less meaningful than such a political term as 'Conservatism' or 'Radicalism'?

What, then, is probability, when we apply this word to a physical system? The structural view divides all possible distinct answers to the question: What will happen when we try this apparatus in a certain manner? into classes, seeking to design these classes so that all of them stand in one and the same ostensible (visible) relation to the character of the apparatus as a whole. This identity of visible relationship to the apparatus, this symmetry, is deemed to allow us to say that the classes of answers are equi-probable. If we are then interested only in the relative probability of results each consisting in one such class, or each combining in some way several such classes, the structural conception, together with the logically derived rules of the calculus of probability, provides us with a formal means of comparison. The structural method leaves in obscurity the question of the link between ostensible symmetry and actual performance. It may even be said to appeal to this obscurity as a means of defining equi-probability. The experimental method avoids this hiatus by directly observing performance itself. The objection to this procedure is its inability to provide a precise and unique answer to the question: How probable is such-and-such a class of results of performance? For in any series of observations, the ratio of the number of observations which fall into some defined class, to the number of all observations made, will fluctuate as the series proceeds. Another series, made elsewhere with a similar physical system, or on another occasion with the same (i.e. proper-named) system itself, will fluctuate in a different manner. The propensity to fluctuate is the unavoidable accompaniment of the need to agitate the system so as to allow it to 'show what it can do'. The experimental method may be deemed to say that the probability of some class of answers to the question: What will happen when we try the apparatus? is like the bed of a swift river, not determining precisely the surges and eddies of the stream but influencing them in a powerful and consistent manner, so that their variations are minor in comparison with their similarities. It further suggests that the probability of our being impressed by their consistency rather than their variation will be greater the longer we sit observing the behaviour of the stream. But this further suggestion is evidently a relapse into circularity.

34.19 *The structural theory cannot renounce concern with methods of application*

Both the structural and the experimental method entail a dynamic element. For the net must be drawn through the water, if it is to catch any fish, and even the structural theory ought to say something of the proposed *manner* of that drawing. The knowledge of the relative numbers of this kind of fish and that kind, which are in the sea, is not in itself sufficient. Movement of the net, or of the fish, is needed too, if the knowledge of the relative numbers is to have any bearing or effect. It is not open to the structural theory to renounce any concern with the method of sampling its supposedly equi-possible, or equi-probable, phase-classes. If no sampling is in prospect, the alleged equi-probability is irrelevant, inoperative and meaningless. The dynamic element must be envisaged. And how is this dynamic element to be kept within bounds?

34.20 *The paradox of probability: a system must vary yet be unchanging*

The paradox of probability as a means of describing the behaviour of a physical system, is that the system is required both to be unchanging and to vary. Evidently (since we are not interested in propounding a genuine paradox or breakdown of logic) the constancy and the variation must have mutually conformable interpretations or else refer to distinct aspects of the behaviour. What we really mean is that there is required to be variation of detail within bounds which remain constant. This character of the system can be interpreted as forbidding certain conceivable features.

34.21 *Characteristics incompatible with the use of probability to describe a system*

A variation from one instance of performance to another in some particular detail must not lead to a greater variation of that detail between the second and third instances, and a greater still between the third and fourth, and so on. There must not, that is to say, be any tendency towards a self-reinforcing or 'cumulative' process. Such a self-reinforcing process could conceivably take the form of a spreading ring of repercussions involving a different set of details at each successive performance. This equally must be ruled out. The system, in short, must have no inherent tendency to explode. Neither must it be inherently evolutionary. We can conceive of a system (such as any population of living creatures) which would have as part of its constitution a mechanism of unpiedictable change in some design-features which were relevant to the results of its performances. This is plainly unacceptable, since the determination of probabilities by either the structural or the experimental method requires a stable, constant and given design of the system. Determination by the experimental method requires a 'long series' of instances of performance, while determination by inspection of the structure evidently requires that structure to be one given thing and not a mere ephemeral stage of a process of unpredictable change. These prohibitions, of explosion and of spontaneous evolution, are easily accommodated in a physical system. The die in its box and the table-top have a sufficient material strength to resist deformation and abrasion for long enough for the purpose in hand. The human wrist is controlled by an intuitive judgement of the appropriate force to use in shaking and throwing the die. What is far more important, it is governed by a knowledge that some manipulations are forbidden. The die must not be carefully placed, with a particular face uppermost, on the side of the dice box and then slid gently on to the table top. This last consideration suggests that a physical system may include a human element, and that the human element must subject itself to a quite special discipline if 'the system' is to remain relevantly *unchanging* in constitution and relevantly *varying* in performance. But if so, what of the application of probability to systems which are entirely human in all essential respects? This is the question which all our discussion of physical systems must have as its goal, since pure physical systems are not the concern of economic theory.

34.22 *Probabilities falsified by concealed changes of the system*

We have suggested that a physical system whose performance is to be interpreted by probability needs to be unchanging in design and constitution. This evidently means no more than that if we have two systems differing in ostensibly relevant respects we shall not count upon their behaving alike; or if we change one system into another we shall need to re-assess by one means or another its propensity to produce this and that result. This may seem obvious and trivial. What is vital is the question *whether we can know* that a given system has been transformed into a different one. A system whose nature does not allow it to tell us whether and when it has been relevantly transformed will be a very difficult object for interpretation by means of probability.

34.23 *Whether probability applicable to essentially unique instances*

Such a consideration brings us to the threshold of questions of an altogether more radical order. Suppose there can be a system which not merely can secretly transform itself but which will of necessity, by its nature, be transformed or even destroyed by a single performance of the kind whose sequel we are concerned with? Does it make sense to speak of probabilities of various sequels to some class of performances, or probabilities of this and that answer to a question concerning that sequel, when the class of performances can, in the nature of the system, only contain one sole and unique instance? Some will say that it does. But we are at least entitled to ask what the meaning of any such probability would be, and above all, what could be its application, or justifiable application, in practice?

34.24 *Probability and epistemic systems*

And finally, what of a world where the systems we wish to understand are affected by a universal and omni-present transforming agent, where the systems cannot stay the same because they involve, and partly consist of, our own knowledge concerning them? Such systems of course would not be merely physical, but, as we may say, epistemic, using this word to include not only demonstrable knowledge but speculative and originative expectation. But it is epistemic systems which concern the economist. Merely physical systems are the sphere of the engineer. Only systems which essentially involve the deliberative choices, the thoughts and desires of human beings belong to the field of economics. Human beings in their momentous choices (it may be difficult to tell whether a given occasion and immediate subject-matter of choice is momentous or not) are looking forward, not to a simple event but to a whole train or path of events or situations, a history. The complexity of such sequels must render it impossible to say in what degree the 'probability' of one is independent of that of another. Two such paths may co-incide over part of their course, yet be mutually exclusive because of a later divergence. They are rival sequels, rival answers to the question: What will happen in consequence of my choosing this policy rather than that? yet they are not independent. Beyond the purely physical, probability seems to drown in a sea of unanswerable difficulties.

34.25 *Crucial choices. Essentially explosive systems*

Let us return briefly to the question of momentous choices. A choice of one step or one policy rather than another can be called momentous if it will drive the course of events down a road from which there can be no getting back to any of the other roads which are available before the choice is made. A choice is momentous when it is crucial. Some choices seem not to be crucial. Does it matter which compartment of the train we get into? All and any of them will land us on the same platform, and get us to the same business meeting in the end. But if at that meeting one product is settled on instead of another, the firm's future may be placed on a track which never rejoins any of those deriving from products which are rejected. The die in its box is not involved in crucial choices, so long as the only sequel ascribed to it is no more than the coming uppermost of a particular face of the die. In the system of dice-box, die and table-top there is potential symmetry. But in human affairs even an ostensibly trivial choice may be a powder-train leading to explosive consequences. In human affairs there lies in wait the possibility of self-reinforcing, cumulative trains of events. Individual human beings, particular thoughts at particular instants, do not lend themselves to safe symmetrization. The die in its box is in a sense a *stable* system. The human intellect and imagination, the power of one human to influence millions of others, to inject thoughts of his own into their minds, to set fire to the tinder of their needs and desires, does not constitute the material and basis of stability.

34.26 *Conditions for the application of probability to physical systems*

Even in the kinds of treatment which we have labelled objective, probability is a mode of thought. It is, in these kinds, an interpretation of the way things seem to happen in a class of contexts. We have been seeking in the foregoing pages to define that class. We have put a gloss, perhaps an audacious one, on a distillation of some established ideas. If the resulting account of the application of probability to physical systems is accepted, probability, in order to be illuminating, requires certain conditions to be fulfilled:

1. The system must be so circumscribed that its performances can necessarily be classified under some list of mutually exclusive and exhaustive headings.

2. Individual instances of performance can vary in detail but not in general mode of occurrence.

3. Such instances are independent of each other, in the sense that knowledge of one such instance throws no light on the character of the next. This stipulation guarantees the system against the occurrence of a train of instances each leading to a successor more extreme, in some characteristic, than itself. That is to say, the system has no capacity to engender a self-reinforcing and explosive process.

4. The system is guaranteed against invisible change of its constitution. To ensure this, we require it to be insulated from impacts from outside itself, and free from any capacity to evolve by some mechanism inherent in its design.

We select and collect these stipulations, from amongst many which suggest themselves, on account of their bearing on the application of probability to human affairs, in high contrast to the milieu of a physical system. Meanwhile let us amplify some of these ideas.

34.27 *Probability is a mode of thought not necessarily a character of the natural world*

The required invariance of constitution of a physical system to which probability is to be applied will consist, first, of constancy of structure in matters directly referred to by those questions, concerning its performance, which probability is intended to illuminate. Thus with a system consisting of a die, dice-box, table top and human wrist, the relevant question is: Which face of the die will lie uppermost after a throw? And here the constancy which we appeal to is, most pertinently, that of the disposition of the faces of the die and of the distribution of its mass. Secondly, constancy is required in the boundary circumscribing those variations of detail of one performance from another, which constitute the element of search, of inquisitiveness, that brings into play, and into actual manifestation, the structural constancy of, for example, the die or the coin. Despite its dependence on the physical characteristics of a system to which it is sought to be applied, however, we regard probability as a mode of thought rather than a character of the natural world. Its use does not imply any judgement as to whether the natural world contains a principle of 'randomness' or, on the contrary, is strictly and precisely determinate. A determinate world might still allow the notion of probability a useful and indispensable role. The need to appeal to probability may arise purely from our lack of insight or of sufficiently sensitive instruments. We may simply not understand, or we may be unable to observe effectively, the mechanism and forces which govern the behaviour of the system. All we can observe, perhaps, is some boundedness and stability of the visible aspects of its behaviour. It may, for all we can tell, be governed in a perfectly determinate manner, given the events which are allowed to impinge on it. Probability is in that case essentially a means of circumventing some part of our factual inability to discern the precise relevant character of those impinging events, or to trace their consequences. If 'randomness' (whatever this may be) is in fact a characteristic of the natural world, our appeal to probability will be a permanent and inherent necessity, and not merely a provisional expedient. Our epistemic interpretation of probability provides for either case.

34.28 Rational *probability*

Our classification of treatments of probability divided them first into those for which the nature, and basis of assignment, of probability is indifferent, and which merely discuss the logical implications of some axioms concerning an entity otherwise undefined; and those which are centrally concerned with that nature and mode of assignment. The axiomatic treatment can give to any one of many concepts of probability a vast reach and range in application. In this chapter, however, it is the nature and basis, and not the formal superstructure, of probability which interest us. Thus we left aside *probability as an indefinable* and turned to the rest of the table. Here we began, at the next stage of classification, with the objective theories which posit some physical system conforming to certain requirements. Now we turn to the next heading at this stage, namely, those which our table refers to as *rational*.

34.29 *Keynes's definition*

In his *Treatise on Probability* of 1920, John Maynard Keynes says:

In the ordinary course of thought and argument, we are constantly assuming that knowledge of one statement, while not *proving* the truth of a second, yields nevertheless *some ground* for believing it. We assert that we *ought* on the evidence to prefer such and such a belief. We claim rational grounds for beliefs which are not conclusively demonstrated. We allow, in fact, that statements may be unproved, without, for that reason, being unfounded. And it does not seem on reflection that the information we convey by these expressions is wholly subjective. We believe that there is some real objective relation between Darwin's evidence and his conclusions, which is independent of the mere fact of our belief, and which is just as real and objective, though of a different degree, as that which would exist if the argument were as demonstrative as a syllogism. We are claiming, in fact, to cognise correctly a logical connection between one set of propositions which we call our evidence and which we suppose ourselves to know, and another set which we call our conclusions and to which we attach more or less weight according to the grounds supplied by the first.*

34.30 *Probable inference,* pace *Keynes, requires origination and judgement as well as logic*

Such an account of our daily and hourly practical habits of mind, expressed with all Keynes's seductive brilliance of style, is almost irresistible. Yet it poses a great question. The formal constructs of logic and of mathematics, by which, given one set of propositions, we show that another set is *equally valid* with the first set, do not constitute the crossing of a bridge from one position to a different one. They consist in taking in the hand, as it were, the first set of propositions as one whole, and turning it abou. 1so as to see it from a different viewpoint. The conclusion of a syllogism *resides already* in the premisses. There is *essential identity* between what the axioms of a Euclidean proof contain, in their relevant bearing on the *demonstrandum*, and that *demonstrandum* itself. But in Keynes's conception of probable inference, this identity is absent. In it, the premisses do not *compose*, and provide the whole substance of, the conclusion, they merely *suggest* the conclusion. This they do by offering *some part* of what would, with the addition of further premisses, constitute the means of demonstrative proof. I feel obliged, therefore, to propose an extension of Keynes's argument, of a kind which would no doubt have been unacceptable to him, since it adds a considerable and essential element of subjectiveness to his conception of probable inference. When he speaks of 'the degree of belief which it is rational to entertain in given conditions', my proposal is that this degree will depend rather on the judgemental, taste-governed and subjective willingness of the mind to supply and treat as true, such additional premisses as would validate the conclusion completely and assimilate it logically with the body, thus augmented, of premisses or axioms. The *rational* part of the business is precisely the same in probable inference as in certain and demonstrative proof. It is simply the pointing out of a structure of logical relationships which, before the proof is traced, may be said to

* *A Treatise on Probability*, Ch. I, pp. 5–6.

be latent in the total construct which embraces both premises and conclusions, both axioms and theorem. But in the case of probable inference, that total construct is partly created by the reasoner himself as a hypothesis. He does not find, supplied to him by observation and unmistakable evidence, a complete set of premises or axioms necessary to the formation of this total construct, but only some evidential materials which, on inspection, seem to offer a beginning in the assemblage of a sufficient axiomatic basis. Then the questions are, first, what extra propositions, what suppositional extra evidence, would be necessary and sufficient to complete the demonstrative basis? And secondly, how difficult or easy is it for the reasoner, with his personal intellectual background, temperamental constitution, educational history, *et cetera, et cetera*, to find and to 'appoint to office' those extra evidential elements? It is in this judgemental resolve, this act of decision, this originative and bold *démarche*, that there lies the subjective element, and the absolute difference of nature, between demonstrative and merely probable inference. Probable inference must indeed be logical. But its logic is, notwithstanding Leibniz himself, *the same* logic as serves Aristotle and Euclid and all the panoply of modern mathematics. Keynes quotes Leibniz at the head of his very first page: 'J'ai dit plus d'une fois qu'il faudrait une nouvelle espèce de logique, qui traiteroit des degrés de Probabilité.' Surely we may say that the real difference between certain inference and probable inference is the need of the latter to *fabricate* some of its needed evidence? Once a complete evidential basis has been assembled, partly by observation and direct knowledge, partly by imaginative hypothesis, then it is the old logic which comes into play, and nothing new is required.

Rational degrees of belief are rational, but founded also on figment.

34.31 *Keynes's meaning for the Principle of Indifference*

Keynes's principal achievement, in those matters in which we are interested for our own purpose, is to have transformed the Principle of Non-Sufficient Reason, which he calls the Principle of Indifference, from its merely negative aspect of 'equal ignorance' concerning the strength of the respective claims of two rival conclusions, into a positive, clear and precise requirement concerning the evidence for the respective conclusions:

There must be no relevant evidence relating to one alternative, unless there is corresponding evidence relating to the other; our relevant evidence, that is to say, must be symmetrical with regard to the alternatives, and must be applicable to each in the same manner. This is the rule at which the Principle of Indifference somewhat obscurely aims. We must first determine what parts of our evidence are relevant on the whole by a series of judgements of relevance, not easily reduced to rule. If this relevant evidence is of the same form for both alternatives, then the Principle authorises a judgement of indifference.*

34.32 *Degree of rational belief depends on* extra *hypothetical evidence required for* proof

It will be seen that this statement has its counterpart in terms of my own interpretation of the meaning of 'rational' degree of belief. It means that a judgement of equi-probability is a judgement that the extra evidence, which if it existed and were known to the reasoner, would suffice to render *demonstrative* the argument for one of the alternatives, must be in some sense formally similar to that which would serve to demonstrate the other alternative. And we may proceed to interpret 'formally similar' as implying that the moral or imaginative effort required to supply the missing evidence will be of equal degree and equal difficulty in either case.

Let us return to Keynes's interpretation of probability as 'the degree of our *rational belief* in the conclusion, or the relation or argument between two sets of propositions, knowledge of which would afford grounds for a corresponding degree of rational belief'. The essential question is whether an incomplete, insufficient set of evidence, or of 'initial propositions' or axioms, a set, that is, such as fail to provide a basis for conclusive proof, can give *any* support, by way of *reason*, to the proposed conclusion. If we deprive Euclid of the axiom of parallels, his

* *A Treatise on Probability*, Ch. IV, pp. 55–6.

whole scheme is able to be transformed into one or other of several non-Euclidian geometries, the conclusions of which contradict the Euclidian conclusions. A bridge with a missing span is not a bridge. A cart with a missing wheel will not offer, in its existing condition, a probability, other than zero, of reaching its destination. All depends on the possibility of supplying, from somewhere, the missing wheel. It is not on the cart alone, with its three wheels instead of four, on which our attention needs to be concentrated, but on the whole surrounding landscape with its possibility of finding workshops or wheelwright's yards, or broken vehicles which can be bought and dismembered for a wheel to repair our own. Keynes says:

While it is often convenient to speak of propositions as certain or probable, this expresses strictly a relationship in which they stand to a *corpus* of knowledge, and not a characteristic of the propositions in themselves. A proposition is capable at the same time of varying degrees of this relationship, depending upon the knowledge to which it is related, so that it is without significance to call a proposition probable unless we specify the knowledge to which we are relating it.*

I feel it necessary to say that the different degrees of probability, which different bodies of knowledge or evidence entitle us to adjudge to a given proposition, take their effect through the different amounts or forms of *extra* evidence which we should need to supply, in order to render the proposition, not 'probable' but conclusively proved; and that the effect of starting with one rather than another set of initial propositions, or corpus of evidence or data, is to oppose different kinds of obstacle, of different degrees of severity, in the way of making that set of initial propositions, evidence or data into a sufficient basis for certain inference and conclusive demonstration. Study of the existing and available evidence is chiefly relevant as the character of this evidence governs the need for additional and complementary evidence.

* *A Treatise on Probability*, Ch. I, p. 3.

34.33 *Existing evidence insufficient for proof cannot*
of itself *determine rational belief*

What must our conclusion be in regard to the possibility of
establishing a logic of probable inference? It must be that, when
the materials of certainty are incomplete, no manipulation of
those that are present will change ignorance into knowledge, or
will obviate the need for an act of thought which is *creative* in
some sense. When there is a gap in knowledge, which cannot be
filled by the securing of further *knowledge*, it can be filled only by
what is in truth a figment. Reason of course has its vital part to
play, in providing a test and criterion to say what figment, or
which alternative figments, would complete the basis on which
deductive certainty could rest. But when imagination has conceived and proposed some materials for filling the gap, and
when reason has tested them to discover whether, *if they were
available*, they would do what is required, then the subjective
and personal act of mind comes in, which depends not on
reason but on temerity, on the gambler's instinct.

The range or region of indeterminacy, concerning the answer
to some question, left by a body of evidence or a set of axioms,
may be in some sense larger or smaller, and, for any given such
gap (if measurable) the effect of adopting as a working hypothesis an answer on one boundary or extremity of such a void
rather than an answer near some other boundary, may in a
particular context of proposed action be crucial or trivial. But
it seems undeniable that the effect upon such a gap (in narrow-
ing, deforming or eliminating it) of adding an extra piece of
evidence, or an extra axiom, compatible with the initial
knowledge, cannot be known until the exact character of that
additional item itself is known. We cannot argue from the
existing data to a datum which is essentially additional to them.
If, on such grounds, we are unable to accept the phrase 'degrees
of *rational* belief' as describing the mind's posture in the absence
of rigid logical demonstration, where are we to turn for a
meaning for probability? We appear to be taking the position
that probable inference is only valid when the degree of probability is certainty. Let us accept this as our position. Is there,
then, any non-trivial meaning of probability in which it

becomes the equivalent, or near equivalent, of certain and guaranteed knowledge?

34.34 *Probability as the equivalent of knowledge: relative frequency*

Probability as relative frequency abandons the endeavour to argue that ignorance can by some quasi-logical alchemy become knowledge. Relative frequencies *are* knowledge. But they are knowledge about a quite different sort of thing from that which is the object of 'degrees of rational belief'. A relative frequency is simply the ratio of the number of the members of a sub-class to the number of the members of the class to which this sub-class belongs. To establish a relative frequency, all we need do is to state a test by which candidates for the main class can be admitted or rejected, and another test by which a similar thing can be done for the sub-class; and to find a means of counting these sets. The result, if carefully obtained, will have an excellent claim to be established knowledge, if of an unpretentious sort. It will be a pure number in the interval from zero to unity including those bounds. But such a frequency-ratio will be knowledge about *the classes which have been defined*, and in face of any real problem or situation, the prime difficulty will be to know how those classes ought to be, or had best be, defined. For, of course, the numerical probability, or relative frequency, will depend on the choice of these classes.

34.35 *The insight derivable from relative frequencies*

What is the thing that relative frequencies give us knowledge of? It is the classes, each taken as a *concept or thing-in-itself*, whose respective numbers compose the relation. Each of the two classes is defined by some test, for example, the possession of a quality or feature, f, characterizing the main class, and the possession of a quality, q, characterizing the sub-class. Every member of the sub-class possesses both f and q; the rest of the members of the main class possess only f. The hypothesis suggests itself that something in Nature makes the numerical relation meaningful and not merely casual or unique; there is, it may seem, some affinity between being an f and being a q. Such a hypothesis has many valuable aspects. It calls upon the specialist or expert whose business is to dissect or anatomize q's and f's to discover in their constitution or essential nature a basis for their partial and imperfect association, to account for both its *existence* and its *imperfection*. It allows the searcher for q's to know how profitable it will be to search amongst f's. It warns the avoider of q's just how many undesired encounters he will have with q's if he exposes himself to a given number of f's. It tells him *nothing*, at any rate nothing usable, about individual specimens as such.

34.36 *A frequency ratio*, pace *Keynes, as a relation between ideas*

There are then both practical and 'pure' aspects of a frequency ratio. It may contain and convey 'scientific' suggestions, it may, or must, relate to each other two entities, each of which is *both* a class or real collection of actual objects or observations and also an *idea*. A class is an idea, and a frequency ratio is a relation between ideas. This view differs sharply from the impression gathered from Keynes's Chapter VIII. He may be said to reject frequency as an interesting interpretation of probability:

The critic [of Venn's *Logic of Chance*] must show that the sense different from Venn's in which the term probability is often employed *has* an important logical interpretation about which we can generalise. This position I seek to establish. It is, in my opinion, this other sense *alone* which has importance; Venn's theory by itself has few practical applications, and if we allow it to hold the field we must admit that probability is not the guide of life, and that in following it we are not acting according to reason.*

* *A Treatise on Probability*, Ch. VIII, p. 96.

34.37 *'Guide of life' versus 'tool of science'*

This passage, though so incisive in impact, raises many subtle questions which must engage us at least briefly. One such question, which does not seem to have presented itself to Keynes when he was writing, is whether probability is to be looked on chiefly as the 'guide of life' or as a tool of science. The two uses and associated meanings are plainly distinct from each other, and this difference would presumably be emphasized by those who speak, somewhat incautiously, of the 'pre-scientific' attitudes and ideas of the ordinary non-logician seeking his way through the jungle of real life. In 1920, quantum mechanics had yet to establish its dominance over physics in the work of Max Born and others, but statistical thermodynamics was already several generations old, while Mendelian genetics had existed for twenty-five years. In the half-century since Keynes's *Treatise on Probability* was published, probability has come to permeate and largely dominate science and scholarship of every kind, from physics to biology, linguistics and literary attribution; but it is, precisely, probability in the sense of statistical frequency which has gained this place. Science is, or seeks, *knowledge*, and its use of probability is as a vehicle of knowledge. The ordered declension from knowledge to 'quasi-knowledge', the stepping down the degrees of rational belief to levels where there is not certainty but only some ground of presumption of the validity of propositions, is what Keynes's treatment envisages and it is something which carries us *away* from knowledge. The central question is whether probability as a 'guide of life' is any more rational than the ordinary man's contemned 'pre-scientific' procedures. For it can offer itself as a guide of life only in the *absence* of knowledge, only when science is not there to be appealed to. The ultimate question, perhaps, is whether probability can ever be 'rational', 'scientific' and so on, except when it encapsulates knowledge, as it does when (and perhaps only when) it states a relation between classes, a relation which has all the certainty and unambiguousness which careful definition and precise observation can confer. The application of such knowledge to situations *not yet observable*, its use in prediction, depends of course on the logically unwarranted principle of induction, the willingness to assume that experience is to be trusted. And what else, within science or outside it, is there to trust?

In his analysis of the Principle of Indifference Keynes concludes (and it is the most striking and brilliant of the general ideas which the *Treatise on Probability* contributes) that Indifference means symmetry of form. In Keynes's presentation, this symmetry belongs to arguments, to the relevance of the evidence to the alternative proposed conclusions. But symmetry is again the basis of equi-probability when we consider physical systems and their potential behaviour. Equi-probability is what enables us to count cases, and we may say that the counting of cases is as much a part of the structural as of the experimental (i.e. the frequency) treatment of probability. It is the equi-probability, in the structural sense, of the six faces of a die that sanctions our judgment that when, for example, we throw two dice at once, the chance of getting a total of five is one in nine. Keynes pays little attention to this link between his study of 'rational' probability, on the one hand, and of physical structural probability on the other.

Chapter VIII of the *Treatise on Probability* emphasizes the *relativity* of judgements or computations of probability. The probability of an argument is relative to the evidence. Different evidence will in principle yield a different probability. He stresses the high significance of the symbol a/b ('the probability of a conclusion a derived from premises b', which we may read for short a given b). One of the chief differences between physical systems, even one which consists, for example, of a body of insurance policy holders together with their accident-producing environment, and rational systems involving a set of premises and a set of proposed 'conclusions', is that the former can, but the latter cannot, be plausibly treated as self-contained. We can assume that the dice-thrower will not cheat, but we cannot assume that the missing elements in a chain of deduction are the ones which validate our 'probable inference'.

Let us return to the question of the *bearing* of frequency-ratio probabilities. What do they tell us *about*? They give us knowledge (differing perhaps a little in precision from some other kinds of knowledge) of the results of cross-classification. They compare the intersection of two classes with one or other of the classes. But they do not tell us anything useful about individual members of either class, except when they represent a probability very near to one or zero, and when we are willing, in the given context of action, to treat a very high or very low chance as the equivalent of certainty of yes or of no.

So far we have discussed those treatments of probability which we have labelled either 'objective' or 'rational'. What the treatments under these two labels all have in common is a claim to indicate in some sense the nature of the link between the evidence in view and the conclusions claimed to be drawn from it. With objective theories this link involves the counting of cases. What cases to count is still partly a matter of judgement, intuition, personal taste, it is subjective. Nonetheless, when the evidence has been specified and the question what class and sub-class are to be counted has been settled, we then have an operational definition of probability: Do so-and-so, and the resulting number measures the probability that the suggested answer is right. 'Rational' theories, amongst which we have confined ourselves to Keynes's, offer a test of equi-probability amongst conclusions from given evidence; the evidence must be of the same form in regard to each. Judgement or intuition may still be called for in applying the test, but perhaps not more so than when demonstrative proof is in question: the question whether a particular step of reasoning is logical or not cannot be answered by logic. We now turn away from all theories where the bridge from premiss to conclusion is described or sketched, to those theories where no such description is attempted. In what sense can treatments, which do not tell us how to assess probabilities, serve as 'a guide of life'? They can do so principally by constraining our probability-judgements, which, so far as these treatments are concerned, are a direct invisible leap from premiss to conclusion, into a mutual coherence. They ensure that such judgements form a system.

34.38 *Subjective probability*

Subjective probability is a formal construction by which an individual can express, on a scale private to himself, his assessments of how far from certainty some hypothesis or answer to a question is. The scale need not be private in every respect. It can consist in divisions, adjudged by the individual as equal to each other, of an interval between 'certainly right' and 'certainly wrong' or 'impossible'. The meaning of the bounds of this interval can be expressed to himself by the individual in such a way that other people would accept his statement as unquestionably correct. For example, when an ordinary coin is tossed and ends by lying flat on the ground, it is certain to show a head unless it shows a tail, or a tail unless it shows a head. If a coin with two heads and no tail is tossed, it is certain that it will not show a tail. Thus the extremities of the basic interval between certainty and impossibility can be a publicly agreed matter. When a coin with a head and a tail is tossed n times, there are 2^n distinct sequences of head or tail which can result. For example, if $n = 3$, the sequences are:

h	h	h
h	h	t
h	t	h
t	h	h
t	t	t
t	t	h
t	h	t
h	t	t.

The individual can be asked to divide the entire series of 2^n sequences (no matter what n is) exhaustively into sets A, B, C, ..., Q, such that the proposition 'My next series of n tosses will give a sequence falling into set A' seems to him as near to or far from certainty as the proposition 'The sequence will fall into set B', '...set C', and so on. He may or may not be found to divide the 2^n series into sets each with the same number of members. This is not to the point. He will have arrived at sets of sequences such that the sets are *for him* equi-probable. If now a proposition in some quite different context is to have its nearness or remoteness from 'certainly right' assessed, the expression of his judgement of it can take the form of choosing more or fewer of the equi-probable intervals to represent the subjective probability (the probability *in his judgement*) of the proposition in question.

34.39 *Subjective probability is a* distribution of certainty over listed items

To use the language of subjective probability is to give to the results of a private, personal and arcane intellectual process an expression in the terms and frame of that probability which is capable of exhibiting and justifying publicly its basis and procedure. This outward form imposes upon subjective judgements of probability one feature in particular: the numerical assessments of different answers to a given question are required, essentially, to be proper fractions summing to unity, that is, together representing the certainty that, between them, the answers include all possibilities. This logically necessary feature of a *distributive* expression of judgements that particular answers are 'nearer to certainty' or 'remoter from certainty' has one implication which seems to be generally overlooked and ignored. It implies that one of the chief disabilities of some proposed answer, regarding its power to influence action-decisions, lies simply in the *number of its rivals*. To increase the number of rival answers is to reduce, other things remaining unchanged, the probability which can be assigned to particular answers. It has even been proposed that subjective judgements of probability need not adhere to the summation rule. To release them from it would be to authorize such statements as: 'In one-third of all the cases the result of a performance will be *A*, in half the cases it will be *B*, in two-fifths of the cases it will be *C*'. Does subjective probability base its claim on avoiding such illogic, or does it base its claim on not condemning proposed answers or hypotheses merely because they are jostled by a great *number* of rivals? Not both claims can be made at once.

Expectation is the business of answering, with one or many answers, the question: What will be the sequel if I embark on such-and-such a course of action? If, in the sense which matters, there are many answers, they will be rivals, mutually contradicting each other. Then the business of expectation is not finished. Some resolution must be found of the anarchic state of thought. A language for expectation is required as a means of performing this resolution. In choosing or designing it, the first crux is whether the rival answers about a given line of conduct are given as a complete and exhaustive list to which nothing will be added, or whether they are a flowing stream of invention and origination, essentially inexhaustible? If the former, probability in some form can serve as this language; if the latter, probability seems to face an essential disqualification. For probability, in all its treatments despite their diversity, engages itself to distribute *certainty*, that the truth will be found amongst the members of some given list of answers, or classes of answers, over these answers or classes. If the list is not given *in a form which provides a basis for such distribution*, how can distribution be performed? Distribution requires that the individual rival answers, or mutually exclusive classes of answer, shall be specified in some way which enables each of them to be put in a relation to a body of relevant data. Not merely the value of the answers or classes of answer, but the character of each in some detailed form, must be specified, if an assignment of probability is to be made. And if there is then to be distribution, the list of specific items must be treated as complete.

34.40 *Probability concerns groups of events, not single critical choices*

Let us assume at first that such a list, relevantly specific and complete, has been arrived at. Then what further requirements must probability, in one or other form, comply with? Keynes, in reporting Venn, propounds a curious inconsistency (it is not perfectly clear whether this is Venn's own or Keynes's):

The two principal tenets, then, of Venn's system are these: that probability is concerned with series or groups of events, and that all the requisite facts must be determined empirically, a statement in probability merely summing up in a convenient way a group of experiences. It will often be the case that we can make statements regarding the average of a certain class, or regarding its characteristics in the long run, which we cannot make about any of its individual members without great risk of error. As our knowledge regarding the class as a whole may give us valuable guidance in dealing with an individual instance, we require a convenient way of saying that an individual belongs to a class in which certain characteristics appear on the average with a known frequency.*

* *A Treatise on Probability*, Ch. VIII, p. 95.

If the *individual instance*, despite its membership of the class, cannot be the subject of some statements without grave risk of error, how can that membership give us valuable guidance in dealing with an individual instance?

Keynes speaks, in the last sentence of our quotation, of a *known frequency*, and in a pievious sentence he speaks of 'a statement of probability' as a 'summing up'. Relative frequencies are knowledge. They are knowledge about groups of events, or series of events, *not* about individual instances. Yet in human affairs or conduct, the critical choices, *ipso facto* of their criticalness, require commitment to a road from which there will be no rejoining of the alternative roads which are open so long as the choice has not been made. In the crucial affairs of life, the choice is once for all, a single instance. A group of instances *taken as one whole* would of course, be a single instance *of a different kind*. But that different kind, in so far as its composing instances were amenable to frequency treatment, would not be subject to rival answers but only to one answer, there would in the relevant matter be no uncertainty.

There is lastly the need of probability to speak in terms of independent equi-probable cases, such as the results of successive tosses of a coin or spins of a roulette-wheel. But in the affairs of business or of life at large, where can we find threads so carefully separated and laid out that they can be said to be *independent* of each other? The 'ravelled sleeve', the eternally tangled skein of things does not lend itself to such simplicities.

34.41 Standing *of hypotheses as adjudged possibility*

Possibility is a character ascribed in thought by an individual to a state of affairs or to the transformation of one state of affairs into another, that is, to an event. A situation or an event is adjudged possible by a person who, having considered the matter, finds nothing in his general or particular knowledge which disallows that situation or event as part of an imagined sequel to some course of action open to him. We divide his relevant knowledge into general and particular in the sense, on one hand, of knowledge of the nature and process of the world, of natural laws or principles and of human nature and institutions; and on the other, of knowledge of the particular circumstances of his present moment which bear on the particular question. He may regard some specified state or event as capable of coming into being, were the date of its doing so of no account, and yet regard this state or event as not attainable from the existing situation within a specified interval of time. History is all the time composing its endless mosaic. What the next picture can contain depends on what it must continue from, and on what is the 'bank' of *tesserae* which are available to compose it. But the answers to these questions, of what is the starting point and what materials are in reach, are thoughts to be formed by the individual.

34.42 *Ascriptions of possibility are essentially* non-distributional

Possibility in this sense can be ascribed, at one and the same time, to situations or events which are mutually exclusive or compatible, and which are independent or mutually involved. But its essential claim to our interest, as a means of escaping from the dilemmas we have seen in probability, is its capacity to be assigned in any degree to any number of distinct ideas at once, any number, for example, of answers to the question: What will be the sequel to my adopting such-and-such a course of action? Its essential claim is the *independence* of its degrees, respectively assigned to different conceived sequels, of the *number* of these sequels. Possibility, in its essential nature, is *non-distributional*.

34.43 *A frequency distribution is a team of answers which* are not rivals

The contrast of meaning between possibility, interpreted as in the foregoing, and probability, interpreted in the frequency sense, can be sharpened as follows. The answers to which frequency ratios are assigned in a frequency distribution *are not rivals*. Each individual answer refers to what can happen in some one instance or another, but the frequency distribution as a whole is a statement concerning the proportions in which the whole of a series of instances all taken together *will* be made up of one particular answer and another and another. A Rugby football team is made up of eight forwards, two half-backs, four three-quarter backs and one full-back, in those proportions. To find in a team a three-quarter back does not deny the inclusion in it of a forward. A frequency distribution is a *team* of answers, a unity with a character belonging to the whole as a whole. The frequencies which make up a distribution are *summaries* of the data which constitute the distribution. They are knowledge. This knowledge is knowledge about a particular, identified set of circumstances in an identified, 'proper-named', historical context, a set of observations made on some occasion which can be located on the calendar and on the map and on a list of persons who made them. If we wish to treat this knowledge of a specific context and occasion as general knowledge applicable to other occasions and contexts, it will be imprecise, and even its meaning will be somewhat vague in the new surroundings divorced from its origin. But it will still have a claim to be knowledge so long as it is applied, as it was derived, to a *series* or collection of instances treated as one whole. If it is sought to be applied to a single instance, it will lose touch with its origin and cease to have a claim to be knowledge. The question may seem to be one of degree. A pair of instances is hardly a series, yet it is plural. But this argument is insubstantial. A frequency ratio is knowledge in the degree to which its field of application is numerous. This proposition again is not meant to bear a highly exact interpretation. In economics and all its concerns, the meanings are to be seen in the misty and shifting lights of the human scene. Human affairs cannot visibly rest directly on the fine structure of the cosmos. Somewhere in the texture of the world, there is a capacity for limitless richness of variety in the particulars.

34.44 *Possibility avoids two chief disabilities of probability as a language for expectation*

In the search for a language for expectation, we find that the notion of *possibility* is exempt from two chief disabilities which disqualify probability. It is non-distributional, and can be applied to the items of an inexhaustible stream of origination recognized as such. Secondly, it can be applied to hypotheses concerning the outcome of a crucial and self-destructive experiment, one which by its nature irreversibly alters the essential conditions which constitute it. In order to do away with any temptation to add together the degrees of possibility ascribed to different hypotheses, in order visibly to renounce distribution, it is best to invert our scale and refer to degrees of *disbelief*. On such a scale, the ascription of perfect possibility will be expressed as zero disbelief. Thence the degrees of disbelief will ascend to an absolute maximum representing the ascription of impossibility.

Let us consider again the texture of thought in which an individual hypothesis, invented in answer to a question of the general order: What will be the sequel if. . .?, comes into being and is entertained. It is, in the first place, an item in a stream of such inventions, a stream which in origin and nature can go on flowing indefinitely. Secondly, it is one of a class of thoughts which are mutually exclusive, since each is an account, in some way distinct from the others, of some aspects of the entire sequel to some present step. Such hypotheses are for this reason *rivals*, the truth of any one denying the truth of all the others. Thirdly, such an hypothesis is a suggested description of the outcome of what it is convenient to call a non-divisable non-seriable experiment. We are not concerned, that is to say, with one instance in a class of instances of a type of performance such as can, in broad character, be indefinitely repeated. The experiment is one which, because of its scale, its complexity, or its irreversibly crucial and self-destructive nature, is unique. These three characteristics, the unlistableness and the rivalry of suggested answers to a question about the sequel to a contemplated course of conduct, and the crucialness of the experiment consisting in the adoption of such a course, impose upon our choice of language a number of requirements, of which so far we have named only one, that the variable which expresses the standing of an hypothesis shall be non-distributional. Let us now consider the second of the characteristics named above.

34.45 *Mode of representing a set of rival hypothetical sequels to a course of action*

The description and analysis of expectation aim at an understanding of the individual's mode of choice amongst rival available courses of conduct. We suppose him to perform this choice by comparing with each other some representations, one for each course, of the respective sets of sequels (each set comprising finitely or infinitely many rival members) which he ascribes to these courses. We have suggested that the sequels belonging to any one such set will be ordered according to two considerations: the desiredness of each, irrespective of its adjudged 'capacity to come true' or 'nearness to (or remoteness from) certainty', irrespective, that is, of its *standing*; and this adjudged standing itself. This formulation leaves us still with the task of explaining the nature and mode of construction of those representations. Desiredness and standing have in some manner to be both brought to bear upon a task of comparison of the rival available courses, an operation of comparison which may consist in some form of valuation of the courses.

34.46 *The* mathematical expectation *of the outcome of a divisible experiment*

The frequency treatment of probability has an established method of performing such valuation and comparison, a method which, for those situations where the frequency treatment is appropriate, is natural and logically necessary. For in such cases the relevant valuation is that of a *series treated as one whole*, of instances of a type of performance or trial made with some system whose invariance against such trials, and whose insulation from outward circumstance, is taken to be guaranteed. When each item in the list of possible distinct results of such a performance or trial (a list assumed to be known) is valued in terms of some appropriate units, the number of these units assigned to each distinct possible result is multiplied by the proportion which the number of trials yielding that result bears, according to past experience, to the number of all the trials composing the series. When the products of all such multi-plications (one for each distinct possible result) are added together, we have the *mathematical expectation*, a *valuation* in terms of the chosen valuation unit. The meaning and necessity of the mathematical expectation rest wholly on its reference to a *series treated as one whole* of instances of the type of performance in question. Such a series treated as one whole is what we mean by a *divisible* experiment, and in such an experiment, the various frequency ratios which experience has shown to be applicable to the different possible results of a trial form a *team working together*. These values of the frequency variable are not rivals, and the hypotheses to which they apply are not rivals. The mathematical expectation is, in its nature, a kind of knowledge. Probability, most especially in the frequency interpretation, is a distributive variable. That is why it can serve the purpose of forming a mathematical expectation. Disbelief is non-distributional. That is the source of its power to express the standing of an hypothesis when this hypothesis is a member of a set containing indefinitely many such ideas, the majority of which are waiting to be thought of; and when the hypothesis concerns the sequel of an experiment which is essentially, irremediably unique, because the making of this experiment will destroy for ever the conditions which constitute it; for example, by giving men new knowledge, which they will be unable, short of total catastrophe, ever to forget; and when this hypothesis, referring thus to a unique occasion, is a rival of all other distinct hypotheses and denies their truth as a condition of its own. Disbelief thus understood cannot serve the purpose of a mathematical expectation. How, then, can it be combined with desiredness in the making of comparisons between rival available courses of action?

34.47 *A selective method to replace the* adding together *of mutually contradictory hypotheses*

A mathematical expectation is a weighted average. It is com-posed of the respective valuations of the hypotheses, each weighted by its probability. It thus implies that each of these hypotheses is 'true in some degree'. And this is natural and correct, because the mathematical expectation refers to the out-turn of a *divisible experiment*, an out-turn which, by the evidence and suggestion of past experience, will be composed in certain proportions of this particular hypothesis and that other one and that other, and so on through the list, the list known to be exhaustive. And these proportions will be the statistical frequencies which past similar experiments have furnished. In the out-turn of a divisible experiment, the various possible results of any single instance of the type of performance which characterizes the system are not rivals within the divisible experiment itself as one whole. Each and all are true *together* in certain proportions. It is because a divisible experiment can be atomized into trials or performances sufficiently alike in the conditions of their occurrence to yield statistical frequencies, that we can have knowledge, in some sense and with some degree of approximation, of the out-turn. In a non-divisible experiment, where the hypotheses are rivals which deny each other's truth, it is a contradiction to treat them as all true together in some degree. It is necessary, not to combine and average these incompatibles, but to select from amongst them those to which attention should be paid.

34.48 *Logical basis of the notion of focus values*

Probability does not supply knowledge out of un-knowledge. It *expresses* knowledge which has been obtained by observation of statistical frequencies, and which, in common with all our technology and the practical wisdom of everyday living, rests on inductive inference, no matter how lacking that may be in logical justification. We rely on it because there is no substitute. When we are finally confronted with irremediable uncertainty, with un-knowledge from which there is no *ex ante* escape, the only expedient of the human mind is to turn it to advantage by seeing it as a freedom, a freedom for the imagination.

Rival hypotheses will be worth attending to, according as they represent some situation whose attainment is desired, provided the supposition of this attainment is not too difficult to take seriously. If all the rival hypotheses which, at some moment, have been formed in answer to a question concerning the sequel of given conduct, are regarded as equally possible; if the evidence which disables one is exactly paralleled by evidence disabling the others; and in particular, if all of them are regarded as *perfectly* possible, with no positive obstacle seen lying in the path of any one of them; then it will be natural and sensible to pay attention only to the best and worst of these hypotheses, to the two items lying at the extremes of an ordering of all hypotheses, formulated up to the moment in question, according to desiredness. For what interest need one take in a moderately good sequel, if a brilliant one seems, for the *unique* occasion with which the expectation-former is solely concerned, to be *equally possible*? Or what concern is it reasonable to feel about a slight misfortune, when as a sequel to one and the same dated, 'proper-named' occasion of adopting particular conduct, a disaster seems *equally* possible?

We shall not here elaborate the notion of focus value, showing how it can be interpreted when the hypotheses are assigned unequal degrees of disbelief, when some are regarded as not perfectly possible. Such a discussion will be found elsewhere.* Here we sought to argue for a language able to conceive expectation as a source and origin of history rather than as a branch of arithmetic.

* For example, in *Expectation in Economics* (1949, 2nd ed. 1952) and *Decision, Order and Time in Human Affairs* (1961, 2nd ed. 1970), both published by Cambridge University Press.

35

Profit

35.1 *Plural valuations of one object in one thought*

A skein of ideas under the name of profit plays so great a part
in the literature of economics as to make it plain that important
meanings are involved. The arithmetical operation common to
all meanings is that of a subtraction whose terms are valuations.
These are in some sense valuations of one and the same thing.
What brings together two such valuations to serve as terms of a
difference? What kinds of circumstance make possible the
assignment of two different valuations to one object? To find
for these questions an answer, or a scheme of answers, will be to
settle our interpretation of profit.

If profit is arrived at by an operation of thought, it must
essentially exist or occur in a single mind. Some circumstance
or reason, the use of some principle, leads this mind to set up
two distinct valuations of one thing, or respective valuations of
two things (two collections or systems), one of which can
transform itself into the other without the addition of any
further ingredient or circumstance; can transform itself, as we
may say, in a self-contained manner. What are the possible
variants of such a principle? An operation of thought takes
place at some one moment, though it can, of course, concern
itself with ideas about any other moments. We have, then, in
the notion of profit, unity of thought, unity of assessor, unity of
object, unity of time of making the assessment; but duality of
valuation. By what variant alternative means can valuation
escape from the four unities into its own duality?

35.2 *Valuations by different assessors cognized by one assessor*

The means which suggests itself most readily is that one valuation is based by our assessor on his own knowledge of the

relevant circumstances, such as that knowledge may be, while
the other is a valuation which he knows to be entertained by
another individual, or by a market. Can the two valuations
both be 'right'? Can both be based on the same knowledge or
assumptions? It seems plain that they cannot both have an
identical epistemic basis (in the broad sense of epistemic as
'content of thought') unless we divide the whole seed-bed of
valuation into what the assessor accepts as true and what is
originated by him within the constraints of that supposed truth.
If we do so, we can evidently suppose valuations based by different persons on identical bodies of supposed truth to differ
from each other because of the different figments with which
they supply the deficiencies of that body as a basis for inference.
In the mind of one or other, or both, of two assessors making
unequal valuations, there must be *imperfect knowledge*.

35.3 *Imperfection of knowledge allowing plural valuations by one assessor*

A second source of freedom to find plural valuations of one
thing at one moment resides in the assessor's recognition of his
own inadequacy of knowledge. If he is aware that his basis of
supposed fact is incomplete, and thus insufficient to support
any valuation at all until supplemented by suppositions originated by himself *ad hoc*, plainly he has freedom in choosing these
supplemental ideas, to reach many rival and mutually contradictory valuations. In this variant also, there is the same
element, imperfect knowledge.

35.4 *Contrast of* ex post *and* ex ante *valuations*

Difference of assessors, difference of conjectures by one assessor,
can account for difference of valuations. There is a third class
of comparisons, namely, of what has emerged and is now part
of a record of the past, in contrast with what, at some date
antecedent to the calendar interval in question, was imagined
as the possible content of that interval. We shall call this a
resolutional contrast of valuations: the resolution of the problem

of the content of the interval. It is the confrontation of assessments of an interval made *ex ante* and *ex post*, the sequence-
analysis comparison which may call for revision of policy.
Imperfect knowledge, at least at the earlier date, is involved
here as in the other variants.

35.5 *Profit requires a language for expectation*

Profit, then, in all such meanings, involves conjecture and
arises from it. The dual or plural valuations are conjectures
conflicting with each other or with a record concerning what
has been, until the lapse of time brought this record into
existence, the subject of the conjecture. Goods which are unstorable, which are produced only in order to satisfy immediately the immediate needs of a consumer, depend for their
value solely on such immedate needs and their own scarcity or
abundance. Regarding such goods, a perfect market can supply
publicly demonstrable knowledge and can thus eliminate conjecture. If such goods can have dual valuations, it must be
because of imperfection of the market, and the 'profit' arising
from this duality will be arbitrage. Imperfection of a market,
its failure to collect, distil and resolve the tastes, endowments
and intentions of its participants, can in principle be amended.
But un-knowledge of the future, the not yet existent, cannot be
amended. Conjecture finds its inalienable scope and field in
expectation, and the analysis of profit requires what we have
sought in the preceding chapter, a language for expectation.

35.6 *Speculative equilibrium depends on contrast of expectation*

Organizational perfection of the market is independent of the
meaning of the results distilled by the market. Its internal
instantaneous communication of all offered or accepted prices,
the terms of all transactions or conditional intentions, to all its
members, can proceed and exist no matter what ideas in the
minds of these participants underlie the offers and transactions.
In the nature of these sources or bases of the events of the
market, however, there can be an extreme contrast. A market

for unstorable goods can pre-reconcile the actions of its members by informing them of prices which, when each member adjusts his flow of consumption of each good so that his marginal rates of substitution conform to these prices, will give each member the most satisfaction consonant with equal knowledge and equal freedom for all members, and will clear the market. In such a market, each member will thus be fully informed of all relevant circumstances and able to act with strict rationality, that is, in a manner which he can demonstrate to himself to be the best for himself. By contrast, a market for storable goods, and in particular for durable goods, is wholly different in its essential nature.

Unstorable goods have a value only in the present moment. There is no meaning in a notion of their value at any later moment. But storable goods can be considered in relation to moments subsequent to that in which they are being considered. It can be supposed that they will have a value at subsequent moments, since this is the meaning of storability. The value assigned to them in the present must, in logic, take account of any value which it is supposed they will have at a later moment. But that future value cannot now be known. These two propositions taken together mean that the market for storable goods is a *speculative* market. In a speculative market, actions to be taken 'now' can be pre-reconciled. But their meanings, the personal valuations and expectations which underlie them, will at most moments be diverse. In a speculative market, it is only the division of dealers into two camps, holding opposite views about the next movement of price, that can hold the price even momentarily steady. For the coming into being of a consensus will be manifested by an immediate movement in the direction which this consensus expects.

In a speculative market, price (the price 'now') is governed or influenced by ideas concerning the prices which will prevail at subsequent dates. Conversely, all markets where such governance in some degree prevails are speculative in some degree. There is in the nature of things an association between the idea of a market which concerns itself with future dates, and the idea of a division of opinion about the next or subsequent movements of price. For present price will be driven up or down until it has thus divided the market. Markets for goods in which storability is present in any form will be in their nature essentially speculative.

35.7 *Inter-personal, inter-conjectural and resolutional differences of valuation*

Essential storability can take many forms. There can be the simple physical possibility of preserving objects unchanged through time. Or goods which are physically perishable can be ingredients in a technological process from which a good will emerge at a later date, part of whose value will represent that of the presently existing ingredient. Or a good can be a durable tool, or item or system of productive facilities, able to be used at any and all moments over some stretch of future time. All such goods are in their essential nature inescapably in some degree speculative. The operation of valuing them involves expectation based on insufficient knowledge. This imperfection of knowledge makes possible differences of valuation of each of our three kinds, inter-personal, inter-conjectural and resolutional. Profit, we may say by a very slight ellipsis, involves and essentially springs from expectation. This conclusion was in essence enunciated by Cantillon.

35.8 *The dimension of profit*

The next question which arises concerning profit is that of dimension. Is it to be conceived as a stock or a flow? Does its measure have to be expressed as so-and-so many money units, *simpliciter*, or as so-and-so many in some time interval? It seems plain that a valuation can be made of either a situation or of the transformation which carries one situation into another. Situation is stock, transformation is flow. Profit can be a balance-sheet matter or a profit-and-loss account matter. Indeed, the profit-and-loss concept is merely the comparison of two balance-sheets, and cannot be reckoned without those expectational and hence uncertain operations of thought which valuation of a storable or durable entity involves. The question of dimension turns out to be less basic than that of the source of freedom to make plural valuations of one thing at one time.

35.9 *The self-consistency of a notion of profit*

If profit is expectational, its analysis must be conducted in some expectational language, and it is for this that we sought, in the preceding chapter, to go into the requisite nature of such a language. We are confronted with an important practical question and dilemma. If profit is reckoned by an operation of subtraction, it is evident that the two terms involved must each be a single and definite number. But uncertain expectation involves the entertaining of plural rival, that is, mutually exclusive and contradictory, hypotheses. How is a single number to be derived from a bundle of contradictions? By summation, by averaging? And if so, what will be the meaning of such an average? Such an average is exemplified by the mathematical expectation; but that has a clear meaning only when the probability concept involved is the frequency concept, and the frequency concept depends on the assurance of repetition, and the assurance of repetition affords the conditions in which, not uncertainty, but effective knowledge, is present or attainable. And what circumstance can supply the assurance of repetition, of repetition in the sense required by the frequency treatment of probability? The alternative to summation is selection. To see what it can offer, we need to consider what is the purpose of an analysis of profit.

We began this chapter by seeking to organize the meanings of profit round a highly abstract notion, that of the formal operation which all such meanings may be held to involve. From this beginning we have sought to draw a unifying thread, consisting of the idea of duality of valuation of what is essentially one thing, viewed by one person at one moment; and the idea that such duality is not merely permitted but positively thrust upon us by the nature of things; by such aspects of them as the mechanism of the ephemeral equilibrium in a speculative market and the participation of almost all real markets in some degree of speculative character; and in general, by the nature of expectation and its essential uncertainty, the power of origination and not merely of discernment of events, which we must ascribe to it if we accept a non-empty role of decision. From this formal argument, which in one sense has been concerned to establish the logical 'existence', that is, the internal coherence and self-consistency, of a notion of profit, we must go on to consider what part of real experience that notion can be applied to. In what real circumstances, with what role and effect, does profit arise? What does profit do?

35.10 *A language for profit*

In Cantillon it provides the merchant's incentive to action. An incentive is something hoped for, a sequel both desired and not despaired of to available courses of conduct. Something hoped for, then, can be ordered on two axes, of degree of desiredness and degree of adjudged possibility, degree of belief; or better (as we have sought to argue), of disbelief. The power of a profit hypothesis as an incentive will depend on both these orderings. But to define profit, we need a selective principle. We have examined one, in the concept of focus values. Cantillon regards his merchant as able to buy goods at a known price with a view to sell them later at a price which, when he buys them, he cannot know. We can equally regard a producer as able to buy the means of production at contractual prices, in order to combine them into a product which will be available only after a lapse of time, and saleable then at a price which cannot at the outset be known. If the known cost were to turn out equal to the eventual proceeds of sale, the gain would be zero. If greater, the gain would be negative, and if smaller, positive. Hypotheses of gain can be arranged on an axis extending to east and west of a zero origin. On an axis at right-angles to this we can arrange degrees of disbelief, increasing northwards from zero disbelief standing for 'perfect possibility'. There will perhaps be a range of hypothetical sizes of positive or negative gain which are accorded such perfect possibility. Outside this range, still larger numerical gain or loss will then be assigned degrees of disbelief increasing with their numerical size; not, of course, in general symmetrically. But the incentive or disincentive power of such hopes or fears, such vectors of hypothesis and disbelief, will not necessarily start to diminish as soon as disbelief rises above zero. For some distance outside the extremes of the inner range defined by zero disbelief, the larger size of an hypothetical gain or loss may still win it increasing attention. But disbelief must surely reach a pitch, at some size of supposed gain or loss, where it will begin to outweigh the accompanying further increases of size. At the balancing point we have a focus hypothesis, a constrained maximum of attention-arresting power. When, in the preceding chapter, we discussed the inner range itself, and supposed all hypotheses to be classed simply as possible or impossible, we argued that only the two extreme hypotheses, one of desired and the other of damaging outcome, would alone have any claim on the expectation-former's attention. We now suggest that an almost exclusive attention-arresting power will reside, for similar considerations, in the two focus hypotheses. The non-distributional language that we proposed in the preceding chapter thus provides us with the selective principle we need. The relevant hope of gain will be that of the focus hypothesis of gain, and similarly the relevant fear of loss will be the focus hypothesis of loss. We shall refer to hypotheses of gain or loss numerically larger than the focus gain or loss as extra-focal, and speak of them as counter-expected.

The focus gain is itself a dual valuation of one and the same thing, of the kind we held it necessary to seek for as a meaning of profit. It is made by one mind at one moment. For it is the difference between the supposedly known money expense of a set of quantities of means of production, and a conjecture as to the market price obtainable for the product into which they can transform themselves in what we have called a self-contained manner. The self-sufficient means of production, and the product, are in the relevant sense one thing. Differences of date of expenses and sale proceeds will of course be adjusted by discounting at prevailing market interest rates for the appropriate terms. The expense of acquisition or production of a saleable good, and the focus conjecture of its saleable price, exemplify what we called, above, *rival* valuations, that is, simultaneously-made mutually exclusive hypotheses *of the saleable price*.

35.11 *Investment gain or loss*

Of its essential nature, uncertainty involves and veritably consists in the entertainment of rival, mutually exclusive hypotheses. These cannot be made use of by adding or averaging them, but only by selection. Focus gain and loss are a first stage in a selective method which can then treat as indifferent all those proposals for action (all those courses of conduct, productions, investments in equipment, enterprises entire) whose respective focus loss is not ruinous, and allow selection to be finally made amongst them by their positive aspect, their respective focus gains. It is when profit refers to an investment in an expensive system of durable equipment, or in a new enterprise entire, that it attains perhaps its most dramatic application. For here, the issue can obviously be crucial. Success or un-success will make or mar the firm for a long time to come. And the range of outcomes which must be entertained is greater because the remote years whose events come into the reckoning are less and less illuminated by the present. Investment gain or loss will be reckoned by taking for each future year of the proposed plant's operating life, some supposition of the sale-proceeds of the product to be produced with its aid in that year, and some supposition concerning the corresponding outlay for the necessary materials, power, labour and other things necessary for operating the plant in that year, and subtracting the latter from the former to obtain one hypothesis of trading revenue for that year. Each year must have its trading revenue discounted for deferment at the going interest-rate for loans of that term (a rate presented to the business man as an objective datum by the bond market), and all such resulting present values, one for each future year of supposed operating life, must then be summed. The sum will be *one hypothesis* of the value to be assigned to the plant. Its construction-cost, contractual or hypothetical, being then subtracted from this valuation, we have a hypothesis of the investment gain from constructing this plant. To the set of such investment-gain hypotheses, thus obtained, the selective process of focus gain and focus loss can be applied.

35.12 Resolutional profit *and plant valuation*

The investment focus gain assigned to a contemplated investment in some plant (system of durable equipment) will rest upon, and may even in some sense summarize, the focus gains of trading revenue of individual future years of the plant's operation. We cannot say quite simply that the focus gains of trading revenue will be simply discounted for deferment and their discounted values added together to give the investment focus gain. For the business man may well have ground for assuming some auto-regressive effect. High trading revenues of early years may be suspected of offering a conspicuous temptation to rival firms and imitators to enter the field and take some of his market, so that the trading revenues of later years would be adversely affected. A *given* hypothetical investment gain can correspond to each of an unlimited variety of hypothetical courses of trading revenue. Nonetheless when, if the plant is actually built and put in operation, successive years lapse into the past and provide a record of what actually occurred in them, these recorded performances will inevitably be the basis for revision of views of the plant's performance during the remainder of its life. It is here that the concept of *resolutional profit* finds its place.

We began by suggesting that the term profit names in our literature a skein of many various meanings. But now we have in some sense perhaps brought these meanings to a unity. A few ideas: those of valuation, of difference of valuations made by one mind at one moment concerning what is essentially one thing; the idea of imperfect knowledge, of the necessity, quite unavoidable in the practical conduct of life and business, to make conjectures and to allow them to influence our conduct; appear to be both necessary and sufficient for a concept of profit. The problem of profit concerns the manner in which these ideas are to be organized and combined. Our method consists in supposing the business man to find pairs of valuations of a proposed product, or a proposed enterprise, by considering the price for which he could acquire such an object, and the price he could obtain for it or its performances. We suppose him to arrange in size order the differences obtained by subtracting one member of each such pair from the other, and selecting from these differences, some of which will be positive and some negative, a pair of focus differences. In his capacity as enterpriser or investor, the business man will be engaged in reviewing a number of possible enterprises or investments.

Having assigned to each of these its focus gain and focus loss, he can segregate those whose focus loss, in view of the size of his resources, does not exceed some acceptable maximum; and amongst these segregated projects he can choose that which has the largest focus gain. Profit now appears, in its first guise, as the focus gain of the selected enterprise. It is thus acting as the incentive of enterprise or of investment. It formulates and condenses the ideas which have led to the adoption of a policy. Beyond the focus gain there is a range of hypotheses of gain which, by definition of focus gain, have been assigned too high a degree of disbelief to be interesting for the choice of conduct. Nonetheless, they have not all been classed as wholly impossible. The business man may be conceived to give some thought to the question whether some kinds of experience in the actual use of his proposed equipment or the actual conduct of his proposed enterprise might not induce a revision of his expectations. The kind of gain, counter-expected in the initial assessment which led to the decision to acquire the plant or launch the enterprise, which might necessitate the re-working of that initial assessment, would be a trading revenue lying outside the focus hypothesis of positive trading revenue for some particular year. We can interpret it, in the terminology of J. M. Keynes's *Treatise on Money*, as a windfall profit. It would be what we have called a *resolutional profit*, emerging from the confrontation of *ex ante* and *ex post* conceptions of the content of some proper-named (first quarter, 1971, for example) calendar interval.

35.13 *Resolutional profit and elasticities of surprise*

The emergence of a resolutional profit in the trading experience of some particular year would, by definition of our non-distributional variable measuring the *standing* of hypotheses, be surprising. It would constitute the actual occurrence of something which had been disbelieved in. The effect of its emergence, upon the fresh valuations and fresh choice of conduct for the further future, would presumably depend upon the ratio of the resolutional trading revenue to the former focus gain of trading revenue for the year in question. We can formulate the matter as something analogous to an *elasticity*.

Let g be the focus hypothesis of trading revenue of a plant in some proper-named future calendar year, i, of the plant's operating life, and let Δg be the excess, over g, of the trading revenue recorded for that year when 'the present' has traversed it and reached the end of it. Let u be the business man's valuation of the plant when he entertains the focus hypothesis g concerning year i, and let Δu be the increase of that valuation brought about by the emergence of the recorded trading revenue for year i. Then we shall call the ratio $\Delta u/u : \Delta g/g$ *the valuation elasticity of surprise for gain of trading revenue.*

If this upward revaluation of an existing plant leads the business man to increase his intended investment in further plant, during an impending year, from I to $I + \Delta I$, we shall call $\Delta I/I : \Delta u/u$ his *investment elasticity of surprise for gain of valuation.* Lastly, $\Delta I/I : \Delta g/g$ will be his *investment elasticity of surprise for gain of trading revenue.* Evidently,

$$\frac{\Delta I}{\Delta g} \cdot \frac{g}{I} = \frac{\Delta I}{\Delta u} \cdot \frac{u}{I} \cdot \frac{\Delta u}{\Delta g} \cdot \frac{g}{u} ,$$

our third elasticity is the product of multiplying the first two elasticities together.

35.14 *Profit as incentive to action, profit as incentive to thought*

In this view of things, Δg exemplifies resolutional profit. It is something whose possibility was considered and in large measure, but not wholly, dismissed. Whereas the focus gain of some investment or some enterprise plays a part in the comparison of this project with rival ones, by expressing one aspect of the selective outcome of a careful procedure of expectation-forming, resolutional profit by contrast suggests and induces a reconsideration of expectations, the abandonment of existing assumptions, policies or plans and the construction of new ones. The expectations thus abandoned may themselves, of course, have been formulated in the wake of an earlier occurrence of a resolutional profit. Whereas profit in its first guise appears as part of the incentive to action, to choice of practical conduct, in its second guise, as resolutional profit, it appears as an incentive to thought. The unity we have claimed for our frame of profit ideas rests partly on their involvement of uncertainty, and partly on their character of incentives to some *démarche*. Where there is profit, in either of our two senses, there is an impulse to activity: to enterprise or to strategic re-thinking. The two senses of profit in this scheme are distinguished from each other by their relation to a focus hypothesis, one sense consisting in the selection of this hypothesis itself, the other in a reaction to the over-running of that focus by recorded events.

35.15 *Expectational leverage*

The mechanism which we have sought to define by means of elasticities of surprise may give to ostensibly small shifts of the visible business scene a powerful leverage on its subsequent development. If the recorded trading revenue of a plant in some half year exceeds by a quarter its focus value, and if the valuation elasticity of surprise for gain of trading revenue is one-half, the valuation of the plant, as compared with what it would have been at this stage of its operating life, will be increased by 12.5 per cent. If the elasticity of supply of equipment of appropriate kinds is high, an increase of this percentage in the business man's valuation of such equipment may imply a high investment elasticity of surprise for gain of trading revenue, and an important contribution to the investment flow of subsequent months or years. *Expectational leverage* is implicit in the nature of investment. Valuation of equipment whose performance lies in future years depends on the suggestions offered by 'the news', the accidents of the immediate scene, the apparently abrupt changes of direction in political, fashionable, diplomatic or technological affairs. In so far as these shifts have already manifested their first effects on the trading revenues earned by existing productive facilities, they will have expressed themselves as resolutional profit in its counter-expected or even its unexpected sense. The wheel of expectation touches the ground of actuality at only one point of a great circumference whose future rolling can only be guessed at from the jolts it now suffers.

36

Game Theory's Exclusion of Tactical Surprise

The theory of games is the product of a superb mathematical virtuosity. It illustrates a great mathematician's originative genius. By an extraordinary paradox, it *assumes away* the whole of that aspect of business, science, art and contest, which allows originative genius to exist. It assumes that business, and life at large which embraces business, is a game with rules, and that the players not only know these rules but have so mastered their complete and assumedly bounded implications that all possibilities can be surveyed by them and that each of two contestants can so conduct himself as to be invincible, or else as nearly invincible as, for example, the entitlement to first move in chess makes possible. The player of a game, of a kind to whom the Theory of Games can be applied, is one who can take into his reckoning every possibility, and does so on the assumption that his opponent will do the same. Where, then, is the scope for that supreme trump in every contest of the world at large (as distinct from the world of game-artefacts), *surprise*? Surprise is that dislocation and subversion of received thoughts, which springs from an actual experience outside of what has been judged fully possible, or else an experience of a character which has never been imagined and thus never assessed as either possible or impossible: a *counter-expected* or else an *un-expected* event.*

Surprise, the supreme achievement of the tactician, is the outflanking of imagination by superior imagination. Its presence, and its absence, in war equally prove its decisive power. Gideon's overthrow of the vast Midianite host with a handful of carefully selected men was achieved by the impact of an *un-imagined* event, an event *unexpected* in our technical sense.

---

* 'The logic of surprise', G. L. S. Shackle, *Economica* vol. xx (1953), pp. 112–17, reprinted in *Uncertainty in Economics*, CUP (1955, 1968), Chapter IV. See also *Decision, Order and Time*, second edition (1970), pp. 282 and following.

Wellington compelled a great army to evacuate Portugal almost without a shot fired, by confronting it, at the end of a long, earth-scorching march, with the impregnable redoubt-system of Torres Vedras, undreamt-of by Masséna until this spectre of defeat rose from the mist. Kept secret until a thousand were ready, tanks could have decided the first world war. Instead, they appeared at first in handfuls, and even at Cambrai there were no reserves.

Surprise is the exploitation of the opponent's lack of knowledge, or of his reliance on what he wrongly believes to be knowledge. If business is a contest instead of a universal co-ordination of action, its supreme secret is *epistemic*, the gaining and use, the denial and disguise, of knowledge. Bargaining, 'bilateral monopoly', is a contest, and success in it is won by the bargainer who best conceals from the other his absolute limits of action (the seller's absolute lowest price or the buyer's absolute highest) and the filling of this gap of knowledge in the opponent's mind by false beliefs. The contrast between the two situations, that of the perfect, anonymous, unnumbered market whose purpose is the distillation and universal diffusion of accurate, relevantly complete knowledge, and that of the face-to-face bargaining poker-game whose method is the suppression and falsifying of knowledge, is astonishing in face of their identity of context, that of exchange. Our literature seems to pass over this paradox in silence. The suppression of knowledge is an aspect also of the exploitation of novelty, new knowledge, which must be denied to rival firms as long as possible while the possessor of it makes his profit.

To declare that business is contest rather than co-ordination, that its appropriate theory is the theory of battle rather than that of pre-reconciliation, was in appearance to subvert the whole basis of economic insight. The economic theoretician of that time was bound to be both arrested by the audacity of this proposal and sceptical of its claims. The leaders of business themselves, if consulted, might well have declared it a belated recognition by theory of the obvious facts of the modern age. Yet this proposal, so sweeping in its rejection of established theory and so technically brilliant and original, nonetheless conformed with tradition in a fundamental respect: it tacitly assumed that there is a closed system of rules of the game whose existence makes possible a determinate limitation of an opponent's power to gain at one's expense; a strategic conduct which blocks the opponent's advance at a certain point. The theory of value, the theory of pre-reconciliation, addresses itself (if adequately stated) to the question how it is possible for every participant to possess all knowledge relevant to his doing the best for himself that his ultimate circumstances allow, subject to every other participant's possession of the same epistemic facilities. And the Theory of Games does the same. The question that is not asked is this: Does *all knowledge*, even *all relevant knowledge*, as a formal verbal expression, have any referend in the Scheme of Things? Is there an existent 'bank' of potential knowledge which is in principle capable of being exhausted, so that a theory of contest can, by way of abstraction and for the sake of uncovering ultimate foundations, assume it to have *been* exhausted, and all its contents become actual knowledge? Or can the theory of contest assume that the two participants, even if not 'fully informed' are in some manner guaranteed to have mutually *equivalent* knowledge which they are prevented from improving on? Is 'complete knowledge' meaningful? Do we hope to exhaust the store of History's ironies and the laughter of the gods?

Knowledge, novelty, surprise, are correlative terms. There can be no surprise where there is knowledge guaranteed to be complete. Novelty is incompatible with complete knowledge, it is the revelation of a gap or flaw in what was deemed to be knowledge. Novelty must engender surprise. In order to reason rigorously and effectively about the outcome of a contest, the theoretician is obliged to assume a complete set of rules, known to himself and to each contestant, such that an invincible strategy, or a best strategy given the opponent's comparable knowledge, logically exists and can be discovered. In a world where novelty is inexhaustible, such a set of rules would be logically impossible. We do not know whether our world is a world of ultimately inexhaustible novelty, but we can, without absurdity, guess that we are far from having exhausted its *potentiae*.

Business, and the General Human Affair, may be a game with rules. But so long as we do not know those rules completely, we shall not be able to calculate victory; to calculate it 'for certain'; nor to form a policy guaranteed to be the best which is 'objectively' possible. The game may have its rules which enforce themselves without appeal, but we have to play it largely in ignorance of what they are. This is the difference between the artefact, such as chess, which despite the immensity of the 'chess maze' (the totality of possible courses of play) is delimited and in principle subject to a maximin method, on the one hand, and on the other the open, creative void, the unsummable potential, which it may even be misleading to call a 'cosmos', since that suggests boundedness and ultimate self-consistency, a coherence which Gödel's result seems to question.

A training in value theory can have a strange effect on the individual mind. It can give rise to a fundamental scepticism concerning the reality of 'events'. The mind which has been taught to suppose that the norm of conduct is rational conduct, and that 'mistakes' or 'failures' are *abnormal*, draws from this inculcated posture the tacit inference that 'perfect foresight' is attainable, that the fully successful individual would encounter nothing in life which he was not prepared for and which, indeed, he had not taken into account from the beginning of his conscious planning of his affairs. Even historians, whose field of study seems, to the ordinary eye, to support so overwhelmingly Macbeth's final disillusionment and his description of life, find a sufficient orderliness to make 'explanation' in some sort possible. Their belief (so far as they hold it) in such orderliness seems attested by their invocation of historical 'accidents', *anomalous* happenings which defy, and even turn aside, the understandable, accountable flow of situations one out of another. It is natural that men, who depend on their gifts of mind and conscious skills in the struggle to survive, should put a boundless faith in those powers. That faith is less an inference from observation than an indispensable condition of tolerable, and continuing, existence.

The notion of providing a contestant with an infallible algorithm for limited vulnerability is a paradoxical one. Is the contestant in question the *general contestant*? If so, since the notion of contestant itself requires that there be at least two of him, it follows that the algorithm must be available to both contestants. Thus success in the contest cannot mean unconditional victory. It means that each of the two contestants, whether the frame of their contest is symmetrical or not, can limit his opponent's degree of success despite anything that the opponent may do. But what does this infallibility imply? It requires that the 'frame of the contest' be a *given* one, invariant against the choices of conduct of the contestants. In the real arena of life, what circumstance do we know which imposes this character on any struggle? The most powerful resource available to a real-life contestant may be to exploit the ignorance of both, or all, contestants concerning the ultimate conditions of the contest. The rules are not known. Until the whole task of science is performed and all that is knowable is known, the real frame of human contests will still be undiscernible in some respects. Contest is more realistically conceived as an endless drawing on the unknown. The most dramatic and spectacular secret of success is novelty, and novelty is that which an infallible algorithm must, by definition, exclude.

37

Kaleidic Economics

37.1 *Orientation: the teleology of an equipment list*

By *orientation* we intend to name the idea of the meaning which the business man sees in his collection of material possessions. His tools in his eyes are purposeful in many senses. Each item or system in his outfit has, in the first place, a technological range. It can accomplish or assist certain physical operations. It can cut, forge, or roll metal, can contain material which is being smelted, can lift or transport loads, and so on in an end-less list. Beyond this, there is at any moment in the business man's mind a scheme of such operations, a scheme more or less complete, precise and far-reaching into coming hours or days, which he intends to execute. And this scheme itself has an end in view, the improvement of the usefulness and thus the value of other things or circumstances. There is also at any moment an organization, a scheme of thoughts which counts upon, and finds dispositions and roles for, all the material possessions of a business or of a society. The organization is an aspect of the technical capacity of the tools. Their effectiveness depends partly on their co-existence and the existence of channels of command by which they can be brought to collaborate on given tasks. *Orientation* thus embraces technical, organizational and expectational levels: general technical capacity of each item, a discipline for the use of these capacities in some defined process, and a particular proposed transformation of one particular situation into another, an identified enterprise or exploit. *Meaning* evidently is thought, or an aspect of thought, and orientation consequently is a product of the mind.

37.2 *Expectation suggested not determined*

The material possessions, the equipment of the business or of the economic society as a whole, would have no more value than the most casual objects and features of the scene, were they not embraced in a technology, an organization, a policy and, at any moment, a plan of action specified as to the persons whose interests it is to serve or whose orders or desires it is to satisfy, and as to its location and its timing. A plan: something conceived or imagined, constructed in the mind, composed of assumptions, beliefs, hopes, conjectures, of all those grades and colours of thought included in the word *expectation*. Whatever can change expectation can change the valuations of equipment and the worth-whileness of producing additional items of it. And expectation is a vast span resting on relatively slight abutments in the visible present. Expectation is of course an application of general principles to particular facts; but those 'facts' are so much the creation of the individual observer depending on a unique personal history and experience, they are so much a matter of interpretation, of the character of their setting or background, that any objectivity ascribed to them must be largely illusory. Even if the supposed facts could be taken at their face value, their pathetic insufficiency as grist for the mill of reason appears insistently when we consider what questions the expectation-former needs to answer. The 'facts' at best are like a few pieces of coloured stone or glass intended for a mosaic, and the task of expectation is to design the mosaic as a whole from the suggestions offered by these few disconnected fragments. A slight, accidental re-arrangement of the scattered fragments can reveal new possibilities and configurations, can call for new *tesserae* of hitherto unthought of kinds and colours to fill out what is to hand, and can produce novelty in a moment of inspiration. The kaleidoscope is a toy whose angled mirrors produce symmetry and an appearance of design out of random configurations of vari-coloured glass. It seems to epitomize in some sense the limitless richness of mutations and the incalculable instability of the task of expectation-forming. The economic society whose affairs depend on its valuations of desirable equipment can perhaps be suggestively labelled *kaleidic*.

37.3 *The subversion of economics by the* General Theory

The process of writing the *General Theory of Employment, Interest and Money* was, by Keynes's own avowal, a struggle of escape from the ideas bequeathed to economists by the preceding course of economic thought. The germ of a total transformation was present, surely, at the outset, but its nature was not then visible to him. The book is a skein of partly incompatible threads and modes of argument, some of them so ostensibly orthodox that it was possible to consider the book a mere gloss on old notions. Since the author himself did not understand the full reach of his conclusions, and did not there express them in any one place with uncompromising and untrammelled force, it is not surprising that readers were, and have ever since been, confused and divided in mind by two opposite suggestions. They sensed the presence of something capable of overturning received theory. The author 'had something'. He was on the track of novelty and revelation, and this revelation would be painful. But again, was this perhaps an illusion on his part, which he was able at times to inject into his reader's mind so that the reader for a time saw something of the vision, and yet was being thereby misled and caused to follow on a path he would later be obliged to retrace? The *General Theory*, if we see it in the light of Keynes's final recognition of his own meaning in his article in the *Quarterly Journal*, was an Economics of Disorder. The analysis of business life as a steady application of reason to changeable, but knowable and coherent, circumstances, the analysis of business conduct as an informed, collected, undismayed response to a stream of understandable and largely foreseen events, was destroyed, rejected, overthrown in ruin and contempt.

37.4 *The restoration*

A generation of years has passed since 1936, and for most of that time the majority of economists, led by certain great figures who were the better able to defend the citadel because they themselves were aware of some defects in its design, and might themselves have led the assault upon it had Keynes's attack given them time to consider their policy, have been able to re-group around an amended version of the former teachings of the subject. The aspect of disintegration, of purely negative and nihilistic resignation, has been successfully cut out of the new body of doctrine. Stable functions, calculable reactions to properly visible and knowable events, such events as stir up a convenient cloud of dust in their approach, have been set up again as the component members of the theory of employment and output as a whole, the 'macro-economics' of today. Fate's mockery by general consent has been ruled out of order.

37.5 *Keynes eschewed both timelessness and diachronic mechanism*

Needless to say, the total abandonment of received theory, even if Keynes's work had in fact called for it, would have implied the abandonment of economics as an intellectual endeavour. If the careful and subtle dissections which are practised in the *General Theory*'s four-hundred-and-odd pages were worth while, there is in the field of economic phenomena a rich material for orderly and precise discourse, there is the stuff of theory in some sense. Keynes gave a wide berth to both the achronic method of general equilibrium, and the pan-chronic method of supposing that all dates have an equal and co-valid reality, and are in a peculiar sense contemporaneous with each other, so that there are two kinds of time, one for the all-seeing analyst and one for the participant painfully crawling from one sudden contingency to another with no bird's-eye view. He was engaged in subverting that value theory in which involuntary unemployment is either assumed away at the outset or concluded to be impossible at the end of a train of reasoning based implicitly on perfect knowledge. Thus, of course, timeless equilibrium was totally irrelevant to his purpose. But there was in existence also an extensive literature developing another line of thought, namely, the theories of the business cycle, the theories which began their structures of reasoning from the unstated axiom that history is governed by its own past, that what happens is implicit in what has happened. Keynes's attitude here was not consistent. The *General Theory* in the mainstream of its argument eschews all reference to relations between differently-dated values of variables. There are occasional departures from this rule. In explaining the Multiplier, Keynes gives two conflicting accounts, one of them deriving the formula by a trivial manipulation of that of the propensity to consume, which itself is treated as involving no lag between income and the related consumption, while the other admits that the Multiplier will not approximate its full effect (its full numerical value) until the business men have had time to respond to successive unforeseen increases of consumption by successive increases of output. A more important case is the claim in Chapter 22 that the theory of employment which has been presented in the body of the work offers an immediate explanation of the business cycle. Here Keynes describes successive *phases* of boom, crisis, slump and recovery, each phase, it is plainly stated or implied, being the natural, necessary and inevitable outgrowth of its predecessor. The necessity is asserted. But it is by no means always explained and established. Here, in fact, is a slurred sketch of just such a diachronic mechanism, a governance of later events by earlier ones, which the *General Theory*'s general method assiduously avoids. Were associative or genetic links between one date's events and another's to be entirely dispensed with? Yes, if we search the central statement of Keynes's theme in Books III and IV. But in Chapter 22 we find these links implicitly, and almost explicitly, invoked. Thus Chapter 22 by its curious anomalies draws attention to the *General Theory*'s most surprising aspect: the contrast between its message and its method. Its message, the irrational, incalculable motivation and dismotivation of investment in plant and equipment, is made to yield its logical consequences by means of a pseudo-equilibrium.

37.6 *The inducement to invest*

It may be claimed that in the *General Theory of Employment, Interest and Money* Keynes hit upon a method of his own for economic analysis. The theme which comes into view in the course of that book is the liability of enterprisers' confidence, and their willingness to invest, to sudden collapse, for reasons no more irrational and no more foreseeable than those which lead them to embark on great schemes for expanding and improving their facilities in the first place. The inducement to invest is incalculable. No matter that Chapter 11, on the marginal efficiency of capital, is devoted to showing its precise mode of calculation. Keynes was faced with a dilemma. His conviction had come to be that the capricious instability of the aggregate flow of investment, and its tendency to remain far below what, with the normal propensity to save, was required for full employment, was the chief defect of a modern economic society. If so, a method was needed for controlling and stimulating the inducement to invest in the enterprise sector, or else for anticipating its fluctuations and making them good by investment in the public sector. But if the profit-seeking inducement to invest is capricious and incalculable, how can it be controlled and how can its moods or movements be foreseen? Keynes needed a formal scheme by which the forces bearing on profit-seeking investment could be displayed. He adopted the method, natural and obvious to a Marshallian, of regarding the marginal efficiency of capital, for the analytic purpose in hand, as dependent only on the size of the aggregate flow of investment, and of treating that size itself as determined by that numerical value of the marginal efficiency at which the latter was equal to the prevailing rate of interest. This analytical scheme had a number of advantages. A superficial one was the suggestion it offered for influencing the size of the investment-flow by manipulating the interest-rate. But since this analytic treatment was an application of *ceteris paribus*, it was of course legitimate and essential to consider what were the *cetera*. They were all those expectational, emotional, superstitious, straw-grasping and star-gazing psychic eddies and turmoils of the investor's mind. Keynes in Chapter 10 takes pains (handicapped by the simplicity and consequent brevity of the statement in question, which allows no impressive using-up of long paragraphs and pages) to insist that the marginal efficiency of capital rests on the whole vista of future years during which the proposed new facility or item of equipment will be yielding its services. Those years, he also insists, (and this is the ultimate core of the whole Keynesian thesis) are beyond any reach of inference or reliable conjecture as to their content of events and states of affairs, 'We simply do not know'. Thus we may just as well embrace them all in the shape and position of the curve which displays the marginal efficiency as a function of the size of the investment-flow. If that unanalysable mass of atmospheric influences undergoes a swift transformation, if the business man's conjectures about the future climate for his proposed investment change or if his emotional response to a specific conjectural prospect alters, then the curve of the marginal efficiency will shift bodily, abruptly and widely to a new 'shape and position'. The *ceteris paribus* method thus shows itself, surprisingly and rather paradoxically, to be able to cope with the intractable problem of representing and formally getting in focus the matter of the inducement to invest. But is there not an inconsistency between the two suggestions we have made concerning it?

37.7 *The kaleidic method*

If the curve is given to unheralded bodily shifts, in what sense can we hope to 'control' the size of the aggregate investment flow by altering (by monetary measures) the prevailing interest-rate? The legitimate answer seems to be that no matter what the shape and position of the curve, we can always try to push investment one way or the other *along* the curve. If the curve shifts, the effect of this on the size of the investment flow must be counteracted, if desirable, by a movement along the new curve. Keynes was justified, we may think, in urging that monetary policy should do what it can in any circumstances to bring the aggregate investment-flow to an appropriate full employment level.

Now the analytic method and policy insight which arise from this line of thought are something different from both the achronic general equilibrium and the diachronic mechanical business-cycle or growth model. The method implicit in the *General Theory* is to regard the economy as subject to sudden landslides of re-adjustment to a new, precarious and ephemeral, pseudo-equilibrium, in which variables based on expectation, speculative hope and conjecture are delicately stacked in a card-house of momentary immobility, waiting for 'the news' to upset everything again and start a new dis-equilibrium phase. It is this interpretation of the latent Keynesian theme which

elsewhere I have ventured to call 'Keynesian kaleido-statics'.*
It is the method to which Keynes seems to me to have been
constrained by two circumstances of his writing.

37.8 *Two influences upon Keynes: distrust of arbitrary formal schemes*

He deeply distrusted formal schemes which imposed their own
lineaments on the face of economic theory. His distrust of
reliance upon algebra was an aspect of this repugnance.
Algebra not merely requires us to take the mere skeleton for the
whole man, but it allows no putting of flesh on the bones by
informal relaxation and qualification of the strict letter of the
assumptions. Its process of implication must be followed
through on algebra's own terms. But Keynes saw the eddying
stream of business life as incapable of such canalization. If
algebra is too precise, many of the tempting formalizations
which our subject-matter can be reduced to are grossly arbitrary. They are insidious traps for thought. We speak of 'the
period', or 'period 1', 'period 2', and so on. By what right do
we impose coherence and homogeneity upon the events of an
arbitrary period? Life is continuous, thought is ever-liable to
catch some scent of suggestion from the unceasing breeze of
existence. Can expectation only make its pounce upon some
new idea, at those moments, which the formal scheme designates
for revision of ideas? May it not make all the difference in the
world to our conclusions, that our dictate requires income to be
earned on one 'day' and not spent till the next? How long is
such a 'day'? Can it be more than a moment, without breaching the fabric of real experience? It is so simple to divide life
into a succession of equal intervals, and call for a clearing-up
and balancing the books of each interval before we clear the
letter-box and open the orders, bills, reports and disconcerting
news of a new interval. It is simple. It may be the only way to
make sense of things, or one way amongst several equally
artificial ways. Keynes said 'Forget about periods'. He was in
effect advocating the attempt to understand life by examining

* G. L. S. Shackle, *A Scheme of Economic Theory*, Cambridge University
Press (1965).

capsules of connected events and accepting them as typical of the stuff of history: study the moment, not the 'period'. In the same category of distrusted temporal dissections comes the 'time-lag'. Keynes by no means applies any subtle analysis of the meaning or mechanism of delayed response. There are many such mechansims which can be pointed to in a quite ordinary scanning of the business scene. But to select amongst them, to elevate any one lag, or a particular structure of several such lags, into a permanent frame of thought, is to fetter judgement and despatch our exploratory ventures down a pre-determined track. Keynes simply disregarded the idea of time-lagged influences. Is it better, someone has asked, to be vaguely right or precisely wrong?

37.9 *Two influences upon Keynes: Marshall and a mathematical training*

The second governing influence on Keynes's method was, per-haps, his Marshallian background as a student of economics, and his own formal training in mathematics. The *General Theory* was necessarily at odds with itself. For its author had been brought up to believe that in order to make sense of things we must have 'as many equations as there are variables', we must have a determinate 'equilibrium'. But 'equilibrium' was the antithesis of the *General Theory*'s inward vision of busi-ness life. To talk of 'equilibrium' in the speculative, competi-tive, cut-throat business game was as though a man should make nice calculations of human buoyancy as a guarantee of survival in the Atlantic rollers which can shake the cliffs them-selves. How could the two 'necessities' be reconciled? Only by the method of studying the abstract adjustments which the expectations and beliefs (of any degree of conflict and diversity amongst themselves) prevailing at some moment would lead to, given a breathing-space or moratorium to work out their logical inter-active consequences, and then of imagining, so far as possible, the cascade of real events which must flow from the inevitable upset of any such state of rest accidentally attained. It is such a method which I seek to designate by the term 'kalei-dic economics'.

37.10 Variables of thought *and their swift mutations*

Keynes's formal, momentary equilibria no doubt have something in common with Marshall's conception of 'the normal'. 'The normal' is what would be the case if the governing, extra-economic conditions stayed still for long enough (and it would be a very long time indeed, in terms even of the human life-span) for 'things to work themselves out'. Marshall's normal is an implication of a set of data, the answer to a sum, not necessarily ever attained in practice or visible reality. A Keynesian equilibrium may have meant for Keynes a set of mutually consistent goals visible, in its character of a configuration, to many of those with power to decide upon large-scale action; a summary of the forces at work at some moment. But he seems also to have regarded it as having a compelling power, as able to draw the evolving state of affairs towards itself, so that the equilibrium would describe or indicate not only a concert of movements but an attainment. If so, the economic society, and its organization and technology, which he envisaged must have possessed a high fluidity and capacity for adjustment. And, indeed, we find in the *Treatise* and the *General Theory* a central role and importance assigned to variables which can adjust themselves virtually in no time at all through large ranges of movement, which can perform discontinuous jumps. These are the *variables of thought*, the valuations and expectations, the valuations *springing* from expectation, such as the worth attached to Stock Exchange securities. These mutable judgements could swiftly compose a picture which made sense of such data as there were, and could as swiftly dissolve that picture when the data were falsified, augmented, re-interpreted or swallowed into the past.

37.11 *Kaleidics and the union of reason and realism*

What claim can the kaleidic method make, and how can the instinctive and unconscious experiment which the *General Theory* presents best be given a precise formulation? We have already suggested that the paramount need which its procedure served was the writing of an Economics of Disorder. Yet by describing equilibria it admits that in all the turmoil, reason is at work. The economics of organized, coherent, pre-reconciled rationality, the value-construct, could not give insight into the massive unemployment which its premises excluded from the outset, or its conclusion showed to be impossible. *Reason in full control* would have been a mockery of the truth in the early 1930s, yet reason in full control is the premiss of value theory; reason *fully informed*. The kaleidic method shows the struggle and frustration of reason in face of those uncertainties which are part of the scheme of things; which ultimately, despite successful efforts which can be made to reduce their effect, are part of the essential and unalterable frame of human affairs. In doing this it plainly surpasses the value-construct in realism. It does so without surrendering the insights of particular equilibrium, for it rests on the classic assumption that the firm is a profit-seeking interest. It presents us with descriptions of equilibrium positions for the economic society as a whole, which differ from those of the value-construct in not being optima, but merely positions which do not contain within their structure an immediate source of movement. It shows how in the nature of things, and in their own nature, these 'equilibria' are vulnerable in the extreme to any expectation-changing news; for they rest upon expectations which naturally and necessarily conflict with each other (speculative prices can only stay at rest on condition of conflict of expectations) and are ready at a touch to break up and dissolve. One step remains: Can theory or measurement throw light on the character of the disintegrative movements which flow from the break up of a kaleidic equilibrium? Can such an equilibrium be described in such terms as will suggest the directions in which variables will move, and how fast and far their reactions will go? Can the equilibrium be described, not as to the numerical values which its variables show at the moment of rest, but as to the latent forces in their momentary relationships and the potential pattern of their dispersal?

. 37.12 *Kaleidics and the bursting of equilibrium*

Such a kaleidics, if practicable or meaningful at all (and we are advancing a suggestion of obviously speculative character) might offer diachronic insights of a very tentative, modest and short-range kind, not seeking to show what must happen, but what is the range of diversity of the immediate developments that various situations are capable of. The description of such situations would be in terms of elasticities. Kaleidic equilibrium is an adjustment to each other of those matters (variables) which are under the control of business men, but above all, an adjustment of them to beliefs and expectations (not by any means likely to be mutually consistent amongst different people) about matters *not* under the individual or collective control of the business men. The notion of kaleidic equilibrium is an explicit recognition of, and draws attention to, the overwhelmingly evident fact that the *economic* affairs of society are not self-contained and independent. They may be compared to a sailing-boat in tempestuous and tide-swept waters. Certainly the boat itself has unity of structure, but what happens to it will be the outcome not only of its design (its capacities for response to impacts of various kinds, its *elasticities*) but of the policies, training and local knowledge of the crew, and the behaviour of the vast forces of the environment: the gales and tides of politics, diplomacy, technology, fashion and social upheaval. We may be able to gain knowledge of how the economic boat will respond to this or that shift of the surrounding forces; we cannot hope to know what those shifts will be.

37.13 *Kaleidics rejects the self-containedness of business cycle theory*

Kaleidic economics would adopt and exploit consciously the method to which the *General Theory* was in its practice constrained by circumstance and by its author's insights, a method which in the years after Keynes's death was misconceived and neglected in favour of a swift return to self-contained systems. Throughout the 1920s, Britain experienced depression and high unemployment, and in 1929 the question was actually being asked: When will the recovery come? Keynes wrote the *General Theory* against the background of what seemed like a settled condition of under-employment, rather than the depression phase of the business cycle. In the midst of it had come the abrupt and catastrophic plunge of the early 1930s. This history was not the regular boom and slump of the cycle, but a permanent mode of life of the economy, like a locomotive unable to raise steam and yet subject to sudden derailments. The United States enjoyed relative prosperity in the 1920s, and some believed it had found 'the secret of permanent prosperity'. The disaster was in consequence more overwhelming. The American national income in money terms was halved in a few years, and even its real income was, incredibly it may nowadays seem, reduced by a third. These things were not cycles but cataclysms. The theory which might cope with them would have to be able equally to cope with periods of settled low vitality in the economic society, and unforeseeable spasms of greater trouble. It would have largely to be a theory of how 'non-economic' events and pressures affected the business world, rather than a theory of that world's supposedly insulated, self-sufficient life capable of accounting for its own vicissitudes by its own internal mechanisms. Theories of the business cycle were inward looking. Keynes's experience of war and peace was too broadly educative to sanction such a hot-house view.

37.14 *Economic society and history as textile rather than rigid structures*

Keynes's practice of his non-diachronic method, his refusal to set out explicitly any formal frame of ideas about time, amounts to a belief that we mainly need, and are best able, to study the *texture* of economic affairs, and of the general economic history-engendering process, its quality and general mode, rather than try to see it as a matter of exact, stable quantitative relationships. The structure and nature of economic society is perhaps *textile* rather than rigidly engineered. Insight can unquestionably be gained (and was transformed in its penetration of reality) by the Stockholm School's device of sequence analysis or period analysis, and above all by means of that method's characteristic and central idea, the absolute contrast of meaning between the business man's (or other economic subject's) *figments* of the contents of the *coming* time interval and his *record* of the contents of the past interval. Myrdal's distinction of the *ex ante* from the *ex post* view, though mainly formal in his presentation, was one of the most transforming insights that theoretical economics has had. Despite its elemental simplicity, its obvious inescapable necessity once it has been proposed, the making explicit of this notion was a stroke of genius. Myrdal did not perhaps go on to insist on the *generative* nature of the *ex ante* view, though this is implicit in his construction. What is imagined for a coming period must, in an ultimate sense or as a link in a train of impulses, help to shape what will, *ex post*, emerge as the facts of that period. The conception as a whole was capable of clearing away a mass of confusion arising from the treatment of economic affairs as mechanistic or hydraulic instead of subjective and, to use Edgeworth's suggestive word, psychic. Yet the Myrdalian scheme has its own problems. It is plain that there are many competing, and somewhat incompatible, criteria for the length of the Myrdalian period. Is it not essentially a mere moment of time? For the very concept of 'the present', intangible by the most delicate gropings of the mind, seems, so far as it can be analysed, to contain something of both past and present, and thus to involve in some degree the visible transformation of what is expected into what is realized. 'The present' is, as it were, not a Myrdalian period but a Myrdalian *moment*.* Yet in our economic application of the idea, it seems plainly appropriate to identify the Myrdalian period with the business man's planning period, the interval between his Board meetings, the stretch of time which he allows for the policy-commitments and revisions to be tried out, to show their practical implications. Does that view not again imprison us, however, in a mechanistic, inflexible frame?

* I use the word 'Myrdalian' as a technical term for the notion of contrasting the expected with the realized.

37.15 *Keynes's neglect of a methodology of time*

Keynes had already, long before the publication of the *General Theory*, shown an instinctive distrust of any cut-and-dried scheme of division of the calendar. In the *Treatise on Money* his Fundamental Equations are an embryonic glimpse of the Stockholm sequence method.* But the word 'period' slips only once into his discussion of them. He preferred to leave calendar-divisions alone. Marshall had devised his short- and long-period concept without any connotation of an 'absolute' length of time. Keynes was deeply Marshallian. He was also a mathematically-trained man habituated to the telescoping of interval-events (the translation of a moving object) into moment-events (the velocity of translation expressed by means of a limiting process). It was natural enough that he should seek to emancipate his thought from too strict a pacing by the calendar. But with no strict division of time or consideration of dates, what is left? The things which are held to bear upon each other, to influence each other, are simply brought together and the analyst shows how they might settle down, given a sufficient undisturbed opportunity. Keynes perhaps gave no careful thought to his methodology of time. He took for granted the broad notion of self-interested forces pushing against each other till mutually brought to rest at a point at which it was no longer worth while for any of them to shift things further. This 'equilibrium', like Marshall's 'normal', pointed where things would try to go. There was no inference that all of them could adjust to it immediately, although those of them which were valuations could so adjust almost instantly, with the speed of thought, for 'thought' is what they were. No doubt the kaleidic method, if I may be allowed so to call it, was invented and used unconsciously and by accident, and exists in the *General Theory* as a mere mute, unformulated possibility. From the *Treatise*, Keynes could have moved in either direction, towards a development of his Fundamental Equations into a full-fledged Stockholm-type sequence analysis, or in the direction of orthodoxy and Marshallian equilibrium. He moved towards concessions of method in exchange for tremendous heresies of

* This thesis is developed in *The Years of High Theory*, Chapter 13.

content. He recognized and understood not at all the necessity and meaning of *ex ante* and *ex post*, near as he had come to it in the *Treatise*. It is a pity that he was not more explicit in his treatment or neglect of time, for his apparent orthodoxy of method gave a ready means to his exegetists to divert his meaning as well into something like conventional economics.

38

Economic Theory Unbound

Economic theory has concerned itself with the sources and consequences of conduct, and has sought in this field what can be conceived as rational, what can be expressed as proportion, what is publicly and unanimously agreed, and what belongs within bounds defined by the notion of exchange in an inclusive sense. For these choices of matter and method it has strong incentives. If conduct is rational, the analyst can directly understand it by applying his own reason to the circumstances and the desires ascribed to the conduct-chooser. By reducing all to proportion, all can be directly related to the operation of exchange, in which proportion is naturally and necessarily inherent. Proportion also lends itself to the construction of a highly austere and abstract axiomatic system, and to the enunciation of tests of success. By confining itself to what appears to be publicly agreed, it can claim something of the objectivity of the physical sciences. Exchange as the focus of its interest gives it a highly definite and distinct criterion and delimiting principle, and marks it off readily from other aspects of conduct and policy. So powerful are the claims of such a programme, that we may almost regard the path which economic theoreticians have followed as inevitable. Moreover, the execution of this programme has given scope to some of those felicities and ingenuities of invention, which are a perpetual delight to the recorder and practitioner of economic theory, for the task of reducing human action to such terms as could equally well apply to the behaviour of inanimate objects is delicate and difficult, as well as being dangerous in the extreme and a potential source of vast error.

The attractions of such a programme are evident and compelling. The cost resides in what, by its nature, it is obliged to neglect or even implicitly to declare unimportant. The title of this volume expresses my own judgement of what is the most serious of those exclusions. It is the brushing aside of the question, a unity though requiring three terms to express it, of time, knowledge, novelty. This trinity of terms would have well served as our title. Economic theory in the form which history has given it follows its own line unhesitatingly. Having opted for the supremacy of reason, it rejects what conflicts with reason. Expectation is origination, not reason, therefore it cannot be understood by the principles of logic alone, and must be excluded. This exclusion is necessary, if economic theory is to avoid *both* losing grip of logic, and making an arbitrary choice of premisses. It is natural and right for the theoretician to reduce to the unavoidable minimum his arbitrary choices of assumption, and for that purpose, to make the few which are unavoidable as incisive and powerful as he can. One great, dramatic stroke and have done with it, is his course of daring and of safety. To tinker with his premisses will exasperate his reader and cause him to abandon any hope of testing the writer's soundness of reasoning. Therefore theory has chosen rationality, whole and unimpaired. And thus it has cut itself off from the most ascendant and superb of human faculties. Imagination, the source of novelty, the basis of men's claim, if they have one, to be makers and not mere executants of history, is exempted by its nature from the governance of given and delimited premisses.

An axiomatics, to attain beauty, cogency and usefulness, needs a certain simplicity. Thus the first policy-decision of the constructors of theory, to assume that conduct was governed by reason and could be understood by it, pre-disposed them to the suggestion offered by their concern with exchange, namely, that economic theory should content itself with quantities and their mutual relations, and eschew entirely that world which, in the most essential and fundamental sense, escapes from number, the world of form and arrangement. The cardinality of the functions of a real variable is more powerful than that of the continuum of real numbers itself. By excluding ourselves from form and spatial arrangement we exclude ourselves from technology, from all the arts of survival and of expression of feeling, we renounce the question How? in favour of sole interest in the question How much? Business cannot afford to neglect the question How much?, and a breakdown of financial control, of accountancy, will reduce to nonsense the most brilliant technological conceptions, because it implies neglect of their *orientation*, the study of their possible and profitable uses, their inter-contributory aptness, their burden of duty in the organism as a whole. But if orientation, the concern of accountancy, studies the purpose of things, it is equally true that there would not, without technology, be any things for it to study the purpose of. Technologies, practical arts, the knowledge supplied by engineers, chemists, geneticists, soil scientists; the questions which only they can ask, let alone answer; the difficulties, dangers and consequences they can warn of; the inventions they can imagine; all these must press eternally upon the business man's consciousness and engage his anxious thought. The production department is as vital as the accountancy department; it is *more* vital, for brute need itself in the last resort determines orientation, but productive arts must be mastered or we perish. Yet economics must limit itself to a coherent set of facets and questions, to attempt everything is to fail everywhere. It chose, let us acknowledge, with high wisdom or supreme good luck.

Economics is the study of the operation of exchange and its implications. Exchange is the means of giving operational meaning to the notion of economic value. By marvellous good fortune, the nature of things turns out to be such, in the law of diminishing marginal utility, that individuals have an incentive to adjust their conduct so that exchange values are universally agreed. The price of one thing in terms of another, after the market has pre-reconciled the respective quantities that individuals, each with his special tastes and circumstances, wish to exchange, reflects the estimations of every participant: the *marginal* estimations. Thus economic value seems to be as publicly and universally meaningful as mass or length, and makes possible the most audacious of the illusions practised by the theoretician, the measurement of 'aggregate income', 'aggregate wealth', 'the aggregate flow of investment', the movement of 'the general price level', as scalar, one-dimensional quantities. These aggregates, statistical fictions, mere shadows which suggest the outline, only, of the assemblages of infinitely diverse items that they embrace, restore to economics, in a sense, the simplicity of the Crusoe economy. The whole society is described in a handful of variables, and large meanings and implications are drawn from the definitional identities which unite them. Macro-economics, the profile of the economy, gives valuable knowledge. It also lends itself to arguments which lose touch with its fictional character, its nature of cardboard scenery concealing the back-stage realities.

Macro-economics has contracted to a study of the mechanics of growth. When theoreticians turn again to the essential nature of conduct, policy and history, they will necessarily make their fresh start from the basis which exists, the scheme of ideas which two centuries have arrived at and which, by luck or inspiration, has miraculously given the Human Affair, in one of its aspects, a semblance of order. That scheme of ideas makes its profound impression on those who study it by the contrast of its utterly simple and mundane origin, namely, the operation of exchange, and the universal reach and penetration of its conclusions. Almost organic in the need and dependence of its ideas for each other, the theory of value may be claimed to be a single idea with a number of distinguishable facets. Conduct, specialized to the act of exchange; rationality, requiring pre-reconciliation; the market, achieving pre-reconciliation; equi-librium, the prescription of conduct for all by consent, and advantage, of all; economy, the utmost advantage for each individual from his given endowment, given the equal freedom and equal (perfect relevant) knowledge available to all. The business of life is thus seen in some degree *sub specie aeternitatis*. Our difficulty is that this conception is too perfect. It shows men as acting rationally, whereas to be human is to be denied the necessary condition of rationality, complete relevant knowledge. So far is knowledge from ever being complete, that conscious-ness consists in the gaining of knowledge.

Fewer than half-a-dozen ideas, distinct but inseparable in meaning, form the whole method and essential content of the still-vital theory that we have received from our founders. The tool they forged is too keen to be dispensed with, the thicket of distracting detail and difficulty through which it cuts a narrow path is too involved to be cleared by any but heroic means. Those few ideas: rational self-interest, exchange, the general market, universal public prices, equilibrium; must be the basis of any improved conception. A theory which denied men *reason* would be an abdication from our claims of humanity; general exchange is the *operation* which gives unity and definition to our field; the market is the source and means of that *knowledge* which makes rational conduct possible; equilibrium names the result of the market's pre-reconciliation of endlessly diverse tastes confronted with an infinite diversity of circumstance. Because successful action of one's own *depends upon* the recognition and exploitation of the desires and intentions of others, a general equilibrium naturally tends to coalesce from the seething initiatives of individual interests. This pattern must forever be discernible in the process of a free society. But those initiatives are engendered and influenced by far more than those things which value theory, in this ultimate abstract form, can conceive of. What that theory neglects is the epistemic problem, the problem of how the necessary knowledge on which reason can base itself is to be gained, the problem of what to suppose that men will do when time's sudden mockery reveals their supposed knowledge to be hollow. How is the *morale* of expectation sustained in face of the *nature* of expectation, its necessary encompassing of rival, incompatible hypotheses? Can we find any general principle that may give insight into men's mode of response to the counter-expected and the unexpected? It is such counter-expected, surprising, outcomes of trading and of investment, outcomes defeating expectation, that give rise to profit in its nature and role as a signal of the need to reconsider policy. Profit (positive or negative), in the sense of an impulse thrusting across the former line of policy and suggesting, with a strong supporting incentive, that the policy must be revised in order to avoid disaster or secure a great success which can be glimpsed as within reach, is the central dynamic or evolutionary element in the market economy. Profit can be looked upon (as by Marshall) as in some sense a regular constituent of income and the reward of a main category of factors of production, namely, 'management', 'organising capacity' or 'enterprise'. But what the initiators and policy-makers of enterprise do is divisible into distinct strands. On one hand they devote their technological and mercantile skill to the choice of products and of methods of production and sale; on the other they shoulder the responsibility for success or failure and stake their reputations, their self-esteem, their lucrative jobs, and even some of their personal wealth, upon their judgement. If the trading revenue, or the investment-gain (discounted expected trading revenues less first cost of the enterprise) lie within their range of expectation, there is 'profit' in the Marshallian sense. If the outcome falls outside the inter-focal range, there is 'windfall' profit, counter-expected profit, policy-discrediting profit (showing policy as wrong in character, when profit is negative, or insufficiently bold in its ambition when profit is positive and remarkable in *rate*). We have even ventured in Chapter 35 to suggest a measure of the strength of the policy-changing effect of counter-expected events. It is, perhaps, in taking the phenomenon of profit more seriously, in analysing its nature, origins and influence as a systematic and an organic part of value theory and as an inevitable product of the inevitable recurring collapses of equilibrium, a natural, inherent and essential feature of the kaleidic economy, that we can best hope to improve economic theory as an insight-tool, as a means of understanding, and also persuade ourselves not to insist too confidently on its powers as a foresight-tool. As to foresight, economic knowledge should surely be applied to each problem on that problem's merits, to each case as something singular and special.

INDEX

bond price (*cont.*)

constancy of, cannot be engendered by any state of opinion which will be confirmed by it, 201

stable only in virtue of two views, 162, 199

bondage to circumstance

as the meaning of determinacy, 220

Bridgeman, P. W.

and *operational meaning* of a concept, 378

building-blocks of conduct,

elemental enough for theorizing, 61

business

a game played largely in necessary ignorance of the rules, 425

and diplomacy, 6

and jigsaw-puzzle problems, 39, 119

and political actions, 6

as applied science, 115

contrast of, with a 'delimited' game such as chess, 425

is necessarily non-rational, 163

prevented by potential novelty from being a *game with known rules*, 424

supreme secret of, is *epistemic*, the gaining or the witholding of knowledge, 423

business cycle theory(-ies)

and a natural sequence of states of mind, 60

can be a unity though centred on expectation, 60

mechanical, are asking to be out-witted, 59

mechanism of, some think it is to be viewed as one whole, 59

show both transformational and analytic aspects, 55

calendar

as a class with natural succession, 277

implies measurement, 278

calendar-axis

and need to study fine structure of history, 280

how filled with content, 279

two dangers in seeking suggestions from the past, 280

calendar-intuition, the

accepts the succession of moments, 278

Cantillon, Richard

and the essential role of the merchant, 92, 164, 364, 415

and the nature of profit, 413

and the start of an economic science, 359

capital

and relation to each other of the technological structure and time-structure of production, 300, 331

and the *average period of production*, 309

and the concepts of *embodied factor-days* and *factor-day embodied days*, 306–8

as an embodiment of productive effort, three ways of viewing, 306–8

as the basis of an input–output matrix, 298, 331

Austrian theory of, 305

Austrian theory of, an illustrative model, 306–12

Austrian theory of, and determina-ion of income from, 314

Austrian theory of, and the stationary state, 315–19, 330

Austrian theory of, and unification with the Leontief model, 332

Austrian theory of, belongs to a world of perfect knowledge, 315

Austrian theory of, bound up with the stationary state, 305, 315

Austrian theory of, can the average period be measured in value terms? 319, 320

Austrian theory of, claims to scalarize a heterogeneous collection, 320

Austrian theory of, contrast of simplicity in essence and com-plexity in detail, 312

Austrian theory of, exists in an *arbitrarily* stationary world, 331

Austrian theory of, has difficulty in accomodating *durability*, 306

Austrian theory of, ignores the orientation of capital items, 315

Austrian theory of, ignores uncer-tainty and novelty, 315

Austrian theory of, is difficult to emancipate from comparative statics, 314, 316

Austrian theory of, regards the value of an embodied factor-day as growing with the passage of time, 313

Austrian theory of, shows income from capital stock determined by impatience and technology, 315, 332

Austrian theory of, whether its difficulties are due to process inter-action, durability, in-definite orientation, or unreality of 'impatience'? 321

can be measured by means of time, 304

choice(s) (*cont.*)
  'the logic of', is it unconcerned with the mode and source of invention of *things choosable?* 355
  uselessness of a test *ex post* as a guide to choice, 123
classification
  and an economics of qualities, 118
  employed even in mathematics 73, 185
  is essential to description, 61
  is not a second-rate technique, 73
classificatory method
  a conceivable resort for kaleidic phenomena, 186
  whether a suitable resort for economics, 30, 118
code(s)
  and temptation to transfer the use of a given code from one discipline to another, 52
  appropriate to science of inanimate events, have misled economists, 53
  as a means of explanation, 51
  as a source of predictive suggestion, 51
  as an instruction for practice, 51
  concept of, 50, 51
  criteria of beauty in, 52
  criteria of power of, 52
  dual character required of, in economics, 72
  efficacy of, 51, 53
  selective light of, 51
comparative statics,
  does not lead to an understanding of movement, 271
  need of the method of, 271
composition of the product wage,
  difference of desires concerning, as the origin of unemployment, 169, 170
  incompatible desires of income-receivers and income payers concerning, 169–76
  incompatible real composition of wages, not cited expressly by Keynes as the source of unemployment, 175
  Myrdal's glimpse of the problem of, 175
concept(s)
  arranged in counterpoint, 131
  consists in a *named class*, 61
  may seem to spring into relief by Nature's own prompting, 343
  nature of, 6
concert of action
  sometimes dependent on a conflict of opinion, 71
conditional intentions, pooling of, for pre-reconciliation of choices, 253

constructive or transformational theories,
  and the business cycle, 55
  nature of, 52, 55
consumer's surplus
  and meaning of market unanimity, 79, 109
  and valuation as a means of scalar measurement, 46, 109, 110
  is a 'particular equilibrium' concept, 110
  paradoxes of, 110
contour-line
  as a tool of economic theory, 65
convention
  as basis of valuation, 68, 221, 222, 223
  beliefs can originate in, 193
  given exact meaning as a technical term in *General Theory*, Chapter 12, 224
  is resorted to in the absence of real clues, 193
  prices as the result of, 268
conventional judgements
  capricious instability of, 225
  naure of, 225
conventional valuation of assets
  principle of, and consequences of, 224, 225
cost
  as displacement cost, 132
  implies the existence of rival possibilities, 132
  notion of, and freedom with determinacy, 132
Cournot, Augustin
  and duopoly, 96
  and the dilemma of perfect competition, 147
co-valid equations
  system of, is an indispensable idea for the economist, 249, 250
co-validity of distinct dates, 57
  as in one of the two aspects of Marshall's long period, 289
co-validity of equations, 149
cumulative process
  any precise description of, requires endless arbitrary assumptions, 337
  Wicksell's, 335, 336
cycle
  and a diachronic fibre in history, 339
  and problem of how the influence of events at one date is carried through time to shape those of another, 339
  co-existence of all ingredients of, 340, 341
  contains the notion of a *gap of time* between states of the system, 338

SEE

duopoly
compels each firm to act on a rule
different from that which it
ascribes to the other, 236, 237
seems to defeat analysis, 96, 97, 236
shows a fundamental limitation of
rationality, 97, 236
durability
and speculation, 12, 79, 112, 412, 413
and valuation of equipment, 14, 47, 79
destroys the basis of rationality, 158,
159
durable assets
price of, can remain at rest only
through opposed views of Bulls
and Bears, 112, 412
durable goods
necessarily constitute a medium of
speculation, 159, 412
value assigned to, can rest only on
supposed content of a stretch of
future time, 183, 412

economic affairs
a purely economic explanation of,
flies in the face of history, 240, 344
a shawl of loosely knotted strands, 240
are not self-contained, 240, 344
do not conform to mathematical
abstractions, 260
General Scene of, can be described
in infinitely many different
languages or taxonomies, 273
no warranty for assuming them
insulated from other human
affairs, 281, 343, 344
response of, to kaleidic shifts, 240
economic analyst
his bent and training lead him to
start at the end, 115
his concerns are a thin gruel, 115
is not interested in *form*, 114
not aware of the degree of abstraction
that he adopted, 151
the object of his study must be
accepted as protean, 255
economic aspect of conduct
is the part guided by valuations, 156
economic conduct
and choice between double-think
and compromise, 255
danger of supposing it self-contained,
281
explained as the dictate of reason, 229
is engendered by *thoughts about
thoughts*, 71
economic man, the
value-theory flows from the
character and conditions of
existence ascribed to, 148

economic theory(-ies)
an illuminant, 118
and the non-conformity of things to
simple schemes, 118
and the 'subjective ideal', 247
contrast of assumptions between
theory of value and other branches,
134
disgust with, sometimes expressed
by the economist, 272
does not deal with tangibles, 177
form a counterpoint, 131
has defined its field as reason,
proportion, public measure, so far
as these relate to exchange, 443
has eschewed direct concern with
technologies, 444
has sought to dispense with questions
of time and acquirement of
knowledge, 444
its claim to be invincible in cogency,
yet real in content, 247
its ingenuities in reducing human
action to the terms of inanimate
action, 443
mathematization of, how possible?
224
must appear to the business man a
summary and commentary of his
methods, 42
must renounce the search for perfect
generalness of its self-representations, 254
needs incompatible sets of assumptions, 246, 254, 255
renounces concern with form and
arrangement, 444
economics
a device for scalarizing heterogeneous
collections, 39, 109, 360
aims to control the average and the
mass, 362
and a unified scheme of ends, 81
and divorce of method from
meaning, 361, 362
and self-consistent action, 80, 81,
84
and superficial facility of measurement, 361
and the static model, 246
and the technique of index-numbers,
36
as a classic maximizing problem, 102
as pure logic of choice, needs to
assume *certainty*, 81
bludgeons the face of reality, 111
deemed itself one of the 'exact
sciences', 65, 66, 361
depends on ideas derived from
universal experience, 246

history *(cont.)*
  flows from ideas and their rivalries, 77
  how can one aspect of it be treated as self-contained? 344
  how to be inferred, if engendered by future *choices*? 123
  is made up of details, 156, 280
  is one whole, 343
  kaleidic conception of, 77
  'loose-textured' and the notion of *cause*, 351, 352
  'loose-textured', may give the economist's short-range analysis some warrant in the origins of history, 352
  Lord Acton's belief in discoverable motives, 350
  need to study fine structure of, 280
  no internal logic of it has been conclusively shown, 343
  paradox of, in its nature of moments seen as sequential yet co-existing, 283, 284
  small portions of, but not the whole, can be unified by theory, 348
  the ready-made assemblies of impressions in, 346
  the store of her ironies, 424
  the 'sub-compositions' of, 346
history to come
  cannot be encapsulated in a model, 26
human affairs
  orderliness of, defended (but indefensible) by orthodox economic theory, 224

ideal allocation of means of production, 252
  and universally reconcilable choices, 252
ignorance
  exploitation of, is called speculation, 12
  region of, is as exploitable as that of knowledge, 12
imagination
  and future time, 25, 67
  and more than infinite possibilities for human volitional conduct, 28
  and tests of efficacy of choices, 124
  and the creation of forms for the sake of their form, 130
  and the inducement to invest, 15
  best accessible state of, 126
  creates the objects of choice, 96, 130
  fired by suggestions of beauty, 114
  of the future, Preface, 3, 67

  rejected by economic theory in favour of rationality, 444
  source and process of, concerns the economist, 130, 131
  the formal, is the originator of science, 187
  the formal, value theory a triumph of, 239
  the present consists partly in imagination of the future, 67
  transforms the problem of accounting for human conduct, 130
  un-knowledge is a freedom for, 407
impatience
  and a threat to dis-invest an existing capital stock, 328
  and impossibility of dismantling a modern society's productive apparatus, 328
  and nature of the production-net, 328
  and the Austrian theory of capital, 320, 325
  as reluctance to accept a short reduction of real income for the sake of a permanent later increase, 327
  as reluctance to build up a capital stock, 326, 327
  doubtful role of, in determining an interest-rate, 202, 203
imperfect competition
  incompatible with rational determinacy, 235
imprecision(s)
  a science of, is indispensable, 362
  and particular equilibrium, 262
  and the economist's art, 9, 48, 49, 72, 142, 359–63
  and the meaning of perfect competition, 142
  language of, a justifiable source of pride for economics, 363
  pervades all human affairs, 403
incentive
  is something desired and not despaired of, 415
income
  nature or meaning of, 66, 67
  relation of, to capital, 66–8
incommensurables
  economics the art of reducing to common terms, 10
indifference-curve, indifference-map
  a master tool, 65
  consistency of, as a source of real knowledge, 121, 122
individual mind, the
  forbidden by science to examine itself, 354

investment-values
  can be based only on suggestive
    evidence, 178
  depend on expectation, 179, 181
  dependent on trading-revenues
    conceived as possible, 181

Jevons, Stanley
  and bilateral monopoly, 98
jigsaw-puzzle problems, 39

kaleidic analyst
  must recognize the real market as
    speculative, 79
kaleidic approach
  sees human affairs as bounded but
    indeterminate, 76, 77
kaleidic effects
  and a conceivable resort to classifi-
    catory methods, 186
  and most dangerous point in any
    investigation, where we seek to
    write the problem down, 184
  cannot be encapsulated by formal
    functional notation, 184
  difficulties of *notation* posed by, 184
  typified by the response of asset
    values to 'the news', 184
kaleidic movement of affairs
  a social response to uncertainty, 78
  landslide phase of, 78, 184
  nature of the phase of stability, 78
kaleidic society
  and struggle amongst rival orienta-
    tions, 76
  as a skein of *potentiae*, 76, 438
  can achieve coherence for each
    member differently, 125, 428
kaleidics, kaleidic method
  accommodates uncertainty and
    precariousness without
    surrendering the insights of
    equilibrium, 437
  and a classificatory procedure, 72, 73
  and Keynes's perhaps accidental
    procedure, 72
  and the character of the break-up
    of equilibrium, 437
  eschews explanation of shifts
    between equilibria, 72
  exists in the *General Theory* as an
    unformulated possibility, 441
  its equilibria described in terms of
    elasticities, 438
  its equilibria rest upon vulnerable
    expectations, 437
  nature of, 72
  regards the economy as subject to
    landslide re-adjustments from one
    pseudo-equilibrium to another, 433

shows the struggle of reason in face of
  ineluctable uncertainties, 437
was an instinctive and unconscious
  experiment, 436
kaleidoscope
  as an anologue of economic society,
    428
  expectational, 9
  its total transformation of patterns
    through slight disturbances, 428
Keynes, John Maynard
  adopted a *ceteris paribus* method for
    the inducement to invest, 432, 433
  and a passage in terms of decision, 172
  and 'kaleidic economics', 435
  and *probable inference*, 387–91
  and the contradiction between his
    two purposes of analysis and policy,
    163, 432
  and the dangers of formal schemes,
    434
  and the fragmentary and mutable
    basis of investment-decision, 364
  and the *insidiae* of value theory, 232
  and the Principle of Indifference,
    389–91
  and the role of *thought-variables*
    capable of instantaneous adjust-
    ment, 436, 441
  and two separate themes on the
    origin of involuntary unemploy-
    ment, 166
  and *windfall profit*, Preface, 419
  condemned scalarization-by-value,
    but resorted to it, 48
  did not ask why money is not
    immediately spent, 207
  encompasses in a coherent system
    the role of an indefinable called
    liquidity, 213
  had no such notion as *ex ante* and
    ex post, 442
  he adapted to macro-economics
    Marshall's method of studying the
    texture of economic affairs, 439
  his handling of essential imprecision,
    72
  his method in the *General Theory*,
    431–3
  neglected any methodology of time,
    441
  sought a quasi-physical measure of
    output, 48
  sought to correct disastrous policies, 35
  sought to unify the theory of money
    and the theory of value, 335
  was influenced by his mathematical
    training, 435, 441
  was steeped in Marshallian ideas,
    163, 435, 436, 441

marginalism (*cont.*)
  subjective, provided the second
    equation for simultaneous deter-
    mination of price and output, 244
  united psychics, mathematics and
    the supremacy of reason, 244, 245,
    248
market
  allows individuals to adjust their
    affairs so that their valuations
    are those of the market, 82
  and advantage of being 'one of few',
    82
  and claim of economics to be an
    independent discipline, 33
  and coherence of the actions of its
    members, 33, 34, 82
  and definition of economics, 5
  and the proviso of 'just' endowments,
    83
  and valuation, 8, 9, 83
  cannot solve the problem of
    expectation, 83
  continuous, involves expectation, 266
  continuous, is necessarily speculative
    in some degree, 266
  distinct in method, not purpose,
    from political institutions, 6, 82
  enables the individual to adapt his
    conduct to his circumstances, 83
  for durable goods, is inevitably
    divided into Bulls and Bears, 83
  in 'futures', leaves opinions about the
    future free to diverge, 112
  its business is a continual patching
    and piecemeal improvement, 268
  makes valuation objective and
    publicly agreed, 9
  mechanisms suggested for, 238
  provides the means and temptation
    to subordinate form to quantity, 39
  solves the problem of the single
    maximand, 83
  unanimity is at the margin, 79
  values, and scalar measurement of
    diverse collections, 9, 39
market values
  deceptive meaning of, 110, 111
Marshall, Alfred
  and a letter to Edgeworth, concerning
    a proposal of Sir Henry Cunyng-
    hame, 292
  and an irreversible long-period
    supply curve, 292, 293
  and Comte's thesis, 33
  and consumer's surplus, 109
  and detailed content of the notion
    of cost and supply-price, 295
  and measurement of the strength of
    motives by money, 113

and overcrowded meaning in the
  long-period supply curve, 291, 292
and the dilemma of 'increasing
  returns', 244
and the dilemma of perfect competition, 147
and the distinction between analyst
  and participant, 290
and the essential imprecision of
  economics, 262
and the inter-generation of needs
  and activities, 130
and the *long-period* from two viewpoints, 289
and the long-period supply curve
  best described in Appendix H of
  the *Principles*, 290, 291
and the long-period supply curve
  designed to accomodate the
  business man's awareness of
  knowledge to be gained, 286, 287,
  290
and the necessary falsity of every
  plain and simple doctrine of cost
  and value, 296
and the 'Normal', 288, 292
and the perfectibility of human
  nature, Preface
and the 'Principle of Continuity',
  288
and the real character of the
  Principles, Preface
and the Representative Firm, 295
and the response of business to new
  technology, 115, 287
and the unity of explanation and
  prediction, 345, 347
and time in the *Principles*, 286–96
does not subscribe to a determinism
  of thought, 348
his long-period supply curve, has
  ex ante and *ex post* meaning, 290
his method not that of the determinist systems, 349
his reliance on the *partial
  equilibrium* method, 347
meant by the Normal an adjustment
  to *given* opportunities, 289
recognized the incompleteness of
  information, 238, 286
said consistently that the business
  man is moved by what he expects,
  364
saw the necessity to spin together
  mutually repellent strands of
  thought, 287
saw the *texture* of economic history
  rather than its outline, 348
says that the selection of facts is part
  of the analyst's task, 349

probability(-ies), subjective
  and a classification of outcomes into
    empty boxes, 22
  and a logically necessary feature of
    distributive assignments of
    standing, 399
  and a strictly endless list of hypotheses
    in answer to some question, 22
  and business men condemned to dip
    in a bottomless bran-tub, 22
  and incompatible views of the claim
    of subjective probability, 399
  and necessary resort to a residual
    hypothesis, 22
  and *number of rivals* as a chief
    disability of any one proposed
    answer to a question, 399
  assumes that all relevant hypotheses
    have been specified and
    enumerated, 15, 21
  can be assigned to rival hypotheses, 20
  directs attention to the question of
    exhaustiveness of list of hypotheses,
    and consistency of judgements, 20
  gives judgement the dress of
    observation, 399
  inclusiveness of list of answers may
    require a Black Box, 22, 23
  language of, ensures coherence, 21
  must sum to unity, in regard to any
    one question, 21
  seem to express a degree of positive
    belief, 21
  uses a private scale, 397, 398
production
  average period of, 309
  average period of, measured
    continuously, 310–11
  cost of, and reason for viewing as the
    explanation of value, 272
  definition and measure of, 166
  money measure of, is income, 172
production-function
  and constant returns to scale, 144,
    145
  exhaustion of the product ensured by
    linear homogeneous form of, 144,
    145
  linear homogeneous form of, is
    implied by ready abstractions, 144
production, theory of
  and the practical arts, 115
  illustrates the scalar concern of
    economics, 44
  is a theory of the incomes of sources
    of productive services, 45
  is chiefly concerned with the distri-
    butive exhaustion of the product, 45
  is not concerned with practical arts
    in themselves, 45

  neglects shape and arrangement, 117
  what question answered by, 44
productive organism of society
  and the time-net of production, 300
  consists in a network of converging
    and diverging channels, 298
  correspondence of sector and phase,
    300
  input coefficients of, 299, 300
  morphology and evolution of, 300
  represented by input–output matrix,
    298
  sectors, activities or industries of, 298
  two kinds of complexity of, intimately
    mutually involved, 300
profit
  a language for, 415
  a list of ideas essential to the notion
    of, 418
  and division of the basis of valuation
    into supposed truth and
    acknowledged conjecture, 410
  and dual valuation, implies imper-
    fect knowledge, 410
  and resolutional contrast of
    valuations, 410, 411
  as an impulse to activity, 421
  as focus gain of an enterprise, 419
  can two valuations of one object
    both be 'right'? 410
  counter-expected, is the central
    dynamic element in a market
    economy, 447
  definition of, requires a selective
    principle, 415
  dimension of, 413
  duality of valuation: how possible,
    409
  expected and counter-expected, its
    essential role in the kaleidic
    economy, 448
  implies unity of thought, of assessor,
    of object, of time, 409
  in one guise an incentive to action,
    in another an incentive to thought,
    420
  is a thought in one mind, 409
  is expectational, 414
  logical consistency of a notion of, 415
  looked upon by Marshall as a
    component of income, 447
  method of employing the concept of,
    in arriving at that of investment
    gain, 418, 419
  most dramatic context of, 417
  operational meaning of, 409
  requires a language for expectation,
    411
  resolutional, and elasticities of
    surprise, 419, 420, 421

profit *(cont.)*
  resolutional, induces a revision of
    expectations, 420
  resolutional, is counter-expected,
    419, 421
  unity of ideas concerning, rests
    partly on their serving as incentives
    421
  what does it do? 415
proof
  economist rightly contents himself
    with something far short of it, 342
  is necessarily concerned with
    abstractions, 342
proportion(s)
  concern with, has distracted the
    economist from shape and
    structure, 40
  of factors of production, 44
  variable, value theory the study of, 114
psychic link between circumstance and
  action, 355
purpose and obstacle
  and scalar character of economic
    theory, 131
  meanings dependent on each
    other, 131
Pythagoras, 30

quantity(-ies)
  are not the whole of knowledge, 104
  concern with, has obscured
    questions of shape and structure,
    40, 114, 329
  economics almost exclusively con-
    cerned with, 39, 40, 104, 114, 329
  obscures *form*, 39, 114, 329
  of factors of production, will be
    decided indirectly, by decisions
    concerning design and methods,
    41, 104
  questions concerning, are often
    summary or secondary questions
    for the business man, 41, 104
  scalar, made possible by price, 9
Quebec,
  capture of, by surprise, 24
Quesnay, François
  and the contribution made by the
    Tableau Economique, 65, 250, 359
  gave to economics the idea of a
    system of inter-organized sectors,
    and that of intra-sectoral balance,
    251, 359
  his system led to Leontief's, 251
questions
  asked by economic theory concern
    situations and *courses of events*, 89
  which are 'no earthly use' but
    release men from frustrations, 54

rational action, discernment of
  only useful *ex ante*, but only possible
    ex post, 85
  value-theory's criterion of, forbids
    the study of the question of
    knowledge, 85
rational action, field of,
  claims identity with that of value
    theory, 120
Rational Calculus,
  can be an illusion, 228
rational conduct,
  circumstances of, must not be *open-
    ended*, 230
  proof of logical existence of, best
    justifies value theory, 143
  requires timelessness, 229, 265
rational degrees of belief
  are rational, but founded also on
    figment, 389
rational determinacy
  excludes money, 233
rational ideal, the
  can be derived from a minimum
    axiomatic base, 127, 128
  cannot apply to speculative markets,
    159
  dissolution of, by the theme of the
    General Theory of Employment, 175
  gives a starting-point of high clarity,
    127
  is at the mercy of *ceteris paribus*, 128
  must exlude expectation, 156
  sets at rest the mind's desire for order,
    128
  undermined by the combined effects
    of money and uncertainty, 176
rationalism
  and conduct as part of the order-
    liness of Nature, 239
  paradox of, 239
rationality
  an idle term until the data available
    to the individual are specified, 37,
    90
  and self-sufficiency of field of
    economic events, 4
  and the claim of self-interest to be
    the central economic principle, 36
  as the application of fully-informed
    reason, 230
  bounds of, 84
  can prevail in a hand-to-mouth
    society, 157
  cannot be ascribed to a speculative
    market, 158, 162
  cannot span a temporal succession
    of situations, 84, 89, 90, 125
  finds expression in equilibrium, 53,
    90

timeless system
  and the *long period*, both treat time
    with disdain, 127
tools
  contrasted with theoretic systems in
    their influence, 62, 63
  use of, implies accumulation and
    lapse of time, 269
Torres Vedras, lines of, 24
  and the effect of surprise in war, 423
Townshend, Hugh
  and Chapter 12 of the *General
    Theory*, 226
  and '*direct* causal influence of
    expectations on *all* prices', 226
  and 'the future not merely unknown
    to the economic man: it is also
    undetermined', 226
  and 'the mechanical analogy breaks
    down', 226
  and the origin of involuntary
    unemployment, 175
  and 'there is no position of equili-
    brium', 226
  and two modes of price formation
    which can be called conventional,
    227
  makes expectations to work on prices
    via *liquidity premium*, 226
Trasimene Lake, battle of, 24
Treatise on Money, The
  and Keynes's abandonment of his
    Fundamental Equations, 441
  and Keynes's essential leaven of
    novelty, 162
  and the bond market, 162
  and windfall profit, 419
  drew inspiration from Wicksell,
    Preface
  Fundamental Equations of, are an
    embryonic sequence analysis, 441

uncertainty
  and interpreting discordant voices,
    19
  engenders its own source, 165
  is alien to statistical probability, 20
  is at some times more oppressive than
    at others, 208
  is the entertaining of plural rival
    hypotheses, 19, 416
  leads to immobility, 78
  neglected by theories which
    separate profitability from safety,
    215
uncertainty-variable, non-distributional
  and feeling of more to be lost than
    gained, 78
  avoids suggesting inclusiveness, 23
  character of, 23

considers degrees of *disbelief*, 23
  expresses adjudged possibility, 23
unemployment
  and desire of income-earners for a
    product-wage composed too largely
    of investment goods, 170, 175,
    233
  and effects of a hypothetical
    general reduction of money wages,
    169
  and product too cheap in terms of
    money, 167
  and the *composition* of the product
    wage, 169, 170, 175, 233
  and the terms *real wage* or *product
    wage*, 168
  and whether reduction of money-
    wage can reduce product wage,
    169, 232
  and unwillingness of employers to
    take the risk of buying specialized
    equipment with borrowed money,
    170, 175, 233
  involuntary, definition of in Keynes's
    General Theory of Employment,
    166–75, 231
  involuntary, is logically excluded
    from general equilibrium, 231
  involuntary, is logically possible in a
    money-using economy with
    certain institutions, 168
  involuntary, necessary exclusion
    from value theory because of
    tacit assumption of 'full informa-
    tion', 232
  involuntary, whether logically
    possible, 166, 232
  the two distinct views of employer
    and employed, 168, 232, 233
un-knowledge
  assumed away by value theory, 232
  disregarded by economic theory, 3
  implies freedom for conjecture, 18
unused permission to over-draw
  difficulty of aggregating, 204

valuation
  and the bounds of economics, 5
  appears as arbitrary in principle and
    theory, 68
  as a personal act, 9, 43
  at the margin, and scalar measure-
    ment, 46
  cannot reduce essential diversity to
    uniformity, 46
  conventional, 221, 222, 223
  conventional, and the *kinky
    oligopoly demand curve*, 222
  conventional, exact meaning of, 224
  dependent on *orientation*, 75